Coping with Excess

Coping with Excess

How Organizations, Communities and Individuals Manage Overflows

---

Edited by

Barbara Czarniawska

Professor of Management Studies, GRI, University of Gothenburg, Sweden

and

Orvar Löfgren

Professor Emeritus of European Ethnology, University of Lund, Sweden

Edward Elgar

Cheltenham, UK • Northampton, MA, USA

Published by
Edward Elgar Publishing Limited
The Lypiatts
15 Lansdown Road
Cheltenham
Glos GL50 2JA
UK

Edward Elgar Publishing, Inc.
William Pratt House
9 Dewey Court
Northampton
Massachusetts 01060
USA

A catalogue record for this book
is available from the British Library

Library of Congress Control Number: 2013944958

This book is available electronically in the ElgarOnline.com Business Subject Collection, E-ISBN 978 1 78254 859 1

MIX
Paper from responsible sources
FSC
www.fsc.org
FSC® C013056

ISBN 978 1 78254 857 7 (cased)

Typeset by Columns Design XML Ltd, Reading
Printed and bound in Great Britain by T.J. International Ltd, Padstow

Contents

Contributors

Helene Brembeck is Professor of Ethnology and Co-Director of the Centre for Consumer Science (CFK) at University of Gothenburg, Sweden. Her research interests are parenthood and childhood in consumer culture, including food and eating, and she has published several articles, books and anthologies in this field. Recent international publications include articles in *Culture Unbound*, *Critical Public Health*, *Distinktion* and *Children's Geographies*, and book chapters in Czarniawska and Löfgren's (eds) *Managing Overflow in Affluent Societies* (2012), in Peter Jackson and the CONANX Group's *Food Words: Essays in Culinary Culture* (2013) and in Belasco, Murcott and Jackson's (eds) *The Handbook of Food Research* (2013).

Franck Cochoy is Professor of Sociology at the University of Toulouse, France, a member of CERTOP-CNRS, France, and a visiting Professor at University of Gothenburg, Sweden. He works in the field of economic sociology, with a focus on the human and technical mediations that frame the relationship between supply and demand. He has conducted several projects and case studies in such areas as the role of marketing, packaging, self-service, standardization, corporate social responsibility and trade press. His most recent publications in English have appeared in the *Journal of Cultural Economy*, *Organization*, *Marketing Theory*, *Theory, Culture and Society* and *Young Consumers*.

Hervé Corvellec is Professor of Business Administration in the Department of Service Management and Service Studies, Campus Helsingborg, Lund University, Sweden. His field of research and teaching is business and public administration, especially organization theory, with a research focus on risk, business ethics and infrastructure services (for example, power supply, public transportation, waste management). He often works with narrative and argumentation analysis. He recently edited *What is Theory? Answers from the Social and Cultural Science* (2013). His articles on issues related to waste management have been published in *Environment and Planning A*, *Waste Management*, *Waste Management and Research*, *Journal of Organizational Change Management* and *Journal of Cleaner Production*.

Barbara Czarniawska is Professor of Management Studies at Gothenburg Research Institute, School of Business, Economics and Law at University of Gothenburg, Sweden. She takes a feminist and constructionist perspective on organizing, recently exploring the connections between popular culture and the practice of management on one hand, and the organization of the news production on the other. She is interested in methodology, especially in techniques of fieldwork and in the application of narratology to organization studies. Czarniawska writes in Polish, English, Swedish and Italian; her texts have been translated into Arabic, Chinese, French, Danish, German and Russian. Recent books in English include *Shadowing and Other Techniques of Doing Fieldwork in Modern Societies* (2007), *A Theory of Organizing* (2008), *Organizing in the Face of Risk and Threat* (ed., 2009), *Cyberfactories: How News Agencies Produce News* (2011), and *Managing Overflow in Affluent Societies*, edited with Orvar Löfgren (2012).

Mariusz Czubaj is Professor of Cultural Anthropology at Warsaw School of Social Psychology (SWPS), Poland. His research interests include popular culture, anthropology of sport and fan studies. He has authored several books: *Biodra Elvisa Presleya. Od paleoherosów do neofanów* [*Elvis Presley's Hips: From Paleo-Heroes to Neo-Fans*] (2007), *W stronę miejskiej utopii* [*Towards the Urban Utopia*] (2007), *Etnolog w Mieście Grzechu: powieść kryminalna jako powieść antropologiczna* [*An Ethnolog in Sin City: Crime Novel as Anthropological Story*] (2010) and *Postfutbol: antropologia piłki nożnej* [*Postfootball: Anthropology of Football*] with Jacek Drozda and Jakub Myszkorow (2012). He also writes crime novels. His novel, *21:37*, has received an award for the best detective story of the year in Poland and has been translated into German, English, Turkish and Ukrainian.

Pierre Donatella is an accounting consultant and Deputy Director of the Municipal Research Institute in West Sweden in Gothenburg. At the same time he is working on his PhD thesis, which addresses the issues related to financial accounting in municipalities. His focus is on the way annual reports are designed and how they are perceived by decision makers.

Karin M. Ekström is Professor of Marketing at University of Borås, Sweden. She is the initiator and former Director of the Centre for Consumer Science (CFK). Her research interests are family consumption, consumer socialization, collecting, consumers' relations to artefacts and the meaning(s) of consumption. She has edited several books, most recently *Consumer Behaviour – A Nordic Perspective* (2010) and *Beyond the Consumption Bubble* with Kay Glans (2011). Recent journal articles include publications in *Journal of Consumer Behaviour*, *Journal of Macro Marketing*, *Journal of Marketing Management* and *Research in Consumer Behaviour*. She has recently published *Nätverk, trådar och spindlar – Samverkan för ökad återanvändning och återvinning av kläder och textil* [*Network, Threads and Spiders – Cooperating to Increase Reuse and Recycling of Clothes and Textiles*] with Nicklas Salomonson, and a book chapter 'Mode på Röhsska museet – Samlande, marknadsföring och varumärkesbyggande' ['Fashion at Röhsska Museum – collecting, marketing and brand building'].

Susanna Fellman is Professor of Business History at the School of Business, Economics and Law, University of Gothenburg, Sweden. She has previously worked as Research Fellow and Professor of Economic History at University of Helsinki, Finland, where she also received her PhD in 2001. She writes in Swedish, Finnish and English and her texts have been translated into Spanish. Fellman is currently working on a project related to competition policy and cartels, but other research interests are the professionalization and modernization of management, questions related to the evolution of the Nordic model of capitalism, and to labour relations. She is currently focusing on methodological questions within the field of business history. Recent publications include *Creating Nordic Capitalism – The Development of a Competitive Periphery*, edited with Martin Jes Iversen, Hans Sjögren and Lars Thue (2008), *Historical Knowledge. In Quest of Theory, Method and Evidence,* edited with Marjatta Rahikainen (2012), an article on trust in the labour market for *Business History* (2010) and a chapter on professionalization in family business, forthcoming in *A Global Revolution. The Endurance of Family Businesses*, edited by Paloma Fernandez Perez and Andrea Colli.

Orvar Löfgren is Professor Emeritus of European Ethnology at Lund University, Sweden. The cultural analysis and ethnography of everyday life has been in focus of much of his research; see, for example, *The Secret World of Doing Nothing* with Billy Ehn (2010) and *Managing Overflow in Affluent Societies* edited with Barbara Czarniawska (2012). Other central research fields have been studies of urban life, transnational mobility and culture and economy; see *Magic, Culture and the New Economy,* edited with Robert Willim (2006). Currently he is engaged in a project on media and domestic life and a study of everyday academic skills.

Lars Norén is Associate Professor of Business Administration at the School of Business, Economics and Law, University of Gothenburg,

Sweden. His research interest is in public administration and management and in qualitative research methods. A recent and relevant publication is 'The private interest of consumers in the health care market', *International Journal of Public Sector Management* (2010, **23**(4): 264–371).

Mika Pantzar, PhD is Research Professor in the National Consumer Research Centre, Finland. One of his current research interests is the economics of sport, health and well-being. Another interest is related to Big Data, large data sets of various forms (for example human physiology, netnography). His former project (2006–2011), Co-production of Innovations – Towards an Integrative Theory of Practice, within the Academy of Finland and Aalto University, Finland was finalized in *Everyday Life: The Dynamics of Social Practice* with Elizabeth Shove and Matt Watson, (2012). Pantzar has published widely in the areas of consumer research, design and technology studies, the rhetoric of economic policy, food and future studies, and systems research in such journals as *Design Issue*, *Design Journal*, *Journal of Advertising*, *Journal of Consumer Culture*, *Journal of Consumer Studies and Home Economics*, *World Futures*, *Journal of Futures Studies*, *Ethnologia Europaea*, *Technology Analysis* and *Strategic Management*. Two major works published in Finnish are *Domestication of Technology. From Science of Consumption to Art of Consumption* (1996) which was awarded a prize by both the Finnish State and the Finnish Science Council; and *Future Home – Inventing Needs for Domestic Appliances* (2000), which is widely used at many universities.

Andrew Popp is Professor of Business History at University of Liverpool Management School, UK. His research has focused on a series of interlocking themes in British business history in the nineteenth century: industrial districts, regional business networks, systems of distribution and patterns of integration, commercial travel and occupational cultures. More recently he has been particularly concerned with the histories of family business and entrepreneurship. He has published widely in the key journal of business and economic history. His most recent book is *Entrepreneurial Families: Business, Marriage and Life in the Early Nineteenth Century* (2012). He currently serves as Associate Editor of *Enterprise and Society*.

Elena Raviola is Assistant Professor of Managing Professional Work at the Department of Organization, Copenhagen Business School, Denmark. She is interested in organizing and technology, especially in the fields of news production and cultural industries. In her dissertation, 'Paper meets web. How the institution of news production works on paper and online' (2010), she investigated the way journalistic professional practices are transformed through technological changes and how the professional logic of journalism meets the logic of management in newspaper organizations. She has also conducted studies on the encounter between management and art in such various forms and contexts as dance and design. She has published articles in international organization and media studies journals – in *Organization Studies* and *Information, Communication, and Society*, among others. She also writes and publishes in Italian and French.

Rolf Solli is Professor of Management at the University of Borås, Sweden. From 2003 to 2012 he was Director and Professor of Management at Gothenburg Research Institute, School of Business, Economics and Law, University of Gothenburg, Sweden. Prior to holding those positions, he was Head of the School of Public Administration, University of Gothenburg for many years. His research focuses on processes of management, leadership and accounting – mainly in the context of public sector organizations. He has recently studied and published articles about financial stress in local governments.

Emre Tarim is a Teaching Fellow in Finance at King's College, London. After receiving his PhD in Sociology from University of Edinburgh, UK, in 2011, Tarım has held research fellowships at Gothenburg Research Institute and the University of Edinburgh, and worked as a management consultant at Arama (Search) Participatory Management Consultancy in Instanbul. Tarım's principal research interest is the development and application of sociological and narrative approaches to understanding cognition and decision making in financial markets. More specifically, he is interested in the ways finance professionals assume collective agencies that constitute of economic, social and cultural capital, and historically delineated and institutionalized market roles; and how these collective agencies underpin financial decisions and numerically observable patterns in market outcomes. Tarım has several publications on the sociology of the Istanbul Stock Exchange and the role of narratives in sensemaking and legitimacy in financial markets.

Jakob Wenzer is an ethnologist and Research Fellow at the Center for Consumer Science (CFK) at the University of Gothenburg, Sweden. His research interests focus primarily on aesthethic economies, but also on issues of consumption and space. Recent publications in include articles in *Distinktion: Scandinavian Journal of Social Theory* and book chapters in Peter Jackson's and the CONANX Group's book, *Food Words: Essays in Culinary Culture* (2013).

Robert Willim is Associate Professor of European Ethnology, Department of Arts and Cultural Sciences, Lund University, Sweden. He works as a cultural analyst and as an artist. Willim's research has primarily dealt with themes such as digital and material culture and cultural economy. He has developed research around the concept of Industrial Cool, and has investigated the ways in which ethnography has been transformed as it has moved within and without academia. Willim has published a number of books and articles. His artworks are positioned close to his practices as a cultural analyst and ethnographer. Several of the works are about experiences of place, landscape and geography, and they often emanate from research questions.

1. Changing perspectives on the management of overflow

Orvar Löfgren and Barbara Czarniawska

What does a stockbroker in Istanbul navigating the rush of incoming trading figures have in common with a mother in Sweden trying to organize a growing pile of baby clothes? They are both coping with excess – with overflow. The phenomenon of overflow opens a rich field for analysing the ways in which people, institutions and corporations define and manage situations of too much – too much information, too many choices, too many commodities or tasks.

This book takes the reader through a range of diverse social and economic settings which illustrate how overflows are created and dealt with – from corporate settings and public administration offices to everyday routines at home and work. We provide a number of analytical tools and perspectives for understanding the complexities of overflow phenomena, which, although ubiquitous, take a variety of forms and shapes. Our material is drawn from an ongoing interdisciplinary research programme in which management scholars, sociologists, ethnologists and historians are exploring the processes through which overflow becomes a problem or a blessing in various social contexts.[1] In an earlier book from the project (Czarniawska and Löfgren, 2012), we made a first mapping of the research territory. This volume takes the analysis into new territories.

THE SCOPE OF THE PRESENT VOLUME

The 14 chapters which follow provide a rich comparative platform, allowing us to develop a more general understanding of the complex dynamics involved. To begin, there is the question of how, why and when overflow is charged with negative or positive connotations. One area in which overflow has a politically negative meaning is the public sector: an excess of money, indicating overtaxing, as explored in this volume by Barbara Czarniawska, Pierre Donatella and Rolf Solli (Chapter 4); or an excess of ageing baby boomers in search of medical care, examined by Lars Norén (Chapter 5). In both cases, though, the modes of management are borrowed from the private sector – the currently preferred source of management models.

Meanwhile, the private sector, especially finance, is having its own problems, not least those caused by traditional ways of managing information inflow. Emre Tarim tackles the issue of framing processes in what is called 'scopic' financial markets (trading based on screen sighting) and reveals that relatively traditional methods are used to manage these overflows. In contrast, Jakob Wenzer (Chapter 7) ventures into a world which is not scopic, but phonic: music. Can the Cloud world be controlled? And can its users manage the overflow it produces?

The idea of interflows launched previously by Gideon Kunda (2012) is well illustrated by Elena Raviola's study (Chapter 9) of the 'Hundred Offices' project, in which the overflow of empty office space is supposed to meet the overflow of creativity – lacking working space. Will the two become connecting vessels, or, as in Kunda's example, will the overflow of one be an underflow of the other? Robert Willim (Chapter 8) goes even further in challenging traditional framing: Is it possible to turn that which was always eliminated – errors, glitches, messes and failures – into something positive?

In exploring new venues, we nevertheless attend to traditional areas of overflow, understood as the overabundance of things, although even in this domain new ways of management are obvious. Helene Brembeck (Chapter 12) inspected young mothers' innovative ways of managing the overflow of 'baby stuff', and Karin M. Ekström (Chapter 11) studied middle-aged Swedes (the first generation which can truly be described as well-to-do) moving from houses to apartments as they age. Inevitably, such topics are closely related to an epitomic issue of overflow: waste. But even in this area new and somewhat surprising developments can be detected. It turns out that food waste can be good; it can be turned into biogas. But is this transformation as positive as it may appear at first glance? asks Hervé Corvellec (Chapter 10).

In the end, we explore areas close to our own profession. Susanna Fellman and Andrew Popp (Chapter 13) share the secrets of business historians confronted with enormous business archives, and Orvar Löfgren (Chapter 14) concentrates on the central skills useful in managing overflow of knowledge: learning to ignore and overlook. In the afterword Franck Cochoy (Chapter 15), himself a specialist on the issues of overflow, performs a sociological mapping of those studies conducted by ethnologists, historians and management scholars, thus helping us to see where the flows originate and where do they go.

NEW DIRECTIONS

In a previous volume dedicated to overflow management (Czarniawska and Löfgren, 2012), we explored a number of ways of addressing the theme, ranging from funeral arrangements in nineteenth-century France (Trompette, 2012) to present-day book reviews on Amazon.com (Pinch, 2012). The studies confirmed Callon's (1986) acute observation that it is the act of framing which actually creates overflow. This observation has been extended by examples showing that framing can also produce something which could be called 'underflow'. Such situations can be helped by a temporary removal of the frame, as in the Swedish cultural institution of 'Cosy Friday' (Brembeck, 2012), in which the usual prohibition on overeating and junk food is suspended in Swedish families. In this case, a hydraulic analogy is not helpful; but it is fitting in other cases, as when Kunda (2012) posited the existence of an 'interflow' between family and work life, in which an overflow in one creates an underflow in the other.

All in all, the studies reported in the previous volume revealed an amazing and varied set of mechanisms and devices used to manage various types of overflow. Many of them, such as bar codes, editorial software and shredders, were typical of the digital era. Not surprisingly, perhaps, it turned out that some of them, such as the digital information on wine bottles (Cochoy, 2012) or the codes used by news agencies (Czarniawska, 2012), produce further overflow. Apart from mechanical devices, a whole series of new or updated skills which help to manage overflow could be detected (Löfgren, 2012). The combination of skills and devices gives rise to a new type of organization of the public and private kind: companies which specialize in ordering, and a whole variety of organizations dealing with waste (Åkesson, 2012). Indeed, waste is the epitome and symbol of present views on overflow, so we return to the topic again in this volume.

This new volume carries some of these themes further, and adds new approaches. When, where and why does overflow emerge, and for whom is it a problem or a blessing?

One lesson we learned when writing the first book is how easily a concept such as overflow acquires a moral dimension. This tendency can be found in much of the literature on excess and surplus, from Veblen (1899/1994) to Lipovetsky (2006). One way of resisting this temptation to moralize is to uphold our pledge to maintain a symmetric attitude (following Latour, 1993) by providing contrasting approaches. After all, uses and definitions of a concept such as overflow are always culturally charged, framed by the given social and historical context to which they are applied. This is why moral undertones or cultural values invariably become part of the argument, both in everyday life and in the scholarly discourse of overflow management – often in indirect or inconspicuous ways.

By way of introduction, we discuss three dimensions of moralizing tendencies. The first comprises a variety of situations in which scarcity is the problem and longing for abundance is the case. The second is formed by debates on overflow – a moral battlefield on which various actors position themselves. The third dimension constitutes varying views on practices and materialities of everyday life at home and at work, where such apparently aesthetic criteria as balance, order, mess or chaos are culturally defined with a strong moral subtext.

LIVES OF SCARCITY AND DREAMS OF ABUNDANCE

Most of the contributions to the first volume focused on overflow as a problem which constantly needed to be managed and controlled in affluent Western societies. But even considering only those societies, one need not move far back into history to encounter situations in which scarcity and the management of want was seen as the main problem, and dreams for the future were dreams of overflow. Such times and places gave rise to fantasies of abundance, opulence and richness of choice. Who could perceive such a blissful state of overflow to be a problem? And why would they? Or, rather, when do such perceptions change?

The ways in which various groups and societies moved from situations of acute scarcity to growing abundance can be easily traced throughout the history of Western mass consumption. It is enough to look at early twentieth-century Europe to encounter settings in which daily life was a constant battle to make ends meet through the management of scarce resources. At the same time, messages about new forms of mass consumption provided material for dreams of another life. Swedish novelist Sara Lidman, who grew up in impoverished Northern Sweden in the early twentieth century, clearly remembered the fantasies of a new consumer society and a much-awaited visit to a country fair. Her little brother was so excited at the prospects that he fainted when they finally made it to the rows of market stands; he was overcome by the dazzling glitter of opportunities and the wealth of offers.

A historical view also demonstrates that the workings of a consumer society require a constant redefinition of scarcity and abundance, which in turn create a longing for new types of overflow. Such dialectical tensions are evident in the recent history of the Cold War and the ways in which ideas and experiences of scarcity and overflow organized much of the relationship between the West and the East in Europe.

The post-war years in Western Europe witnessed an unprecedented affluence, even among the working class (Löfgren, 2012). The post-war world of the so-called Soviet bloc was dramatically different. As the US anthropologist with Hungarian roots, Krisztina Fehérváry (2009), has noted, the ideological battle between the two blocs was often centred on everyday consumption. Another scholar of Hungarian origins, economic historian György Péteri, suggested that the notion of the 'Iron Curtain', coined by Churchill to suggest a divide between the Christian West and the new Barbarian menace of the East, ought to be replaced by the term 'Nylon Curtain'. Péteri (2006) alludes here to a famous satirical work of David Riesman (1951), who wrote a fictional piece called 'The nylon war', in which the US, within the framework of Operation Abundance, was bombing the Soviet Union with consumer goods for many months:

> The curtain was made of Nylon, not Iron. It was not only transparent but it also yielded to strong osmotic tendencies that were globalizing knowledge across the systemic divide about culture, goods and services. These tendencies were not only fuelling consumer desires and expectations of living standards but they also promoted in both directions the spreading of visions of 'good society', of 'humanism', as well as of civil, political, and social citizenship … Nylon, as opposed to Iron, was the epitome of industrial modernity in the early post-war decades. (Péteri, 2006: 4)

The socialist state ideologues did not neglect this state of affairs, even if they were still 'obsessed with counting the tons of iron and coal produced' (Péteri, 2006: 4). Although those states were indeed keen on producing a situation of overflow within the traditional industries, both Péteri and Fehérváry emphasized that the aim in the 1950s and 1960s had been to create a specific socialist modernity, a modernity characterized by 'socialist abundance'. People in socialist countries were to be educated into becoming modern, rational consumers, learning to live without bourgeois kitsch and irrational opulence. The state promised to provide rational socialist consumer abundance, as opposed to the decadent and wasteful hedonism of Western consumer societies. Socialist consumption was to be restrained, and should avoid unnecessary waste. The state, on the other hand, must maintain a constant promise that socialism would deliver the goods – a good and well-planned abundance.

Failure to fulfil this ideological promise began to kindle the dreams of Western consumer life in the East. Small consumer objects – a pair of jeans or a bottle of Coca-Cola – became icons of abundance, quality and trendiness, while the ideological battle over abundance (was it good or bad?) was conducted in everyday consumer life. State planning often resulted in hoarding, creating overflow of the wrong kind of commodities, while people had to invest a great deal of energy in finding and acquiring such scarce goods as toilet paper.

Mika Pantzar (Chapter 2) offers another example – of poor, war-devastated Protestant Finland, which, expecting a post-war affluence, started to introduce framing devices even before this affluence was realized. Thus it becomes obvious that abundance and scarcity can be framed differently in different geopolitical contexts, producing a multiplicity of moral economies. In contrast, Mariusz Czubaj (Chapter 3) describes times since 1989 when the Polish economy moved from 'socialist scarcity' into 'capitalist abundance' – an excellent example of overflow being perceived as positive in a Catholic country. Two decades later, in September 2012, Polish ethnologists organized a conference with the title 'Plenty can be a plague: an overflow in the times of scarcity'.

If the management of overflow calls for a number of specific skills, as illustrated in the following chapters, the management of scarcity develops its own arsenal of strategies and tactics. In a recent study of household economizing in Havana, Maria Padrón Hernandez (2012) discussed the wide range of skills required to make ends meet under conditions of constant scarcity of the most basic resources. Household economizing consists not only of learning to stand in line or work the system by activating various social relations, but also of knowing how to move between the state market and the black market. It calls for a wide range of competencies: making do with less and making ends meet – learning to differentiate between short-term and long-term needs, for example.

OVERFLOW AS A MORAL ECONOMY

Maria Padrón Hernandez (2012) demonstrated how moral norms and economic practices are tightly interwoven in economies of scarcity. Deirdre McCloskey (2012) observed that moralizing creeps into the discussion in the Western world when overflow is unfailingly connected to the making of the new bourgeoisie. Thus discussions of class, whether intended or unintended, formed an arena in which the concept of overflow became an ideological weapon.

As Polish sociologist Maria Ossowska (1956/1986) noted long ago, the prejudice against the bourgeoisie is as old as the bourgeoisie itself. At the end of the nineteenth and the beginning of the twentieth century, various European countries witnessed a sharp critique addressed to what was called a 'bourgeois morality'. This critique was equally strong in countries dominated by the middle class and in countries where the middle class was insignificant. Furthermore it came from at least three ideological perspectives: the leftists, the gentry and the bohemians.

After having briefly summarized those critiques, Ossowska began a search for the epitomic descriptions of bourgeois morality in literature. The results were rather startling: no conspicuous consumption, no pride in excess, and no decadence. As McCloskey did later, Ossowska chose to focus on Benjamin Franklin, whose model of a human being included 'financial reliability' based on hard work, thrift, orderliness, prudence and monetary calculation, and a 'non-elitist' independence based on everyday gain. Ossowska showed how these ideas were transformed into the petty bourgeois bible as illustrated by the Lynds (Lynd and Lynd, 1929, 1937) in their *Middletown*, among other works. It is no wonder, therefore, that the bourgeoisie felt the moral right to criticize excesses of both the upper and lower classes.

In Sweden, for example, the emerging bourgeoisie of the nineteenth century conducted a battle on two fronts, in which arguments of overflow were directed at the old elite – the gentry – and at the lower classes: workers and peasants. The new bourgeoisie defined itself as morally superior in many ways, a superiority which was demonstrated not only by thrift, restraint, productivity and investments in the future, but also by projecting the vices of overflow onto other groups. The old gentry lived a wasteful life, squandering their resources on luxuries and unproductive forms of consumption; the lower classes, which really needed to plan and husband their meagre resources, could squander them on carnivalesque bouts of overconsumption: overeating and overdrinking at festive occasions. Against those two categories of overspenders, restraint and the rationality – virtues of the bourgeoisie – were defined (Frykman and Löfgren, 1985).

There were also internal class conflicts, in which different branches of the bourgeoisie battled others with the help of overflow arguments, often centred on consumption and taste. Two symbolic enemies often singled out and ridiculed were the nouveau riche and petite bourgeoisie. Gendered polarities were also produced, sometimes positioning male restraint and rationality against female spending and irresponsibility in many middle-class settings, whereas the reverse roles were often ascribed to husband and wife in working-class settings of the early twentieth century (Frykman and Löfgren, 1985).

Instead of linking overflow to the bourgeoisie, it may be more fruitful to ask why debates on overflow often contain a moralizing dimension of 'Othering'. From a historical and comparative perspective on the Western world, overflow is often used as a weapon, an accusation, which can be used by very different groups targeting Others and become part of different arguments. Who is accusing whom of overflow, in what ways, in what social contexts and for what purposes? What types of overflow are defined as harmful, wasteful or morally bad? This kind of moralizing can change over time, occur in various forms and be used by different groups.

What is more, morals and aesthetics can become interwoven, resulting in the presentation of the cult of flow as a pleasing, seamless and smooth phenomenon, in contrast to a wasteful, messy and uncontrollable overflow. This polarization takes us into another prominent theme of this volume: the ways in which flows may be turned into overflows and vice versa.

Several chapters in this volume focus on specific kinds of transformations. When the situation changes from flow to overflow or vice versa, the transformation is often framed in questions of control – or lack of it. In the production of biogas, Hervé Corvellec (Chapter 10) shows how an overflow is transformed into a neat flow of fuel; the wealth of materials in the archives can be disciplined into an orderly and accessible resource (Susanna Fellman and Andrew Popp, Chapter 13) or into a manageable market resource such as music on the Internet (Jakob Wenzer, Chapter 7). During such transformations, there is often room for the special skills of brokerage, a capacity of directing overflow. This was the case in Elena Raviola's study (Chapter 9) of empty office space offered to artists; her example also illustrates how the polarities of lack of control or established control can carry different cultural charges according to the context. There are situations in which controlled flow stands for a disciplining limitation of potentials, and in which a chaotic overflow has stimulating and rich potential – as when creativity was defined as an energizing force in the office project, for example.

MATERIALITIES OF EVERYDAY LIFE

The third type of moralizing dimension is often buried in discussions of the practices and materialities of everyday life. In many attempts to manage overflow there is an underlying notion of balance, harmony and order. The ambition of many people in both private and public life, at home and at work, is to reach and maintain a situation at the intersection of overflows and underflows: neither too much nor too little. As mentioned previously, moral arguments are often disguised in aesthetic terms, as when overflow is defined in terms of overspill, waste, disorder or an unappetizing mess. The aesthetics can then transmute into existential fears, related to lurking chaos or the feeling of losing control. Overflow management is then seen as a constant existential and aesthetic battle, in which the imposing of a pleasing and comforting order is crucial in both private lives and professional planning.

Consequently, materiality plays a decisive role here. Thus the chapters in this volume address a variety of materializations of overflow, from the overflow of numbers on the investment bankers' screens and the flow of baby clothes and toys in and out of family homes, to the logistics of streaming music or turning unpleasant waste into beautiful biogas. It becomes crucial, therefore, to explore how such different materialities impose possibilities and restraints; how, in the vocabulary of actor-network theory (Latour, 2005), they become actants in the action net which we called the management of overflow.

Several chapters explore various devices with which overflow is handled and framed. The flow metaphor works better with some material forms, such as liquid, than it does with others. The same goes for filtering mechanisms: compare, for example, Jakob Wenzer's discussion of filters in the music market (Chapter 7) with Lars Norén's discussion of complex administrative systems created to filter and redirect patients in an overcrowded health system (Chapter 5). In the case of music, it is fascinating to see what happens when the flow is transformed in analogue and digital settings.

Overflows can comprise very different ingredients, blocking, complementing or blending into each other. As Helene Brembeck's and Karin M. Ekström's studies illustrate (Chapters 12 and 11), householders trying to sort out an excess of belongings when moving house may find that the real problem is not the material abundance of things, but all the mixed emotions accompanying them.

Franck Cochoy's 'Afterword' (Chapter 15) indicates a new direction for our future studies: following leaks rather than overflows. It is certainly a fascinating metaphor, strongly related both to morality and materiality. We will consider this suggestion. Complex phenomena demand a variety of perspectives in order to be understood. Our deliberations over the variety of possible ways of coping with excess and managing overflow are to be treated as a beginning, rather than the end of the exploration.

NOTE

1. The programme is financed by the Jan Wallander and Tom Hedenius Foundation, and we thank them for their support.

2. 'What are we to do with our new affluence?' Anticipating, framing and managing the putative plenty of post-war Finland

Mika Pantzar

When the first internationally known 'garden city' – Tapiola, near Helsinki – was being developed some 50 years ago, warnings about forthcoming prosperity, excessive consumption and urban sprawl came into the picture from the very beginning. In retrospect, deciding what to do with a 'new affluence' – overflow management, in other words – was not the most obvious problem in one of the poorest countries in Europe and one, moreover, which was just recovering from the heavy losses of war. The affluence was more utopian dream than any kind of reality. Nevertheless, standards of the 'good life' and 'proper' consumption in Finland began to be defined by professionals from relatively new fields such as home economics and sociology, together with urban planners and architects. In the course of the Tapiola building project, the discursive frames of the different professions involved converged by means of fairly ambiguous concepts such as 'biological function', 'catching up', dormitory town', 'cross-sectional society' and 'neighbourhood unit'. A closer look at the reality behind these terms reveals a seemingly shared view of the necessity, as well as a deterministic theory, of social progress, and the aim of restricting the wrong kind of growth.

Today Tapiola, with its 20 000 inhabitants, exemplifies a rare persistence of Ebenezer Howard's original term 'garden city' (Aario, 1986; Ward, 1992). When in 1952 Tapiola's construction work began under the supervision of the Housing Foundation (Asuntosäätiö), a journal published by the Family Federation of Finland (Väestöliitto) saw Tapiola's future as follows:

> The planned area of Hagalund is not intended to become any kind of 'dormitory town'; instead, it is intended as a daughter city of Helsinki that

> will be as self-contained as possible … It is estimated that at least 12 000 residents can be located in the area, 700 of them into detached houses, 3000–3500 into row houses, and the rest into apartment buildings, four stories high at most. (*Asuntopolitiikka*, 1951, 3: 4–5)

The large body of written material that has been produced in connection with Tapiola Garden City provides the main sources for the present chapter (for further references, see Pantzar, 2010). Tapiola's early developers favoured holistic design, whether it was a question of national planning, housing design or education (Nikula, 1994; Nupponen, 2000; Tuomi and Paatero, 2003). In the Finnish context, Tapiola was the first example of highly systematic and organized planning and living. My view, however, is partly personal, as I spent my adolescence in Tapiola, from 1967 to 1981. It was the young who were the objects of the discourse of the model city. We children were the plants of the garden city, to be watered, fertilized and activated (see also Jerram, 2011).

In creating the Garden City, oppositions between the necessary and the superfluous, real needs and bric-a-brac, and active and passive leisure were frequently evoked. Forces such as bureaucracy, self-interest and the economy needed to be restrained (Pantzar, 2010). Therefore the main focus of this chapter lies in identifying how a threatening overflow was framed and managed with a specific discourse about 'urban sprawl', 'excessively materialistic culture' and 'idle time'.

BUILDING A MODEL CITY

Tapiola's builder, the Housing Foundation, had been established by a number of non-governmental organizations (NGOs) ranging from trade unions to the Finnish tenants' union and the Family Federation of Finland. The Housing Foundation's multidisciplinary planning and building teams consisted of experts in education, sociology, household economics, architecture, town planning and garden planning – actually the first housing project in Finland to include sociologists and home economists. The Housing Foundation acted as a point of intersection in the planning process, packing and unpacking bundles of ideas and models from home and abroad (Czarniawska and Sevón, 2005). Meetings, workshops and team palavers along with discussions in the local newspaper acted as fora where ideas were spurred forward from one place to another or, alternatively, prevented from moving any further.

Tapiola's early phases were described in most revealing terms by Wolf von Eckardt (1967: 351), architecture critic for the *Washington Post*, who dedicated his book 'To Heikki von Hertzen whose great example is surely making the whole world a better place to live'. What built Tapiola was not a system but a man, a man of simple beliefs, great organizational talent, civilized tastes and great energy. His name is Heikki von Hertzen. Prosperity came late to Finland, von Hertzen told me, as we lunched in the excellent restaurant on top of Tapiola's tower. Until 1952, the year its planning began, the country had to pay exorbitant war reparations to the Soviet Union:

> When we finally caught up [with the West] we asked ourselves: What are we to do with our new affluence? We can't eat more. There is a limit to the automobiles and gadgets we really need. So I started to persuade my countrymen that we should build a beautiful and suitable environment for everyone.

This citation exemplifies the selective manner in which the inhabitants of an impoverished country were beginning to talk about building a new kind of consumer society of plenty. More developed countries were not viewed uncritically as objects of imitation; overeating, cars or gadgets were clearly not part of life in an ideal society. 'Consumerism', consumption of the wrong kind or 'idle time' were seen as threats to be fought against.

As will be seen, when Tapiola was being created, it was not just a question of constructing new houses; there were numerous other human and material building projects ongoing at the same time. Interestingly, what started out as an anti-urban, anti-consumerist and anti-individualistic utopia in the 1940s had developed by the 1970s into an urban, consumerist and individualistic community, heavily reliant on private transport. Coincidentally or not, the head office of Nokia, economically the most successful company in contemporary Finland, is situated right next door to Tapiola. In a sense we can say that utopian plans to create new types of citizens were never realized. The motto of the current Tapiola 2010 development project is 'All good things together', and in future there will be a considerable increase in commercial space, more department stores, megastores, speciality shops, cafes, restaurants, cultural activities, leisure and recreation facilities and, finally, underground parking space for 3000 cars.

The Family Welfare League of Finland was established in 1941, during the war, to ensure homes and welfare for the population; Heikki von Hertzen, then a young lawyer, was invited to be its executive director in 1943. He had begun his career in banking and had succeeded in surrounding himself with leading politicians representing different sides of the political field. The Second World War had led to an urgent shortage of housing in Finland and new homes had to be built for hundreds of thousands of evacuees from the ceded part of Karelia. My conclusion is, however, that in the planning and making of Tapiola Garden City the shortage of housing played only a minor role once building actually commenced.

In time, perspectives widened and deepened as the (material) work progressed. On the one hand, the builders' perspective broadened from individual houses to optimizing entire blocks and service complexes of blocks (shops, schools, cultural services). On the other hand, the developers turned their attention more to residents' everyday life. The Family Federation of Finland was the most important organization behind the idea of Tapiola and emphasized the need to produce citizens who were more cultivated, not so much in self-centred economic terms but rather in moral terms. What was required, and to some extent achieved, was not just quantitative growth of population but also qualitative developments within individuals and communities. Unspecified growth was considered dangerous.

In most European countries investments, both private and public, were prioritized in the post-war period (see, for example, Kroen, 2006; Daunton, 2007): the doctrine of the economic policy was that the citizens' activities ought to serve the balanced development of the national economy. Capital formation, through both human and industrial investments, was also the main doctrine in post-war Finland and Tapiola.

The pro-investment doctrine was not the one defended when Tapiola Garden City was envisaged. Von Hertzen pointed out wherever possible that Tapiola was a collective project in which the principal aim was one of developing a welfare-state prototype, but without either state bureaucracy or technocracy. This resonates with what Scandinavian institutional theorists have said about benchmarking and imitating best practices in terms of models and prototypes (Sahlin-Andersson, 1996; Czarniawska and Sevón, 2005). The different professional interest groups involved in the building of Tapiola all sought to convince others of the merits of their particular understanding of how the world is, how it should be, and what kinds of policies would make it better in the future (see also McCann, 2003; Vitale, 2009). Political persuasion worked through different discursive frames: simplifications of the world which selectively identified and attached meanings to certain actions, experiences and events in order to impact politics and policies.

The case of Tapiola demonstrates how imitating ideas that had been developed elsewhere represents an unusual mixture of creativity and disciplined copying of existing models. Kerstin Sahlin-Andersson (1996) refers to the principles governing such simultaneously creative and disciplined processes as 'editing rules'. She identifies commonalities shared by many success stories (that is, benchmarking of organizations): success is typically communicated in a form of story; it is described as having followed a careful planning process and specific rationality; and it is decontextualized. Indeed, the Tapiola success story (especially that of the early developers) was told in terms of rational planning. Specific local prerequisites were de-emphasized, both when the garden city model was imported, and when the experiences of the Finnish version were exported. However, Tapiola's case adds an important aspect to Sahlin-Andersson's editing rules: new and less acknowledged concepts that do not fit any pre-given categories can occasionally act as 'boundary concepts' (Star and Griesemer, 1989; Löwy, 1992) with the potential to integrate different discursive frames. The most important ideas and ideals came from the fathers of the garden city concept: Lewis Mumford and, to a lesser degree, Ebenezer Howards and Patrick Geddes, whose texts about the promises of social progress and the condemnation of the passive lifestyle were carefully read by the developers of the Finnish garden city.

What made conceptual packages travel so smoothly from one place to another had partly to do with the fact that the studied time period witnessed the triumph of a whole new kind of team concept; a team consisting of multiple professions – in this case lawyers, architects, gardeners, home economists, sociologists and engineers. Occasionally, ideas were transformed into abstract entities such as two-dimensional maps and graphs, or even into laws such as the New Towns Act 1946 in the UK, or the Arava (state-subsidized loan arrangement) Act 1948 in Finland. Some of the ideas were expressed in symbols and brands. For instance, huge gardens and spectacle lawns in Tapiola's centre were intentionally designed to characterize a common identity. Another function of these lawns was to function as greenbelts to restrict the city's overgrowth.

MANAGING OVERFLOW: THE ORIGINATORS' VIEW

> We wanted to build a town that was dedicated to man and to his home life, his leisure, and his recreation.' (von Hertzen, 1965: Planning, Design, and Management of Tapiola. University of Pennsylvania European New Towns seminar, as quoted in Heideman, 1975: 11)

For Ebenezer Howard (1898/1965), the originator of the concept, the 'garden city' represented an optimal combination of the urban and the rural in the early 1900s, at a time when the countryside in Britain was in danger of being emptied of inhabitants while cities faced the risk of congestion from growth. But there was no risk of either in 1950s Finland. When the war ended in Finland's defeat, von Hertzen and the the Family Federation of Finland began to look for new models and guidelines from 'more developed' countries to create what was to become Tapiola. International publications as well as excursions within Finland and abroad encouraged new perspectives on building. In 1945, right after the war, the Welfare League's representatives made an extensive tour of Finland's population centres to hear about their housing situation and town plans. They also collected a large number of maps and photographs (*Asuntopolitiikka*, 1961: 2, 6–7). On excursions abroad they learned about the achievements of Finland's Western neighbours in the field, particularly the Swedes.

One of the outcomes of the tours was a polemic 'flyer booklet' entitled *Koti vai kasarmi lapsillemme* (Homes or tenements for our children) by von Hertzen (1946), where it becomes apparent that von Hertzen regarded the countryside as the only healthy place in which to live. In addition to housing solutions, the booklet approaches the lives of children and young people more broadly. It is easy to see, looking at the photographs, many of which were taken by von Hertzen himself, that happy children live in the countryside: scampering around in the fields and woodlands, smiling, constantly on the move. These photographs, with their rounded edges, speak clearly of the softness of the organic world (see Figure 2.1). In contrast, the photos of urban children are square-cornered. The children are pictured standing motionless, smoking cigarettes, in the narrow courtyards of city blocks or inside within four walls (see Figure 2.2).

Von Hertzen's commentary about Mumford's famous film *The City*, originally made for the 1939 New York World Fair, is indicative of the import of Mumford's thinking to Finland:

> Naturally I had read his books, but the biggest impact he made upon me was through his film, *The City*. I first saw it when I was invited to a showing by the Finnish Ambassador to Denmark … Since then I have used the film's theme quite often, underlining the fact that we are biological beings and the most important environment for the majority of our lives is the town or city … At the moment it is not the right environment: With pollution it is not biologically correct, it is not a sociologically pleasing place either, and we can be quite certain from a mental or spiritual point of view that this environment doesn't give the right impulses for a happy kind of life. (as quoted in Alanen, 1983: 43–4)

Source: von Hertzen (1946). Reprinted with permission of the Family Federation of Finland (Väestöliiton kuva-arkisto).

Figure 2.1 Homes or tenements for our children I

Source: von Hertzen (1946). Reprinted with permission of the Family Federation of Finland (Väestöliiton kuva-arkisto).

Figure 2.2 Homes or tenements for our children II

Thus the excess of whatever was wrong with the city had to be managed or removed.

MANAGING OVERFLOW: TAPIOLA'S ARCHITECTS DEFINING BALANCED SPATIAL DEVELOPMENT AND THE GOOD LIFE

> The architect is not only a builder, however; he is an artist, and as artist he carries the burden of prophesy and the compulsion to tell what the good life is. (von Eckardt, 1967: xii)

The architect who was foremost in importing international influences on Tapiola was Otto-Iivari Meurman (1890–1994), a professor of town planning (1940–1959) and the father of Finnish townscape thinking. As early as 1915 he had taken part in preparing a town plan for Greater Helsinki together with the architect Eliel Saarinen (1873–1950) (Saarinen, 1915). Both Meurman and Saarinen had been involved from the early 1900s in the international movement which Mats Deland (2001) has referred to as the 'Social City'. Its central reformist idea was that town planning is at least as much a question of controlling masses of people as it is of technology and aesthetics, and that a better physical environment produces better people.[1]

The fathers of the Finnish garden city movement took their stimulus from problems originally encountered elsewhere, and the local differences were barely recognized by the developers. The solutions created to alleviate problems of urban sprawl, slums and violence in Edinburgh (Geddes), London (Howard) and New York (Mumford) were assumed to be directly applicable to the Helsinki region, with the scale, for instance, not seen as an important characteristic of the model. This is one aspect of disembedding (Sahlin-Anderson, 1996) as it relates to the Finnish version of overflow management. Another aspect lies in the fact that models of town planning (that is, context-free prototypes) originated from general models used to represent living systems. Saarinen followed Patrick Geddes, a student of Charles Darwin and one of the most important pioneers in town planning, when he generalized biological models directly to the cases of giant cities, using terms such as 'organic decentralization'. He even used graphical representation of cancer taken from the pathology textbooks: 'Now slums are a cancer in the urban body, and it is a well-known fact how cancer must be cured' (Saarinen, 1943/1958: 147). He defined the community unit as a place 'where the bulk of the population can exist without being compelled every day to rush back and forth into the congested heart of the city or elsewhere to make a living' (Saarinen, 1943/1958: 208).

In accordance with this view, several articles in the journal *Asuntopolitiikka* [*Housing Policy*] and *Valtakunnansuunnittelu* [*National Planning*] written by O-I. Meurman, a close friend of Saarinen, emphasized that a city is like a tree: a tree's overgrowth makes the distance from the bark to the core grow too large, thereby eroding the bark and congesting the core. Meurman, as a regular contributor to *Asuntopolitiikka*, wrote articles on urban planning issues such as the need for towns to comprise 'residential cells' (Meurman, 1951, 1954). Like the annual rings that form around the central pith in a tree, so new residential cells with their own nuclei will form around a city. The nucleus of an individual cell would create a sense and feeling of a common destiny among the residents. Meurman saw this communal feeling as vital for a nation recovering from two wars: a civil war in 1918 followed by the Second World War. 'Under such circumstances social contrasts will be mitigated and optimism will gain more ground' (Meurman, 1950: 7). Moreover, he was emphatic that the cellular structure should be explicitly social, not administrative (Meurman, 1947: 79) and that 'a residential area should have a home-like spirit' (Meurman, 1947: 76).

In his writings Meurman frequently referred to the urban-critical views of Lewis Mumford and Ebenezer Howard, who considered green belts necessary to restrict growth. It was also Meurman who introduced the three levels of urban planning to Finland – neighbourhood units, residential units and communities – through his articles and his 1947 book *Asemakaavaoppi* [*Town Planning*] (Saarikangas, 2002: 392).[2] This classification was very visible in the subsequent building of Tapiola (Figure 2.3) (Meurman, 1950). Here Meurman followed Saarinen (1943: 208), who had suggested that 'in the functional community, walking must be considered the basic system of individual transportation'.

Accordingly, issues such as optimal positioning of the service network received serious attention in Tapiola. Services had to be located within residential cells so that neighbourhood facilities such as grocery stores and schools were at a maximum distance of 250 metres from residents' homes. Young, 'fresh' architects were selected to plan neighbourhood units intended to house approximately 500–1000 residents each,[3] and because the units were bigger than individual buildings, these new-generation architects began to double up as town planners.

Considering the remarkable number of people taking part in the design and building of Tapiola it is problematic to assume that inspiration flowed in as if through a single pipeline – which is what the official archive materials (of the Housing Foundation) would imply. Instead,

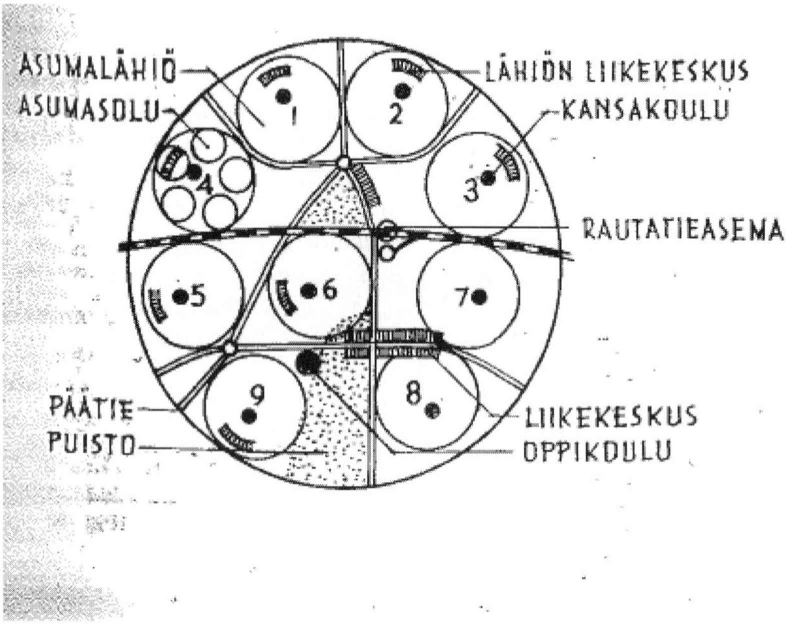

Source: Meurman (1950). Reprinted with permission of the Family Federation of Finland (Väestöliiton kuva-arkisto)

Figure 2.3 Two 'models' of Tapiola

inspiration came from numerous sources and numerous individuals.[4] For instance, Aarne Ervi, Tapiola's principal architect, deviated from the pattern of many of the so-called 'hero architects' of that time (Aalto, Corbusier, Saarinen) by non-theoretically, even popularistically, stressing life's small, everyday details. To him, nature was an essential source of pleasure and enjoyment, but he felt that the recreation offered by movies, restaurants and shopping malls, for example, was equally important (Lahti, 2006). In puritan Finland of the 1950s this kind of attention to everyday comforts combined with a genuine enthusiasm for technological advances such as personal helicopters was rare indeed.

HOME ECONOMISTS, SOCIOLOGISTS, LANDSCAPE ADMINISTRATORS AND TEACHERS AS OVERFLOW MANAGERS

The best models from abroad were adopted to build Tapiola (at least, this is the story as told by the early developers themselves, such as von Hertzen and Itkonen, 1985). Engineering experts from Sweden, for example, were hired from the early 1950s onwards to design (or mainly to supervise) the novel centralized electric power and heating systems, inspect the Finnish plans and calculate prognoses for future heating systems. Thus, in the first instance, Tapiola was modelled on examples from Sweden (housing design, collective spaces, electrical and heating systems), but best practices were additionally sought from other countries: Denmark (garden design, landscaping), Great Britain (new suburbs in accordance with the garden city ideology, the New Town movement), and the United States (roads for light traffic, a schooling system based on youth activity) (von Hertzen and Itkonen, 1985). But when Tapiola was 'exported' into the wider world, the origin of such ideas was obscured; for example, the Swedish techno-bureaucratic approach to building soon began to be seen as an outright antithesis of Tapiola's development (von Eckardt, 1967; von Hertzen, 1971a).

The home economists in the foundation's multidisciplinary teams, some of whom had been employed in the Household Work Efficiency Institute that had been established during wartime, contributed to Tapiola by commenting on matters such as kitchen and bathroom design to standardize the work of the housewife. Chronic fatigue among housewives was one of the pressing social problems of the 1950s. Experts emphasized that housewives had a right to domestic appliances and equipment to make housework easier. Tapiola's home economists also defended this equipment in the name of rationalization (*Asuntopolitiikka*, 1954; Ritvala, 1958). It was representatives of home economics who first proposed the collective provision of storage, laundering and deep-freezing equipment, for instance, as an alternative to more individualized ways. Besides common laundry rooms and cold stores in apartment houses, they also imported to Finland ideas such as the American bar kitchen in apartment houses, fair-faced brick walls in interiors and narrow air vents, many of these as early as in the 1950s. The masses were introduced to the newest trends in architecture and domestic technology in local housing exhibitions featuring fully furnished apartment interiors.

In the 1950s, the ideals of better-equipped homes were similar in many Western countries. Managing time and money was a central concern, especially for the mother of the family. The washing machine, for instance, made it possible for her to devote more time to her family (Pantzar, 2003). However, as one of the pioneers of efficient housekeeping and director of the Work Efficiency Institute proclaimed: ‘it is not only equipment, machines and appliances that make people’s work easier. People themselves have a crucial position: their capability to organize, to think, to understand’ (Janhonen, 1986: 5). The housewife should be encouraged to reflect on her work so as not to tire herself out unnecessarily, whereupon she could spare ‘resources to improve herself and create the home’s atmosphere’ (ibid.). Household appliances were part of the promise of progress. Progress, but not just any kind of progress: the woman’s workplace was still at home.

In consumer expenditure the share required by ‘necessities’ such as food, clothes and housing started to diminish fast in the 1950s and the elite began to worry about the wrong sort of consumption. In Finland the key text expressing the ideal of an investment-driven economy was published in 1952 by Prime Minister Urho Kekkonen. The name of his book is very telling: *Onko maallamme malttia vaurastua?* [*Does Our Nation Have the Patience to Prosper?*]. Kekkonen’s central concern was how to make private households defer the satisfaction of their consumer desires. Characteristic of the period was that, in real terms, interest on bank savings was negative, and public institutions were channelling funds into investments. The building of national infrastructures, roads and communication networks, and state-run industry, was of primary importance. The ‘patience’ required for making the nation prosper meant investing in durable goods such as refrigerators and washing machines, and especially private apartments. Therefore, somewhat paradoxically, consumer goods – refrigerators, automobiles and washing machines – and houses became important means of controlling the excess and the impulsiveness of the population. Banks and the leading figures in economic policy regarded saving for owner-occupied homes, and even for household appliances, as a way to restrain the desire to consume, to induce people to save their wages, and thus to enable the country to finance industrial investments (Lehtonen and Pantzar, 2002).

Household appliances were durable tools, and thus much more appropriate to the industrial mode of the times than would have been, for example, Mediterranean tours or exotic foods. Their time would not come until the 1980s. One could speculate that the unique combination of Eastern planning and investment-driven economic thought, and of Western dreams of consumption, could be one of the reasons why

Finnish households accomplished an exceptionally swift transition from an agrarian surplus-saving culture into a Western consumer and 'credit culture'.

Throughout his life von Hertzen maintained a critical position in his writings towards the dangers of the 'wrong' kind of progress (material growth) that placed too much emphasis on economic concerns (that is, production and consumption). For instance, when the oil crisis broke out he continued to stress education as the question that would determine the fate of the whole nation:

> We see spiritually underdeveloped individuals and groups of individuals fighting to destroy one another in a way that may end in the total demolition of human culture ... Due to an underestimation of the education process, society is teeming with frustrated and character-disordered individuals, families, and homes that are falling apart. (von Hertzen, 1973: 2–3)

It is no surprise that this kind of thinking had led the founders of Tapiola to emphasize educational activities from the very beginning (von Hertzen, 1962).

MANAGING TIME: ACTIVE VERSUS PASSIVE LEISURE

The role of professional youth workers and teachers was to provide advice on how to keep the children off the streets. Like the plants growing in its gardens, Tapiola's youth also had to be tended in subtle terms. Von Hertzen explained the delicate rhetoric of freedom and discipline in von Eckardt's (1967: 355) book as follows:

> Was there any adult supervision and management of these activities? 'Of course,' smiled von Hertzen, 'we have a very imaginative young man on the staff. But we don't call him a youth activities officer, or anything like that. That we fear would only scare the very kids that need involvement most. His title is assistant town engineer.'

At the end of the 1950s, when new Finnish-speaking schools were established with the help of the Housing Foundation, the conflict between the old and the new era grew: an experimental school, Tapiola Co-educational School, became feasible only after the more traditional forces withdrew – that is, when an American-type pioneer spirit and openness overcame the bureaucratic and hierarchical Swedish-German system (Opintiellä, 1998). The chair of the school board had a background in consulting in Los Angeles and it was he who introduced new terms such as 'team work' and 'innovations' to the teachers.

The overall innovative pattern of the garden city is also evident in the discussion of controlled spontaneity in the founding of the youth theatre: in the absence of finished manuscripts, everything was done collectively, on the young people's own initiative. The same encouragement of individual initiative was repeated in Tapiola's schools, which were among the first in Finland to teach a special subject called 'oral presentation'. At the same time business English and engineering drawing were also introduced into the curriculum.

The record sales of pianos in the shopping mall, the audiovisual equipment in the schools, team sport activities and cultural exchange (mainly with the US) all demonstrate the kinds of things that were appreciated in the model town. Car driving, spending time in idleness, watching TV, and generally staying locked up within four walls represented 'bad' consumption and the wrong kind of time use in Tapiola. The risk of dormitory towns or bedroom suburbs was pointed out in many public statements published in the journals *Asuntopoliiikka* and *Valtakunnansuunnittelu*. Heikki von Hertzen was editor-in-chief of both journals. Though initially, in the 1950s, the term 'dormitory town' only referenced the contrast of job self-sufficiency and traffic problems in the city centres, by the 1960s it began to refer to all forms of passivity associated with the suburbs.

A lively debate about the activity or passivity of Tapiola's residents continued throughout the 1960s. In a 1967 seminar of the Finnish Society of Architects ('What can we learn from Tapiola?'), sociologist Paavo Seppänen reported on time-use surveys indicating that people were likely to choose idleness if services were not located within walking distance from their homes – which posed the risk of such areas degenerating into dormitory suburbs. Accordingly, optimization of the service network was an issue that received serious attention in Tapiola. At the same time, trifles were juxtaposed with real needs. Self-interest was seen as a force to be controlled, while new residents moving to the community were greeted by newsletters sent to them by Tapiola's 'public relations officers'. According to a brochure entitled *Tapiola Garden City* (Tapiola Housing Foundation, 1957: 14), 'These newsletters also use dry humour on occasion to inculcate lessons of good behaviour and consideration for one's neighbours, both upon the young and their parents. They also bring together people with similar interests and hobbies.'

As already noted, the initial expectations, interests and plans of Tapiola's originators, and especially of von Hertzen himself, were targeted at anything but an urban consumerist way of life. Of course, in reality, the variety of opinions on the requisite conditions for a happy life was wider among the developers than official history writing leads us to understand, and perceptions of a 'proper' lifestyle also transformed in the course of the building process. Nor could conflicts be avoided. The architect Alvar Aalto, for example, attacked the home economists by remarking that individually owned refrigerators, deep freezers and washing machines were taking the race for household equipment much too far at the cost of commonly shared facilities (Aalto, 1952).

MANAGING OVERFLOW: CONTROVERSIAL VIEWS

The propaganda films about Tapiola made in the 1960s usually picture a family – mother, father and two children – on a ski track that leaves right from their own doorstep. This kind of romantic image of Tapiola attracted a lot of criticism, especially from young architects and sociologists. In the seminar 'What can we learn from Tapiola?' mentioned above, young architect Kirsti Nordin mused at the applied rhetoric:

> Typical features of Tapiola's institutional ideology are hermeticalness, organizational isolation, transformation of organization into social reality, fierce opposition to any attempt at criticism, use of slogans, invoking of emotions, traditions, wishes, and obscure theory – I still haven't figured out whether the 'biological function' refers to reproduction or to skiing – and a striv[ing] to control people instead of things. (Finnish Association of Architects Seminar, 1967)

One of the most notable controversies that arose concerned the role of 'lower' social classes. Von Hertzen felt that the involvement of sociologists was necessary so that the area could be approached both as a population issue and as a way to promote national unity. In a theme article on Tapiola in *Reader's Digest*, von Hertzen used sociological terms to depict Tapiola as a 'cross-sectional society' where class differences had lost their meaning (Taylor, 1966). He expressed his pride at the achieved success in a book published a few years later: 'Foreign visitors find it hard to believe that so many people with low and middle incomes live in Tapiola and this had had practically no negative influence on the appearance, cleanliness, level of culture, or spirit of the community' (von Hertzen and Spreiregen, 1971: 170). Sociologists, however, did not accept this kind of story at face value. One of them, Professor Paavo Seppänen, for example, interviewed in the book *Tapiola – A Village of Better Folks*, expressed the view that:

> the environment that the children [of Tapiola] are socialized into is a community of people who represent a particular lifestyle. Were such a sphere of experience some kind of absolute ideal, the solution might be optimal also from the children's viewpoint. But with no guarantee of this, there is at least a danger that the children's worldview in a community of this type tends to become one-sided – restricted, in a sense. (Hiisiö, 1970: 148)

Von Hertzen expressed his dissenting opinion in an unpublished memo entitled 'Hiisiö's compliments' (von Hertzen, 1971b):

> What's wrong if the upper middle class becomes an object of imitation: if it isn't the upper middle class that is taken as the benchmark to pursue, then where do you get the benchmark? Does everyone have to descend to the level of social class IV? And is that what citizens are now asking us to do? It certainly isn't. Citizens want advancement, not descent, and if we are truly realistic this advancement is usually targeted at reaching the upper middle class. In a way it is strange, even outright depressing, that sociopolitical and sociological thinking is still so undeveloped that a statement like this cannot even be made without belittlement. As a matter of fact, it is a question of one of the very greatest achievements of the Tapiola project. But even that would be belittled, were it only possible.

Von Hertzen's comment partly explains how it was possible several decades before there was any material (democratic) affluence to raise the question of what to do with affluence when it arrived. Von Hertzen saw material progress advancing inevitably in a linear way, like many other people in the Finnish elite. What was seen as 'trickledown' in the social sphere was seen as a 'catching-up' phenomenon on the scale of nations. In retrospect he was right, but there could have been another turn of events, such as that in post-war Latin America, where promises of material wealth and democratization were not realized. This observation requires further examination: how to explain the unison of so many people in the idea of making a model town in a relatively poor and peripheral country such as post-war Finland.

MAKING A MODEL FOR MODERN-DAY PEOPLE: THE STRENGTH OF WEAK CONCEPTS

The Housing Foundation used its powerful mediatic position to control the changing content of the garden city story. The discourse on Tapiola actually abounded with much-repeated new, and therefore ambiguous and flexible, concepts such as 'garden city, 'real needs', 'modern-day people', 'cross-sectional society' and 'dormitory or bedroom suburb', as well as 'overplanning' (with particular reference to Sweden). These terms were especially favoured by the early developers, Meurman and von Hertzen. It was partly through ambiguous concepts and through positive and negative references to other countries that the various professional discourses (of expectation management) and disciplines became integrated and activists were mobilized.

Although unanimity was not total and critical voices were heard, nonetheless the majority of Tapiola's builders shared a strong belief in a better future. International comparisons provided the raw material for self-assessment (Pantzar, 2010). The evolution of a consumer society in Finland, a country that had recently lost the war alongside Germany, had much in common with corresponding development in Germany, and the United States became an important model to follow in both countries (Heinonen and Pantzar, 2002; Kroen, 2006).[5] Aarne Ervi, in particular, who designed the area's main shopping mall among other things, brought American thinking into the planning of Tapiola. It was also he who managed to change the founding fathers' original understanding of the good life to include facilities such as the new type of shopping centre that offered all kinds of recreation and activities. Even von Hertzen, who in the 1940s had been highly critical of urban pleasures, was forced to 'edit' his attitude towards bars and restaurants along with the arrival of the shopping mall. Very similar developments towards tolerance were taking place all over post-war Europe (Jerram, 2011).

Many of Tapiola's ideals were generally compatible with those equating technological advancement with quality of life, but no single model of prosperity was adopted. Illustrative of this diversity is the way Alvar Aalto in the 1940s questioned his American colleagues who proudly pronounced that American homes were at the forefront of progress: 'How many rowboats are there in the United States per thousand people? And how many American hairdressers are able to go skiing from their doorstep? How many Americans are able to reach clean fishing waters just 15 minutes from their home?' (Schildt, 1989: 107). The Housing Foundation had purchased a rowboat for use by all residents as early as the 1950s.

Tapiola could hardly have materialized as a result of the purely top-down plans and orders of overflow managers. Indeed, apart from much elitist philosophizing, a specific feature of Tapiola was the lively public discussion in the local newspaper about very concrete details such as the upkeep of clubrooms in buildings, the preservation of individual trees during construction works, and the need for audiovisual equipment in the schools. Tapiola's uniqueness in the Finnish context was in its powerful emphasis on community planning and activities. As has become evident, the exceptionally strong commitment to the development of the community and communal activities introduced a new organic terminology:

> Many people still think that planning ends with the drawing of the master plan and town plan … What happens during the actual construction period is also vital. And life must be breathed into everything that has been planned. A community … must be a living organism, its heart must be made to beat. (Von Hertzen, 1965, as quoted in Heideman, 1975: 12)

This terminology, largely borrowed from Mumford (and indirectly Geddes), generated and emphasized concern about the reproductive qualities of the community. In different fields of expertise these became translated somewhat differently but the main idea was shared. Table 2.1 summarizes and simplifies the main ingredients and implications of the biological or organic metaphor of living community in the context of overflow management.

Table 2.1 Living community as seen by urban planners, educators and economists

Excess	Frame	Solution	Managers
Urban sprawl, slum	Biology, overgrowth of a cancer cell	Greenbelts and cells with functioning centres	Architects and urban planners Engineers Landscape administration
Discretionary expenditure Affluence	Rational non-myopic behaviour	Saving, economizing and long-term investments in durables	(Home) economists Sociologists
Idle time	Dormitory vs. active leisure	Organized free time Educational institutes	Educators Sociologists

Tapiola's founding fathers believed that people could and would change in the processes of living and building. However, they did not always understand either the changing activities (or actually passivity) of ordinary people or the autonomous development efforts of the business world.

The well-known architecture critic Jane Jacobs (1961/1993) also pointed out that both Howard and Mumford had quite a static view of city life. Their approach to commerce, for instance, was in terms of a standardized supply of goods, with little attention paid to the tendency of businesses to expand, or to human conflicts. Good planning was conceived as a series of static acts that were based more on averages than deviations. In a quite similar vein, the main difficulties that Tapiola's developers faced were both attracting business companies into the area and changing human character permanently. The clubrooms and other youth facilities in many housing companies, for example, were quickly closed down due to noise disturbances, and also for financial reasons.

The Mumfordian idea of starting from a pristine state was most obvious in the lack of concern on the part of Tapiola's builders with private car-ownership. This may, in fact, have been the biggest error in the design of Tapiola. The developers were as unenthusiastic about, even disinterested in increasing traffic requirements and the use of private cars as Mumford had been. In this sense Tapiola was unlike the rest of Finland, where American influences favouring private car use were adopted much more readily. Von Hertzen felt, for instance, that it sufficed if a removal van was able to drive up to a house once in a lifetime. The majority of traffic would move along pedestrian walkways and bikeways. He did not foresee that Tapiola would be taken over by private cars, especially after the area became part of Greater Helsinki with the completion of the Länsiväylä freeway connecting it with central Helsinki.

CONCLUSIONS

In this chapter I have discussed little-known aspects of the birth of consumer society in Finland, with special focus on forthcoming riches, idle time and overused land area. Tapiola's developers were eager to copy models that had proven successful elsewhere. Models and ideas travelled as elements of larger ideological complexes developed by Mumford and other thinkers of the early twentieth century, and found their own shape and place of attachment in the perhaps unexpected contexts of post-war Finland. What had been a concern over the quantity of population (the 'population crisis' of the 1930s) turned into a concern over its quality in the 'human capital discourse' of the 1950s and 1960s.

At the start, Tapiola's building process was shadowed by thoughts evoked by the war economy as well as by worries over the detrimental effects of cities on the masses, fitting well with what was known to be happening elsewhere in Europe. In retrospect, the emerging rhetoric emphasizing the active participation of citizens, and young people in particular, may seem to have been highly calculated, having subsequently fanned the growth of the national economy. But in fact the wishes, interests and plans of the first developers of the area comprised anything but an emphasis on an active, urban consumerist lifestyle.

Findings in this discussion underline that even in a small and relatively open economy modernization (or Americanization) was far from a simple process of imitation. The analysis supports Frank Trentman's thesis (Trentman, 2009: 209) that globalization of consumption is more than financial flows and commodity trade: 'It involves human actors whose ideas, identities, anxieties and power can facilitate, manipulate or contain global exchange.' In processes like this certain languages of description, explanation and calculation came to acquire the value of truth, and specific kinds of action and techniques become possible by such truths. Meanwhile, maps, charts, diagrams and graphs make things stable, mobile, durable and comparable, and they convince others (Rose, 1999).

The chapter adds a not so widely acknowledged aspect of modernization to the insights of Trentman and other commentators on modern consumerism (which ignored the role of the home economist, for example): the role of a relatively new profession in mediating the future, in this case in managing and anticipating a forthcoming overflow. In Tapiola's case the highly specialized division of labour of its planners and builders influenced the way 'proper' consumption was defined. In the encounter of many different professions with their own internal communication patterns, ideas of the good life within a garden city were translated into many different sublanguages of various historical origins. Residents probably failed to realize that the greenbelts linked their community to Ebenezer Howard's idealistic thought and through him to Leonardo da Vinci's early visions, Thomas More's *Utopia*, or Edward Bellamy's faith in techno-optimism, classless society and the cooperative movement. These utopian thoughts acted as background and origin of fuzzy terms such as 'biological function', 'dormitory town' and 'urban sprawl' with which overflow management was exercised. The fact that these terms were loosely defined explains why they functioned as boundary concepts, adaptable to local sites, and facilitating communication across various professions.

EPILOGUE

My parents' generation was guided by the ideal of progress and a naive belief in a better and more civilized society. In our upper-middle-class family of six the shaping of a young person's life and ideals was surprisingly consistently steered by modern Western consumption culture. However, the Tapiola of the 1960s was not yet an individualized consumer society; it was more of a Mumfordian and Galbraithian model community, embracing a sense of collective responsibility and collective upbringing – which, paradoxically, created an excellent ground for the emergence of a society of almost limitless consumerism. In fact, many of the leaders of the Finnish 'mobile information society' are former classmates of mine, who had adopted Nokia's values long before Nokia itself. Good public performance skills, internationalism, tolerance and pragmatism were at the core of Tapiola's pedagogical philosophy. Tapiola's schools were the first in Finland to teach business English and engineering drawing, and children were made familiar with computers on class visits to the University of Technology a few kilometres away. This was where several of my classmates would continue their studies and even today many are living somewhere in the neighbourhood.

NOTES

1. The association that later came to be known as Asuntoreformiyhdistys (Housing Reform Society) was established in Finland as early as 1910 to promote building activity that aimed at 'the public good' and 'more social and healthy' housing.
2. A neighbourhood unit was defined as the area within walking distance from home to school and a basic shop. It also referred to the kind of social community (*Gemeinschaft*) emphasized by sociologists in the 1950s worrying about the loss of community (for example, Mann, 1954: 163–168). The neighbourhood unit concept formed an important starting point in the 1952 housing reform competition where many of the young architects for the Tapiola project were found.
3. In the winning plans, potential residents were classified by household types: 'The results of the competition indicate that family dwellings should generally not be located into high tower buildings, but into low apartment houses or row houses, whereas dwellings for single households or families without children are more suitable in tall buildings' (*Asuntopolitiikka*, 1953: 5). In any case, this was how Heikki von Hertzen (the editor-in-chief of both *Asuntopolitiikka* and *Valtakunnansuunnittelu*) saw it.
4. For example, the architects who designed the area were quite diversely oriented: Meurman represented the 'old school' where German influence was predominant, while younger designers such as Aarne Ervi (1910–1977) drew most of their influences from the United States and Great Britain. Ervi was an important actor as a town planner as well. He realized what exceptional freedom Tapiola enjoyed in being able to develop as part of Espoo municipality, a district with almost no housing regulation in the post-war period. Part of this freedom came from the fact that land prices were fairly low because the border of Porkkala, an area leased to the Soviet Union after the war, was just 15 kilometres away.
5. Generally speaking, Finland was not 'Americanized' by a flow of physical objects, but mostly in the form of ideas and cultural goods. For instance, of all the countries of

Europe, it was Finland where Donald Duck and *Reader's Digest* drew their largest audiences. Small artefacts such as records, comics and cosmetics were not only materializations of the notion of the modern society but its carriers as well (Heinonen and Pantzar, 2002). It is also symptomatic that American ideas and ideals were imported and translated for Finnish audiences mainly through books that were critical of American society, for example through the writings of Mumford, Galbraith and Packard.

FIELD MATERIAL

Aalto, Alvar (1952), 'Rakennammeko liian valmista?' ['Do we make too ready-made homes?'] *Asuntopolitiikka*, 2: 8.

Alanen, Arnold (1983), 'An interview with Heikki von Hertzen: the man behind the Garden City of Tapiola, Finland', *Landscape Journal*, **2**(1): 40–51.

Asuntopolitiikka (1951), 'Ihanteellinen puutarhakaupunki suunnitteilla Helsingin liepeille' ['An ideal garden city being planned on the outskirts of Helsinki'], 3: 4–5.

Asuntopolitiikka (1953), 'Asuntoreformikilpailu ratkaistu' ['The winner of the housing reform competition'] D391, 2: 6–9.

Asuntopolitiikka (1954), 'Kerrostalojen yhteistilat' ['Collective provision of storage'], D 1460, 2: 8.

Asuntopolitiikka (1961), Väestöliiton asuntopoliittinen toiminta ['Housing policy initiatives of the The Family Federation of Finland'], 2: 6–7.

Finnish Association of Architects (1967), 'What can we learn from Tapiola?', seminar report, 16 September, Helsinki..

Heideman, M. Lawrence (1975), 'Tapiola: model, myth, or happenstance? A personal investigation', *Urban Ecology*, **1**(1): 5–47.

von Hertzen, Heikki (1946), *Koti vai kasarmi lapsillemme. Asunnontarvitsijoiden näkökohtia asunto- ja kaavakysymyksissä* [*Homes or tenements for our children*], Helsinki: WSOY.

von Hertzen, Heikki (1962), 'On investoitava ihmiseen', (pääkirjoitus) ['We have to invest in people' (editorial)]. *Valtakunnansuunnittelu*, **1**: 1.

von Hertzen, Heikki (1971a), *Miksi Tapiolaa ei rakennettu Ruotsiin, miksi se on rakennettu Suomeen?* [*Why could Tapiola not be built in Sweden?*], unpublished manuscript.

von Hertzen, Heikki (1971b), *Hiisiön kiitokset* [*Praise from Hiisiö*], unpublished memorandum, 13 January.

von Hertzen Heikki (1973), *Ihmiskunta, yhteiskunta, perhe ja yksilö olemassaolonsa vaikeimmassa kriisissä* [*Mankind, Society, Families, and Individuals Facing the Worst Crisis of Their Existence*], paper delivered 21 October to a seminar of women members of the conservative National Coalition Party.

von Hertzen, Heikki and Uolevi Itkonen (1985), *Raportti kaupungin rakentamisesta, Tapiolan arkea ja juhlaa* [*A Report about Building a City: Daily Life in Tapiola*], Tapiola, Finland: ArtPrint.

von Hertzen, Heikki and Paul Spreiregen (1971), *Building a New Town. Finland's New Garden City, Tapiola*, Cambridge, MA: MIT Press.

Hiisiö, Ossi (1970), *Tapiola – parempien ihmisten kylä* [Tapiola – A Village of Better Folks], Helsinki: Tammi.

Janhonen, Hille (1986), 'Kotitalouden rationalisointitutkimuksen uranuurtaja, Maiju Gebhard 15.9.1896-18.7.1986' ['Maiju Gebhard, the pioneer of the home rationalization movement'],*Teho*, **9**: 4–5.

Kekkonen, Urho (1952), *Onko maallamme malttia vaurastua?* [*Does Our Nation Have the Patience to Prosper?*], Helsinki: Otava.

Lahti, A. Juhana (2006), *Arkkitehti Aarne Ervin moderni. Kaupunkisuunnittelu pääkaupunkiseudulla* [*Urban Planning in Helsinki Area. Modernism and Architect Aarne Ervi*], *Taidehistoriallisia tutkimuksia*, 34. Helsinki: Taidehistorian seura.

Meurman, Otto-Iivari (1947), *Asemakaavaoppi* [*Town Planning*], Helsinki: Otava.

Meurman, Otto-Iivari (1950), 'Asumasolu ja asumalähiö' ['Residential cell and a community'], *Asuntopolitiikka*, 1: 5–7.

Meurman, Otto-Iivari (1951), 'Asuntoalueiden suunnittelusta Englannissa' ['Town planning in England'], *Asuntopolitiikka*, **2**: 4–5.

Meurman, Otto-Iivari (1954), 'Asemakaavoitus sivistyksellisenä ilmiönä' ['Town planning as a civilizing process'], *Asuntopolitiikka*, **4**: 4–5.

Nupponen, Terttu (2000), *Arkkitehdit, sota ja yhdyskuntasuhteiden hallinta* [*Architects, War and Town Planning*], Helsinki: Suomalaisen kirjallisuuden seura.

Opintiellä (1998), *Tapiolan yhteiskoulu, koulu ja lukio 1958–1998* [*History of Tapiola Schools*], Jyväskylä, Finland: Gummerus.

Ritvala, Riitta (1958), 'Kotitalousasiantuntijan havaintoja nykyaikaisesta asuntotuotannosta' ['Notes by a domestic scientist concerning modern housing'], *Asuntopolitiikka*, **4**: 8.

Saarikangas, Kirsi (2002), *Asunnon muodonmuutoksia. Puhtauden estetiikka ja sukupuoli modernissa arkkitehtuurissa* [*Metamorphosis of a House. Gender and Aesthetics in Modern Architecture*], Helsinki: Suomalaisenkirjallisuuden seura.

Saarinen, Eliel (1915), *Munkkiniemi-Haaga suunnitelma* [*Munkkiniemi-Haaga Plan. A Proposition*], Helsinki: M.G. Stenius Oy.

Schildt, Göran (1989), *Inhimillinen tekijä. Alvar Aalto 1939–1976* [*Human Factor. Alvar Aalto 1939–1976*], Helsinki: Otava.

Tapiola Housing Foundation (1957), *Tapiola Garden City*. information leaflet.

Tuomi, Timo and Kristiina Paatero (2003) *Tapiola. Elämää ja arkkitehtuuria* [*Tapiola: Everyday Life and Architecture*], Tampere, Finland: Rakennustieto Oy, Tammerpaino.

3. Potlatch à la Polonaise or consumption cultures in times of transformation

Mariusz Czubaj

Anthropology depends upon the play of details. It should focus on mundane, everyday, boring events at least equally as much as on spectacular events and events that occur on holy days or significant days. What frequently happens is that small, local events become bigger events, unexpectedly acquiring new meanings; and are transformed into something that could be called a cultural metaphor. I begin this chapter with such a small local event.

Between 2012 and 2013 a great deal of media attention was dedicated to Weekend – a band from the small Polish town of Sejny, Poland – and their disco-polo song, *Ona tańczy dla mnie* [*She Dances for Me*].[1] It was soon possible to say, without great exaggeration, that the whole of Poland was talking about it. Weekend's vocalist was portrayed on the cover of the Polish edition of *Newsweek*, numerous press articles were dedicated to the group and the phenomenon of disco-polo, and, at the time of writing, 14 February 2013, a video of the song has been seen 51 million times on YouTube.[2] Apart from the original clip, there are many parodies, documenting the entry of Weekend into the fan culture.

This is what you can see on the YouTube video. The vocalist wears a white t-shirt, a shiny jacket and a thin golden necklace (disco-polo is not rap!) and has a solarium-tanned face – in short, a variation on Don Johnson during his days with *Miami Vice*. He enters the club. There are sofas, some lights, a bar, and a dance floor. Long-legged and long-haired young women attract the eye, but the sense of eroticism is subtle; these are not vamps dripping sexuality. Disco-polo contains a visible trait of small-town conservatism – it is populist yet puritan. The vocalist starts to sing, and the song's key phrase is repeated many times: 'I adore her/She is here/She dances for me/ Because she knows/that I am going to kidnap her/and hide her deep in my heart.'[3]

A universal and forceful declaration of love, intended to transport listeners to the land of pure feelings, to a country existing beyond time and space, where everyday troubles never enter. A perfect song for a time of economic crisis, which, in spite of what the Polish government says, did not spare Poland. Even if the billboard advertisements of jeeps encourage 'Life. Take it!', the fans of Weekend know better. We live in times when it is best to concentrate on small pleasures, on the consumption of emotions, on relationships – all on a small scale, with no extraordinary expectations and aspirations.

But observe one peculiarity of the song. It says 'She dances for me', not 'She dances with me'. Her body is a commodity; its movement conveys temptation and promise, which will produce new desires, as in Schopenhauer's circle of desire and partial fulfilment. In this way, and certainly unplanned by the creators of the hit, 'She dances for me' becomes a metaphor of consumption, realized on a small scale. It is also an unexpected commentary to Zygmunt Bauman's statement in *Razem, osobno* [*Together, Apart*] that 'the present sufferings of *homo sexualis* are in fact the sufferings of *homo consumens*' (Bauman, 2003: 142). It can be also read as an illustration of the following observation by Polish sociologist Tomasz Szlendak, who studies the transformation of sexual customs of young people in the epoch of consumerism:

> Sex had been moved from the 'sphere of production' to its consuming environment and it became exactly that – consumption. Young people are clients in a supermarket and choose only that which attracts them or that which – they are told – they need. The more magic, the more fairy-tale-like atmosphere, the better for the supermarket. (Szlendak, 2004: 113)

And 'She dances for me' offers exactly that magical atmosphere of erotic and emotional fulfilment as *pars pro toto* in these difficult times, when other forms of consumption may be scarce.

CIRCLES OF CONSUMPTION AND SECOND-DEGREE GLOCALIZATION

The popularity of the small-town band has been discussed here in order to illustrate varying levels of consumption aspirations – in contrast to the usual discussions of consumption conducted on a general, global level. In Poland at least, it is absolutely necessary to speak about the differentiation of consumption practices, caused by economic differentiation on the one hand and lifestyle differences between big cities and the rest of the country on the other hand. This differentiation is not new, and ought to be analysed in Braudelian categories of *longue durée.* In 1938 barely 30 per cent of the Polish population lived in big cities – a figure that has nearly doubled now. It needs to be added, however, as culture historians have noted, that it is not merely that the Polish countryside has become more urbanized; many Polish cities preserve their rural character (Szpakowska, 2004: 15). Thus the issues of consumption must be considered in the frame of local knowledge, as recommended by Clifford Geertz, and 'the humanist coefficient', as suggested by Florian Znaniecki.

Common fields of consumption practices undoubtedly exist, even in strongly differentiated societies. One of those practices is tourism, and Poles are no different in this way to any other 'nomadic consumer tribe', to use the expression coined by Cova et al. (2007). Again, students of customs indicate that the contents of the wallet can no longer serve as a gauge of the opportunity to consume space as a tourist:

> This is quite striking: the complaints about poverty and the proofs of hardship are accompanied by relations from recent travels abroad, and these are pleasure travels. It shows without doubt that travelling belongs no longer to luxuries. (Szpakowska, 2004: 205)

Poles have gladly adopted various 'consumer holidays': the days of St Valentine (the saint of love), St Patrick (the saint of beer) and Santa Claus (the saint of all things). This is but one more proof that the sacred and the consumed can collaborate in harmony (Czubaj, 2007).

Like many others, Poles participate in bodily spectacles. Bodies have acquired a special value in postmodern or late modern times as both tools and objects of consumption, as documented by local salons (called nail studios or beauty institutes, however) and exclusive spas. Foucault would consider them yet one more kind of heterotopia, this special place-no-place, of which there is more and more in contemporary societies. Universities in Poland now offer a specialty in 'Manager of Spa and Wellness'.

It happens that the same or similar cultural practices are performed differently in a big city than they are in a small town. Marketing oneself on Facebook is typical for the inhabitants of big cities, whereas the inhabitants of smaller communities use local media for the same purpose – the Polish portal *Nasza Klasa* [*Our Class*], for instance. Citizens of Polish metropolises meet in such places as large malls (Golden Terraces in Warsaw, Old Brewery in Poznan), whereas the inhabitants of small towns choose the premises of retail chains (especially one called Biedronka, or Ladybird[4]). Perhaps shopping and dating elicit similar feelings of uncertainty, which render such places ideal spaces for encounters.

Consumption customs and habits also contribute to a phenomenon that can be called 'glocalization of a second degree'. More and more often, consumption practices contribute to a local taming of global trademarks and products. McDonalds in Poland offers WieśMac [*CountryMac*], and the sale of hamburgers in Germany's McDonalds was originally supported by a quote from Feuerbach: '*Der Mensch ist, was er isst*' [*Man is what he eats*]. Second-degree glocalization concerns the relationship between the centre and the periphery, or perhaps the centres and the periphery. It is necessary, therefore, to speak about consumer societies in the plural.

WEDDINGS AS A CONTRIBUTION TO THE THEORY OF CONSUMER SOCIETY

Every culture likely contains some key practices that, like a magnifying glass, illustrate its most characteristic traits. Some scholars claim that Europe experiences an atrophy of rituals of passage, with the result that there are few ceremonies and rituals marking crucial passages in the life history of an individual: birth (and its new and incredibly developed 'newborns industry'), and death (although the funeral industry has a long history, as described by Pascale Trompette, 2012). In Poland, as in Sweden and Italy, the wedding remains the special occasion.[5]

It is exactly the wedding that deserves the moniker 'potlatch à la polonaise',[6] because it belongs to an old and solid Polish tradition that defines the wedding as an occasion to put on the table more than necessary, and more than one can afford. This is 'that one time', when one can afford madness (worse, however, it is usually more than one time nowadays). I see a similarity to Ruth Benedict's descriptions of the incredible potlatches of the North American Kwakiutl tribe. In her *Patterns of Culture* (Benedict, 1934/2006), she dared to call the potlatch an expression of 'a megalomaniac paranoid tendency'. I am fully aware of and in agreement with later commentators who, like Clifford Geertz, suggested that Benedict's analysis actually concerned contemporary US, and could be read together with Karen Horney's *The Neurotic Personality of Our Times* (1937). Potlatch can therefore be seen as a metaphor for megaconsumption, and I use the term in this sense. The Polish culture historian Małgorzata Szpakowska spoke of 'wedding fetishism' (2002: 202).[7]

A Polish wedding is a specific combination of the tradition and its games, plays and music (currently often disco-polo) and an ambitious logistics task. One of many websites offering the organization of weddings and marriage ceremonies guarantees that its professional personnel will:

- guarantee an exceptional marriage ceremony in the church;
- prepare an elegant party with particular attention to detail;
- help to lower the costs of the ceremony;
- offer a wide choice of companies in this industry (specializing in the very 'detail' mentioned above).[8]

Every part of the wedding is critical, not least the logistics. The advice concerning the organization of the honeymoon says that it is 'extremely important that all matters concerning the wedding must be ready before the departure. Only then will your thoughts not be wandering through the list of things that you were supposed to do but did not.' But there are two elements tied by an economic thread, in which a crucial role is played by *signum temporis* – the world financial crisis. The website contains an article entitled 'Wedding in times of crisis'. There readers are told how to save money in preparing the wedding, or even how to recuperate some of their expenses. But even more interesting is the information about discounts:

> Many companies offer discounts to the newlywed. Often you can learn about them by visiting wedding fairs. It is also recommended to hire a *wedding planning* [the English words with a Polish construction] company, which usually has many subcontractors, more willing to offer a discount to the clients of the company than to another couple.[9]

It is clear that the suggestions for economizing would not exist if it were not for the economic crisis, but they would also be unnecessary if there were no tendency to turn the wedding into a hyper-feast.

The second element is related to possible ways of describing the consuming society. There are quite a few to choose from: Baudrillard's orgiastic consumption in *The Consumer Society* (1998), which suggests the emergence of a hyperreality; Ritzer's description of McDonaldization (1993/2008), claiming that the hamburger producer incorporates Weberian iron cage rationality in the design of the chain; or Bauman's (1998) ethical propositions and his search for support of human subjectivity in these times, tainted by postmodern sins – including consumption. Nevertheless, as Löfgren and Czarniawska (2012) have noted, these models and images are relatively close to one another. In order to speak of a 'consumer society', it is not enough to highlight intensification of processes and practices that were always present, albeit on a lesser scale. All these authors attempt to show that these practices and processes presently form a more or less coherent system.

The example of the wedding, when treated as the contemporary epicentre (and not the only one) of consumerism, permits formulation of yet another systemic quality of the consumer society. To use computer vocabulary, the essence of consumption lies in its partitioning and fragmentation. In the case of the wedding, there is a whole list of products and services: dresses, jewellery, makeup, catering, flowers, dance schools. One must choose the restaurant, the car or cars, the type of music and the band, photo or film services, accessories and accessories to accessories. Proper consumption requires a sophisticated analysis; therein lays the 'special attention to detail'.

This overflow of offers, this overgrowing need of analysis, needs to be tamed. The dam is provided by the group of professionals who would frame the overflow and help to convert it to a coherent stream, which will flow pleasantly and without disturbances. A key aspect of consumption is that it is done right, as it should be, as the rules of art dictate. It can be claimed that the professionals help their clients to reach the level of metaconsumption, where they acquire a feeling of control and a final synthesis of fragmented and partitioned bits of the overflow of offers. And although both 'consultant' and 'wedding planner' are words of foreign origin in Polish, the former is too well known and too well integrated to play an effective symbolic role (Lévi-Strauss, 1977). The dam – or, in the vocabulary of this volume, the frame – must be constructed from effective elements.

THE ANTI-CONSUMPTION NOVEL

The awareness of the fact that Poles joined the global consumption network has been documented in fiction. Between 2003 and 2005 a great deal of attention and some awards were given to novels gathered under the common name of 'anti-consumption literature'.

One of these novels is called *Zwał*, which means *Dump*, but also, in the newest slang, the psychophysical state of drug withdrawal (Shuty, 2004). The protagonist and the narrator of the book, when not indulging in activities potentially leading to the 'dump', works in a new, modern 'Hamburger Bank' (thus McDonaldization), organized and working according to all 'European standards'.[10] After hours, and under the influence, the bank employee flees into a better world, while reflecting over the one he inhabits during his working hours:

> Let's face it – all the rules of the game are decided by large corporations, strategically related to one another. They decide what product should be chosen this year, they determine the character of the market, its scope and territory. And do you want to know who, exactly, does this? Sons-of-the-bitches who control the image and the big advertisement campaigns in the media; it is them who have all the buttons to push. Those who produce both concrete and chocolate. Soya bigwigs and maize bosses … Incredibly rich and frustrated, who, like gods from yonder years, now and then cross the city in their armoured limousines. (Shuty, 2004: 36)

The narrator is probably an economist, so it is possible that he also wants to express disappointment with discovery that the 'producer's market' of the previous regime has not been replaced by the 'consumer's market', regardless of the new ideology. It is, again, the producers – of goods and services – who rule, and are more powerful than ever. Observe also that Shuty anticipated David Cronenberg's science-fiction film *Cosmopolis* (2012) by eight years.

Other novels have focused on transformation of the countryside. In his novel, *Nic* [*Nothing*], David Bieńkowski tells the story of an old bar ('dirty and stinking of hamburgers and fat hags') that acquires a new, international name through its inclusion in a chain: 'Positive' (an English word). And though the changes are dramatic, the new state of affairs still does not reach the model of service of the consuming society:

> Yes, it is clean, the work in the kitchen is well organized, and so is the cash flow, deliveries and accounts … they are able to manage all this, but they still lack certain subtleties … A smile, for example. They are unable to smile, unable to project an image of people who are content … And yet everybody in Positive has to smile … they need to infect the clients with their smile … the smiling client has the highest value for Positive. (Bieńkowski, 2005: 46–47)

Yet another image comes from a Mariusz Sieniewicz novel set in a small town, paralyzed by poverty, unemployment and apathy. There is an awareness that very close, within reach, is another world, which is not unambiguously better:

> If they do not speak of Jews, TV or gays, it is always about money – about credits, about discounts, about pensions, about steady jobs and about debts. How to earn, how to make money, how to make do. Dough in the ears, dough in the eyes, dough in the hands. Wherever you turn, you hear 'I bought', 'I rented', and 'I earned'. Dough like erection and like ejaculation … Dough

> and its altars, its monuments, its icons, its fetishes. In this country, only churches and banks are constructed really fast. (Sieniewicz, 2003: 146)

The anti-consumption messages can be heard only where and when consumption dominates (or at least is strongly felt). It is no accident, therefore, that those novels were written by young authors who did not experience or remember times of shortage and empty shelves in the shops, before 1989 and the beginning of the transformation. These are the voices of the first generation for which capitalism and the market society was a natural environment. It can also be added that the peak of Polish anti-consumption novels coincided with protests of the alter-globalists during the European Union (EU) Economic Summit in Warsaw on 29 April 2004. It seems that the first decade of the twentieth century hosted the strongest expressions of anti-consumption reflection. The following economic crisis and international Occupy movements (which took place in 82 countries) have not, at the time of writing, seriously influenced either the form or the range of similar initiatives in Poland.

One of the literary critics claimed that after having read Bieńkowski's novel, nobody would ever buy a hamburger again. Of course the critic was wrong, because is impossible to imagine any message that would prevent members of a society that lived for so long with scarcity from reaching for the goods that are now available. Tomasz Szlendak and Krzysztof Piotrowicz were likely right when they wrote in their book with the significant title of *Na pokaz: o konsumeryzmie w kapitalizmie bez kapitału* [*For Show: On Consumerism in a Capitalist Society Without Capital*], published at the same time as the Polish anti-consumerism novels:

> We have never had real capitalism, so there are no possibilities of consumption on credit. Let's repeat: Poland does not suffer from *affluenza*, does not have problems with excess and does not witness a sickly dependence on buying goods produced by international corporations, at least not on a wider, societal scale. Buy Nothing Day (which the ethnocentric Americans call 'international') can possibly reach the consciences of metropolitan experts, or to be more exact, of our isolated and precious Warsaw elite. (Szlendak and Piotrowicz, 2004: 9)

Szlendak and Piotrowicz were referring to a book by De Graff et al. (2001), *Affluenza. The All-Consuming Epidemic*, the authors of which claimed that this 'sickness' has many dimensions – from the sociological (weakening family ties and cooling neighbourhood relations) to the emotional (related to the stress caused by various excesses and the escalation of consumption desires). Szlendak and Piotrowicz were wrong, however, in what concerns the Polish 'life on credit', as demonstrated by the growing popularity of shadow banking and other companies lending money on usurious interest.

CONSUMPTION PARADOXES: SHOPPING CARTS AND THE SYMBOLIC CARGOS

But changes and transformations do occur, and quickly. It seems light years ago when a well-known Polish anthropologist so wrote about shopping carts[11] in an article on supermarkets and the rhetoric of consumption:

> The shopping cart is a medium that transforms our status within the supermarket … Taking a look at typical supermarket situations makes it clear that the shopping cart uniformizes our presence there; allots us all the same space (about 100 × 50 cm), which is within the reach of our arms. The shopping cart is our extension. It also separates us from other people … With the shopping cart in front of us we do not experience crowding. The fear of being touched diminishes. (Sulima, 2000: 177)

One could add, alluding to the notion of extension as introduced by Edward T. Hall (1976), that moving or touching someone else's shopping cart is treated like a bodily intrusion or an invasion of privacy. Even if avoidance is the rule and interaction the exception, however, Franck Cochoy (2008) noticed that the shopping cart also acts in the opposite emotional direction when used by a couple or a family. It serves as a meeting point after individual picking-up operations; as an observation point for those who wait; as a playground or a resting place for children; as a safe place for the parents to deposit their children. As the tool of separation or integration, the shopping cart is a reminder that shopping is an emotional endeavour.

Supermarkets, hypermarkets and malls are thus spaces for a complicated play of emotions; another such space, also suggesting modernity, globality and civilization is offered by covered football arenas. Their emotional weight was especially visible in 2012, when the European Championship was being played in Poland and Ukraine. In another text (Czubaj et al., 2012), I compared the cult of such objects to cargo cult in Malaya, as described by Kenelm Burridge (1960/1995) in his famous study of Melanesian practices.[12] Even if Poles, in contrast to the inhabitants of New Guinea, do not construct mock-up ships, their pride in their football arenas can be seen as a symbolic cargo. These objects signal that stage of the civilization which is still in the future – that stage of consumption which Colin Campbell (2003), after Lefebvre (1991: 394), called 'a desire for desire', and which more prosaically can be called a widening of the horizon of consumption expectations.

TRANSFORMATIVE CAPITALISM AS AN OBSERVATION FIELD

Contemporary consumption practices occur at the interface between private experiences (shopping in the mall) and group ecstasies (during the championship in 'supporter zones', in the company of Carlsberg beer, Coca-Cola and the images of a great many sponsors), but also at the interface between the virtual and the real and the interfaces between metropolises and small towns. The space extends between the small scale of Weekend concerts and their disco-polo, and the monumental arenas or the symbolic cargos. It can be argued that the phase of transformation, which in Poland is far from completed, allows for a better view of such differentiated consumption practices. The 'mature' capitalism homogenizes more, or perhaps only effaces differences between the forms and the contents of various well-established practices, which are taken for granted. The differentiation of consumption processes in such countries as Poland is, in itself, a sign of that transformation; but because it continues, because it is happening as we watch, it renders observation possible. What emerges is not one, but many consumption cultures, where overflow is still being defined.

NOTES

1. Disco-polo is a type of pop music characterized by a simple 4/4 rhythm and a simple melody and arrangement, and is usually sung by a soft and calm male voice. Disco-polo is considered to follow the aesthetic preferences of small towns and villages, as opposed to the big cities' club culture, and has become significant in Poland over the past 20 years. Music critics call it 'kitschy'.
2. http://www.youtube.com/watch?v=m5XYMGjZOQ8.
3. All translations from Polish by Barbara Czarniawska.
4. http://www.biedronka.pl/about_us/biedronka/who_we_are/.
5. I am not going to discuss the weddings of celebrities here, for they have both global and local character, although the common participation in such events (*per procura*, via gossip magazines and portals) is, in itself, a significant new cultural practice.
6. I am using the term in its usual anthropological meaning: a gift-giving festival originally practised by indigenous peoples of the Pacific Northwest Coast of Canada and the United States.
7. She also pointed out the emergence of new customs, such as following the lives of celebrities and the necessity of gift-giving on the occasion of the First Communion.

8. http://www.wyjdzzamnie.pl/Konsultanci;;;organizacja;wesela-artykuly-23.html.
9. The next paragraph, however, reverts to the potlatch frame, emphasizing that one must not economize on everything during a wedding, and especially not on food, which must be 'plentiful and of good quality'.
10. On the organization of such a bank in this satire, see Czarniawska (2009).
11. For the history of shopping carts, see Cochoy (2009).
12. A cargo cult is a religious practice observed first in pre-industrial tribal societies in the wake of interaction with technologically advanced cultures. The cults focus on obtaining the material wealth (the 'cargo') of the advanced culture through magic and religious rituals and practices. Cult members believe that the wealth was intended for them by their deities and ancestors. Apparently, cargo cult activity in the Pacific region increased significantly during and immediately after the Second World War; http://en.wikipedia.org/wiki/Cargo_cult, accessed 16 February 2013.

FIELD MATERIAL

Bieńkowski, David (2005), *Nic*, Warsaw: Wydawnictwo W.A.B.

http://www.biedronka.pl/about_us/biedronka/who_we_are/, accessed 15 February 2013. http://www.wyjdzzamnie.pl/Konsultanci;;;organizacja;wesela-artykuly-23.html, accessed 15 February 2013.

Shuty, Sławomir (2004), *Zwał*, Warsaw: Wydawnictwo W.A.B.

Sieniewicz, Mariusz (2003), *Czwarte niebo*, Warsaw: Wydawnictwo W.A.B.

4. Help! We have too much money!

Barbara Czarniawska, Pierre Donatella and Rolf Solli

It is commonly assumed that economic organizations strive to accumulate as many resources as possible. Private companies aim at maximizing profits, and public administrations and other non-profit organizations attempt to acquire an adequate basis for performing their statutory activities. Yet at some time (generally at the end of the budgetary year) they all encounter the problem of having accumulated too much. They may be concerned about having to pay too much tax or, to the contrary, of being accused of collecting too much money from taxes paid or of not using their donations and grants before their year end. How do they manage their overflow? This chapter attempts to answer this question in relation to the public sector of one country – Sweden – and suggests that definitions of overflow and ways of framing it may be locally and culturally determined, and time-related.

The phenomenon of earnings management[1] is well known in Western economies (see, for example, Healy and Wahlen, 1999; Libby and Seybert, 2009; Dechow et al., 2010) and exists even in the financially prudent Swedish economy. A series of Master's theses from Uppsala and Lund illustrates this problem, but from a macro perspective (Backlund and Dahlöf, 2006; Weich and Pietilä, 2008; Andersson, 2009; Hermasson and Olofsson, 2009; Wall and Wiik, 2010; Bergmark and Gårdenberg, 2011). Earnings management is a sensitive issue, and it would be difficult to obtain direct access to accounting practices used for that purpose in private companies. The Swedish public administration, in contrast, is ruled by a transparency principle, and researchers are often allowed a close look at various ways of managing financial overflow in municipalities and municipal companies. Earnings management is obviously not an officially approved method in the public sector, but a number of scholars suggest that it does exist (Anthony, 1985; Ballantine et al., 2007; Stalebrink, 2007; Pilcher and Van Der Zahn, 2010), and, as these authors demonstrate, public administration also has its ways of dealing with financial overflow.

In the following sections, we first present the handling of overflow in a Swedish municipality in the late 1980s, then cite an example of a municipal company managing its profits in the late 1990s. Finally we describe recent developments in the first decade of the 2000s, during which reported surpluses in three municipalities were among the most extreme in the history of the Swedish public sector.

THE RICHES OF NORTHTOWN

One of us (BC) conducted a multi-site study of public sector organizations in Sweden in the late 1980s (Czarniawska, 1996, 1997). One of the sites was the municipality of Northtown, where as the next year's budget was being prepared, finances were found to be exceptionally strong. The Head of Finance related (in a study using the diary-interview method; Czarniawska, 2007) that the council was perplexed by the fact that instead of the usual question, 'How can we find the money for what we want to do?' they had to address the question, 'How can we spend the money sensibly?' This task produced a general feeling of uncertainty, especially as the central government decided at the same time to postpone the section of the budget bill concerning municipalities, and to include it in the supplement to the bill, which comes later.[2] There was nowhere to turn for advice and instructions. As the Head of Finance said:

> We had a very unusual and somewhat problematic situation with the budget directives for the coming year. We hadn't needed them much over the past few years, as we could use the existing long-term plan and budget directives, and our task as officials was simply to translate this into monetary terms. But now we have something like 10 to 15 million extra kronor, and it's the politicians' job to decide what to do with it. We came up with a proposal, but it received poor support, even within the governing party. So there were problems.

As the Head of Finance saw it, the problems were twofold. The governing party faced difficulty in achieving internal consensus, and the politicians were unused to establishing priorities among potential operations – operations that did not yet exist. Consequently, the mayor hastily accepted the officials' proposal as it was, without any political consultation. As the proposal was based upon earlier political decisions, it was 'coherent but not topical', which provoked the opposition when the proposal was presented in a political setting. The Head of Finance continued his story:

> There was a long debate for three or four hours. It was very similar to a debate in Parliament, where the government says that the situation is fine and the opposition tries to show that it is very bad indeed. But this time, everybody agreed that things were, in fact, very good, so the issue was how good they were and if we have to economize even when times are good. It was the Moderate Party that demanded that, in spite of healthy finances, the committees must be required to economize. According to their opinion, economizing is the only way to increase efficiency. Besides, strong finances today do not mean strong finances tomorrow. Everybody seems to be afraid of that positive budget directives will lead to demands which will greatly exceed all the limits. A positive presentation of the financial situation has the psychological effect of increasing level of aspiration.

It needs to be added that the Moderate Party traditionally heeds most of the recipes produced by economists in which scarcity is supposed to be the norm. Most importantly, the situation run against a set of well-established routines: the opposition party must prove that the economic situation is bad, or at least worse than when it was running the ship; and the budget process consists of reducing demands, not of encouraging or increasing them. Additionally, positive directives run counter to a certain control philosophy which is popular within and beyond the public sector: In order to tighten control, a situation of crisis must be created (Czarniawska, 1989). As the Head of Finance formulated it:

> In my experience, one has to create a crisis situation to be able to induce thinking about economies. If you want to introduce changes, you must begin by building a sense of crisis. This is the basis of all change – changes that are to lead to economizing, at any rate. What makes it difficult is the fact that it isn't enough to lie and say that there is a crisis. It has to be a credible crisis.

Overflow is not the right kind of crisis. Luckily for Northtown, the strong financial situation turned out to be illusory (how this is possible is shown in the next section). Soon, to everyone's relief, they were able to return to the 'same procedure as last year':

> A proper budget process addresses only one theme: How great are the economizing requirements? Usually, it is a discussion about 'Shall we take 1 or 2 per cent off the demands of this committee?' In a more grandiose variant, the request is for a reappraisal of all the activities. Then we know what we're doing.

Although the commonly accepted truth is still that the Swedish municipalities have an 'expansive mentality', 'expansion' was actually replaced by 'stagnation' several decades later. The fact that budget requests are higher each year than they were in the previous year does not necessarily reflect a financial situation or an expansive mentality. It may have more to do with the role of the administrators (Anton, 1967).

As Brunsson (1989) noted, the negative reaction to surpluses in public administration has also to do with a more general question of legitimacy within a given field. A strong financial situation in a private company may indicate work well done, whereas the same thing in a public organization can be interpreted as proof that taxes were too high or that the job had not been done.

The following case of overflow management was studied a decade later in a hybrid organization: a municipality-owned company. It was not the taxes in that case, but the fees that could be perceived as too high when money overflows.

HOW TO STOP MONEY FROM OVERFLOWING

What follows are excerpts from field study conducted in the late 1990s in a Big City in Sweden by one of us (BC). Among many other things, the study involved two weeks shadowing the Head of the Environmental Department at one of the big city utilities, owned by the municipality (Czarniawska, 2002). It should be added that during the period described in the previous section, this Utility was accused by the opposition of charging citizens too much for its services.

Following are excerpts from the observations of the final stage of a budget process at the Utility. BC participated in budget meetings conducted at various levels in the company, which gave her the opportunity to see how the same issues were handled in different contexts. The first scene is from a meeting of top management, preparing themselves for a meeting with the Board of Directors. Present were the Chairman of the Board, Vice-Chairman of the Board, Head of the Staff Office, Head of Finance, Head of the Environment Department and the Vice-Managing Director:

> *Head of Finance* (presenting an overhead showing an economic prognosis): Production volume is much higher than we expected. That is, sales didn't fall as low as we believed they would. Costs even developed in such a way that finances are in much better shape than predicted in the previous budget. Loans are smaller and salaries lower than we had counted on. Still, we should not be too optimistic…

Chairman: Is it better than expected?

Finance: We still have an enormous tariff reserve. But I'm not intimidated by it. At some point we'll have to use it up.

Chairman: But is this reserve a fictitious sum?

Finance: No, but we must strive to maintain a zero balance. When we have too much money, we consider it a tariff reserve. This means that we are borrowing money from our clients, as opposed to a bank.

Chairman: But the City is going to demand an investigation into the tariff structure in order to encourage financial stability … .

Finance: The new tariff is independent of income revenue. We're building up the reserve because we're anticipating a merger [with a Utility from a neighbouring municipality]. The merger will become fact by the turn of 1997/98, and it's not unusual to have this kind of reserve. It's just that this one is so big – much bigger than planned …

(the Chairman continues to describe how these issues are to be presented to the Board.)

This excerpt illustrates the paradoxical role of economic information in public sector organizations. On one hand, it should inform organizational actors about their operations in economic terms – a controlling function, which the Head of Finance once called 'monitoring'. On the other hand, it should inform shareholders (in this case, the taxpayers) about the results of this activity (the controlling function known as accountability). The first function exists as continuous information, whereas the other is simply information which has been accumulated and processed at a certain time (a translation of continuous information into information about results). In principle, the events, along with the continuous information about these events and the accumulated information about their consequences, should all correspond exactly to one another. As identified by several scholars of accounting (Hopwood and Miller, 1994; Jönsson, 1996; Power, 1994, 1997), this correspondence does not happen automatically.

The observation about the paradoxical nature of accounting information contains the first indication that correspondence between two systems of information (not to mention the events they signify) may be far from perfect. The exchange between the Chairman, who represented external actors, and the Head of Finance, who represented internal actors, is quite telling. The company is a non-profit organization, which means that the budget must maintain a balance of zero. As we have all experienced with our own household finances, it is a rare and random event when incomes and expenditures equal zero. Such a scenario would certainly be difficult to predict or create at any given time. Waiting for this random effect to occur would be impractical, of course, especially when one is required to present a balanced budget to a Board of Directors. So the balance must be manufactured – a feat which can be accomplished by counting unexpected profit as tariff reserve (a minor translation, from one term to another, using the same language). The Chairman reacted as most laypeople would, wondering whether it was real or fictitious money.

The Head of Finance responded that the money was of course real or true. But as we shall see later, it was both real and make-believe. The bottom-line figures listed in the economic report were fictitious, because they were intended to produce a specific result for that report; but they were also factual, because they had real consequences.

The next excerpt is from an observation of the budget meeting of the Utility's top management group. All department heads were present, as was the Vice-Managing Director:

> *Finance*: When the budget was ready, it became clear that this was not a budget the Board could accept. Additionally, I don't think that the point has been to get the budget pushed through the Board as soon as possible. The budget is important for all of us, and we should discuss it in detail before we present it to anybody else. It gives us an opportunity to consult one another. Now, we took the three-year economic plan and the Board's comments on it, corrected it for diminished inflation, for the higher sales volume, for lowered interest rates, lower costs and the merger. We now have a tariff reserve of 10 million kronor.
>
> This result shows that we need to increase fees by 4 per cent and not, as we thought, by 2 per cent. We suggested the increase, but the suggestion was rejected. The politicians vehemently oppose it. Their alternative is to keep the same tariff and fee structure. Other alternatives were not discussed. But who knows, they may accept the 2 per cent increase.
>
> At any rate, something must be done about costs. Are you able to create a budget that can be accepted by the politicians?

Too much money has now turned into too little money, which should come as no surprise to anybody who ever attempted a balanced account. Once a sum has been safely tucked into one category (for example, tariff reserve), it cannot be used in another (budget expenditures). The Head of Finance also shows here the basic difference between financial information for internal use and financial information for external use. The internal represents declared needs; the external signifies the limits of political acceptance. This discrepancy is commonly acknowledged as the difference between what one wants and what one gets. But how one is transformed into the other?

> *Environment*: At the beginning of the three-year plan, we assumed no increases. After a year, we asked them for permission to raise fees by 2 per cent. I don't believe that they'll accept 4 per cent now. Besides, I wish I could compare the present budget with the plan from the previous year.
>
> *Finance*: I can finish what I was saying with a summary of financial results for 1995. Look at my overhead. We said that we would save 38 million kronor by 1999. Now we're halfway there, and it should look like this [shows an overhead with budgeted and realized costs of operations for the previous three years].
>
> *Production*: We never said that we would diminish costs by X amount, but that we would make operations more efficient by X.
>
> *Finance*: Well, X could mean 'so many people and so much money'. I have simply translated it into money. This picture does have an educational function. We have to explain, to ourselves and to others, why we've deviated from what we'd promised, so that the next time we say something, we'll be better at it. [It was unclear whether Finance meant that they should become better at avoiding deviation or at offering more convincing explanations for their deviations.]
>
> *Personnel*: We need to lower the budget by 30 million kronor or 3 per cent.
>
> *Environment*: But we've also said that we need to lower our ambitions for greater efficiency, because we've received new tasks and we have certain new objectives. We must attend to those.
>
> *Production*: As I see it, this picture indicates that, compared to the three-year plan, things have changed. We have an educational task, which is to explain these deviations, and that's the right thing to do. But I don't see what this has to do with the budget. It's also an obvious impossibility to demand a 4 per cent fee increase in the tariff, especially when faced with the coming merger. But why should we all of a sudden not demand an increase? I also think we should stop increasing the tariff reserve.

The Head of Production can understand, as most readers would, why it is an educational task to present the budget in a way that the politicians will accept and to explain deviations convincingly. According to Production, however, composing such a presentation should differ from the actual budget deliberation; rather it should be a discussion about what is needed and what is possible.

> *Finance*: Obviously, reality changes, but every time we add something new we need to find something to take away. The investigation of any consequences needs to lead to a zero-sum. Plus and minus figures should routinely

> balance each other out. At the same time, we must describe what has happened regarding the merger, increased production volume, lowered interest rates, etc.

'A living document', a fashionable expression in today's accounting and often used at the Utility, requires constant correction. Budgets, account balances, and long-term plans are not supposed to be 'living' in the same way, however. The two types of accounting are governed by opposite kinds of logic, which means that it is difficult to compare them. Yet a comparison is a necessity if financial information is to have a controlling function, although it makes presentation less credible (fiddling with numbers in retrospect, is considered a less than elegant manoeuvre). The magic of numbers – the illusion that they stand unambiguously for the world – crumbles when numbers are changed. Unfortunately for numbers and their magic, reality changes constantly. Indeed, numbers are unstable, in contrast to what Power claimed: that 'numbers are objective because they are stable' (1994: 21), and in contrast to the common belief that they are stable because they are objective. And, as they do not 'speak for themselves', the changes in numbers must be explained:

> *Production*: Why can't we argue that it is impossible to use a long-term plan as a basis, because there we had assumed a 2 per cent income increase, but we now know that it is going to be a zero increase?
>
> *Finance*: We have experienced an increase in production volume, lower interest rates and lower inflation; there's a coming merger and a whole new host of activities. We've also been assuming that the merger wouldn't have any influence, but we now know that isn't true. We're going to lose 1 per cent of revenues because our merger partner will have to lower its fee level to match ours. And this was a political decision.
>
> *Production*: Well then, this is a good argument.
>
> *Finance*: That's exactly why it's a bad argument. I'm allowed to talk about it, but I can't put it down in writing.
>
> *Production*: But it's obvious that the merger conditions have been changed, and not by us. What's the problem with using that as an argument?
>
> *Finance*: We can say it. We just can't put it in writing.

Why is the Head of Finance unable to use this political decision as an argument in the Utility's defence? Likely because the very people who caused the change will determine the validity of the argument. Making them responsible for disappointing developments at the Utility will not make them sympathetic to the company's worries. If another type of external circumstance causing changes were at stake, Finance would be first in line to bring the circumstances to the attention of everyone involved. But the dialogue between politicians and economists is caught in a delicate web of unspoken but institutionalized assumptions which should not be overtly questioned.

The participants in the meeting eventually grew bored, and wanted to get to the real core of the matter: How does all of this affect their operations?

> *Environment*: Even if we lose 1 per cent of our income, it doesn't mean that we have to raise fees. What about reducing costs?
>
> *Finance*: We can take 1 per cent from the tariff reserve. As for the rest, I don't know. We lose 2 per cent. We'll have to lower our budget ambitions before we suggest the raising of fees. We must lower our ambitions. Or increase our efficiency. Work during lunch hours, run faster … [nobody laughs]
>
> *Personnel*: Do you have any suggestions? …
>
> *Finance*: First of all, we must look at those areas where the budget exceeds the given framework. After that, we'll begin thinking about economizing.
>
> *Environment*: Personnel wants us to cut more than the others. But I simply can't cut more than two million kronor. I have too many new tasks … It's impossible.
>
> *Production*: We're all going to feel it.

After all the department heads had negotiated the cuts within their units, there was a top management meeting where the budget proposal had to be decided:

> *Finance* [reports to the MD, who is now present]: We needed to have this extra meeting to be able to adjust the budget in time. The budget proposal must be ready by December 10. We checked everything and decided to cut 30 million out of the 40 million kronor we were lacking. We'll then take 10 million kronor from the tariff reserve. If we could raise fees by 1 per cent, it would give us the additional 10 million kronor which are missing because of the merger.
>
> *MD*: The Chairman told the press that there would be no change in fees, and the City Council is going to suggest an unchanged fee structure. So we'll have to decide which would be the better tactic: to swallow this right now and announce a 5 per cent increase next year or prepare a special proposal demanding a 1 per cent increase.
>
> *Finance*: Don't forget that the budget proposal must be accepted by December 10.
>
> *MD*: Well, of course we won't spring it on them without preparation.
>
> *Finance*: Push the 'external circumstances' argument.

Perhaps it would be helpful at this point to explain why there was a need for those preparatory meetings and why the politicians would have to be prepared for what was to come. One does not need to assume backstage intrigues or conspiracies in order to find the answer; rather it is a demonstration of the pragmatic, Scandinavian way of doing things, in contrast with the way things are done in, say, Warsaw or Rome (Czarniawska, 2002). The meetings at the Utility took place two weeks before the Board met. At the end of the Utility meeting, they discussed their strategy:

> *MD*: The elections are in 1998. The budget for 1999 is drawn up in 1998, after the elections. This makes 1998 a sensitive year. Which means that we have to raise fees in 1997. If we don't, what will we do? Would it be unreasonable to say we could live off the tariff reserve that year?
>
> *Finance*: We have developed various techniques for dealing with the tariff reserve in order to prevent it from growing unnecessarily, but we can't simply empty it either, or we'd have to raise fees sky high.
>
> *MD*: OK, the budget debate in the City Council is on Wednesday, Thursday and Friday. The Council will accept a three-year plan on Friday. Along with the proposal, they'll receive our suggestion for a 2 per cent increase. At the same time, the Board will notice that our income is higher than expected, which means that they'll suggest that we use that income to finance our activities and leave the fees as they are. That will be quite correct. Looking at it strategically, I think we should say that we accept the idea of unchanged fees, but in exchange we expect their openness in discussing the fee structure. They can't do both – keep the fees stable and the fee structure immovable. I'm prepared to sacrifice the tariff reserve for 1997 and 1998. But if the Board says that it's better to increase the fees by 2 per cent, well, then we'll just have to agree. [everybody laughs.]
>
> *MD*: Strategically speaking, however, it isn't worth going after 1 per cent, which is nothing. Better to give that up altogether in order to gain a better position for the future. That's what I think. And you should also remember that the three-year plan is nothing to evoke in our defence, because it hasn't been decided by the present majority.
>
> *Production*: We'll have to make it clear to them that the company is going to show a loss.
>
> *MD*: Exactly. We'll have to negotiate that with the City Holding Company and then explain it pedagogically to the politicians.
>
> *Finance*: Given this situation, it's really important what our Chairman says to the press.
>
> *MD*: Which will have to include an explanation of how we're going to use the tariff reserve. OK. Is everyone happy with the proposed savings?
>
> [*All together*]: Oh no, no. We haven't even discussed them yet.

A layperson (and that includes the Chairman) may get somewhat confused by this situation. The Utility obviously has too much money and is going to hide it in the tariff reserve, in order to avoid accusations of charging too much for its services. Then it will reach into that tariff reserve to cover part, but not all, of its needs because, in this way, the Utility will lose negotiating ground when the time comes to demand a fee increase. Or, it may even cover its needs from the reserve – but only as a tactics showing compliance with political demands and therefore establishing a better ground for increased demands next year.

This is but one example of overflow management: finances mix with politics, educational ambitions with operational needs, the past with the present and the present with the future. Each has its own vocabulary, but the final document will have to speak in the same tongue. And once the document is completed, all traces of translation will have been erased, and the overflow will vanish. It is no wonder that the Head of Finance referred to the budget and balance account as a pile of 'dead documents'. As has been noted previously (for example, Czarniawska, 1997), it is the preparation of a budget rather than the budget itself which is of importance to operations. Once decided upon, a budget becomes an inscription of the past which will be activated only during the preparation of the next budget. Financial information has the greatest influence on actual work processes while a budget is being produced, not after it has been presented in its final form. And, as in the previous example of Northtown, the basic norm for a public sector company is breaking even.

Another decade has passed since this study was conducted. In the past two decades, many things changed in the Swedish public sector, including the ideology of the 1970s and the 1980s. The public sector started to imitate the private sector, as the latter has become a model of efficiency and effectiveness. One thing has not changed, however: too much money remains a problem. But the ways of dealing with this problem have also changed over time.

NEW PREMISES, OLD PROBLEMS

The rules of public sector accounting have changed substantially in Sweden during the past two decades. In one of the first countries in the world to do so, Swedish municipalities began, in the middle of the 1980s, to test corporate accrual accounting voluntarily (see for example, Brorström, 1997). Accrual accounting requires revenues to be counted when they are earned (not when they are received) and expenses when they are incurred (and not necessarily when they are paid). And although the declared purpose of this innovation was ‘to increase the degree of facts’ in public accounting, to Olson and Sahlin-Andersson (1998: 270), ‘accrual accounting opens up the possibilities for income-smoothing’. In spite of, or because of, that, accrual accounting began to spread within public administration in many countries (see for example, Carlin, 2005; Lapsley et al., 2009), replacing cash-basis accounting.

Under cash-basis accounting, revenue is recorded when cash (or another form of payment) is received, and expenditures are recorded when they are paid. Assume, for example, that a computer company delivers an information system in November and receives payment in January. In cash-basis accounting, the income is recorded in January, and in accrual accounting, the revenue is accounted in November. This means that the focus in the accrual-based accounting model is on the results (net use of resources) rather than on the cash flow (Brorström, 2007). Furthermore, the different placement of revenues means that it is possible to manage the financial results to be accounted for through appropriate periodization.

After a wave of experimental and voluntary applications of the accrual model in Swedish municipalities, the growing practice was stabilized by law in 1997 and introduced as obligatory in 1998 (Brorström et al., 2008). The Municipal Accounting Act of 1997 has been interpreted as an indication that the central government decided to introduce sharper and more distinct rules for the administration of economic resources by municipalities. The beginning of the 1990s was marked by what, in retrospect, was a relatively mild financial crisis. Yet it convinced the Minister of Finance at the time of the necessity of tightening up public sector expenditures. The demand for a balanced economy in municipalities was formulated, requiring that the annual municipal budget should incorporate a plan for revenues to be higher than expenses (Brorström, 1997). As an accrual model emphasizes the results, the balance sheet, unsurprisingly, has become a relatively unimportant document. Furthermore, the introduction of the law meant the end of the open and experimental attitude which had earlier characterized municipal accounting. Representatives of the central government said openly that the goal of the reform was to introduce standardized accounting forms, in place of the local creativity often shown in preparation of annual financial statements aimed at balancing the books (Brorström et al., 2008).

After 1997, the Municipal Accounting Act was changed and revised, but the main requirement of a balanced economy still exists. A municipality which prepares a balanced budget but then reports a deficit at the end of the year, must compensate for it over the next three years. There is one permitted exception: 'justifiable causes' may explain the necessity of accepting an unbalanced budget or the impossibility of not compensating a reported deficit. To simplify, it can be said that the requirement of a balanced economy is asymmetric. A surplus strengthens the financial position of a municipality, but, unlike profit in private companies, must not be used unless justifiable reasons are cited; whereas a deficit (loss in private companies) must be compensated in some other way. These are the rules under which Swedish municipalities must operate in the 2000s.

How, then, can an overflow ever ensue? Financial overflow is a result of a specific periodization of income and expenditure reported as revenues and expenses in an annual report. Yet that situation seems impossible to imagine in public administration, where the demand for municipal services is always large and growing. Nevertheless, a large number of Swedish municipalities found themselves in financial overflow in the second part of the 2000s. This situation was due to a combination of at least two events: unexpectedly high tax payments (in Sweden, the major part of income taxes goes to municipalities) and a perceived need to build financial reserves.

The need for reserves is related to demographic changes in Sweden. As a population ages, the longer life span creates a growing demand for more and better services, even as the existing infrastructure requires extension and renovation. As seen in the Utility example, building financial reserves is not an easy task within the public sector. At any rate, this was the shared opinion of three Heads of Finance in three relatively large municipalities, all of whom were interviewed by one of us (PD). When the Heads of Finance were asked to describe the financial position of their municipalities, their stories – just as in the previous examples – concerned problems caused by financial overflows, and they stated a need to reframe these situations.

An interview with the Head of Finance in Easttown was conducted just after they prepared an annual report, which had been sent to the media:

> Today we have presented our financial results for *Easttown News*. Our result is 95 million kronor … But actually, although we aren't too eager to tell it to the press, our surplus is something like 270 million kronor. Well, we've made some provisions, put some in the future for covering the forthcoming debt in the pension fund … then defined some other things as liabilities that are actually on the border of that definition. In other words, we did what we could.

In the remainder of the interview, Easttown's Head of Finance described how the reported results were diminished by anticipating future costs, including various expenses for the next year. If the next year were not to produce profitable revenues, therefore, the municipality would still show good results and fulfil the requirement of a balanced economy. The Heads of Finance in Westtown and Southtown mentioned the same ways of managing overflow: earnings management. The discretionary realm of interpretation related to periodization (in technical terms, discretionary accruals) has been exploited in order to account for future expenses, especially those related to infrastructure investments and pension funds. These expenses could have been accounted for in a different manner (that is, left for the future), but the surplus would be even higher and the future expenses higher as well.

The Head of Finance in Easttown mentioned one key element in this situation: not everyone who uses accounting information has the same possibility of discretionary interpretation of the results. Were that so, there would be no point in attempting to manage overflow through this type of temporary reframing. Such reframing is obviously a prerogative of the Heads of Finance.

Is this type of earnings management legal? Or at least in tune with general recommendations? Opinions differ. The Heads of Finance do not hide their actions, and they emphasize that their behaviour is reasonable and compatible with present rules and regulations. An interviewer has no basis for passing judgement on the correctness of such utterances, but there is no doubt that the phenomenon is worthy of study. Accounting requires judgements and interpretations. It is likely that the earnings management which occurred in Easttown, Westtown and Southtown is correct, at least to some extent, within the present rules and regulations. Nevertheless, it is obvious that the realm for discretionary judgement is large – and larger than most laypeople would imagine.

Do they do the right thing? And is earnings management necessary? There are no easy answers to those questions, but at least it is possible to identify their motivation for using earnings management. In general terms, there is a requirement to frame the flows, which translates into striving for a balanced economy. This requirement goes hand in hand with the technical restrictions that municipalities with surplus must observe, just like other municipalities do, because their future resources may otherwise be limited as punishment. Thus a vicious circle is created, which Heads of Finance try to break. The Head of Finance in Westtown commented on this situation:

> When we saw that we had about 200 million kronor as the annual result, knowing that our goal is to reach some 70 million kronor … we were forced to think about ways to balance the books. We are not allowed [to] use

> reported surplus in the future, so naturally we started to think about possible provisions [as a way of advancing expenses].

Easttown's Head of Finance was of a similar opinion: 'When we reported a good result, we had to decide if it should be frozen or put to some good use'.

Here, as mentioned previously, asymmetry in the requirement of a balanced economy becomes visible. True, the Heads could report that the deficit was caused by 'justifiable causes', but they see it as politically infeasible. Politicians do not want to report 'justifiable causes' which can be questioned and later analysed. It is therefore simpler to smooth surpluses, to frame flow through periodization – by anticipating future expenses and by building a financial reserve in prediction of future expenses and investments. As seen in Utility, however, the building of reserves is not likely to be viewed with a friendly eye by taxpayers, and therefore by politicians. Whereas Utility was afraid of being accused of setting its fees too high for its services, municipalities are afraid of being accused of overtaxation and of not delivering proper services in the present. The Head of Finance in Easttown said this about preparation of the annual report and the way of deciding how to report results:

> It is politically impossible to make a big surplus acceptable. Taxpayers would immediately say: 'So why do you tax us so much? Almost 300 million [kronor surplus]!' This is an unthinkable situation, so we twisted and turned a bit, and ended up with 95 million kronor instead.

It was also explained to us that 100 million kronor is a magical border above which one is not supposed to land. This is where the overflow begins in Easttown and probably elsewhere. Interestingly, this limit seems to be applied no matter how big the municipality; if the result is compared to the revenues from taxes, smaller municipalities have much larger surpluses. But such relative differences play no role when the Heads of Finance use the expected reactions of taxpayers to legitimize their ways of managing overflow.

The Heads of Finance are also afraid that the acceptance of a large surplus will lead to an escalation of expense, which in turn will render it difficult to argue for the need of economizing and raising efficiency. They do not believe it possible to convince the officials responsible for service production that a surplus is needed for future expenditures which will grow because of demographic changes. They expect a spending spree at the very announcement of an overly positive result. The financial flow must be tamed, and they see that their actions are necessary and justifiable.

SWEDISH MAGIC

What makes 100 million magical? Here is one possible explanation. One of us (RS) participated in the giant transformation of a big city organization, replacing its previous division into functional units for a geographic division into submunicipalities (Jönsson et al., 1999). It was a long project, comprising a series of subprojects, with various researchers collaborating according to their specialties. RS's task consisted of following the organizing process initiated by the 21 Heads of the new submunicipalities.

At the start of the reform, the city in question was in financial straits. The reform was presented under the slogan of increased democracy, but it was hoped that the reorganization would also improve control processes. The 21 Heads of Submunicipal Committees took to the task with great enthusiasm, and were soon able to document a reduction of the running costs by 15 per cent. That is, most of them did. Some did not manage that task well, and they left their positions soon afterwards.

A few years later the financial position of the city changed dramatically. The new system of state subsidies was especially beneficial to the three largest cities, so the municipality in question could not only enjoy its previous savings; it also increased its income. Nevertheless, the Heads of the 21 submunicipalities were still expected to demonstrate thrift and effective control.

As the project was ending, the researchers regularly reported their observations and insights, which the Heads usually met with great interest. During one of those presentations, a man entered the room and, without attending to the ongoing presentation, began to distribute 21 envelopes among the listeners. The presenter stopped, but the chairperson asked him to continue. At first the Heads continued to listen, but then, surreptitiously, one by one they opened their envelopes, looked at some table on the piece of paper, then closed the envelope. They seemed to be checking a poker hand.

The envelopes contained the results of the citizens' survey, which is a standard evaluation method used by the Swedish municipalities. This procedure is not without its complications: the response ratio is usually low, and the formulation of questions is not always the most felicitous. Nevertheless, in the audit society in which we live (Power, 1997), any evaluation is of great interest, and such was the case with the citizens' surveys, which constituted the basis of ranking the submunicipalities. But this ranking was interpreted in a particular way. As explained by one of the Heads, number 1 was not an attractive position to be in, because it could be interpreted as a proof of overspending, with a possible resource cut in the next period. Understandably, landing on the bottom of the ranking list was not good either, as it indicated that the submunicipal unit did not perform its duties properly. The most desirable was a place in the middle – not too high and not too low – because it attracted least comments.

Commenting on the survey and the resulting ranking, the Heads used the Swedish word *lagom*, which does not have a direct equivalent in English. It means something like 'just the right amount'. It is variously translated as 'enough', 'sufficient', 'adequate' or 'just right'; or as 'in moderation', 'in balance', 'optimal' or 'suitable' (when it concerns an amount of something). But words like 'sufficient' and 'average' suggest scarcity or failure, whereas *lagom* carries the connotation of appropriateness, although not perfection. There is a Swedish proverb, *Lagom är bäst* [*lagom is best*]. It seems that 100 million is just *lagom*.

An apocryphical story, told to all new Swedish immigrants, would have them believe that this word is a remnant from Viking times, when the whole group drank beer from one vessel. The skill was to drink enough for oneself, but only enough that a fair amount was left for the whole team: *laget om*. *The Urban Dictionary* suggests, however, that this version was coined as a student prank in Lund (http://www.urbandictionary.com/define.php?term=lagom). The more serious *Swedish Academy Dictionary* relates it to an expression in Old Swedish meaning 'according to the law' (http://g3.spraakdata.gu.se/saob/), but with the admission that in the most-used sense of the term it indicates something which is not too much or not too big. Thus, it can be seen as a culturally specific framing device, of obvious relevance in situations defined as overflow.

POWER TO DEFINE

The various Heads of Offices did not seem to see what Ruth Hines pointed out when addressing accountants:

'It seems to me, that your power is a hidden power, because people only think of you as communicating reality, but in *communicating* reality, you *construct* reality' (Hines, 1988: 257). This hidden power enables Heads of Finance, but also top managers and politicians like those that conferred with them in the Utility, to construct an image of reality that is non-controversial and requires no complicated explanations. They do it in the name of the need to communicate the results of their activities – up and down the hierarchy, to professionals and laypersons. What they seem to forget, or perhaps do not bother to mention in conversations with the researchers, is that this image becomes the basis for decisions and priority settings concerning the services their organizations provide, as well as the basis for accountability of decisions and evaluation of priorities regarding services rendered.

The power to define is not the sole prerogative of Heads of Finance in Swedish municipalities and utilities. As Richard Harvey Brown (1978) noted over 30 years ago, decision-making is focused upon by both organization actors and observers, but it constitutes a second step in a process which begins with the introduction of a basic definition and consequent labelling of actions and events. What is more, he observed that the power to define is not always, or perhaps only seldom, limited to those at the top of the hierarchy. Together, and before any official decision-making, 'a subtle, diffuse, hierarchically low-level complex of negotiations' occurs (1978: 376).

> What emerges from those subterranean activities is a redefinition of the official paradigm in the very process of its application. In putting the official rules of relevance into practice, there emerges a set of unofficial, inarticulate 'rules of irrelevance' by which information entering the official organizing frame is screened and manipulated. (Brown, 1978: 376)

This is exactly what we have seen in our studies. But Brown did not perceive his comments as a critique of organizational practices, but as a critique of the rationalistic – and therefore unrealistic – model of organizational functioning. This model is taken to be a correct description of practices by the media, some organization theorists and some leaders. Commenting on this discrepancy between the model and the practice, Michel de Certeau (1988) has suggested that strategy is what leaders want to do, and tactics are what subordinates do in order to subvert this strategy. Steps are taken to prevent such subversion and to induce a friction-free road of official definitions down to the last steps of the hierarchical ladder. Wiser bosses and many organization theorists inspired by the work of, for example Karl Weick (1979, 1985), understand however, that the process of defining, labelling, interpreting – and, in general, sensemaking – is at the very core of organizing. Reality is enacted by these symbolic procedures.

A reader outside the field of accounting or even the Chairman of the Utility may protest, saying that it is not reality which is being managed – merely symbols. But *symbolein*, as Umberto Eco (1985) reminded us, means 'half of the coin', standing for the missing half, so this interpretation is tautological. Money is the symbol of our times, and the ways in which the overflow of such symbols is managed is of utmost importance. Further, periodization is a way of managing overflow which is not limited to Swedish municipalities. Overflow is usually considered in the frame of spatial metaphors, but it needs to be considered as a notion in time, as well. The flows are also regulated in time, and what is overflow at a certain time is not overflow at another. *Lagom* as framing device, however, seems to be particular to Sweden.

NOTES

1. The use of accounting techniques to produce financial reports that may present an overly positive picture of a company's business activities and financial situation.
2. The Budget Bill announces the amount of state contribution to municipal finances. Usually, the contribution is very small, as each municipality is an independent taxation unit, but the bill indicates priorities and preferences.

FIELD MATERIAL

Andersson, Göran (2009), *Resultatmanipulering i svenska börsföretag*, Lund, Sweden: Ekonomihögskolan vid Lunds universitet.

Backlund, Samuel and David Dahlöf (2005), *Earnings Management i svenska börsföretag*, Uppsala, Sweden: Företagsekonomiska institutionen vid Uppsala universitet.

Bergmark, Björn and Andreas Gårdenberg (2011), *Earnings management. En jämförande studie av 363 företag noterade i Sverige, Finland och Danmark*, Uppsala, Sweden: Företagsekonomiska institutionen vid Uppsala universitet.

Hermansson, Niklas and Ola Olofsson (2009), *Resultatmanipulering i svenska börsföretag. Styrelsesammansättningens påverkan på Earnings Management*, Lund, Sweden: Ekonomihögskolan vid Lunds universitet.

Wall, Johan and Magnus Wiik (2010), *Earnings management och finanskrisen*, Uppsala, Sweden: Företagsekonomiska institutionen vid Uppsala universitet.

Weich, Andre and Jenni Pietilä (2008), *Kapitalstrukturens inverkan på Earnings Management i svenska börsföretag*, Lund, Sweden: Ekonomihögskolan vid Lunds universitet.

5. Management of and by overflow: the example of primary healthcare

Lars Norén

The flow of patients into the healthcare system has long been regarded as overflow, generating healthcare problems in many countries. As Jönsson et al. (2004) described the problem in Sweden:

> In order to match increasing opportunities and requirements, increasing health care resources are needed. Despite available resources there are requirements that can not be met because resources are limited. It is not possible to fully meet limited resources with greater efficiency and rationalizations. The requirements for health care will probably always be larger than available resources. (Jönsson et al., 2004: 119; translation LN)

Healthcare costs in Sweden have traditionally been strictly controlled (Diderichsen, 1995), rendering it impossible to increase resources to deal with the overflow of increasing requirements. The prevalent method of managing the problem of an ever-increasing flow of patients is to prioritize, and queues have come to be seen as an inevitable part of Swedish healthcare.

The overflow of patients can also be described in a positive way, however, as a consequence of new and better treatment methods, improved pharmaceuticals, improved methods for diagnosis and the fact that people live longer. People who come from the baby boom generation also want more healthcare, which tends to strain the loyalty of the taxpayers. Something else seems to have happened during the past few decades, however: politicians no longer accept long queues for healthcare and are determined to shorten them. At the beginning of the 1990s, Sweden introduced a guaranteed waiting time (Hanning, 2005) and later in 2010 a choice-of-care model which allows patients free choice of care centres for primary care. These reforms relied on the development of overflow devices which permitted the identification and assessment of queues based on statistical methods; the existence of such devices strengthens the mood among politicians to fight the queues.

Following Callon's reasoning, queues can be seen as a consequence of management in terms of framing conducted by actors in healthcare. For Callon (1986), it is framing that produces overflow. Providers of healthcare manage by using frames, resulting in patient queues. Primary healthcare centres are forced to manage through framing, although their members do not believe that they have enough capacity to treat the complete inflow of patients. Because this type of management based on frames is usually introduced via means of a political process, however, it can be questioned. Devices for the identification of overflow and its management are key factors in this process, which can contribute to the introduction of new management principles with consequences for framing. New framings lead to other types of overflows, which will later be questioned by new overflow devices.

In this chapter, I describe a sequence of actions, beginning with the identification of overflow in the form of queues, connected to the previous way of framing. Framing and the resulting queues are therefore challenged by the development of overflow devices. My description continues by showing how new management principles for framing are developed in a market context, which may potentially lead to future overflows.

The example used in this chapter is a market reform in primary healthcare in Sweden, based on an accreditation which can be seen as a new model for the management of overflow. An accreditation document typically describes a required service concept, a formula for funding, the rules for patient choice and evaluation criteria for service quality. A provider cannot enter the market unless it meets the requirements of the document. The accreditation document is seen here as a core actor, based on overflow devices. The document supports the new management principles used for framing, while simultaneously preventing queues. Thus, the chapter highlights the temporary and fluid character of both overflow and framing processes.

This chapter is organized as follows. I first provide a short presentation of some theories that seem to have been used for inspiration for new management models of primary healthcare in Sweden. I then briefly present a description of Swedish primary healthcare and how the overflow of patients began to be specified by using overflow devices, beginning in the 1990s. Next comes a description of existing framing and how the use of queues has been challenged by ideas and devices taken from New Public Management (NPM). This section is followed by a discussion of the construction of new frames and the type of overflow that may result as a consequence. Conclusions are then presented, together with the chapter's contribution to this volume. Finally, the Appendix describes the methods used.

NEW MANAGEMENT MODELS FOR THE PUBLIC SECTOR

During the 1990s, an escalating political debate arose over the problem of overflow in the form of healthcare queues – a debate which could be addressed through the ideas behind NPM, which was introduced at the time. Most observers have claimed that these rationalization models were borrowed from the private sector (see for example, Brunsson, 1991; du Gay and Salaman, 1992; Forssell and Jansson, 2000). It could be expected, therefore, that models and theories from the 1980s and beginning of the 1990s – models about private sector management – would be used by actors in the public sector for rationalization purposes, and could be germane for understanding what is happening today. Such potentially relevant ideas as the notion of 'the market' and consequently 'the customer' were at the centre of healthcare reforms.

Management Models for the Private Sector

In Search of Excellence by McKinsey consultants Peters and Waterman (1982) can be seen as a trigger for the lively debate on management which followed. The primary message of the book was that organizations must be more customer-oriented in order to prosper. Later, scholars such as Piore and Sabel (1984) argued along similar lines, claiming that it was time to abandon Ford's traditional ways of production, in favour of more flexible and customer-oriented options.

A slightly different view of the customer was presented by Toffler in his influential book, *The Third Wave* (1980). He launched the concept of a 'prosumer', claiming that, in a society of the future, consumers would also become producers to a greater extent. A critical review of these various ideas of the customer was presented by Ritzer (1996), who suggested, somewhat satirically, that the McDonald's chain can be seen a prototype for the rationalization of all types of organizations. Consequently, the customer is included in management ideas about the process of rationalization, and both apologists and critics seemed to agree that the customer has the potential to be productive – and to be used as a resource in production.

In another critical review of the new management ideas, du Gay and Salaman (1992) argued that customers are key because of their usefulness for management purposes. When the customers' requirements are determined, they can be used for the rationalization of organizing processes in companies and public utilities. In this critical view, however, customers are not seen as value-maximizing individuals. Rather, Rose (1993) has argued, for example, that processes of rationalization often rely on the regulated choices of individuals. Regulation means that such choices usually conform to the rules established in a political process.

The idea that customers can be connected to internal organizing processes found its most obvious expression in the concept of 'lean production', 'lean thinking' (Womack and Jones, 1996). As they said in their book on the healthcare sector:

> What happens when you go to your doctor? Usually, you make an appointment some days ahead, then arrive at the appointed time and sit in a waiting room. When the doctor sees you – usually behind schedule – she or he makes a judgment about what your problem is likely to be. You are then routed to the appropriate specialist, quite possibly on another day, certainly after sitting in another waiting room. Your specialist will need to order tests using large, dedicated laboratory equipment, requiring another wait and then another visit to review the results. Then, if the nature of the problem is clear, it's time for the appropriate treatment, perhaps involving a trip to the pharmacy (and another line), perhaps a trip back to the specialist for a complex procedure (complete with wait). (Womack and Jones, 1996: 50)

This excerpt indicates that the queues in healthcare are seen as a form of waste to be eliminated. It also says that the customer is at the centre of the streamlining of care production.

It may be concluded that many new management models introduced in the 1980s and 1990s focused on customers and processes. Consequently, overflow was regarded as a resource rather than a problem. Customers could be used for management purposes – to generate an overflow of requirements, which the organization must meet with rationalizations. The idea of process is crucial for this rationalization, exactly because activities can be related to customers. It was soon discovered that such ideas could have relevance for the management of overflow in the public sector.

NEW PUBLIC MANAGEMENT

Many trends of the 1980s and early 1990s which were relevant to the private sector also exerted their influence on the public sector. One of the most influential books in this regard, Osborne and Gaebler's (1993)

Reinventing Government, espoused the basic argument that politicians should 'steer – not row'. They emphasized the managerial role to be played by politicians and core civil servants, referring to many of the ideas that were popular in the private sector and encapsulated in the concept of NPM. Their book was almost immediately translated into Swedish and seems to have been extremely influential.

So what are the basic ideas inherent in NPM? The claim is that a fundamental shift is occurring in public administration – from a bureaucratic form to a market-oriented one. Osborne and Gaebler's book contains many examples of customer orientation, showing how the public sector can adapt to the desires of the customer, and introducing many explicit references to Peters and Waterman and to Toffler. A related claim was that the market, in contrast to bureaucracy, is the relevant form for control in the public sector. Organizational regulation should be replaced by market regulation. The introduction of markets is associated with the introduction of customers in the centre.

Osborne and Gaebler also addressed the issue of process management. They suggested that because a focus on the customer is the point of departure for Total Quality Management (TQM), it would be a good fit for the public sector. All the organization's activities should be evaluated on the basis of their contribution to 'customer value', they argued. There can also be internal customers, however, of which the public services' purchaser–provider model is a prime example (Walsh, 1995).

A focus on processes is not a completely new theme in the public sector. A half-century ago, for example, Donabedian (1966, 2003) described quality in healthcare in relation to processes by distinguishing three aspects of quality: structure, process and outcome. He was unsure whether outcomes were the only measure of quality, but concluded that 'Outcomes, by and large, remain the ultimate validation of the effectiveness and quality of medical care.' As to processes, he saw them as comprising a set of organized activities. The quality measures of processes in healthcare production could require, for example, a calculation of the number and time spans of activities, for time spans can be valuable in the management of processes. He also provided a number of tools for process or flow management.

Osborne and Gaebler also noted that citizens must engage themselves in the public services. One critical task for providers in the public sector, they argued, is to engage citizens and users in activities tied to the production of services. Toffler's ideas about a future prosumer were key to this discussion. It is possible to see connections between suggestions on how to make a patient 'productive' and, for example, Ritzer's (1996) idea of 'McDonaldization'.

Thus customers and processes seem to be significant notions in the rationalization of the public sector. But how are customers and processes connected to the concept of overflow? In Callon's (1998a) opinion, overflow must be measured to become a fact. One of his examples was the economics concept of externality or transaction spillover. It is usually defined as a cost or benefit which is not transmitted through prices and is incurred by a party who was not involved as either a buyer or seller of the goods or services causing the cost or benefit. Thus, argued Callon, externality is a consequence of a certain process of framing. Actors' calculations in a market may exclude environmental issues outside the frame. But pollution can be measured, and thereafter included in the calculations inside the frame of a market.

In this chapter I use the concept of overflow devices to describe ways and apparatuses that can quantify, construct overflow and, in general, be used to manage overflow. NPM can be seen as a source of inspiration for the construction of these overflow devices, whereas customers and processes in the public sector can be seen as raw material – resources – for their construction.

THE STUDY: FRAMING AND OVERFLOWING IN SWEDISH PRIMARY HEALTHCARE

The Identification of Overflow

Sweden's healthcare system, financed by the government through income tax payments, is similar to Great Britain's National Health Service; it comprises 21 county councils and regions (I use the word 'region' in this chapter). The regional care centres began providing primary healthcare in the early 1970s when Sweden's primary healthcare policy was reformed (Hjortsberg and Ghatnekar, 2001; Saltman, 2006). A care centre typically comprises a number of general practitioners, nurses with specific specialties, district nurses, social workers and psychologists. The care centres are not responsible for housing the elderly, however, or people with intellectual disabilities who have somatic and mental illnesses. Thus, primary healthcare contrasts with the specialist care provided by hospitals and other medical facilities. Yet for at least 30 years, there have been political initiatives aimed at concentrating healthcare in these care centres, in order to avoid the more costly specialist care provided elsewhere (Anell, 2005).

This way of organizing primary healthcare was challenged at the beginning of the 1990s, when the baby boomers of the 1950s began to age. A number of overflow devices were developed, sometimes independently, to quantify and evaluate queues. One example of such an overflow device was Sweden's 1992 waiting time guarantee (*vårdgaranti*) (Hanning, 2005), the major political intention being the limiting of long healthcare queues. After a series of modifications, the guarantee took a shape best described by the formula 0–7–90–90. Patients would make contact with the care centre the same day, visit the clinic within seven days, and visit a specialist clinic within 90 days, where they would be treated within the next 90 days. There are a number of fascinating aspects to this formula. It says that queues are not acceptable in primary care (0 + 7 days), but that they are accepted in specialized care (90 + 90 days).

One aspect of this guarantee is the assessment of time limits, the results of which are published on a regular basis. Queues become objectified and 'real' after this quantification. The waiting-time guarantee can therefore enable politicians to fight queues, and care centres with long queues can be identified and managed. Another political goal is to reduce the total time of treatment programmes. Although it would be possible to use such flow data for management purposes, these data are not yet available for specialist care.

Another device for managing overflow was developed by insurance companies in the mid-1980s: a private health insurance (Norén, 2010), introduced under the argument that it assured short waiting times. It now became possible for patients to calculate the cost of waiting times – a highly relevant goal, as insurance is often funded by private enterprises that want to see their employees back at work as soon as possible. Private insurance also made it possible for the companies to calculate the cost of absenteeism and set a price on queues. The cost of overflow could now be counted, and these formulas perceived as overflow devices. Long queues were no longer associated merely with patient costs; they now had identifiable implications for other groups, such as employers. Here one can see connections to lean thinking and a focus on processes and costs for stock.

New management ideas relevant to primary care were introduced at the beginning of the 1990s, and the introduction of market mechanisms in healthcare became an issue in Sweden (Bergmark, 2008). In their book on strategic reform in Northern European healthcare systems, Saltman and von Otter (1992) exerted a strong influence on the Swedish system, with their argument in favour of internal healthcare markets in which public authorities owned the providers. By the mid-1990s, public procurement as a way of promoting competitive markets (Walsh, 1995; Caldwell et al., 2005) was becoming increasingly popular in Swedish healthcare, especially in primary healthcare. Politicians, in their role as healthcare purchasers and internal customers, saw an opportunity to specify provider requirements and to introduce the notion of an internal customer. They issued 'invitation to tender' documents which allowed providers from the private sector to compete with public providers – documents that can also be regarded as an overflow device. It became possible for politicians to measure the flow of patients, and to negotiate, for example, the number of patients a healthcare centre was expected to receive.

Such were the various overflow devices in Swedish healthcare introduced since the beginning of the 1990s. They contribute to the specification of patient overflow, thereby rendering explicit the question of how to manage this overflow. NPM had an answer to that question.

A New Management Model Based on Overflow Devices

In early 2009, following an amendment to the Healthcare Act, a new type of market mechanism was introduced (Anell, 2011). As of 1 January 2010, it was now obligatory for regions to use a new model for the organization of primary healthcare. This reform permitted free entrance by accredited healthcare providers. The role of the politicians was now to develop the principles for funding and the service evaluation criteria. Overflow devices were key to that work. An accreditation document (AD) which was introduced at the time, the goal of which was to provide guidelines for the construction and regulation of this market. I therefore interpret the AD as a new management model for primary care.

In late 2009, I was lecturing at a meeting of care centre managers from the Västra Götaland Region. I brought the AD with me and placed it on the lectern. After a break, one manager who walked by the lectern pointed at the AD, and announced: 'This is our Bible'. The interviews (see Appendix) confirmed this assertion: the managers were extremely knowledgeable about the AD.

Here is a short description of the management model used in the two regions studied here. They have four main sections, which specify the following:

1. The basic functions at the care centres are defined, including details for recommended actions and policies. The manager should be a general practitioner, for example.
2. Patients have the right to choose, including choosing the number of times they may change centres annually. Some regions have restrictions, however.

3. Both regions use a capitation model, by which payment is based on the number of patients enrolled at the care centre.
4. A mandatory quality system uses indicators to measure responsiveness to patients and their medical issues and evaluates cooperation with the larger healthcare system.

The ADs are fundamental in the accreditation process for care centres. If a care centre's application is approved, the region notifies the care centre that it is allowed to enter the market.

Mobility as a Fundament for the Fighting of Queues

NPM presented the argument that patients must be liberated from a bureaucratic model relying on queues. One way to accomplish this goal is to transform the patient into a 'mobile consumer of primary care'. The AD contributes to a construction of patient mobility by allowing the patient an unlimited or certain number of choices to change care centres each year. As a central civil servant in the Region of Halland described the situation:

> *LN*: Can the care centre tell the patients to go somewhere else – is that acceptable?
>
> *Civil servant*: Yes we know that this happens, but if so we call the care centre. They aren't allowed to say no to patients.
>
> *LN*: It is not acceptable?
>
> *Civil servant*: No – not for any reason. They have to say yes to all patients who apply to them. They aren't allowed to say that the care centre is full either. We don't have that restriction. (civil servant, Region of Halland)

All care centres, then, must be prepared to welcome all types of patients, and this rule contributes to patient mobility. Up to four times a year, the patient has the option of choosing another care centre, and cannot be turned away. Another rule that contributes to flow is the fact that the funding follows the patient. The care centre must recruit patients in order to obtain funding. A third way for politicians to create mobility is to build information systems that guide patients to the most highly rated care centre (Ranerup, 2008). All these initiatives coming from the ADs contribute to the flow of patients.

Patient mobility is organized in other ways. The care centre is just one unit in an action net (Czarniawska, 1997) in which the resources of hospitals can also be included. Thus a care centre can be seen as a customer in relation to more specialized care units. It is transformed into a customer on behalf of the patient, thereby allowing new care providers to enter the market with alternative concepts of specialist care.

In sum, the mobility of patients is essential to the new ways of managing overflow because patients can be expected to move away from 'bad' to 'good' providers. Their decisions are expected to be based, for example, on statistical data about queues provided by politicians, which, in theory, may lead to greater efficiency. Quality monitoring can, to a certain extent, be delegated to the patient. The patient is also key in the care process – but more about that in the next section.

The Construction of Customer Requirements as a Way of Challenging Queues

The formulation of customer requirements is a complex process with a number of actors and procedures involved. Rose (1993) has described how this type of market is based on the regulated choices of patients. A regulated choice means that people other than patients – politicians and civil servants – are involved in the formulation of requirements.

Authorities at the national level are clearly involved in the formulation of requirements. One example is the National Board of Health and Welfare, which has developed a system of quality indicators (Swedish National Board of Health and Welfare, 2005) covering such areas as patient satisfaction and medical and organizational issues. The National Board of Health and Welfare prescribes that all county councils and regions must have a quality assurance system, but allows recommended indicators to be modified by regions. In this section, I focus primarily on the interplay between patients' formulation of requirements and the specification of indicators in which the politicians are involved. This interplay is key because the management of overflow involves the construction of requirements that patients are expected to enforce. The results from the measurements of indicators are published in web portals and available to patients. The intention is that they would be used as a basis upon which patients could choose their care centre.

There are primarily two sources of indicators. One is based on the overflow device tied to the 0–7–90–90 formula and all the statistics that are generated by the Swedish Association of Local Authorities and Regions. It is used by politicians to create information about the way care centres receive their patients. Västra Götaland, for example, constructed an indicator based on the number of patients that receive contact with the healthcare system the same day – a '0' contact, and Halland constructed an indicator based on the number of patients that are received by the care centre within seven days.

A second source used for the construction of indicators is the national patient survey (Institutet för kvalitetsindikatorer, 2009) initiated by the National Board of Health and Welfare and sent every year to a sample of patients who are expected to respond to questions which provide opinions on such issues as reception and involvement in the treatment process. These data are also published on web portals and are expected to be used by patients in their choice of a centre. As a politician from Halland said about the patient survey:

> One also realizes that there are problems, and it is interesting when the patient surveys arrive, to compare with how patients have signed in to care centres. Then one realizes that it has nothing to do with private or public. For care centres that score badly in the surveys, patients have already started to leave. You can see that immediately. (politician, Region of Halland)

Thus politicians contribute to the construction of differences between care centres with their choice of indicators. Politicians also rely on the media in their creation of differences between centres. As a politician from Halland said: 'We soon realized that when the media focused its attention on an indicator, a care centre that scores badly in the survey starts to lose patients … That means that patients realize these scores when the media reports about them.'

Thus the media also contribute to the formulation of patient requirements, which can be seen as an example of regulated choice and potentially as a construction of overflow of patient requirements. Therefore it also represents one way of working with management by overflow from the politicians' point of view. Politicians have the opportunity to modify patient requirements through the introduction of new indicators.

The patient's own formulation of requirements in the role of consumer is also critical, however. Patients' wishes seem to have some relevance for the care centres. As a politician in Halland told me:

> Competition has the consequence of requiring public authorities to think in a new way, but there are also private care centres that have contributed with innovative initiatives. One example is to be open on Sundays. We have care centres that are located in areas where people leave for work at 7 in the morning and come back at 7 in the evening and what can they do for their healthcare? So the centres started booking time on Sundays, and suddenly they were able to list a number of patients. (politician, Region of Halland)

This politician describes how this care centre expanded its opening hours from weekdays to Sundays in order to attract patients. Initiatives tied directly to the requirements formulated by patients were not always welcome, however. A politician in Västra Götaland described one potential problem:

> What do we do if – how do we deal with – an application to start a Muslim care centre? All possible prejudices come into one's head. Is it open for all patients? The care centre has the obligation to accept all patients that apply. (politician, Region of Västra Götaland)

Thus, customer requirements are generated partly by the AD, although this situation can also be seen as a problem for the management of overflow. Patient choices can come into conflict with political goals.

A New Framing and Future Overflows?

In the previous sections, I described how politicians introduced a new market model that identified an overflow situation and challenged an existing framing. Does this mean that the overflow of patients is eliminated when framing through the use of queues is no longer acceptable? Or is it the case that a new management model leads to a new framing that will in turn lead to other forms of overflow? For Callon (1998a), a market needs framing in order to function, although this framing inevitably leads to overflow.

I previously described how politicians attempt to manage overflows. In this section, I change perspective by describing management by overflow and how is it exhibited by managers at care centres. These are examples of producers of care that risk the meeting of a large flow of patients, but are not allowed to work with traditional queues.

First, what happened when patient choice was introduced and patients became mobile? A politician in Västra Götaland whom I interviewed just before the reform had been introduced in the region said, 'The factor that I think will be the most important for most patients is closeness – to have a care centre close to where I live.'

The politician's statement could suggest that this new patient mobility is not crucial. A manager for a care centre in Halland who had some years of experience with the choice-of-care model had another view, however:

> *LN*: Has your care centre a stable stock of patients?
>
> *Manager*: It is dangerous to regard it that way. People are mobile today. You can see how long people are prepared to drive to shop, for example. No one hesitates to drive 20 to 30 kilometres to go to the supermarket. (manager of care centre Region of Halland)

It is also noteworthy that this care centre lost a number of patients when the choice-of-care model was introduced in Halland. Thus it became vital for managers of care centres to try to retain their patients. As a manager of a care centre in Västra Götaland said, 'so we have good availability, continuity and quality – this is what I see as the most important'. Managers try to keep the patients happy and avoid long queues.

Patients who left a care centre and registered at another centre, however, sometimes contributed to the problem of an increasing flow of patients to the second care centre. One manager described the following situation:

> Since choice of care was introduced, we have expanded from 5000 to 10 000 inhabitants who have registered. The primary care we worked with before the choice-of-care reform worked well, and we served a population that consisted of both healthy and sick persons. Since the reform, 5000 new people have registered [which they can do at any time], but almost all of them are sick. These 5000 new people generate three times more work and generate three times higher costs. Therefore we now have economic as well as organizational problems. (manager of care centre, Region of Halland)

Both regions use capitation models for funding, whereby the budget is divided by the number of patients. The groups differ by age in both Halland and Västra Götaland, but Västra Götaland also includes a differentiation by socio-economic group. In both regions, a fixed amount of money is allocated for each registered inhabitant, which means that it is easy for a care centre to run into economic trouble when a large number of new (sick) people are registered.

From the politicians' point of view, it is easy to see some advantages to capitation. They can allow patients to flow into the care centres that seem to be the best according to the quality indicators that they themselves have chosen, and they can obtain better control over healthcare costs. They can also decrease the subsidies for healthcare and in this way exert pressure on the care centres.

So what can the care centre managers do to deal with an increasing flow of patients? There are a number of possibilities. One is to improve the internal flow of patients – to treat more patients per hour at a lower cost – or, in other words, to increase productivity of the unit. Another is to find treatment programmes that are effective but cheap – employing personnel with lower wages, like specialist nurses instead of physicians. A third is to support patients in the management of their own treatment. In the next section I elaborate upon this last theme.

To Make the Patient Productive: An Example from a New Framing

It has been argued that patient overflow can be managed by increasing the entrepreneurial spirit of the patient – by making the patient productive, like at McDonald's (Ritzer, 1996). In Västra Götaland, 'self-care' is part of the choice-of-care reform. As one politician said:

> I want citizens to make an active choice, to confirm that they have been offered the care centre in, for example, Partille. A confirmation gives some type of contract, and not only this passive registration. I will encourage a confirmation because this means that I put my trust in your care centre when I need you. (politician, Region of Västra Götaland)

It is noteworthy that the politician is talking about 'passive registration', meaning that inhabitants who do not make an active choice are listed at the closest care centre.

The contract is key in this situation, as it represents a mutual contribution. The contribution of the patient is perhaps more than payment. Åkerström-Andersen (2003) has argued that we live in a contract society, even for social services; the patient who agrees not to commit suicide, for example, will receive treatment.

The idea of self-care seems to be relevant for care centres and for the management of overflow. As a spokesperson for a patient association for diabetes reasoned:

> What are the preconditions for a patient to get a good blood value (HBA1C)? Well, it is to have a good knowledge as a patient – that one gets that knowledge – that one gets the tools such as a blood glucose testing kit, etc. – so that one can follow up and see and to make improvements. (spokesperson, patient association)

The quote says that a blood glucose testing kit enables patients to take greater responsibility for their own treatment. This is also in line with National Board of Health and Welfare guidelines, providing standards for the treatment of diabetes for the entire country.

The care centres also try to place restrictions on the number of visits to care centres for patients with diabetes. As the manager of one care centre said, 'If we have a patient with diabetes, he or she will meet me once a year and a nurse specialized in diabetes once a year – it is two visits.'

These visits are combined with self-care, which allows politicians to let patients go to care centres that have the best track record in developing the patients' self-treatment. For care managers, it is a way of managing the flow of patients. Thus framing activities may lead to overflow that must be managed. It is perhaps a bit early to discuss the type of overflow that will result from this new framing, but one problem seems to be equity. Management by overflow is based on the supposition that patients are active – that they can and do make their own choices. As Hirschman (1970) has argued, market models like the one described in this chapter are built on the assumption of an exit of patients from an unwanted provider, and that active patients using their exit option leave behind passive patients with poor providers. In countries like Sweden, where the law provides its citizens with the right to equal care, this model presents a problem.

FROM MANAGEMENT OF OVERFLOW TO MANAGEMENT BY OVERFLOW

This chapter describes a transformation of a management model based on prioritization that was questioned and replaced by a management model based on the control of patient flows. Another way to characterize this transformation is from the management of overflow to management by overflow.

The traditional model of management of overflow was based on a prioritization, resulting in queues. The use of queues was questioned at the time, but became politically sensible at the beginning of the 1990s, after a number of overflow devices had been developed to fight the queues. Overflow devices were incorporated in a new management model, called management by overflow in this chapter. The mobility and requirements of patients are used for management purposes. Politicians try to control the flow of patients and lead them to the 'best' providers according to their evaluations. Consequently, these providers receive an overflow of patients and deal with them by using such procedures as working with patients' self-treatment. Yet this strategy can be seen as an example of framing that may lead to new forms of overflow, which can be described in terms of equity problems. Patients who are not mobile risk being left with providers of insufficient quality. New overflow devices that use statistical methods to measure inequalities in healthcare may be developed and included in new models for the management of overflow. The story continues.

APPENDIX: FIELD STUDY

The primary care sector has been chosen as an example of new ways of managing overflow in healthcare. In 2009 the Swedish Parliament amended the Healthcare Act (Swedish Statute Book, 1982: 763) to require that all regions use a choice-of-care model (CCM) for primary healthcare (Government Bill, 2008/09: 74). This bill allows care centres to enter the market and, following their accreditation, to choose a location freely. All regions must present accreditation documents (ADs), specifying their requirements for approval of such centres. The regions are required to publish their ADs on a dedicated web portal: http://www.valfrihetswebben.se/startsidan.aspx.

The study focused on two such ADs – one from the Region of Halland (Region Halland, 2009) and one from the Region of Västra Götaland (Region Västra Götaland, 2009). Halland was chosen because it was the first region in Sweden to use a CCM (adopted in 2007) and because it is a rural region. Its CCM has been a blueprint for the entire reform and is used by many other regions (Anell, 2009). Västra Götaland, which adopted a CCM in late 2009, was chosen as a contrast to the Region of Halland, because it is an urban region, yet uses a model patterned after Halland's. A number of new care centres have been established in Västra Götaland.

I interviewed policymakers, civil servants, care centre managers, and patient representatives in these two regions. I first interviewed two policymakers and eight civil servants who were involved with the preparation of the ADs. I then interviewed six care centre managers and, later, three patient representatives. The purpose of the first set of interviews, which were conducted in the Region of Västra Götaland in 2009–2010, was undertaken in order to understand the expectations of the primary healthcare reform. The purpose of my second set of interviews, in the Region of Halland in 2010–2011, was to acquire data on the experiences of policymakers and civil servants with the reform. Each interview, which was tape-recorded and later transcribed, lasted between 60 and 90 minutes.

One could ask the question of why the case of Swedish primary healthcare could be of interest to readers abroad. The Dutch scholar Annemarie Mol (2008) answered a similar question which was addressed to her study of a Dutch hospital:

> Good case studies inspire theory, shape ideas and shift conceptions. They do not lead to conclusions that are universally valid, but neither do they claim to do so. Instead, the lessons learned are quite specific. If one immerses oneself

long enough in a case, one may get a sense of what is acceptable, desirable or called for in a particular setting. This does not mean that it is possible to predict what happens elsewhere or in new situations. Dealing with whatever is different always requires work and logics do not do work. They are not actors, but patterns. Thus, the logic of care articulated here only fits the case that I studied. It does not apply everywhere. This is not to say that its relevance is local. A case study is of wider interest as becomes a part of a trajectory. It offers points of contrast, comparison or reference for other sites and situations. It does not tell us what to expect – or do – anywhere else, but it does suggest pertinent questions. Case studies increase our sensitivity. It is the very specificity of the meticulously studied case that allows us to unravel what remains the same and what changes from one situation to the next. (Mol 2008: 9)

FIELD MATERIAL

Akerström-Andersen, Niklas (2003), *Borgerens kontraktliggöresle*, Copenhagen: Hans Reitzels Forlag.

Anell, Anders (2009), *Vårdval i primärvården,* Lund, Sweden: Economic Research Institute at Lund University.

Government Bill (2008/09:74), *Vårdval i primärvården.* http://www.riksdagen.se, accessed 22 March 2010.

Institutet för kvalitetsindikatorer (2009), *Nationell patientenkät primärvård,* http://www.indikator.org/publik/default.aspx, accessed 20 November.

Region Halland (2009), *Vårdval Halland. Modellbeskrivning 2009*, http://www.valfrihetswebben.se/startsidan.aspx, accessed 15 December 2009.

Region Västra Götaland (2009), *Krav och kvalitetsbok*, http://www.valfrihetswebben.se/startsidan.aspx, accessed 15 December.

Swedish National Board of Health and Welfare (2005), SOSFS 2005:12, *Ledningssystem för kvalitet och patientsäkerhet i hälso- och sjukvårde,* Stockholm: Socialstyrelse.

Swedish Statute Book (1982), SFS 1982:763, Hälso- och sjukvårdslag, http://www.riksdagen.se, accessed 11 January 2010.

6. Taking Michel Callon to the Istanbul Stock Exchange: frames, overflows and storytelling

Emre Tarim

In this chapter, I describe the role of storytelling as a framing device for helping to manage information flows in financial markets. In doing so, I draw on Michel Callon's conceptual discussion of the importance of framing to the success of market-based exchange relationships. Callon has argued that frames imposed on phenomena and their relationships can disentangle things and render them calculable. To summarize his arguments, I begin with Callon's discussion on framing in financial markets (1998b, 1999), in order to highlight the neglected role of storytelling in the framing of market phenomena and overflow management in financial markets. I then take this theoretical conversation with Callon to Istanbul, where I have conducted fieldwork research on the ways in which investors and brokerage firms have made sense of financial markets. I thereby demonstrate how storytelling has served to manage flows of information by generating and maintaining shared frames and interpretive templates (Czarniawska, 2008), and how these frames were subjected to occasional overflows.

CALLON ON CALCULATIVE AGENCY, FRAMING AND OVERFLOWS

Overflows in Markets

Callon has suggested that a market is a coordination device by which individuals can enter and leave the economic exchange as strangers (1998b, 1999). Frames, a notion Callon borrowed from Goffman (1974), can be seen as brackets or stabilizing devices which create 'a clear and precise boundary' (Callon, 1999: 187) among connections to be considered, and connections which can be ignored by actors in their calculations on market exchanges. Thus frames allow actors to disentangle things – and their own actions – from myriad connections and contingencies. They can then calculate their possible courses of action and the outcomes related to things that are subject to exchange in a market. Frames can therefore take the form of classifications, rules, cognitive and calculative equipment, and other mechanisms by which markets allow individual actors to act as calculative agencies (Callon, 1998b: 3–4).

Callon described overflow by using economics' account of externalities. In economic parlance, externalities refer to negative or positive outcomes which are not considered when agents calculate their courses of action and the associated outcomes. The crucial point here is the 'the impossibility of total framing' (Callon, 1998b: 17): not all possible outcomes and the plethora of underlying connections can be considered within a specific act of framing. To exemplify this overflow, Callon (1998b: 25–26) referred to Mitchel Abolafia's (1996) study of three US financial exchanges, claiming that the finance professionals described in the study faced overflow for two reasons. Their existing and prospective asset situation is affected, on the one hand, by the actions of other professionals; and, on the other hand, by the potential reaction of others to the specific asset decisions of a given professional. But thanks to measurement equipment which can assist individual actors in framing the intentions of others en masse while allowing them to pursue their own framed interests, it is possible to manage these types of overflow (Callon, 1998b). Callon has mentioned Chartism in this context: 'that strange calculative practice … starting with the aggregated curve which records prices, analyses its shape and attempts at revealing the hidden dynamics of the different individual decisions behind it' (1998b: 25).

At this point, I can add a third reason for overflow in financial markets: economic and political events outside the marketplace. This type of overflow can be managed by different frames, such as calculating the intrinsic value of assets or evaluating them with the help of charts or models that measure what others think and do about these flows (Smith, 1998; Beunza and Stark, 2005). All in all, this three-pronged overflow situation implies two things. First, there is an information load in financial markets that results in ambiguity or uncertainty about the current and future states of assets, with which an individual human may be unable to cope (Abolafia, 1998; MacKenzie, 2009). Second, this individual incapacity sanctions the distributed use of various frames, cognitive and calculative equipment, and institutional resources, all applied in order to manage the informational overflow and to reach individual judgements and make individual decisions about assets (Abolafia, 1998: 74–5).

The Master Frame in Financial Markets: Scopic Systems

Although contemporary financial markets operate under highly diverse rules, regulations, types of contracts traded and geographical reach, one unifying feature, at least from the perspective of market participants, is the 'scopic systems': the dominant framing and representation technologies (Knorr Cetina and Preda, 2007). The scopic systems are assemblages of material and algorithmic equipment for information and data generation, collection and dissemination, in and outside financial markets. They also facilitate remote exchange participation without the necessity for spatial contact among market actors.

Scopic systems convert a plethora of market and outside events and actions into information and data format, and stream them in designated channels on computer screens. This conversion includes the calculation and trading of market actors, which are then channelled back to the scopic system's representational components. Owing to these framing and reflexive features, flows represented on computer screens are 'not chaotic or marked by an undefined heterogeneity' (Knorr Cetina and Preda, 2007: 132), but are individually framed by such concepts as price, trading volume, volatility, news and charts, thus capturing the aggregate of actions and intentions in a market at any given time. Knorr Cetina and Preda (2007: 132) have also posited that the sequential and multiple-channel architecture of scopic systems influences the way market actors cope with information flows. They have argued that this coping mode assumes a similar sequential format in actors' observations and in the content of actors' interpretations, which are characterized by both intuition and anticipation, rather than by a purely numerical calculation mode.

Storytelling in Scopic Systems

Because humans have a strong tendency to know and explain their experiences in a narrative mode (Bruner, 1986; Polkinghorne, 1988; Tilly, 1999; Herman, 2003), and because a scopic market system processes intuition and anticipation as well as financial data, market actors frequently resort to storytelling in their interpretations (Zaloom, 2003; Levin, 2005). Sassen (2005: 27) has argued that the ubiquity of simple data in digital financial markets provides no meaningful advantage for its receivers. For this type of data to be useful in individual investment and speculation in financial markets, a 'higher datum' in the form of 'interpretation/evaluation/judgment' is necessary. Storytelling around market screens, as in other realms of life, contributes to higher datum generation by sequencing instances across simple data flows beyond a mere chronology, in accordance with their perceived contribution to the outcome being explained (Polkinghorne, 1988). Using such emplotment (White, 1973), storytelling helps bring a sense of social, historical and economic contexts into digital financial markets and their ubiquitous simple data. Plots serve as explanations, embedded in causal and intentional dimensions. Emplotment can thus be seen as further framing, contrasting and complementing the framing provided within the logico-scientific mode (Bruner, 1986), in which events and actions are explained as manifestations of universal laws or logics pertinent to the operations of financial markets.

Narratives can be seen as 'fickle' or 'weak interpretations' in the face of an ever-present stream of simple data (Rebonato, n.d.: 6; Zaloom, 2003: 268). In practice, though, they contribute to the calculative agency of market actors and help them in the precarious task of managing the three-pronged overflow in a sustained manner, because narratives about shared experiences systematically draw upon and modify more stable sensemaking resources in organizations (Boje, 1991; Weick, 1995; Orr, 1995; Abolafia, 2010). Narratives propagate shared cognitive frames – classifications, schemata and interpretive templates – generating explanations of the relationships among phenomena and scripts for action which offer solutions in specific circumstances. Narratives can therefore be seen as concrete products of these cognitive resources that characterize the 'framed world' of finance professionals. They can therefore be studied as a way of understanding these 'framed worlds', and their associations with patterns and overflows in market outcomes. In the following sections, I present my research on the Istanbul Stock Exchange, including a direct account of the way narratives and their underlying frames and interpretive templates have, in diverse ways, come to characterize and sustain the calculative agencies of various types of investors and intermediary organizations in this emerging equity market in the global financial system.

MY STUDY OF THE ISTANBUL STOCK EXCHANGE

My fieldwork in the Istanbul Stock Exchange (ISE) was conducted between 2008 and 2009. The overall aim was to explore market actors' cognition and decision making in scopic financial markets. During the preparatory fieldwork at ISE headquarters in the summer of 2007, I began to familiarize myself with the field by conducting interviews, attending seminars for summer interns given by ISE staff members, and perusing publicly available statistics.[1] Through this process, I learned about the types of investors and brokerage firms and the general investment modes of actors in this market. I discovered that the large capitalization Turkish company stocks traded in the ISE in the last decade, which constituted the bulk of the ISE's total market capitalization, were owned predominantly by institutional investors outside Turkey. Liquidity in these and other stocks, however – the daily flow of funds in and out of the Turkish stocks in the ISE – were generated by Turkish retail investors. This type of liquidity provision in the ISE is a curious one; in most developed stock markets, both the ownership figures and the liquidity provision have been dominated by institutional investors in recent decades (Erturk et al., 2008; Preda, 2009). Although Turkish retail investors and Turkish institutional investors have comparable ownership figures in the total market capitalization of the ISE, the institutional investors have not made a significant contribution to the ISE's liquidity provision (Tarim, 2010).

Fieldwork in 2008 and 2009

In January 2008, I approached a number of brokerage firms operating in the ISE as sole intermediaries for all investor types, requesting permission to observe their dealers, who served different types of investors directly. The dealing service provides investors with investment advice and executes their trading orders for the Turkish stocks traded on the ISE. Over the next ten months, I secured access to an asset management company (Turkish institutional investor) and three mid-sized brokerage firms (Firm A and Firm B for Turkish retail investors with different investment preferences, and Firm C for foreign institutional investors).[2] Together, these firms generated around 5 per cent of the annual trading volume of the ISE in 2008. In May 2009, I returned to Istanbul to observe indirectly the wealthy Turkish retail investors and foreign institutional investors in Firm D, one of the biggest brokerage firms in Turkey. Firm D generated approximately 3.5 per cent of the annual trading volume of the ISE in 2009 – similar to 2008. In each organization, I stayed for three weeks and devoted no less than five working days[3] to direct observation of the trading room and dealers. I used notebooks and a digital voice recorder (wherever permitted) to record dealing-room events and conversations. I then analysed these data according to an operational definition of sensemaking narratives, in order to capture my interlocutors' narrative reactions to market events. I used two criteria for operational definitions of narratives: (1) at least two sentences about observed and/or predicted market events and actions;[4] (2) which attributed meanings to each event and action in relation to their possible contribution to the outcome under scrutiny. Under these operational definitions, the narratives went beyond a mere chronology of events and actions. Narrative theorists call this type of meaning creation 'emplotment': the transformation of temporal order into causality (Czarniawska, 2004).

I then analysed the narratives for their plots and for their human and non-human actors, trying to ascertain common and divergent narrative frames and interpretive templates across the observation sites. At the end of my observation period, I had collected 1261 stories over 74.5 full observation days in seven observation sites. Moving beyond the specific observation sites, I then interviewed or had informal discussions with more than 50 finance professionals and leading investors in the ISE. I selected interviewees who would best allow me to explore their accounts of cognition and decision-making in the ISE, and how these accounts compared with my observation-based findings.

What Were the Narratives Like?

To begin with, the narratives I collected were not always complete stories – characters and plots resembling dramaturgical conventions with their usual protagonists (Gabriel, 2000). They were what Boje referred to as 'terse stories' (1991: 106): 'A terse telling is an abbreviated and succinct simplification of the story in which parts of the plot, some of the characters, and segments of the sequence of events are left to the hearer's imagination'. They were short interpretive reactions of narrators to events and actions as they unfolded, usually between two and five sentences long, connecting aspects of the multiple flows observed on a dealer's screen, with a view to predicting the future. The screens, fed by local or global data vendors' data-streaming software, represented flows in multiple dimensions and placed them in virtual frames, with columns and rows for such figures as price (stock, index, commodity, currency), volume (trading) and codes (of shares, indexes, brokerage houses, banks). A virtual frame for news – the newswire – was also standard on the dealers' screens. The data software could make simple and more sophisticated analyses of this information and these data flows, by converting price and volume data into charts, alerting the user to an increased momentum in price and trading, and calculating a plethora of second-order indicators on a company's economic performance data. The only thing missing from this scopic system of framed flows was an automated commentary, which would explain why a number of flows happened as they happened and what they would imply about the future of asset values. This type of commentary was instead generated by my interlocutors, predominantly in narrative mode.

The following conversation between Dealers T and B, and Strategist U, all working for Firm A, comes from my first observation day in the field (19 February 2008). I believe it shows the need for such commentary and the narratives provided. I italicized the two sentences that I take as constituting part of a narrative that I included in my 1261-story database.

> Dealer T: *What's the deal behind Germany?*
>
> Strategist U [glances at his screens]: *It's profit realization.*
>
> Dealer B to Dealer T [in a tongue-in-cheek tone]: Does everything have to happen for a reason?
>
> Dealer T: Then the guy [his client] would be asking on the phone and I'd have nothing to say!

The phrase 'the deal behind Germany' referred to an observed event on the computer screen – a fall in the Deutscher Aktien Index (DAX), an index which comprises the stock prices of 30 large capitalization companies quoted at the Frankfurt Stock Exchange. The dealer used 'Germany' as a metonymy to refer to the DAX. Again it is uncertain in that sentence to what index direction 'the deal' refers, but the explanatory response of the strategist 'profit realization' suggested a sale in the Frankfurt market, and hence a drop in its index value.

Intertextuality of Sensemaking Narratives

Of course I was unable to interpret this narrative reaction in this way when I was taking notes in real time on my first day of observations. I could do so only after I was exposed to similar narratives about market events over the following days, and had the opportunity to discuss with my interlocutors their methods of analysing and playing the market. Following Boje (2001), I could say that I was gradually immersed in the field in the intertextuality[5] of my interlocutors' case and mine, which permitted me to understand sensemaking in the ISE. After all, Dealer T's use of metonymy did not lead to a break in the conversation; everyone knew to what he was referring. And as for Dealer B's tongue-in-cheek reaction to T, in spite of my impression that he saw no value in this narrative explanation, it was only during my first day of observation that B used the DAX a few times to explain to his client and others in the room what was happening in the ISE. And, as a reminder to the reader, none of the Turkish retail clients of my dealer interlocutors actually traded or invested in the Frankfurt market; they were trading only in the ISE. So there was no reason for them to look at the Frankfurt market, if it were not for the following local market phenomenon. A frame of a correlation or causation between market events abroad and the ISE's events, as I would discover later in my research, was one of the most dominant sensemaking and decision-making frames in the ISE.

How did I make this discovery? For the collected narratives, I subjected my 'story dataset' to plot and character analysis. Taking causality as the master logic of emplotment, and in accordance with a close reading of the captured narratives, I was able discern other plots, such as correlation (between market indexes), similarity (between a past market event and the current market situation used to make a prediction about the current market situation), randomness (a situation in which none of the other plots seemed to work), and protostories (those narratives in which there is no explicit plot; see note 4 for a more detailed explanation). Finally, I found in my story database a special kind of narrative: counterfactual stories with strong plots, which intimated what should have happened, given the state of the flows on which the narrators focused. Such stories usually exuded a sense of anger on the part of my interlocutors (some randomness narratives had a similar effect). I also identified characters in each narrative, which helped me to see how their features were framed in relation to the logics of emplotment.

The Globalized ISE

Having completed an analysis of the narrative dataset and my observations and interviews, I concluded that in order to make sense of the ISE's movements and to predict its future states, my interlocutors in all seven sites looked afar: to information flows in the USA and Germany and, to a lesser extent, in other significant global hubs of financial and economic activity. This interpretive sequence or template with reference to the way my interlocutors observed the flows on their screens constituted the essence of the 'globalized ISE' frame, and it delimited the field of intertextuality used for sensemaking in the observation sites. The frame's narrative outcomes could be observed in all the plot categories, as the narrators took a specific market event or news from abroad as the direct or implied cause of what had been and would be observed in the ISE. Some of them, as in the utterance about 'the deal behind Germany', did not mention the ISE directly, but all were informed by the frame.

Despite its ubiquity, the frequency of the globalized ISE frame in selecting and emplotting a number of simple data flows observed on dealers' screens differed appreciably across the observation sites. I came to this conclusion by calculating the frequency of the framing of these flows in each site. The frequencies were calculated by aggregating all globalized ISE narratives from a site and dividing them by the total number of narratives collected in that site. The highest frequencies in the framing of these flows were observed in the three sites where wealthy or high-frequency-trading Turkish retail investors were served. They constituted 54 per cent (Firm A – concentration of high-frequency retail investors in the ISE index futures, longing and shorting these contracts many times a day),[6] 48.5 per cent (Firm B – concentration of wealthy, medium-frequency long-only retail investors in large- and middle-capitalization ISE stocks covered by securities analysts), and 42 per cent (Firm D – concentration of wealthy, high-to-medium-frequency long-only retail investors in similar liquid and analyst-covered ISE stocks).[7]

Some Dissident Views on the Globalized ISE Frame: Parrot Talking about the German Market

Only in the fourth Turkish retail investor site – a Firm A branch – did the frequency of the frame decrease appreciably: to 23 per cent. The residents of this site represented those 'marginal' Turkish retail investors who are more interested in lower-liquidity, small- and middle-capitalization Turkish stocks quoted in the ISE which are generally not covered by securities analysts and are not on the institutional investors' radar.[8] In fact, the residents of this Firm A branch were poking fun at the dealers in Firm A's headquarters who frequently invoked the globalized ISE frame as a trading strategy for their clients trading the ISE index futures. As one investor in the branch said, 'They [the dealers in the headquarters] are like parrots you know, "The DAX is up. The DAX took off." It means nothing; we look at the fundamentals [of a company's economic performance-intrinsic value] here' (Informal conversation, 5 March 2008).

Yet, as my observations and discussions with them made clear, those 'fundamentals' also referred to what the powerful retail investors were doing with those shares, which generally went unnoticed by the institutional investor. Thus in this observation site, in contrast to the remaining six, private information regarding powerful retail investors (not available on the dealers' computer screens but gained through social connections) was much more frequently used in the narratives (20 per cent of the 93 narratives collected in Firm A branch). As the assistant manager of Firm

A's branch network put it, 'Here [in the branches] everything is done with information, but not the information that passes through Matriks [local data vendor]' (11 March 2008). Firm A branch residents seemed to invoke the globalized ISE frame only to make sense of the movements of the ISE's leading indices, which did not concern them as much as it would the dealers in the other Turkish retail sites described previously. On the other hand, during my field studies in these 'mainstream' sites, the globalized ISE frame seemed to be invoked naturally, with little sarcasm, and occasional counterfactual narratives about the ISE's movements which did not conform to the direction of the markets abroad.

The Origins and the Future of the Globalized ISE Frame from the Retail Investors' Perspective

As can be inferred from the previous discussion, I attributed the differences in frequency of frame usage in the four retail investor sites at least in part to the specific Turkish retail investor preferences observed at these sites. These frequency differences can also be attributed to the changing global market conditions, however. I conducted my observations in Firms A and B during the chaotic months preceding the global economic and financial meltdown in the autumn of 2008, and the dealers in Firm D were observed during the global economic and financial lull in the first few months of 2009. Nevertheless, the globalized ISE frame did not emerge merely in the time leading up to the 2008 meltdown, and it will not necessarily wane with better global economic conditions (which are yet to come at the time of writing this chapter in the autumn of 2012). As my interlocutors from various sites and brokerage firms serving all three types of investors had repeatedly mentioned, for them it was the 2001 financial crisis, the largest economic crisis in the history of the Turkish Republic, and the ensuing political, economic and financial reforms in government and society which made the ISE a globalized stock market. And one of the foremost measures of this globalization for my interlocutors and other investors in the ISE was the inflow of foreign funds into the ISE and a steadily rising 'foreigners' share' in the ISE, calculated and broadcast daily by data vendors in the post-2001 era.

This new political and economic era in Turkey was marked by a strong contrast with the 1990s, when the nascent ISE, which had started trading in 1986, had been subjected to the negative effects of persistent high inflation, high budget deficits, strong state presence in financial markets, and frequent political and economic instabilities and crises in Turkey. In the 1990s, the ISE seemed like a market that was inherently local and volatile, despite increasing interest among those pioneering and more adventurous foreigners in the ISE who saw it as an exotic market (Tarim, 2010). This was especially the case for Turkish retail investors, who have historically provided the bulk of the liquidity in the ISE, owing to their short-term investment preferences.

It can be argued that the globalized ISE in the post-2001 crisis era, which coincided with the full 'scopization'[9] of the market in late 2001, has been one of the key frames for the Turkish retail investors (the highest liquidity providers in the ISE) in their management of information flows. One measure of this consequence is provided by various econometric studies of the ISE. These studies point to short-term one-way volatility and return effects or 'co-movements' between developed-country stock markets and the ISE during this period – without the researchers being aware of my qualitative findings on the ISE and the globalized ISE frame (see Korkmaz and Cevik, 2008, for a review; see Berument et al., 2011, for a ten-year analysis of the US markets and the ISE indices in the new millennium). Considering that the Turkish retail investors have generated the bulk of annual trading volume during this period, just as they had done in the preceding periods, the possible underlying contribution of the globalized ISE frame of the Turkish retail investors to these short-term index movements cannot be denied. I believe that the Turkish retail investors' contribution to the ISE's econometric feature will probably continue as long as the steady dominance of foreigners in the ISE's market capitalization continues.

The Frame as a Tool of Coordination: Dealers Protecting the Foreigners from the Domestics

The globalized ISE frame plays a significant role in information flow management among the Turkish retail investors and in the ISE's econometric features. But what role, if any, does the globalized ISE frame play in the institutional sales departments of brokerage firms that serve foreigners – an equally important investor type in the ISE, as they own the bulk of the ISE's market capitalization? To begin, frequencies of the frame usage were appreciably lower in the two such firms where I made my observations: 17 per cent in Firm C (July–August 2008) and 20 per cent in Firm D (May 2009). Despite these lower figures, the dealers at both sites used the frame to make sense of and to predict the ISE's movements, similar to the way their retail sales counterparts used the frame with reference to sensemaking. This frame was used primarily for adjusting their daily trade execution strategies on behalf of their foreign institutional clients. The trading adjustment was generally made against the high-frequency-trading Turkish retail investors, or 'the domestics' as the dealers called them – traders who tried to benefit from the perceived large buy or sell orders of foreigners. Otherwise, there was little attempt by the dealers of foreign institutional investors to generate impromptu trading and investment advice by using the globalized ISE frame – unlike the case of the dealers of Turkish retail investors. Nor did their clients, the foreigners, regularly ask for such narratives and the associated advice.

The more dominant sensemaking frame in these institutional sales sites was the calculation of the Turkish companies' and the Turkish economy's middle- to long-term growth and financial prospects – calculations of the securities analysts and macroeconomic analysts in their research departments, using universally accepted valuation and forecast models. I sometimes witnessed dealers and research analysts at odds over obvious trading opportunities stemming from both short-term ISE flow dynamics and company-specific market flows. If analysts did not find any of these opportunities worthy of incorporating into their existing calculative frame for the stock in question, they did not communicate them to their clients. As became clear from my observations and interviews in the institutional sales scene, there was one core service principle for the sales and research teams in these two observation sites and in other similar institutional sales departments in Istanbul: 'generate numerically and qualitatively accountable calculations on future asset and index values, communicate them to your clients concisely and promptly, and never tell them anything that they already know – what happened abroad!' As my interlocutors from the leading institutional sales and research teams in Istanbul made clear, the foreigners were busy investment professionals who did not tolerate irrelevant information and unjustifiable trading ideas in reference to the universally used calculative frames on asset values. After all, most of the foreign institutional investors were in the ISE, not because of the globalized ISE frame – the belief that the ISE moved in tandem with global markets – but because there were economic and financial growth opportunities in Turkey that could be reaped by long-term investors in the ISE.

This investment approach of the foreigners to the ISE contrasted strongly with the widespread retail investor and dealer perception that foreigners would flee the Turkish market if the developed economies in their home countries underwent economic and financial difficulties. For many of my interlocutors from the Turkish retail investment scene, such a pessimistic view or its optimistic projection has become one of the justifications behind the frame and the short-term investments it encourages. Nevertheless, publicly available statistics on the foreigners' investment movements in the ISE do not justify this view. The Association of Capital Market Intermediary Institutions of Turkey provides telling data.

Between 2008 and 2010, a turbulent period for global economy and financial markets, the proportion of foreigners in the total market capitalization of the ISE stood steadily around 66 per cent – following a historical peak of 72 per cent in 2007. Between 2011 and the time of writing, in the autumn of 2012, in the midst of the euro crisis, it has hovered around 63 per cent. It appears, then, that most of the foreigners are in the market for the long run.

Turkish Fund Managers: 'When They Fart in the USA, We Soil Ourselves Here'

As mentioned, the Turkish institutional investors have played a peripheral role in both ownership and trading profiles in the Turkish stocks traded in the ISE. In April and May 2008, as I began my investigation of sensemaking and decision-making profiles from this peripheral role, I observed five fund managers working for Asset Management Company (AMC). I then interviewed several fund managers from AMC's peers and examined publicly available documents and analyses in order to explore more of the sector. AMC was a medium-sized company within the sector, which then constituted 23 companies that issued financial products containing stocks, bonds, currencies and derivatives. Three of the fund managers in AMC had greater exposure to Turkish stocks among the AMC's financial products which they managed; the remaining two managers had greater exposure to Turkish fixed-income assets, such as bonds, among the AMC products which they managed. In both product categories, the regulations set by the Turkish financial regulator in the Turkish asset management sector rendered these financial products relatively conservative, multiple index and benchmark trackers. The aim of the managers, like their peers in the industry, was to beat these benchmarks in financial returns. The benchmarks dictated the frame regulating their sensemaking and decision-making activity. The second effective frame was the globalized ISE. It was not that the managers in AMC found the globalized ISE totally convincing, as suggested by the retail investors' reasonings reported previously. Like their peers, however, the managers had to anticipate how various ISE indices and several of their significant benchmarks would move in the face of information flows; the managers were then required to make trading moves accordingly, to ensure that their managed products continued to perform better than these benchmarks.

Otherwise, the three equity fund managers in AMC were relatively dismissive of the globalized ISE frame. One equity manager made the joke quoted in the heading of this subsection to communicate his feelings when I asked him what he thought about the reactions of Turkish retail investors in the ISE to information flows from abroad (personal communication, 18 April 2008). Nevertheless, 31 per cent of the equity managers' stories invoked the globalized ISE frame directly or indirectly as part of their benchmark-beating strategy.

The situation for the two fixed-income managers was more challenging, partly because the assets in which they invested – bonds, currencies and derivative contracts were linked to macroeconomic indicators, or at least the fixed-income fund managers believed that they were. They therefore framed any market dynamics into periodic information and data flows about macroeconomic conditions from Turkey and abroad. They followed foreign economies and markets, mainly because they wanted to gauge the direction of global capital circulation by examining the state of the global economic output and the interest rates attached to hard currencies like the euro and the US dollar. They believed that these factors would affect the global investors' appetites for risk and eventually affect the value of such higher-return-yielding but riskier assets, such as the Turkish currency and bonds, to which these fixed-income managers were heavily exposed in their financial products. Furthermore, the computer screens which the fixed-income managers studied did not provide information as deep and detailed as that provided to their equity manager counterparts or to any other dealers and investors in ISE stocks. The fixed-income managers, or any other actors in the Turkish fixed-income markets for that matter, could not see the names of organizations that were active in the Turkish bond market. Nor could they see the quantities in which the Turkish currency was traded in the interbank market. This type of information was available only in ISE stocks and futures trading, and was used as crucial information by stock dealers and investors alike.[10] This lack of both information and depth of data also pushed the fixed-income managers' framing of the fixed-income and currency markets in Turkey towards a more paradigmatic mode, based on their universal macroeconomics knowledge and the available but limited information flows. As a result, the fixed-income managers invoked the globalized ISE frame in 38 per cent of the narratives they told. Yet 70 per cent of the globalized ISE narratives told by fixed-income managers focused on macroeconomic news and/or foreign news about large corporations, and they served to make sense of the state of large economies.

On the other hand, in only 12 per cent of the equity managers' narratives that invoked the globalized ISE frame was such news from abroad emplotted. The other narratives emplotted the daily index and stock price movements abroad with ISE events. Similar to what the dealers of Turkish retail and foreign institutional investors did, the equity managers' narrow reasoning was based on whether or not the news announcements were in accordance with the analysts' consensus. Then they adjusted their trading strategy accordingly for a short time – sometimes as short as a day or even an hour. The fixed-income managers, on the other hand, seemed to have a longer-term view of the global and local macroeconomy and, consequently, on the fixed-income assets and currencies. They therefore tried to incorporate each piece of new and relevant information in the constant simple data flows into such a long-term outlook on economies, fixed-income assets and currencies.

The analysts' consensus predictions on macroeconomic and microeconomic data were compiled by global data vendors such as Reuters and Bloomberg. Incidentally, during my fieldwork in Istanbul's local TV channel, CNBC-e, a local business news TV channel, was conducting similar consensus surveys on the Turkish macroeconomy and on companies. My impression was that my dealer and investor interlocutors at all the sites and beyond had greater interest in macroeconomic and market events in distant places than they had in local economic announcements.

The Overflow from the Globalized ISE Frame

From the framing-and-resulting overflow perspective, the factors or information that market actors bracket out by their frames are those that cause uncertainty and ambiguity in financial markets. Bracketing out can be done by applying various frames – such as a valuation formula that has only a certain number of factors incorporated into it or such as the globalized ISE and the interpretive template and the scripts for action associated with it. In any case, it is done in order to make sense of and to act upon a select number of flows observed on the dealer screens. In the case of my interlocutors, the indication of overflow on their globalized ISE frame was the existence of the counterfactual and randomness narratives.

At the sites where I made my observations, I witnessed 69 narrative reactions that contained counterfactuals (42) and randomness (27) as explanation. Most of the counterfactual and randomness narratives were associated with the globalized ISE frame; 33 counterfactual and 15 randomness narratives indicated an overflow on the frame. These narratives, together with the curses that occasionally accompanied them, made it clear that the select number of events and outcomes observed within the constant information flows from the ISE and from abroad did not make sense within the frame.

There were 48 narrative incidences of overflow from the globalized ISE frame. Considering that in the 1261-story dataset there were 432 narratives (34 per cent) that invoked the globalized ISE frame, the fact that only 48 narratives (11 per cent) indicated overflow from the frame can be taken as a sign of frame robustness. The investors and their dealers, whom I observed, could use this frame in most of the market instances I observed, not merely to make sense of a plethora of information flows on their computer screens, but also to predict the future states of Turkish stock prices and ISE indices.

CONCLUSION

Finance Professor Richard Taffler suggested to me that narrative frames such as the globalized ISE constitute a myth (Richard Taffler, personal communication, 10 September 2007). Unlike a finance professor, my interlocutors, and especially the Turkish retail investors who used the frame as an investment strategy, have not bothered to systematize it scientifically or to establish its econometric properties and effects on the ISE's movements. In this respect, the globalized ISE is a shared story-generating and story-maintaining frame, describing what are believed to be appropriate price movements and correlations in the ISE. The frame also contributes narrative underpinnings to historical structures and practices in the Turkish brokerage sector, which have encouraged Turkish retail investors to take a short-term perspective. On the other hand, the frame seems to be used by Turkish institutional investors and Turkish dealers of foreign institutional investors, primarily for interpreting and anticipating the effects of the Turkish retail investors' significant trading presence and their short-term investment preferences in the ISE. For these institutional investors and dealers, the frame does not seem to be associated with any fundamental economic reality that could justify its use, or any organizational response to this 'reality'. It is merely a model of how the Turkish retail investors, as the biggest liquidity-providing investor type in the ISE, would react to certain types of information flows.

Although the globalized ISE frame may be deemed 'unscientific', at its epistemic core lies the narrative mode of knowing and explanation observed in the dealing rooms of the ISE. Yet one should not see the narrative mode of knowing and explanation as peculiar to this market and its participants. As the humanities and social sciences demonstrate, narrative-knowing and explanations provide a universal logic of explanation generation. Nevertheless, as this chapter also demonstrates, the narrative content, purpose and extent of use vary across contexts, professions and groups of people. The ubiquity of scopic systems and their real-time spectacle of simple data flowing around the global financial system is factual; yet they seem to require storytelling as one of the several framing devices, permitting the management of information overflows in financial markets. Such narrative devices have contributed to the emergence and reification of the idiosyncratic investment and market patterns found in the ISE. More research is necessary to ascertain their possible role in the management of overflow in other financial markets and economies.

ACKNOWLEDGEMENTS

This chapter was written during my stay at the Gothenburg Research Institute in 2011 and 2012, which was funded by the Swedish Institute. I benefited from the useful comments and recommendations of Barbara Czarniawska, Orvar Löfgren, Hervé Corvellec and Lars Norén.

NOTES

1. The publicly available statistics on these aspects are collated and analysed by the Association of Capital Market Intermediary Institutions of Turkey. These statistics and analyses are published annually and are available on their website, www.tspakb.org.tr.
2. I was a participant observant only in Firm C, where I helped the securities analysts in their routine intrinsic value analyses and observed the dealers serving their foreign institutional clients. At the other sites, I was a non-participant observer.
3. There is one exception. I observed three Turkish retail investors and a dealer in a Firm A branch for three-and-a-half days in early March 2008.
4. Gabriel (2008: 194–5) provides a succinct overview of agreements and disagreements about the composition of a narrative among the leading narrative theorists (chronological accounts vs. emplotted stories). In my fieldwork data, I encountered narratives that comprised mere chronologies, but of selected events and actions, yet without discernible references to their contribution to explicit explanations or predictions about market events. I counted them as narratives too, but under the 'protostory' (Gabriel, 2000) category in my plot categories.
5. Julia Kristeva (1980) suggested the notion of 'intertextuality' as a replacement for 'intersubjectivity'. Meaning is not transferred directly from writer to reader, but is mediated through or filtered by codes imparted to the writer and the reader by other texts.
6. A future is a type of contract traded in financial exchanges. It gives the parties to the contract the right and obligation to receive and deliver an underlying asset at a specified date and price agreed upon at the time of exchange. In all index futures markets, including the ISE, contracts are settled in funds rather than in the underlying asset, as an index is not a deliverable entity.

7. In financial market parlance, 'long' simply means 'to buy'. 'Short', on the other hand, refers to selling in general, but also selling borrowed assets: short-selling. Short-selling in the ISE equity market is not easy for the Turkish retail investors whose stock ownership records are kept at the Turkish custodian bank. These difficulties seem not to apply to foreigners, however, as many of them bypass the ISE's short-selling rules by using international custodian banks. In Firms B and D, there were few short-selling retail investors who had significant wealth or courage to trade in this way.
8. There are more than 350 companies quoted in the ISE. Around 100 of these, however – generally large- and middle-capitalization companies – are covered by the institutional sales and research departments of some 30 brokerage firms in Istanbul which serve institutional investors in Turkey and abroad. Their stocks constitute a large part of the ISE's total market capitalization. The uncovered stocks, in which the institutional investor's presence is extremely weak, are more easily subjected to guided movements and control by powerful Turkish retail investors and groups, also known in ISE parlance as 'domestic speculators'.
9. Although the trading floor was digitized in 1994, reliance on floor brokers in ISE's main trading hall continued until the end of 2001.
10. In the ISE, Turkish retail investors and their dealers would generally use this type of information on brokerage firms and traded quantities to gauge the activities and intentions of the foreigners (with the frame on certain brokerage firm activities being 'foreigners-only'). They would then predict what the short-term stock price dynamic would be, given the traded volume figures, the bid/ask prices and the aggregated volumes at these price levels. The dealers serving the foreigners would generally use this information and depth of data to take defensive measures *vis-à-vis* Turkish retail actors when they executed client orders.

FIELD MATERIAL

Berument, Hakan M., Zuzzal S. Denaux and Yeliz Yalcin (2011), 'The effects of the US markets on the Istanbul Stock Exchange and its components', *Journal of International Finance and Economics*, **11**(2): 85–94.

Erturk, Ismail, Julie Froud, Sukhdev Johal, Adam Lever and Karel Williams (2008), *Financialization at Work: Key Texts and Commentary*, London: Routledge.

Korkmaz, Turhan and Emrah I. Cevik (2008), 'Cointegration relations between Turkish and international equity markets and portfolio choices', *BDDK Bankacilik ve Finansal Piyasalari Dergisi*, **2**(1): 59–84.

Rebonato, Riccardo (n.d.), 'What models do we need for risk management?', *Qfinance*, available at http://www.qfinance.com/contentFiles/QF01/g956u8c7/10/0/what-models-do-we-need-for-risk-management.pdf, accessed 26 July 2012.

7. Cloud control: the capture and escape of music as information overflow

Jakob Wenzer

THE MATTER OF MUSIC: FROM COPY TO CLOUD

Music is a special type of matter. It occupies a key position in the study of modern overflows because of its material format within a specific type of artistic content and the way it connects information. Thus music may be loosely defined as sound organized to make it recognizable as a melodically, harmonically and/or rhythmically thematic for human listeners. Hence, music can be considered as transcendental – existing even when it is not played – but also physical, tied to the medium in which it temporarily occurs. By this definition, music is not saleable, but the materials acting as its medium (magnetic tapes, vinyl records, CDs) are. Music, therefore, is not its medium; the medium is what allows music to flow, both by providing the reproductive conditions and by being operative in the process of determining what music is. This chapter focuses on issues of control of this medium and how it is monetized, capturing it in marketable material forms in a variety of ways. At every historical point of capture, part of the flow is framed as a legitimate musical flow and everything else is deemed illegitimate, thus overflowing some type of boundary.

At least since the birth of recording technologies around the beginning of the twentieth century, music as a commodity has been found in the midst of a maelstrom of flows: social, discursive, economic, political, juridical and technological. The categories of 'music' and 'the musician' have emerged and transformed, partly in accordance with changes in technology and access to this technology, rendering the economic aspects of access highly relevant.

The last century constitutes the history of analogue musical formats, each of which provided its own way of allowing music to flow. The legislation that has accompanied the diverse formats attempted to confine music to these formats. The formats and the laws and regulations can be considered ways of 'damming' the overflow and thereby creating it. In this chapter, these attempts are called 'moments of capture' and 'moments of escape' of the musical flow.

The concepts of capture and escape originate with French philosophers Gilles Deleuze and Félix Guattari in their book *A Thousand Plateaus: Capitalism and Schizophrenia* (1988). In their vocabulary, the 'apparatus of capture' is a device for converting a free, qualitatively differentiated and unique flow into quantified, manageable units. They use terms such as stratification, territorialization and coding to describe similar processes – moments when something is captured by a force of certain superiority, and therefore begins to act in accordance with the tendency dictated by this force. But there is another moment in every stratum, territory or code: a spontaneous destratification, deterritorialization or decoding. This is because no capture is total; every stratum, territory or code leaves open certain 'lines of flight' – lines of escape – certain connections to the wider 'machinic' system of the world, providing an ever-present potential for change (Deleuze and Guattari, 1988). In this chapter, the concept of escape is used in this way.

Music defies total capture. Its nature is flowing. But as an element that affects human beings deeply, it is also a subject of constant attempts to be captured into quantifiable units which could easily be subordinated to economic quantification, and made monetizable.

What, then, is music? Can it actually be owned, or is every attempt to make it an individual property destined to be at the mercy of economic actors trying to regulate the availability of technologies necessary for making, distributing and listening to it? Is it the property of the crowd? Every new music technology, whether technical, juridical or discursive, has both potentials: the potential of being captured and the potential of escaping from capture. How the apparatus of capture is expressed differs and changes along with history.

Ideas about music and musicianship are related to the technological changes which alter them, feeding back, in turn, into techno-economic systems. The initiatives here are constantly shifting. Music producers, publishers and audiences continuously attempt to adapt to changing technological environments from their respective points of departure, all of which have an impact on that environment. Rapid technological development is certainly the watchword of 2013, yet no singular solutions as to the juridical status of music has yet appeared. In this chapter, I attempt to demonstrate how three actors, with different interests and acting at different levels of the music industries, all tried to adjust the flows and themselves to adapt their properties, in order to tap into those flows.

ANALOGUE FLOWS

Towards the end of the nineteenth century, the premier medium of music was music sheets, which were sold individually. Music was played at home directly from those sheets; it was an interpersonal phenomenon, tied to socially shared occasions. Benkler (2006) claimed that the invention of the phonograph – a machine acting as a medium for music reproduction – changed all of this at the beginning of the twentieth century. With the phonograph, music itself was given physical form; a form which could be copied, owned, bought and sold. Thus an historically new link between the artist and the music came into being; a link that could materialize because of the sudden possibility of defining one musical recording as an original, of which copies could be sold. From this point onward, the association between an individual person and a musical piece began to hold pre-eminence over the older account of music as a social phenomenon linked to shared experiences. In the words of Tschmuck (2006), a 'playing regime' was replaced by a 'listening regime', mediated by a 'copyright regime'. Tschmuck examined technological and juridical innovation in the music business around the end of the nineteenth and twentieth centuries. His research suggested to him that the copyright regime is directly related to the technologies of production, and that the interactions between copyright and production have a significant influence over what is to be considered music (Tschmuck, 2009). In terms of this chapter, this was a moment of capture: copyright legislation confines music to the expression of an individual and, thereby, to the property of that person. This capture was made possible by the new technologies allowing a piece of music to be recorded, copied and sold.

Concerts and other occasions where music was played to an audience were transferred from the status of moments when music is really happening to an occasion when an original piece of music was more or less authentically and faithfully reproduced before a passive audience. This also enabled the publishing companies – the new powerful actor – to enter the scene and strengthen the link between the musician and the music, in order to promote an artist. According to the listening regime, even when music occurred at such social events such as large concerts, the social gravity was fed by the grandeur of the individual artist performing. Sociality came to depend on a technologically mediated and juridically supported individualism. This was also another moment of capture: music was divided into originals and copies, with the recording acting as the original and their public performance as copies of the original. Music began to flow via artists and not via the collective singing and playing crowd.

Tschmuck (2006) demonstrated that even though individual musicians could benefit financially, the most substantial profit was made not by the musicians, but by those who controlled the wildly expensive technology required for producing and reproducing the music. They were the publishers, who surfaced at this point as the arguably most powerful segment involved in the then-emerging music industry.

Since then, the power of the publishers has been threatened at times, most often by new technologies which have placed the tools for reproducing music directly in the hands of the music consumers, thus creating the means to escape capture of the flow of music. These technologies, such as reel-to-reel audio tape recorders, cassette tape recorders and mini-disc players, have been unable to match the sound of the vinyl record, however. The central source of income in this history of corporate protectionism was the control of material copies, because vinyl records, as selling copies – the material substratum of music – have generated money. The tool for this purpose has been the juridical institution of copyright – the prime mode of capture pertaining to the liberating possibilities offered by new technologies.

Despite many threats, the copyright regime has remained firmly in place during most of the twentieth century. It has also contributed to a concentration of ownership. Towards the end of the century, there were countless recording labels, yet 72 per cent of the market was controlled by four firms known in the business as the 'Big Four': Universal Music Group, Sony Music Entertainment, EMI and Warner Music Group (Wikström, 2009). Thus, the capture of music by copyright legislation has channelled money to the Big Four.

To this point, the protagonist of this story has been the analogue musical format. During the twentieth century, the recording industries controlled the prime productive and reproductive technologies of recording studios and record presses. Other, more publicly accessible technologies were inferior to vinyl records in sound reproduction, but the rise of digital technologies of musical production and reproduction in the 1990s changed this situation. The sound quality of the compact disc proved a real challenge to the vinyl record, and in time, this format turned out to be copyable with relatively simple home technology. At first it was merely a means of even more pervasive capture of the monetary flows associated with music. But then, as home computer technology developed, it became a more common means of massive escape – the escape of prospected monetary income, but also of musical authorship.

DIGITAL FLOWS

When the first digital formats for music reproduction appeared at the end of the 1980s, they created a huge boom for the industry. Consumers not only bought the new and more expensive compact discs; they also started to convert their record collections to CDs. The boom reached a worldwide peak in 1998 (Wikström, 2009). By then, the vinyl-to-CD conversion was considered finished, but something else was happening: the Big Four's control of the technological means of reproduction had begun to slip. With the file-sharing programmes of the late 1990s, most notably the 1999 introduction of Napster, the personal home computer had suddenly become a powerful tool for reproducing and distributing copyrighted music. The new, digital format converted any piece of music into an infinitely multipliable copy, with almost no data loss; the format contained the potential of overflowing the constraints of copyright legislation.

These technologies provided the means for producing music at home. But if individuals could extract a music file from a CD medium and share it, a sequencer or studio recording programme could do it just as easily. Thus by the middle of the first decade of the 2000s, the technologies of both production and reproduction were out of the hands of the established music industry. Between 1999 and 2009, total revenue of music sales and licensing in the USA decreased from $14.6 billion to $6.3 billion. In 2009, Goldman (2010) projected that the decline would continue until at least 2014.

The initiative seems to have shifted from music industries dominated by the Big Four to those which have previously been viewed as a passive audience: the listeners – the consumers of music. As the tools of production have become more readily available to the common person, the function and role of the consumer have also begun to change: production, forms of consumption and the dominant definition of music as the expression of a musical author, tied to a material medium possible to be bought and sold.

Thus the emerging consumer culture is, in most key aspects, a participatory culture (Deuze, 2006; Baym, 2011) – just as it was in the days before recording technologies, and before music publishers entered the stage. Digital community-based music listening began in decentralized communication networks in the 1990s, with users sharing individual files. This tendency has increased in the 2000s.

The BitTorrent technology, which has superseded personal peer-to-peer programs as the most commonly used technology for illegal file-sharing, allows users to download fragments of one file from multiple sources. When downloading a file, the user is simultaneously making the downloaded data available for other downloaders; all downloading is also passive uploading. But most of the legitimate music service business models such as logging the number of listens and tagging and rating music assume a more or less actively participating consumer. Last.fm is one such service. Merely by listening to music, listeners are providing their listening data to a database, which compares it to logs of the listening habits of other users. Based on their music preferences, suggestions of similar music are returned to the user. By using the service in order to obtain recommendations, the user is unintentionally generating data to be used in the recommendation system. Last.fm also offers a paying service which is also growing in momentum: access to a 'cloud', from which music data are 'streamed'. When access is granted, availability to everything in the cloud is free, regardless of data quantity.

This shift from peer-to-peer file-sharing to a data cloud sounds primarily like a technical move, but it may actually signal another paradigm shift. The shift from vinyl to digital was a shift in the format of copies, as the music, if infinitely multipliable, was contained in these copies. Access to a cloud means that copies became obsolete; the music has lost its material substratum. Just as consumer culture has shifted back to a participatory phenomenon, music has shifted back to something more ephemeral, no longer confined to the materiality of the copy format.

The idea of the cloud also defines flows in a new way. One is led to believe that everything is in the cloud. With access to the cloud, one has access to all music, for 'free'. But a cloud is above the ground and separate from the ground; the computer does not contain it. What the computer does contain is a port through which a channel to the cloud can be opened. The contents of the cloud are then streamed through the port, not to the computer, but through the computer. Then it supposedly escapes back to the cloud, leaving the impression that nothing was ever downloaded. (Which it was, but then erased again, and nothing can be played on a computer. It is as if it were never there.) Nothing seems to be multiplied, as nothing remains in the computer after playing the sound clip that was streamed. The cloud does not leak, it just circulates the material that comprises it in what appears to be a cycle between the ground (user/listener) and the sky (container/data cloud). Because it is part of the atmosphere, there is no need to own any part of it; access to it belongs to everyone.

SURFING THE FLOWS

This section attempts to demonstrate how three actors in Sweden, enjoying different levels of popularity and occupying different positions in the music business, adapt to the new situation. Even though they roughly correspond to the categories of musician, producer and publisher, the situation is more complex than that: they must all fill each of these functions in their different ways. My examples are brief, as they serve only to illustrate the possibilities of converting labour to money in Sweden's contemporary musical ecology in 2013. They also represent four ways of surfing at the intersection of flows of money, music and practices, for which music production becomes a point of coalescence.

Daniel Gilbert is a vocalist and guitarist who has been appearing in some of Sweden's most successful independent rock bands for the past 20 years. He began his musical career as a teenage bass player in Broder Daniel, a band he co-formed in 1988, and which was the subject of great hype in 1994. Three years later, Gilbert left Broder Daniel to play in smaller bands; but in 2002, he appeared as a guitarist in the back-up band for Håkan Hellström, one of the cofounders of Broder Daniel. Hellström achieved immediate and enormous success, playing in festivals to critical acclaim and enjoying sold-out concerts on tour in Sweden, Denmark and Norway. Hellström has performed as a solo artist, but the same band, with a few changes, has backed him since the beginning of his career. Most of the members came from independent bands with relatively successful national or international careers in the 1990s or the first decade of the 2000s: Broder Daniel, Souls and The Soundtrack of Our Lives, for example. Gilbert has been a member of the touring band from the outset. Hellström is still one of Sweden's most popular artists, playing sold-out tours for every new record, which still sells a decent number of copies. Although he made his breakthrough on the brink of the MP3 revolution, his record sales, along with those of virtually every other artist have declined ever since.

In 2010 Gilbert recorded his first solo album under his own name for EMI. The record did not sell well, and although it received good reviews, EMI did not offer him a follow-up contract. At the time I interviewed him, in the winter of 2012, he was attempting to underwrite the cost of recording and release of a second solo album through a crowd-funding site on the Internet. Crowd-funding works in this way: each funder receives a small reward based on the sum of money donated: a copy of the album, free download, access to a limited or unlimited number of concerts or a similar incentive. In this way Gilbert managed to finance half the album. The funding went well at first, but began to dry up after a while, and he had to face the fact that he had probably reached the limit of his ability to attract funds in this way.

During his entire career, Gilbert has always had to work outside the field of music. At the time of the interview, he worked in a music store, mainly selling t-shirts, and had temporary employment as a resource person in a school for children with neuropsychiatric diagnoses, half an hour's bus journey outside his home town of Gothenburg.

Making money from music has never been easy in Sweden. Even musicians successful by the standards of the national independent scene have had to supplement their income with other activities. Musicianship tends to consume more money than it generates. Through crowd-funding, an artist may work closely with fans to generate funds, but the critical mass is quickly reached. And if donations do not add up to the sum required for recording and distributing the music, times are hard. It seems that the basic need of independent musicians is to recruit external flows in order to create music; otherwise their music will flow away from them.

Without the support of the music industries, there is no efficient apparatus of capture to convert music into monetizable units. Yet music is capable of creating alliances with people who can make money flow back to the musician by means other than economic transactions for individual copies of musical pieces. It does so through its capacity to create relationships among those who appropriate it – relationships among supporters and between the artist and supporters. These monetary streams are not the same as those that pass through the music industries; they depend upon quality (human appreciation) rather than quantity (saleable units). The spirit of music allows for both these modes of streaming.

Karin Dreijer Andersson is an independent music producer who uses the buzz-building capacity of the Internet. She lives in Stockholm and is famous as the lead singer of the internationally renowned electro duo, The Knife, which she runs with her brother, Olof Dreijer. Together they have made three full-length albums, released on their own label, Rabid Records. In the 1990s, she was a vocalist for the indie band Honey is Cool, and after The Knife's third and most successful album, *Silent Shout* (2006), was released, she began lending her services as a vocalist, producer and composer to a variety of projects. She has also written, performed, produced and released an album alone under the moniker Fever Ray.

Dreijer Andersson has set herself apart from most other independent artists. Although she uses Internet forums in a creative way and builds communities around her various musical personas, she does not partake in the activities of these communities. Still, without becoming a figure of godlike unattainability, she manages to create an aura around her diverse musical projects which is unmatched by any other musician.

In late 2008, Dreijer Andersson took the same technique a step further with Fever Ray. Long before any songs were released, rumours about a Dreijer Andersson solo album and short bits of sounds started circulating the Internet. A MySpace site under the name Fever Ray contained minimum information, except for a minute-long piece of slow, instrumental music, with hardly any rhythm. Then free MP3 remixes by well-known techno-producers of a Fever Ray song began to emerge, sometimes with fragments of Dreijer's characteristic voice, but there was not yet an original version of the song to refer to. The remixes made their way to the playlists of influential DJs and journalists, and the intensity of the rumours and the anticipation accelerated. No interviews about the project were yet made.

When the track 'If I Had a Heart' was released in December 2008, it contained an entirely new sound; a difficult sound, but one that matched the expectations created by the slow build-up, the leaked remixes and the sound clips, which in turn created a sonic reception for the sound. When the album *Fever Ray* was released in 2009, it received good sales and positive reviews.

All this time, Dreijer Andersson had been combining her artistic ambition with commercial branding – or perhaps branding in order to promote her artistic ambition. Through practices such as leaking free remixes, building word-of-mouth and viral marketing, communities were created, anticipation built and a secretive persona on which everything seems to converge had been created. But Dreijer Andersson does not communicate much with participants in these communities and is not really the person to which the moniker Fever Ray refers. What is unusual in her case is the possibility of using the Internet to circulate free digital material, which encourages people to attend her concerts, her main source of income. Yet she dislikes the concert form enough to convert it into something with minimal personal contact between spectators and artist.

The potential for creating mystery appears at the intersection of music and the Internet. Handled subtly, the Internet format allows for the orchestration of information, visuals and bits of audio, creating a gravitational pull, which releases just enough for people to want more and keep waiting and searching for it. Giving away free remixes is a way of making songs heard without actually letting go of the version that will appear on the album (the 'original version') and creating the opportunity for people to connect to the song in more ways than one (on the dance floor, for instance, and at home through earphones, in tailored versions). Just like Gilbert, Dreijer Andersson operates by creating intimacy with the audience, utilizing the communicating capacity of the digital format. But unlike Gilbert, who uses the capacity of the digital format to create a personal relationship with his audience, Dreijer Andersson uses its capacity to be impersonal with them, making them feel that they are part of something big but exclusive. An aura is created that hinges on the unattainability of its creator.

Gilbert's career has been on a national scale, whereas Dreijer Andersson has worked towards an international audience. Digital media is boundaryless, and the Internet provides the opportunity to build a collective buzz, targeting few individuals in many locations.

Many major multinational companies began to practise viral marketing as the opportunities for viral marketing expanded along with widespread use of the Internet in the 2000s. Viral marketing is one of the recent, post-industrial marketing techniques intended to make people integrate brands as a natural ingredient in their lives and identities. Discrete advertising is prioritized when targeting a young, urban middle-class group – one that has great cultural influence, but is often highly sceptical of commercialism. Viral marketing and related marketing techniques involve such features as the building of informal word-of-mouth buzz among the desired public segment, discretely situating the brand within their life-world. Successful viral marketing results in many people talking about and recommending the brand without realizing that they are working to promote it. The technique of 'context branding' is similar: a whole context is discretely marked by its association with a brand, but is not overly demonstrated in the context.

One brand that has utilized such techniques is the energy drink producer Red Bull. Since its introduction in the early 1990s, the brand has expanded its range of branded context advertising with, for example, the Red Bull Music Academy (RBMA) event, which occurs once a year. Red Bull GmbH sponsors 60 young aspiring musicians or music composers from around the world to spend a number of days in an international metropolis, with nothing to do but live together, make music and attend seminars with renowned artists or music producers. And, of course, partying and drinking Red Bull, which is freely available 24 hours a day. Everything is filmed and transcribed for publication on RBMA's website, functioning as both a magnet for the academy and a source of inspiration for people sitting in front of their computers, wishing they could be one of the participants. The format is borrowed from one of the televised reality shows, but the concept is even more elaborate, as it includes a semi-public ('invitations only') club evening for an ostensibly exclusive crowd.

During the RBMA Sessions, an existing club venue is used to promote the RBMA (or, in fact, the Red Bull brand); the word is spread through the relevant Facebook groups, inviting people to an evening event at which some of the past years' attendees are present. In Gothenburg, a town nationally and internationally known for its music producers, an RBMA session was held in 2011 at a newly opened but highly credible venue located between the city's main street and the more 'alternatively oriented' quarters to the west. The evening started with a public conversation between the previous year's RBMA participants and a well-known radio DJ, and concluded with a late-night dance party with free Red Bull-based liquor. No representatives from Red Bull GmbH were visible during the evening, and explicit branding was minimal; the intimate, semi-legal club format was borrowed in order to make money for Red Bull.

The example shows how a format designed and traditionally endorsed by the independent scene can be appropriated by a multinational actor. Creating a gravitational pull by introducing an aura of exclusivity is similar to Dreijer Andersson's strategy. Actually, there are many similarities in these marketing techniques: they operate through intimacy, they give things away in order to pull monetary flows indirectly, and they create relationships with a public without actually providing a face to which the public can relate. This is a sophisticated way of utilizing the capabilities of the new media technologies in order to convert non-material labour into money. As the new media also means that music has escaped the capture of the material copy, these methods generate money indirectly.

These examples are all taken from a Swedish context. They might have come from anywhere, but the fact is that Sweden holds a specific position in the world, as it is a relatively small country which has had a great impact internationally in both music and technology. The next section outlines the way the Swedish scenes of independent music and computer hacking were intertwined in the 1990s, and how similarities in their structures generated a situation that culminated in the 2009 trial of The Pirate Bay; three young men with little money were required by the courts to compensate the music industry with the incredible sum of 46 million SEK (€5.4 million).

AGENTS OF MUSICAL FLOW ESCAPE AND CAPTURE

In the early 2000s, Sweden became the site of several captures and escapes. The internationally best-known case is undoubtedly the 2009 trial against the operators of The Pirate Bay website. This example shows just how intertwined music and information have become, and how common features of the Swedish music scene and the hacker culture in the Swedish context have provided conditions for an actor such as The Pirate Bay.

Sweden has had some great musical successes, considering that it is a country of a mere 9.56 million population; the country can boast several international successes since ABBA's international breakthrough in 1974. In the 1980s, Europe and Roxette both had Number 1 hits on the US singles list; and in the early 1990s, Ace of Base and The Cardigans had a string of Number 1 hits as well. In 1997, Sweden came third in the export sale of music, behind the US and the UK. Swedish producers such as Denniz Pop and Max Martin and video producer Jonas Åkerlund have all worked with some of the world's most successful musical artists. From the 1970s to this day, independent Swedish music has also had international success, if on a smaller economic scale.

When it comes to Swedish file-sharing, the most renowned story internationally is The Pirate Bay, a Swedish BitTorrent tracker site launched in 2003. At the time of the launch, it was pioneering BitTorrent technology as a means for peer-to-peer-based copying and spreading of digital material. BitTorrent technology frames data streams, the name alluding to the flow metaphor that became common in the 2010s when people were talking about music. Many small torrents together become one river; there is no 'original source', but numerous small sources. The data file is not copied from another file, but is streamed together from many. It is impossible to download a file from BitTorrents without simultaneously making it available for download for other users; when one downloads, one is automatically sharing. The technology is, without option, reciprocal: the data flow in all directions.

As well as being a server, The Pirate Bay is an ideology. The ideology was promoted by Piratbyrån, an organization promoting the right to free information, and therefore critical of copyright laws. The name, 'The Pirate Office', provocatively alluded to the name of Svenska Antipiratbyrån [Swedish Anti-Piracy Office], a Swedish lobby group acting against copyright infringement on behalf of companies and organizations within the Swedish film and computer game industries. As the Swedish Anti-Piracy Office was an obvious apparatus of capture,

The Pirate Office was seeking every possible way of releasing music flows from both material and legal confinements.

The spokespeople of The Pirate Office took part in public debates and were often seen in the national news media. At the time, Swedish legislation had no means of addressing this new form of file-sharing, but in 2006, laws were instituted allowing the police to storm the servers, and declaring the new forms of file-sharing illegal and the users legally chargeable. Even though the connection has not been corroborated, charges were soon made against the Swedish judiciary that a raid had been made at The Pirate Bay after what was supposedly severe pressure from the US government and the Motion Picture Association of America (MPAA). In 2009, the owners of The Pirate Bay were charged and found guilty of crimes against the copyright legislation. The verdict was that the four accused young persons were to pay compensation. In an attempt to capture the overflow, the recording industries had found a way to render the BitTorrent technology illegal.

In 2008, the streaming service Spotify was launched. The hype around the launch had been massive; the service was marketed as a 'legal alternative' to illicit file-sharing, over which a great deal of discussion occurred in virtually every Swedish news medium since The Pirate Bay round-up in 2006. The service functioned in this way: after being personally invited by someone entrusted with a limited number of invites, the users were given free access to the entire cloud of music that Spotify had at its disposal – most of the mainstream music ever recorded, with several thousand songs added every day. Users could create playlists from the music according to their own preferences. After a number of songs, the stream was interrupted by a number of commercial messages; then it took off where it ended. The paying service consisted of the same thing, but without commercials. Thus the commodity which was sold was not a mass of listeners to be envisaged as potential receivers of commercial messages from 'sponsors', as in conventional radio or television commercials. Instead, the commodity was the possibility for the user to choose from almost any music without having to have the stream interrupted by annoying commercials. The logic of this business idea was quickly given the nickname 'spotification' by commentators from The Pirate Office.

Much like the RBMA event, Spotify initially played on the dynamic between inclusion and exclusion. What came to constitute the specificity of Spotify, however, was the offering of total access to the music cloud and exposure to commercials versus total access to commercial-free music cloud. The cloud seemed to be limitless and disembodied, making the owning of files on one's hard drive obsolete and unnecessary.

Everything exists in the cloud. Nothing needs to flow between users. No file content needs to be copied or downloaded. The only thing the user needed in order to retrieve any music ever recorded was access to a stream from the cloud, in which all content was already copyrighted, independent of who streamed it. With its logic of absolute digital access, it was also a realization of Kusek and Leonhard's trope of music as water from their manifesto book, *The Future of Music: Manifesto for the Digital Music Revolution* (2005). Access is like turning on a tap, and the music of one's choice flows like a stream right into the living room or mobile headphones.

The public success of Spotify was enormous, perhaps not only because of its own merits, but also because, being a 'legal alternative', it was supported by the Swedish government, the biggest Swedish Internet providers and the music industry's lobby organizations. After the initial buzz, invitations were released to the entire public, and in 2012 the service was still Sweden's most commonly used Internet-based music service. As a means of overflow management, it marks a new shift – one that downplays the consumers' role as active co-producers, but integrates them by providing them with new means to circulate ready-made music to other consumers. These means include the possibility of creating playlists and discussing music with other music fans as a part of the program interface or the more discrete function of generating user data that are later used in generating new statistics or new listening recommendations for listeners.

After the trial of The Pirate Bay, public discussions about file-sharing receded, but discussion on the status of digital information continues. The generation growing up with Napster and The Pirate Bay has spawned a number of intellectuals who are academics and journalists today, and are still participating in shaping the discourse on the freedom of information.

In an article on how Sweden, as an integral part of the global music industry, has coped with changes in market conditions brought about by regulatory changes, Burnett and Wikström (2006) listed three reasons why peer-to-peer file-sharing services have been especially successful in Sweden:

> First, the Swedish government has for many years supported the deployment of a sophisticated Internet infrastructure. Due to this policy, a large percentage of Swedish households have sophisticated computers and Broadband Internet connection … Second, Internet-savvy young Swedes have little compassion for record companies whose reputation is deeply ingrained … Lastly, legal download services … were not really widely available in Sweden until 2005.

> This has not given the consumers who would like to purchase their music on the Internet any choice other than the illegal services. (Burnett and Wikström 2006: 578)

The Swedish case had proven problematic to the music industry because it combined an unusually high computer literacy with availability, made possible by generous legislation. This combination rendered the country a gravity centre of constant leaking, wherein music has flowed outside the international containers that held it. In terms of overflow management, Spotify became a new version of the apparatus of capture, permitting a redirection of the flow of music through an entirely new channel. Capturing the overflow of individual files was accomplished through The Pirate Bay trials. The overall manoeuvre of capture, however, was the creation of this new channel, controlled by the established music industries. In order to do this, another manoeuvre was necessary. Separating Spotify from the cultural context from which the file-sharing phenomena arose amounted to a discursive conversion of the sharing culture into a culture of free access to all music. And yet the context from which the Swedish file-sharing sprung was not the mainstream music listeners, but two cultural circles that began to intertwine with the introduction of information technologies in the 1990s. This process continued after The Pirate Bay trials. These two cultures were the hacker culture and the independent music scene, both having histories of communal, horizontal sharing.

In her extensive work on the Swedish independent music scene, Baym (2011) has described the emergence of a 'gift economy': the digital music scene of the first decade of the twentieth century. As mentioned by Burnett and Wikström, legally paying for services for downloading music in Sweden arrived relatively late in a country characterized by a high degree of computer literacy, making other ways of communicating music a necessity for artists and publishers. Baym interviewed musicians and publishers in the middle of the first decade of the 2000s, and showed how songs were given as gifts on the websites of bands and recording companies, and how the MySpace forum was used as a means of horizontal personal communication between fans and musicians, who tended to run the MySpace sites themselves. The communication structure was flat. No hierarchy seemed to exist among band, publisher and audience, and band members and recording company managers often made friends with fans because of their common love of music. Several musicians interviewed by Baym even refused to use the old established term 'fan' when referring to their listeners.

In these social circles, relationships are built between the artist and the audience. The artist does not appear to the audience as a godlike rock idol; the audience is not regarded by the publisher merely as a revenue source to be exploited and monetized. Rather, they all are allies in a common and shared love of music. Money is not made from publishers selling music to the fans, but from other sources of income, such as clubs, concerts and the sale of physical records or t-shirts. It could even come from selling the music to commercials and TV series, an enterprise that would not have been tolerated by the independent music fans of precious decades. But now, given that most fans realize the small incomes that their favourite bands earn from their music, the practice is accepted. Still, the income of most of Swedish musicians comes not from music, but from working in some other field in order to be able to afford to play – even for those musicians with international hits and international tours.

There is a common denominator between such Swedish informatic activists as those of The Pirate Office and those of Swedish musicians: What has been aspired to and idealized is not the hierarchical revenue exploitation, but communality and sharing between equals. Rasmus Fleischer, one of the founders of The Pirate Office and currently a postgraduate researcher in contemporary history, is an often-heard voice in public debates. In the anthology *After The Pirate Bay*, he reminded readers of the early standards of The Pirate Bay. The motto of The Pirate Office was always *kopimi*, a Swedified abridgement of the English words 'copy me', meaning that information is supposed to be free, and that whatever could be copied should be copied (Fleischer, 2010).

Fleischer also told readers that the point of starting the servers had never been to make money, but to inspire others to do what The Pirate Bay had done: spread information further. Despite the MPAA's assertions and the juridical prosecutors during and before the trials, The Pirate Bay would probably never had made huge profits. Media discussion about the 'pirate movement' was polarized: the 'pirates' were presented either as people displaying double standards who were making money on the work of others; or they were presented as idealists, unselfishly acting on their inner convictions. Fleischer said that neither of these was the case: the Pirate Office and The Pirate Bay were characterized by a pragmatic approach towards the organization itself and the management of the entire project.

Fleischer also reminded readers that members of the Spotify team were eager to propagate their own service as a legal alternative to illicit file-sharing. This was necessary, in the light of media discussions about The Pirate Bay and people's right to free information; without this discussion, the same assertion could not have been made so convincingly. They also implicitly claimed that file-sharing had but one key attribute: people getting things for free. Swedish authorities responded with a great sigh of relief at a time when they were hard-pressed by the US government and lobby organizations representing the Big Four. At last, a way out of the trap! Thus Spotify was hailed as a solution to a political problem on an international level, and many politicians and industrialists did their best to promote the service. But there was one thing missing (or hidden) through both the public debate and the Spotify propaganda: that the ideology that had always been promoted by The Pirate Office through The Pirate Bay was one of democratic equality in sharing. The logic of The Pirate Bay was horizontal. The logic of Spotify is hierarchical.

The aim of The Pirate Bay was to provide people with the possibility of sharing information they wished to be shared with other people. The choice made by many users – to utilize the technology for sharing music, movies and video games – was not the choice (or the aim) of The Pirate Office. Yet many other types of information was also shared – almost anything that could be digitalized, whether legally or illegally. Fleischer suggested that Spotify's business model was used as a handy solution for the question: 'How are the artists going to get paid for their work?' The digital activists had long since moved on, and issues now being handled had nothing to do with file-sharing or Internet 'piracy'. Furthermore, whereas more and more independent musicians had made their music available on Spotify, the hinted-at economic dividends turned out to be small.

Accordingly, although Spotify had added such features as compatibility with Facebook and Last.fm in 2012, a rating system and a user-generated 'Similar Artists' function, it has not proved to be a useful resource for independent musicians. The customers to whom Spotify appealed were not actively engaged social beings, but passive consumers who desired only to be fed with music. Only the 'free music' aspect of informational flatness proposed by The Pirate Office remained, which is why musicians and music publishers had gone elsewhere to build communities in less hierarchical sociotechnical ecologies. Even though the popularity of MySpace had faded, there were other forums through which similar communication could occur. Artist or recording company blogs are having a renaissance; artist pages on Facebook run by the artists and labels are being used as a social interface; videos can be quickly posted at Vimeo; high-resolution music can easily be uploaded and downloaded to such sites as Soundcloud and then linked by aggregators with mobile phone compatibility such as The Hype Machine. 'Gift economies' are everywhere. Many of the services provided by these sites still have semi-legal status and are run by enthusiasts, driven more by the will to create conditions for people to express their passions than by a desire for extracting revenue streams from them.

As the new music-containing formation of the cloud was a means of capture, it also provides new modes of escape – new lines of flight, on which music is released to once again flow among users of different orders. In 2013, Soundcloud seemed to function according to the same cloud and streaming logic as that of Spotify and similar services, but horizontally rather than vertically. Music creators upload new musical pieces such as songs, mixes or remixes to Soundcloud – pieces which are open for the public to comment upon or sometimes even to download and remix the tracks. Most of the songs uploaded to Soundcloud are not copyrighted, which presents the opportunity of an exchange between the audience and the musician. Furthermore, Soundcloud pages are often run by the artists themselves; they can choose to be present as persons or not. Soundcloud and similar sites can therefore be seen as lines of escape from the apparatus of capture, and thus the dynamic between the music industry and the horizontal networks of users continues.

CONCLUSIONS

In this chapter, I have intended to demonstrate the interconnectedness of the economy, technology, ideas and cultural practices through the example of musical production. Music cannot really be owned; its materiality consists partly in the listener hearing it. Because the hearing of sound which is recognizable as music cannot be reconciled with a cost, it is the intermediaries between the musician and the listener which can be controlled and monetized. Music is constantly flowing, changing its materiality, framed anew with every technological shift. As most of these shifts are user-driven, the established music business always seems to be two steps behind, hurrying after and trying to capture and dam up the escaping overflow by whatever means are at their disposal: money, legislation and attempts to influence public opinion.

With the shift from analogue formats to digital formats, there has also been a shift from a relatively homogeneous materiality of intermediates to an extremely heterogeneous one; the digital format of intermediaries seems to be able to spawn innumerable new digital formats by itself. As the established recording industry can deal with only one digital format at a time, the velocity of the capture and escape moments are constantly increasing in the first decades of the twentieth century. As the digital technologies continue to provide new formats, new captures and new escapes of the musical flow spring forth faster than ever.

I asked the reader in the beginning of this chapter to consider the nature of music: 'What is music?' Deleuze and Guattari (1987) have used a cosmologic definition, according to which music is the 'deterritorialization of a refrain'. Thus music is able to create and dissolve territories through its capacity to connect across registers. Even if I do not wish to follow Deleuze and Guattari that far, I can conclude that the capacity of music to connect humans to each other is what drives both its tendency to be economically over-coded by the apparatus of capture and its ability to create lines of escape from this capture.

It also seems to be this capacity that renders music an element with a specific way of flowing and overflowing, and to be managed in relation to the way it overflows. In contrast to such other digitizable formats as books or movies, music also has an inherently social component. Even if it can be listened to in solitude, it pertains to matters of the self by appealing to private emotions and to group identity. The latest technologies have added a social element to both composition (Soundcloud often is used by artists by uploading drafts for songs or rehearsal recordings) and final production (through the possibility or sometimes-occurring public offer of remixing an artist's songs). Many people still consider the concert and the dance floor the ultimate purpose of music; these are indisputably social events. Thus, music has connective properties, but is still easily movable between situations. Its definition may change, however, following the technologies with which it is communicated; it still gains its power through specific ways of connecting people, to each other and to themselves, in ways that continually prove to be impossible to capture fully and to over-code with economic logic.

FIELD MATERIAL

Burnett, Robert and Patrik Wikström (2005), 'Music production in times of monopoly: the example of Sweden', *Popular Music and Society*, **29**(5): 575–82.

Fleischer, Rasmus (2010), 'Femton gastar på död mans kista – om framtidens nätpolitik', in Jonas Andersson and Pelle Snickars (eds), *After The Pirate Bay*, Stockholm: Mediehistoriskt arkiv.

Goldman, David (2010), 'Music's lost decade: sales cut in half', *CNN Money*, web edition, 3 February, available at http://money.cnn.com/2010/02/02/news/companies/napster_music_industry/.

8. Transmutations of noise

Robert Willim

> I couldn't hear my baby crying over the noise of the hairdryer. (www.quietmark.com)

> For sleeping, there's nothing like the ultimate white noise Fan CD and Fan Noise mp3 download! Let the gentlly [*sic*] purring hum sound of a running electric fan noise lull you to sleep without actually running a fan! Sounds of a window fan is [*sic*] an exceptionally effective white noise sound to fall asleep by in any season of the year. (www.purewhitenoise.com)

Noise is commonly understood as an excess of undesired sound. But just as definitions have often been problematic in the other cases of overflow discussed in this volume, it is difficult to define noise. What is experienced as noise in various contexts? The two websites from which the previous quotes were taken described noise as either annoying or pleasant.

The first of the two quotes is to be found on the website of Quiet Mark, which, according to the text on the site: 'is the international mark of approval award programme from the UK Noise Abatement Society encouraging worldwide companies in the development of noise reduction within the design of everyday machines and appliances'. Its aim is to reduce what it calls excessive noise in people's surroundings, in order to improve health and reduce stress.

The second quote is from the Pure White Noise company, which, according to its website:

> is an audio research and development company studying and recording white noise and its many applications, solutions and benefits to children and adults since 1985. As audio specialists, we combine the science of both sound and relaxation technology with the art of white noise to create superior audio solutions and sound files to successfully promote relaxation and sleep in babies, children and adults.

Noise belongs to the sonic and the visual realm, but can also be located in any process of communication in which someone is trying to distinguish signal, message and meaning from random fluctuations. Noise is a polysemic concept. It is usually defined as unwanted – glitches, hiss and buzz – messing up a message. But it is not merely the polysemy that makes it such a thought-provoking concept; it is also the difficulties of capturing and delineating the nature of noise once it has been defined. It appears to shift, both by definition and by the ways in which people approach and experience it. When noise is framed or delimited, it becomes charged with meaning. Framing practices, such as the application of noise filters to clean an electronic signal, force people to decide when noise begins and when it ends. Similarly, definitions of what is experienced as a convenient and preferable sonic environment by different people show what is experienced as noise and by whom.

When the UK Noise Abatement Society defines a sound as noisy, it is automatically framed as a problem – as something to be reduced. The aim for Pure White Noise, on the other hand, is to sell noise as a packaged product. Its products are available on CDs or in MP3 format, and the noise produced by this company is meant to mask and block other noise. By packaging and defining noise as a commodity, the company is transforming unwanted noise into appreciated noise. On a CD entitled *Calming Electric Fan* (from the previous quote) or *Soothing Air Conditioner*, sounds have been transformed from annoying and disturbing to valuable.

In this chapter, I scrutinize shifting understandings, framings and experiences of noise, with the help of the term 'transmutation'. The word provokes associations to mercurial shapeshifting, alchemy and cultural complexity (see for example, Löfgren and Willim, 2005). By using the word 'transmutation', I want to emphasize that the unwanted or the unexpected is transformed into the appreciated and, to some extent, the manageable.

I focus here on noise in relation to sonic and visual media. The products of Pure White Noise serve as examples of transmutations of noise, but I concentrate on ways in which noise is approached within electronic music, visual arts and the use of digital media. I start with a broader discussion about noise, and then present various artistic approaches, ending with some reflections on how the concept of noise can be used as a cultural analytic tool.[1]

THE ALLURING ABUNDANCE OF NOISE

Loud sounds can be overwhelming and disrupting, revolting and nausea inducing. Such uncomfortable sounds are commonly defined as sonic noise. But a discreet low-intensity background hum, like the analogue hiss from a radio when a station is not tuned in, can also be called sonic noise.

Visual noise is an expression used to suggest that an image is uninterpretable, but it can also be experienced as a slight blur of an image. In signal theory, the 'noise floor' is the background against which communication occurs. Its source can be atmospheric radiation, interference among various types of equipment or the limitations of electronic circuitry and components. The noise floor is the inconspicuous and overlooked background that people normally ignore in order to concentrate on what they consider to be significant in a certain situation. According to Douglas Kahn, who introduced the issue of noise in his seminal work on the history of sound in the arts, noise 'can be understood in one sense to be that constant grating sound generated by the movement between the abstract and the empirical' (Kahn, 2001: 25). In order to create meaning, people need to delimit, cleanse, overlook or abstract. Noise:

> needs not be loud, for it can go unheard even in the most intense communication. Imperfections in script, verbal pauses, and poor phrasing are regularly passed over in the greater purpose of communication, yet they always threaten to break out into an impassable noise and cause real havoc. (Kahn, 2001: 25)

In this sense, noise is conceptually related to clutter, waste and irregularity.

A universal definition of noise is probably impossible. As Kahn said, noise indeed exists, but 'trying to define it in an unifying manner across the range of contexts will only invite noise on itself' (2001: 21). A good sample of the wide spectrum of noise studies and thoughts related to the history of music is presented in Christoph Cox and Daniel Warner's *Audio Cultures*: everything from the political visions of Jacques Attali to accounts from experimental musicians.

When noise is mentioned without specification, the first association is often with sonic noise. All sounds, if experienced intensely, or loud enough to be distressing or painful, are probably experienced as noise. But, as Kahn stressed, noise need not be loud. In his more than 900-page exposé of the cultural history of sonic noise, Hillel Schwarz wrote about everything from the Big Bang and reverberating echoes to tinnitus and hearing loss. Noise can have a monumental eruptive character or be peripheral and inconspicuous. He proposed that noise is manifested in relationships:

> noise is never so much a question of the intensity of sound as of the intensity of relationships ... As a register of the intensity of relationships, noise has a fourfold history. First, the chronicle of changing soundscapes: how each era and culture lives within its own ambience of sounds. Next, the annals of sounds earmarked as pleasant or obnoxious: how each era, culture, and rank hears (or does not hear) and welcomes or disdains the sounds around it. Next, the career of noise itself as variously apprehended: how each era, culture, occupation or discipline reconstitutes the notion and nature of noise. Contingent upon these, finally, are narratives of noisemaking and noisebreaking: how noise in each era, culture, and class has been denounced or defended, defiantly produced or determinedly deadened. (Schwarz, 2011: 21)

Noise is culturally charged, therefore; evoked by definition, by the earmarking and categorizations of sounds, depending on settings and situations. It is often associated with an historical trajectory in which people create environments time after time, with more sounds than had existed previously. Noise can be associated with places, with cultural distinctions, with age or gender, with ideas about convenience and the rights of people. Urbanity (and the modern industrialized society) is often coupled with noise, associated with (noise) pollution, with sounds out of control, in overflow, in conflict. There is no doubt that a number of human activities typical to urban settings – large-scale systems of construction and transportation, for instance – are sources of sounds experienced primarily as discomforting. When, in the 1960s, R. Murray Schafer introduced the term 'soundscape', one of his purposes was to point to what, he contended, was an overabundance of acoustic information in the present world. Urban environments were especially identified as problematic and described as lo-fi – in contrast to rural settings, which according to Schafer are generally more hi-fi.

> The country is generally more hi-fi than the city; night more than day; ancient times more than modern. In a hi-fi soundscape even the slightest disturbance can communicate interesting or vital information. The human ear is alert, like that of an animal ... In a lo-fi soundscape individual acoustic signals are obscured in an overdense population of sounds. The pellucid sound – a footstep in the snow, a train whistle in the distance or a church bell across the valley – is masked by broad-band noise ... There is cross-talk on all the channels, and in order for the most ordinary sounds to be heard they have to be monstrously amplified. In the ultimate lo-fi soundscape the signal to noise ratio is 1 to 1 and it is no longer possible to know what, if anything, is to be listened to. (Schafer, 2004: 32)

Schafer advocated practices and competencies of careful listening, through which the cacophonic sonic textures of various places could be tuned out in favour of a concentration on sound which he called well tempered and balanced (Kelman, 2010). Schafer's ideas about soundscapes have provided inspiration for later practices of noise abatement and sound design. The notion of 'the tuning of the world', from his book of the same name (Schafer, 1994), and of sanitized and organized soundscapes versus noisy lo-fi disorder may be stretched to more unpleasant ideas about social and spatial order and about various people and cultures being noisy, loud and disquiet. Since the 1960s, the word 'soundscape' has been utilized in many contexts, and has differed in meaning and range, often quite disconnected from Schafer's ideas (Kelman, 2010).

Noise abatement is an obvious example of overflow management in relation to the sonic noise. If a sound environment is experienced as being out of control and unmanageable, it is likely that it is defined as noisy. Transmutation – turning bad noise into good noise – is a method of management. And, to some extent, the processes of transmutations I write about here can be seen as a kind of noise abatement; but not a simple one. In spite of its strong associations with the unwanted, with discomfort and disgust, noise can be associated with pleasure, as accentuated in the marketing of Pure White Noise. An association of noise with pleasure is also evoked in a number of creative practices.

The Pure White Noise company frames the noise it sells as something authentic and pure. Within acoustics white noise can be defined as:

> a complex signal or sound that covers the entire range of audible frequencies, all of which possess equal intensity. White noise is analogous to white light, which contains roughly equal intensities of all frequencies of visible light. A good approximation to white noise is the static that appears between radio stations on the FM band. ('Noise', *Encyclopædia Britannica. Encyclopædia Britannica Online Academic Edition*, n.d.; see also Krapp, 2011: 69)[2]

White noise is a complex signal or sound, yet it is not necessarily experienced as complex and varied. The possibilities for interpreting white noise, whether loud or not, are limited (or endless). Its complex variations create what can be experienced as static similarity. The rapid flow of water is one of the sources of sounds experienced as white noise. In a waterfall, the overflowing and crashing of the water induces a wall of sound, experienced primarily as static. A similar sound is produced by heavy rainfall, or even by electric fans, air conditioners or vacuum cleaners.

White noise may be experienced as intrusive, but also as relaxing. Hillel Schwarz, for instance, wrote about soothing, low-intensity white noise. He referred to Pure White Noise and to white-noise machines, which according to him:

> became the mainstays of birthing chambers, nurseries, offices, and bedrooms, like The Sharper Image Heart and Sound Soother, 'your own personal sound environment,' 'with buttons for rain, ocean, brook, summer night, and white noise', 'Real digital recordings. Not tape.' Or maybe a CD for fussy babies, each track with 'nine peaceful minutes' of 'the soothing hum of a vacuum,' 'the constant whir of a hairdryer,' 'the continuous rumble of a lawnmower.' 'Or truly Pure White Noise® baby CD and MP3 baby audio files in baby's nursery, or wherever you hug or rock your baby. Our collection of baby soothing sounds includes Baby's First White Noise, a variety of nature sounds (ocean waves, surf, brook, rain), motor noises (vacuum cleaner, dishwasher, blow dryer, clothes dryer, washing machine, fan, car motor).' Motor noises? What an odd turn of events, that sounds once heard as obnoxious and disruptive should become a sonic backdrop marketed without qualm as 'pure white noise'. (Schwarz, 2011: 835)

As noted previously, when the issue of noise is raised, it is often the sonic that is meant. But there are also noisy images. Visual white noise is often referred to as 'snow' or 'static' – the type of image that occurs on a television screen when no broadcasting channel is tuned in. Both sonic and visual white noises are difficult to interpret. The complex character of white noise can be soothing, but these complex sonic or visual textures can also be the source of paranoid interpretations. It is virtually impossible to locate the source of white noise if no cue is presented, which gives white noise an enigmatic aura, resulting in various occult speculations. The search for hidden paranormal messages in the static complexities of white noise is a common theme in popular culture. In several movies, ghost hunters or similar characters look into the static of TV screens or listen to the static noisy hiss of some aural signal, in search for hidden messages from other dimensions. A web search using the words 'white noise' and 'EVP' results in a large number of pages and sites about spiritual communication. The abbreviation EVP stands for 'electronic voice phenomenon' and describes a concept based on the assumption that paranormal voice messages are being transmitted in the noise of electronic media. The random complexities and overflow of white noise is an alluring invitation to apophenia – to the search for patterns or meanings that may not exist.

THE ART OF NOISE AND MALFUNCTION

Filter it out or amplify it. (Krapp, 2011: 60)

The history of media and communication technologies reveals a long quest for pure messages and signals. High fidelity (hi-fi) and high definition (HD) are two terms which have been used to label certain technological qualities of representation and mediation of audiovisual content. These terms evoke associations of purity, accuracy, distinctness and faithfulness towards what is being represented. Various noise-cancelling technologies have been developed in order to eliminate unwanted interference and overflow.

Once noise has been defined and therefore framed, one can choose either to filter it out or to transform it into valuable noise. Within the art world, and subsequently within digital culture, utilizations of the noisy and erroneous have become escape routes from the predictably structured and from mundane processes of business as usual.

In his book *Noise Channels: Glitch and Error in Digital Culture,* Peter Krapp discussed the relationships between digital culture and creative processes. He noted that 'the productive ambiguity of noise emerged from the consideration that it is too much information – and precisely unexpected information' (Krapp, 2011: xi). According to this statement, noise is an overflow of information. But such an overflow is difficult to manage. Krapp quoted N. Katherine Hayles, who suggested that noise can interfere with signal, thereby becoming part of the message (Krapp, 2011: x). It is this potential intermingling of noise with both the background and the foreground that renders it fascinating. Noise is always lingering at the border of manageability.

One's experience of noise is dependent upon context and upon the way attention is directed. In most cases, the so-called noise floor or background is ignored. But when attention is directed towards it, noise will become the foreground. It is at this point that it can be either filtered out or appreciated.

When noise is framed as appreciated, it can be used to contest concepts of purity. In the history of music and art, questions about purity, norms and conventions, have been intrinsic to the development of new forms, genres and expressions. The hybrid, the irregular and noisy, has also occurred in the borderland between ethnographic methods and literature (see e.g. O'Dell and Willim, 2011). At the end of the last century, Ulf Hannerz wrote about the ways in which flows and hybridity were related to anthropological ideas. He quoted Salman Rushdie as saying:

> The Satanic Verses celebrates hybridity, impurity, intermingling, the transformation that comes of new and unexpected combinations of human beings, cultures, ideas, politics, movies, song. It rejoices in mongrelization and fears the absolutism of the pure. Mélange, hotchpotch, a bit of this and a bit of that is how newness enters the world. (Rushdie quoted by Hannerz, 1996: 65)

The overthrowing of previous ideas of purity and high quality has been pertinent to much art since early twentieth century Modernism (Krapp, 2011). Expressions once considered unwanted and problematic have been appropriated, used in creative processes and subsequently often commodified.

All of this has happened within a number of creative practices, from the early twentieth century 'noise art' of the Italian Futurists, to the Dada bruitism and other strands of artistic avant-gardes (Kahn, 2001). The borders of what to consider art (and music) have been stretched and moved. Artistic boundary work has characterized practically all of the twentieth century; composers such as John Cage and Pierre Schaeffer have contested the boundaries among noise, sound and music, and borders have been challenged within genres and movements such as conceptualism, fluxus and *musique concrète* (Kahn, 2001; Toop, 2004).

Art can view noise as uncontrolled and metaphorically wild, to be domesticated and transformed into something manageable. Playing with the wild and that which is out of control has often occurred in artistic boundary-bending. The making of art is, to some extent, based on combinations of controlled methodological work and the utilization of chance and serendipity (Willim, 2013). Such approaches to noise are related to the utilization of failure and error. According to Lisa Le Feuvre, who edited an anthology of writings about art and failure, failure has achieved a different currency in the realm of art than in other parts of the society:

> Failure, by definition, takes us beyond assumptions and what we think we know. Artists have long turned their attention to the unrealizability of the quest for perfection, or the open-endedness of experiment, using both dissatisfaction and error as means to rethink how we understand our place in the world. (LeFeuvre, 2010: 12)

Accidental discoveries have often been mentioned as the genesis of various artistic concepts. Such stories frequently report an accidental action or an unexpected event as the spark that ignited a process of transmutation, through which noise was remade into something valuable. The description of German music producer Stefan Betke (also known as Pole) on the website of Matador Records serves as an example:

> Structurally, the music of Pole is based on abstract, irregular rhythms created by a defective analogue sound filter Betke uses, namely the 'Waldorf 4-Pole' filter. These rhythms principally are defect frequencies full of interference (in audio terms commonly referred to as 'noise'), not unlike the crackling sounds of vintage vinyl, except for a harder, purely digital quality, which makes them very immediate. (Matador Records, 2000)

According to the story, Stefan Betke accidentally dropped a Waldorf 4-Pole filter device, thereby discovering that the clicks, cracks and pops of the malfunctioning apparatus could be used as raw material for new compositions. The resulting music became a minimalistic 'post-techno', wherein the small glitchy sounds from the filter were used to engender an empty spacious sonic atmosphere. He utilized these glitches from the malfunctioning device, thus turning an accident into an opportunity.

There are many stories of accidental discoveries, but there are also stories about the intentional misuse of tools and technologies. In the 1990s, some musical practices utilizing noise were associated with post-digital aesthetics.

> 'post-digital' aesthetic was developed in part as a result of the immersive experience of working in environments suffused with digital technology: computer fans whirring, laser printers churning out documents, the sonification of user-interfaces, and the muffled noise of hard drives. But more specifically, it is from the 'failure' of digital technology that this new work has emerged: glitches, bugs, application errors, system crashes, clipping, aliasing, distortion, quantization noise, and even the noise floor of computer sound cards are the raw materials composers seek to incorporate into their music. (Cascone, 2000: 12–13)

Kim Cascone wrote about the 'aesthetics of failure' and 'post-digital tendencies' in 2000, but artists and musicians had already been experimenting with the ways digital technologies could be utilized as machines of noise and glitch creation for some years. A genre called 'glitch' had emerged within electronic music, often associated with the German record label Mille Plateaux.

Many types of digital malfunction were sought by artists in the late 1990s. Cascone mentioned Oval, who manipulated the surfaces of CDs to create glitches when the discs were played (2000: 13). The skipping CD was also mentioned by other writers:

> If there were an emblematic sound of today's digital music, it would be the sound of a skipping CD. First encountered as an error in a playback process, then utilized as musical material in itself, this sound-meme spread like a virus through the network of electronic music producers. What distinguishes this

> strand of laptop music from its predecessors (both academic and popular) is the explicit use of the concept 'glitch' by its producers and the whole conceptual framework of digitality surrounding this music. (Vanhanen, 2003: 46)

Utilizations of malfunctioning CDs had been preceded by similar uses of earlier analogue technologies. Phonographs and analogue turntables were favourite tools of a number of artists who used them to turn noise into music. The opportunity to interact physically with and misuse the stylus, the needle and the turntable rendered them suitable equipment for stage performances. Practices such as the scratching of records had been used within hip-hop for some time. The (noisy) sounds of scratched vinyl were widespread, accepted and commodified in ways similar to the earlier sounds of fuzzboxes and the distortion of electric guitars.

Noise and glitches, encountered as errors, have subsequently been utilized as material in creative workflows – something that has characterized several practices. And although noise and malfunction can be transmuted into intended output, these practices are debated. Rosa Menkman, who has written about glitch art and software artists, demonstrated how some critical glitch artists avoid the domestication and commodification of noise and error.

> There is an obvious critique here [from some artists]: to design a glitch means to domesticate it. When the glitch becomes domesticated into a desired process, controlled by a tool, or technology – essentially cultivated – it has lost the radical basis of its enchantment and becomes predictable. It is no longer a break from a flow within a technology, but instead a form of craft. For many critical artists, it is considered no longer a glitch, but a filter that consists of a preset and/or a default: what was once a glitch is now a new commodity (Menkman, 2011: 55)

Menkman's discussion of the commodification of glitches is reminiscent of the discussion about pure noise and various commodifications of noise. The noises and shortcomings of earlier technologies have been turned into aesthetic effects, and subsequently incorporated into such products as guitar pedals and software plug-ins, the pedals delivering distortion and overdrive and the plug-ins adding vinyl record crackle, tape distortion or speaker cabinet noise to sounds. There are also examples of computer-based sound glitches and noises being emulated and packaged into products – such as the plug-in Glitch by Kieran Foster (a.k.a. dblue):

> Glitch features a pattern-based effects sequencer that takes the incoming audio, breaks it down into user-defined slices, and then applies different

> effects to each slice. The sounds it generates range from quite subtle to extremely bizarre, depending on how much you tweak the controls. Effects can either be programmed by hand to create specific desired patterns; chosen pseudo-randomly based on each effect's probability level, with a user-defined seed value that optionally allows the same sequence of 'random' effects to be chosen each time; or combined into a mixture of both methods to suite your own tastes. (Foster, 2008)

A similar example of visual software marketed as a way of intentionally creating glitches is the After Effects plug-in, Data Glitch,[3] aimed at film makers and visual artists interested in prefabricated glitches. The plug-in could be used to make glitches or to 'corrupt' moving images:

> Simulate Realistic Digital Image Glitches with Ease!
>
> Data Glitch is a native After Effects plugin that creates awesome realistic digital image glitches with total ease. Something you would see during a satellite transmission or a cable broadcast or from a damaged disk. Bad TV plugin is great for analog TV look, but this is 2010 and you hardly see anything that's analog anymore. This plugin simulates a realistic digital glitch effect.
>
> In real-life most of the glitches occur due to problems in encoding/decoding and sometimes data corruption. This plugin does exactly that. It encodes the data, glitches the data and then decodes it similar to the real life situation. (Aeplugins, 2010)

> Murphy's Law states
> Anything that can go wrong
> Will go wrong.
> Why wait for it to happen? (From Data Glitch demo video, 2010)

The marketing blurb says that one can create 'awesome realistic digital image glitches with total ease' with this tool. Yet when a tool aimed at creative practices is associated with 'total ease', it often loses credibility among practitioners, as Rosa Menkman implied in her quote (above). With tools of 'total ease', the associated practices of transmutation may be coupled with ideas about 'cheap gains' and prefabricated design – distant from ideas about pure noise and unpackaged glitches. The question once again is how to draw the line at what is really manageable (see Willim, 2013).

AUTHENTIC NOISE?

Some obvious commodifications of noise are the products of companies like Pure White Noise, which evoke feelings of authenticity in their commodities. This notion is well illustrated by the marketing text for the product, *Calming Electric Fan*:

> This fan sound doesn't just sound like a fan; it is a recording of a real fan! There are no fan sound effects or other sound gimmicks here. Our Calming Electric Fan sound captures the sound [of] an actual running fan, which [has been] digitally remastered to optimize its white noise benefits. (www.pure whitenoise)

The ad stresses that this is the recording of a real fan, with no artificial effects or gimmicks, marketed as real, pure noise. But, one could legitimately ask, to what extent is a CD with fan noise more authentic than the unrecorded sound of a real fan whirring in the room? The authenticity of the CD is evoked by associations, not merely to real-world noises, but also to a process of professional engineering and design of noise. When the company states that it is a better noise provider than other noise providers, it is describing its skills and its thorough methods of noise making.

> As pioneers in the field of white noise, we have been working refining our Pure White Noise® for over 20 years. By researching, developing and testing version after version of our pure white noise, making improvements in quality and effectiveness with each new version, we have perfected the science of relaxation and noise masking with pure white noise. What we offer now is simply the finest white noise available period. (www.purewhitenoise)

This designed noise is made to be consumed. If one compares this noise to audio plug-ins like Glitch, by Kieran Foster, some similarities become obvious. Using a designed plug-in for noise means using a predesigned tool for creating sounds. These sounds relate to accidentally arising electronic glitches, similar to the ways in which the recorded and designed noise of a fan relates to the sound of a real fan. The qualities of these sounds are thought not to be disruptive or annoying to users. The tool is meant to be used in an intentional, controlled way, but the sounds it produces can still be called noise. If the sound of an electric fan were to be played at a high volume, however, disturbing neighbours, it would regain some (more genuine?) qualities of (irritating) noise. Furthermore, suppose that the *Calming Electric Fan* CD were scratched, and began to skip while being played. The playback of the glitchy sound from the malfunctioning CD from Pure White Noise would be a good case for questioning: 'What are the parameters of noise?'

NOISE AS A TOOL FOR CULTURAL ANALYSIS

Notions of noise are based on what people call noise and frame as noise. The framings are culturally engendered and dependent upon the ways in which people relate to, conceive and use technologies. In this sense, noise can be used as a culturally analytic tool for understanding when technologies would be experienced as intrusive. When do people feel and think that a medium distorts or enhances? When is unwanted noise induced or when is noise transmuted into an appreciated effect? A technology can be used to filter out noise, but the filtering can, in itself, be experienced as intrusive.

In his book on the use of broken media technologies for the creation of music, Caleb Kelly referred to multimedia artist Paul DeMarinis, who had suggested four dimensions or sets of sounds which can be distinguished when records are played through a phonograph (Kelly, 2009: 297). The first set is the intended sound of the recording of the performance; the second refers to all the environmental sounds captured by the recording equipment: background noise and ambient sound, for example. According to DeMarinis, the phonograph made people more aware of recorded background noises and their relationship to the intended recorded sounds. The third set of sounds is that of the phonograph itself, or of the recording equipment used: the noise of moving components and electric circuitry, the sound of the medium. DeMarinis called this dimension 'the shadow of technology' (Kelly, 2009: 297). The fourth dimension is what DeMarinis called 'autobiographical': sounds created from the use of records; sounds of wear and tear; inscriptions, such as scratches and ingrained dirt on the surface of a record. The act of playing a record causes the slow destruction of the medium.

DeMarinis's demarcation is one way of scrutinizing notions of noise. The division into sound sets provides a tool which helps to map the way certain sounds (or concepts, for that matter) related to media use can be approached, perceived, conceptualized, described and brought to one's attention. To what extent can noise be designed? This question is relevant for the theme of managing overflow. To what extent is overflow out of control? When noise or another kind of overflow is managed, it changes, in the sense that it is conceived differently.

In discussing the cultural value of noise, its relational aspect is of particular importance, as Hillel Schwarz has suggested. What is heard as pleasing and wanted or as abhorrent and irritating depends on the way different cultures, occupations and disciplines 'reconstitute the notion and nature of noise' (Schwarz, 2011: 21).

The relational aspect of noise, the ways in which it is connected to the uses of technologies and media as well as to processes of transmutation, filtering and framing, may help in our understanding of the way people approach and experience the sonic, the visual and other sensory experiences. But noise is related not merely to sound, image and the sensory; nor is it easily captured in models of communication and information transfer. The fluidity of noise, seen as overflow, renders it intriguing, and applicable as a conceptual tool in several contexts. It can be a help in reconsidering what is actually examined in investigations of technology or in studies of the role of sound, the visual and the sensory. There is an intriguing tension in the interplay between noise being at times abated, and at other times packaged and sold. There are many further questions based on the conceptions of noise: what is noise in an organization, for example, in an economical transaction, in a story or in a variety of everyday situations?

NOTES

1. My work with this text has been made possible partly through financing from Riksbankens jubileumsfond, through the project Runaway Methods: Ethnography and Its New Incarnations. This chapter has also been inspired by some of my art projects. In 2003 I started the Industrial Cool project, which was a way of examining the transformations of industrial society, primarily in North-Western Europe. The first part of the project was based on audio recordings from a Swedish sugar refinery. Sounds that were considered as noise in the factory context were used as raw material for a CD, with 20 contributing electronica artists who used the sounds in their works. In several of my other works made with video artist Anders Weberg – *Elsewhereness*, *Surreal Scania* and *Sweden for Beginners*, for example – I have also dealt with notions of noise, the overlooked or the uncanny (www.robertwillim.com/portfolio).
2. There are a number of other types of noise: pink noise or brown noise, for instance. This is not the place to delve more deeply into the complexities of describing different kinds of noise mathematically; it is enough to state that white noise has similarities to white light, from which it draws its name.
3. After Effects is a digital motion graphics and compositing software product by Adobe for use in the post-production of film and television.

FIELD MATERIAL

Aescripts + Aeplugins (2010), *Data Glitch*, http://aescripts.com/data-glitch/, accessed 27 December, 2012.
Foster, Kieran (2008), *Glitch*, http://illformed.org/, accessed 2 April 2012.
Matador Records (2000), *Pole 3*, http://matadorrecords.com/pole/biography.html, 25 December 2012.
Pure White Noise (n.d.), http://www.purewhitenoise.com, accessed 25 December 2012.
Quiet Mark (n.d.); http://www.quietmark.com/, accessed 25 December 2012.

9. Creators meet companies: Hundred Offices and the opening of frames

Elena Raviola

> Creativity is a crucial component of our capacity to innovate. And innovation is a key factor not just to become more competitive but also to improve our quality of life and the sustainability of our development.

> The progress of societies depends on innovation and creative people: these two elements contribute to collective and individual well-being, ensure long and sustainable economic growth and can provide new answers to the current financial, economic and social crisis.

This was how President Barroso of the European Commission (EC) opened the EC's 2009 conference, Can Creativity be Measured? which was held during the European Year of Creativity and Innovation. He related creativity first to innovation, then to economic growth, without missing the opportunity to flavour this relationship with a touch of sustainability. Some of the most fashionable words of current times and of Western countries were mentioned in Barroso's opening address right after 'creativity'. Creativity is believed to have an indirect influence on sustainable economic growth, and as the distinctive feature of the so-called creative sectors, to produce direct economic value. The programme Creative Europe, for example, slated to begin in 2014, is justified by the need for Europe to 'invest more in its cultural and creative sectors because they contribute significantly to economic growth, employment, innovation and social cohesion' (http://ec.europa.eu/culture/creative-europe/).

The European discourse on creativity, innovation and economic development has been nationally and locally translated into a number of initiatives. Consider, for example, how the West Sweden Region, with Gothenburg as the main urban centre, communicates its responsibilities on its website:

> We are responsible for your having access to good health care, and we create the conditions for good health for everyone in West Sweden. Our second

> responsibility is to work with culture, growth, and sustainable development in West Sweden. (http://www.vgregion.se, my translation)

By setting culture, growth and sustainable development as priorities in its agenda, next only to good health, the Region has, in fact, articulated its ambition of becoming the most creative region in Sweden, and works both on the economic development of the cultural sector and on creativity in industrial sectors.

Some voices in the Gothenburg area claim that the city is already the most creative region in the country. Or, as the following quote from Erik Nissen Johansen suggests, the most creative city in the world. Johansen is Director of the local design and communication agency Stylt Trampoli. As he stated in a promotional video for a 'Boundary-less West Sweden, full of possibilities for everybody' (www.100listan.se), a vision formulated by the Chamber of Commerce:

> Gothenburg would be better off if one could tell the true story of the City of Gothenburg. Gothenburg is absolutely one of the most creative places in the world. Specialists from Gothenburg produce special effects in movies. It is also a hard rock city, maybe the hard rock capital city of the world. (www.100listan.se, video, my translation)

The true story of creative Gothenburg seems to be a counter-story to the other, better-known story of Gothenburg: the story of industrial development; the city of Volvo, Saab and SKF; the city to which the next passage in the Chamber of Commerce's promotional video is dedicated. The distinction between 'creative Gothenburg' and 'industrial Gothenburg' has been emerging recurrently in a number of regional events aimed at merging the city's two stories. The commonly posed question is, 'What happens in their encounter?' What happened, for instance, in the encounter formulated in the invitation to the West Sweden Chamber of Commerce Day in October 2012, dedicated to 'Creative West Sweden'?

> Can chief financial officers at a machine factory be as creative as an art director at a hippy advertising bureau? Certainly, all can be creative in their own way.
>
> But the real excitement occurs when the two meet; it is in the meeting between individuals that ideas arise and business is created.
>
> At the Chamber of Commerce, we go from words to actions. Welcome! (http://handelskammaren.net/sv/evenemang/handelskammardagen/, my translation)

Stressing the excitement of the encounter between those I have called 'creators' and the 'regular' businesses, which I have called 'companies', this initiative fits with a regional discourse expounding upon the need for exchanges between 'modern creative competencies'[1] and companies, 'artists and people in active work life',[2] 'creative design processes' and companies', 'innovation and change processes';[3] a discourse endorsed by a number of other private and public initiatives. The term 'creator' is the English translation of the Swedish *kreatör*, which refers to people working independently in such creative industries as design, arts or the media. Although the creators can be either individuals or companies, I call them all 'creators' and use the word 'companies' to refer to what most people would consider to the non-artistic businesses with which the creators are paired.

This chapter focuses on one of the creator–company initiatives: the Hundred Offices project. Hundred Offices was launched by the West Sweden Region as part of the Programme for Business Development of the Cultural Sector and included in the Programme for Cultural and Creative Industries that the Swedish Agency for Regional and Economic Growth developed at the national level between 2009 and 2012. The aim of the Hundred Offices project has been formulated as follows:

> Hundred Offices aims at encouraging companies in West Sweden to accommodate creators in their non-utilized facilities. Creators get free workspace. Companies contribute to a better society while gaining access to new competencies, new spheres of influence and inspiration. Everybody wins. (Think Tank Kombinator's report to West Sweden Region, October 2011, p. 2, my translation)

The idea behind the project is to connect creators who have creativity to share with companies that have more workspace than they need. As explained by one of the two Hundred Offices project managers (Project Manager A) I interviewed:

> I buy the notion of creators, because it is broader than artists. We usually use the notion of artist. But today the boundaries move more than ever before. There are still the traditional artists, sculptors, painters, etc., but otherwise boundaries are fluid. (Hundred Offices Project Manager A, interview, 8 March 2012. This and all other quotes from my interviews are translated by me, ER)

Locating creators and companies which are physically close to one another should allow for the flowing of workspace from companies to creators and the flowing of creativity from creators to the companies. In this chapter, I continue the reasoning of Gideon Kunda, who introduced the notion of 'interflows' and asked: 'What forms of experience emerge or disappear in the cross-currents of multiple flows?' (Kunda, 2012: 100). Taking his question as a starting point, I use the Hundred Offices project as an illustration of cross-currents of multiple overflows (creativity and workspace) between two frames (creators and companies). Whereas other scholars in this volume show how various types of overflows may be managed by circulation (see Brembeck's study of the way parents deal with baby 'stuff', Chapter 12 in this volume), filtering (see Willim's Chapter 8 on the transmutation of noise), mobility (see Norén's study of patients' overflow management, Chapter 5) or forgetting (see Löfgren's Chapter 14 on academic practices), I am investigating the Hundred Offices project as a way of managing overflows of workspace and creativity by opening frames and thereby creating interflows – at least in theory.

This chapter focuses on an ongoing pilot project, launched in the autumn of 2010, between a recycling management company, Hans Andersson, and a creator – the design organization, Creatables. The study is based on my three visits to Hans Andersson; 13 interviews with nine people working with Hundred Offices, four of whom were directly involved in the creator–company pairing; and various documents (West Sweden Region's plans and reports) and press materials on Hundred Offices.

HUNDRED OFFICES: SCARCITY MEETS ABUNDANCE

Within the West Sweden Region's Programme for Business Development of the Cultural Sector, the think tank, Kombinator, was created with the task of establishing the needs of the cultural sector and its workers. In line with the regional discourse praising the exchange between creators and companies, the initator and leader of Kombinator explained the rationale behind the work of the think tank and the programme:

> There is a lot of talk about exchange of competencies nowadays. I believe in creating the conditions for exchange rather than prescribing behaviours. I believe in creating conditions for the meeting of different competencies rather than creating artificial situations like seminars, where people are supposed to meet and competencies are supposed to be exchanged. (Kombinator's leader, interview, 12 November 2011)

In a Kombinator report delivered to the region at the end of 2010, lack of workspace was identified as a serious problem for creators in the region. The programme management team concluded that as the region as a whole does not suffer from lack of workspace, there must be somebody who has more space than necessary. They believed that finding a way to pair those who have too little with those who have too much, and allowing the excess to flow over and fill the lack, would be a solution to the problem that would benefit everyone concerned.

So the Hundred Offices project came about as a solution to the problem of creators lacking workspace – a solution initially conceived by Claes Boman, a creative project leader and designer in the region.[4] The idea was to place 100 creators (individuals or small groups of collaborators) in 100 companies in exchange for each creator's contribution of an agreed-upon amount of work. Pointing to the self-evident wisdom of the idea, Project Manager B, a young creative entrepreneur (or, as he defined himself, 'commercial artist') told me: 'One side needs space. The other one has empty spaces.' He saw value in the pairing for the entire West Sweden Region, which seeks to become 'the most attractive region for creators and artists' (Hundred Offices Project Manager B, interview, 18 November 2011).

It is, in fact, real estate that experiences both abundance and scarcity, because of limited access to available space: a frame. Hundred Offices attempts to open this frame with a simple idea. At least, that is what Project Manager A, who referred to this simplicity as 'genial', told me:

> In my work, I try to start from the pure core in the project, to get companies to make their unused rooms or workspace surfaces available for free to creators, in the broad sense of the term. It is important to think about the basic concept, which is so simple and genial. (Project Manager A, interview, 8 March 2012)

The main idea of the project – 'the pure core', as it is called in the previous quote – is represented in two main images, which are reproduced in several outlets. Figure 9.1, which constitutes the cover of Kombinator's report on Hundred Offices (similar versions appeared in other media outlets) represents the floor plan of an office.

This image presented the original goal of the Hundred Offices project – the use of unutilized office facilities by creators lacking workspace. The flow of excessive workspace from companies to creators is the basic and obvious overflow in the project. There are, however, a number of interflows associated with this overflow. The other image, used several times in media outlets and information material about Hundred Offices, pictures the multiple flows between *företag* [company] and *kreatör* [creator], as shown in Figure 9.2. Free workspace, direct contact with the industry, and new colleagues flow from companies to the creators;

Note: Figure taken from the Hundred Offices open Facebook page.

Figure 9.1 The cover of Kombinator's 2010 report on Hundra Kontor (Hundred Offices)

inspiration, new competencies under the same roof and access to the creators' network flow from creators to companies. Both lists of flows in the picture end with the Swedish abbreviation *m.m.*, meaning 'and much more', pointing to the possibility of many other interflows.

The project managers of Hundred Offices believe that the win–win situation indicated at the intersection of the two ovals is 'naturally'

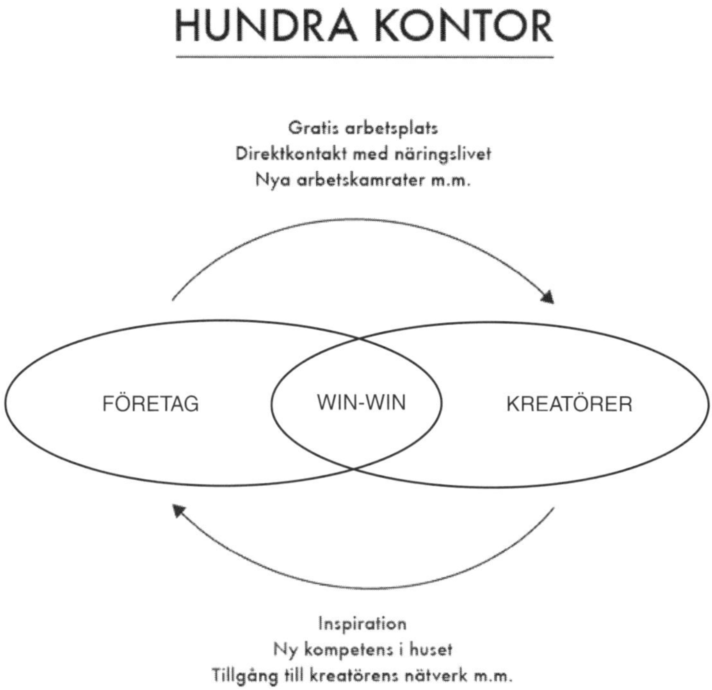

Note: Figure taken from the Hundred Offices open Facebook page.

Figure 9.2 Image used to represent Hundred Offices as a win–win situation

produced by the crossing of these overflows, once the flows have been paired and the frames opened.

The mandate of the Hundred Offices project is to connect flows, in lack or excess of creativity and workspace, which would 'normally' be separated, thereby evening out workspace and creativity on both sides. The overflows are expected to be naturally managed once the frames are opened to each other. Hundred Offices project managers deliberately work to keep the connections as simple as possible, by grounding them in the need for or excess of physical space. In the following quote, Project Manager A describes the beauty of the simple concept:

> The hope is that it will be a win-win situation for both partners when the creators are at the workplace because of their inspiration, the new environment, sharing of each other's networks and making concrete collaborative

> spinoffs. But what is beautiful about the concept is that we can start from a really simple base – making non-utilized working surfaces available to creators for free. Start there; there is no other commitment. It is beautiful indeed. (Project Manager A, interview, 8 March 2011)

His experience from other projects taught him that there are many suspicions and prejudices against creators in the business world. It is good, therefore, that the concept is 'stripped down' and simple at its starting point. It is only later that it can begin to produce 'many exciting things', probably as indicated by the 'and much more' in Figure 9.2.

Hundred Offices project managers have developed a theory of managing overflow 'by simple connection', which seems to be based on the principle of communicating vessels in hydrostatics. Given that they are subject to the same gravity and pressure, the levels of the liquid in connected vessels will automatically balance when the liquid settles. Nothing other than the connection is required. All my interlocutors involved in managing Hundred Offices insisted on this self-regulation of interflows, stressing the necessity of creating conditions for exchange rather than prescribing them. In the pilot case, for example, the creators wanted first and foremost to have a place to work, and Hundred Offices provided them first and foremost with the workspace they needed. The business deals and economic support that emerged from the connection with the company were considered a pleasant bonus.

In other words, the Hundred Offices management philosophy and slogan seems to be: 'Keep it simple, and some unexpected interflows will happen'. Are the interflows, however, really that simple to manage? The next section describes the work required to open frames and regulate overflows, focusing, in particular, on the experiences of the project managers and their logic of connection.

REMAKING FLOWS INTO INTERFLOWS

Hundred Offices had two project managers between the autumn of 2010 and the summer of 2012, with a third one assigned after the summer of 2012. During its first year, the project was located both financially and operationally under the West Sweden Regional Authority, within the programme for the Business Development of the Cultural Sector. The leader of the programme had intentionally hired a young entrepreneur in the creative sector as a project manager.

Since the autumn of 2011, the management of the project has been assigned to the consulting company TILLT – from the English word 'tilt', to indicate the change of perspective necessary to incorporate these new ideas. A previous partner of the Region's Department of Culture, a part-time manager within TILLT, was assigned to the project, but the final responsibility remained with the Region. TILLT's core activity is the organization of artistic interventions in organizations – to foster their development or to implement change – by bringing the creators into organizations that are not usually considered artistic and to cross-fertilize competencies of the two worlds. The managing of the Hundred Offices was assigned to TILLT because 'we are a bridge between work and cultural life and we have the reputation of making things happen' (Project Manager A, interview, 8 March 2011). It seems to imply that TILLT will develop Hundred Offices from one pilot case to multiple cases; my interlocutors said, in response to my repeated questions, that they were to reach 50 cases. They are also to build an independent website for partnerships between the companies and the creators.

In order to create interflows, there need to be two frames which lend themselves to being open to one another. The work of the project managers has thus been focused on the identification of creators in need of workspace – creators who are willing to join the project – and the identification of companies willing to host creators in their facilities. And then they must connect them with each other, case by case. The project managers work first as connectors, then as support for any practical issues which could present an obstacle to interflow. In the eyes of Project Manager B, the development of Hundred Offices creates the conditions for the creators' development, listening to people's needs in order to fulfil them, and 'giving people local support rather than money. People are competent. They know best what they need' (Project Manager B, interview, 18 November 2011). And he continued:

> There is a gap between the two, the big and the small, the young and the old … I thought that we should pull down all the thresholds, in order for them to meet, and that we should merely provide a support function. Like, if you have a problem, we'll help you. We help with all problems. (Project Manager B, interview, 18 November 2011)

Although the theory of managing overflow by opening frames espoused by Hundred Offices assumes self-regulating interflows, the theory-in-action (Schön, 1984) shows that project managers acting as 'connectors' and 'supporters' play an important role in setting and maintaining the connection.

A significant part of the project managers' work was dedicated to spreading information to both creators and companies, in order to make the project 'a buzz around town', as Project Manager A expressed it, and to attract potential participants. The biggest challenge, according to them, was to find companies with excessive workspace that were willing to engage in the project. Both project managers experienced difficulty in convincing companies to make themselves available to a connection with creators, and convincing them to make their excess space available. After the first year Project Manager B had a list of 25–30 creators, but hardly any companies. In order to attract them, he undertook a number of actions. Together with the regional programme leader, he contacted the Chamber of Commerce, which declared itself interested, and had a long promising meeting with them, without following up with concrete actions. They also contacted the public administration to explore the possibility of finding some non-utilized space in city offices. They talked to people at Röhska Design Museum, because they thought creators could work there in rotation, making this space a showcase. This, however, had not been realized yet at the end of Project Manager B's mandate. 'It is for the future', he said to me at the end of November 2011. Following a similar line of action, Project Manager A started to spread information about Hundred Offices through art centres, universities, Chambers of Commerce and other associations.

As the self-functioning online platform was not yet running, and the buzz about town was still around other fashionable projects, Hundred Offices project managers had to work harder in order to procure connections. Once a company and a creator or creators have registered their interest in the project, however, whether on a Facebook page or by e-mailing registration forms downloadable on TILLT's website to the current project manager, attempts at specific connections are made according to a certain logic. This logic differs from the principle of communicating vessels in physics, which states that homogeneous fluid in vessels of any form will even out as soon as the vessels are set in communication. Hundred Offices plans to put together non-homogeneous fluids by opening previously existing frames, hoping that interflows will just happen.

Project Manager B explicitly emphasized the importance of contrast between paired organizations if the desired exchange is to happen. He did admit that he looked for a similarity of interests, but not for a perfect overlapping. He insisted on the importance of gaps between the two parties and emphasized the advantages of interflows between big and small, bureaucratic and creative, wealthy and struggling. He managed to make a first connection between a company, Hans Andersson AB, and the designers' network Creatables. This pilot case, described in the next section, was a success according to all parties involved. Explaining this success, the project manager claimed that a visionary leader is needed as a host if interflows with hosted creators are to occur. He seem to believe that flows must be different, but frames need to be somehow compatible if they are to be opened to one another.

Partly as a reaction to the success of the pilot case and partly due to his attachment to the simplicity of the project, Project Manager A then developed a slightly different theory of connection and the differences and similarities required. Once he has received a company's or a creator's registration of interest and information about space availability or needs, he looks for possible connections. In contrast to Project Manager B's procedure, the second manager starts from practical conditions at the potential host organization and then tries to find creators whose needs may be fullfilled by these conditions:

> I have an organization that has places available in an open space – it is a real estate company – where there are different businesses. Thus they sit together, but manage their own businesses. They are all women, and the space is big. All men are gone. Then I have those who are looking for office space and can sit with others. An artist who wants to have an atelier or a photographer who wants to have the use of a dark room. They are not suitable. (Project Manager A, interview, 9 May 2012)

In his opinion, this is opposite to the TILLT managers' usual procedure of organizing artistic interventions in companies in the other projects that TILLT manages. TILLT usually spends a great deal of time determining exactly the right competence for the specific organization, in order to create the complex collaboration between creator and organization. It could be a good thing to have the company and the creators in potentially related areas of business: 'in the first place I start from the concrete needs', he said. He also explained that the difficulty in finding companies willing to be connected to creators depends on the level of risk that they perceive in participating in the project, because it involves 'a strange guest. Shall I let a stranger sleep on my sofa?' Thus he attempts to convince companies that the project involves little risk for them, hoping to achieve 'a ketchup effect', by hammering away, even with nothing happening, until many demands suddenly come, all together.

On the other hand, TILLT's chief executive officer (CEO) believes in a self-selected compatibility between companies and creators, who should be able to choose each other through what he calls a 'digital solution'. There will be a website on which interested organizations with extra workspace and creators lacking workspace could list themselves. This list would work as an overflow self-management tool and, in the case of

Hundred Offices, would replace the one-to-one non-electronic connections which the project managers were required to make.

But, what happens once the connections are made? Do frames open? Do the interflows take place? I answer these questions using the pilot case of the Hundred Offices project.

PROMISING DESIGNERS CONNECTING WITH RECYCLERS

The pilot case of Hundred Offices was the connection between the company Hans Andersson AB and a small, creative organization, Creatables, made by the first project manager of Hundred Offices in 2011. He had met one of the owners of Hans Andersson at a lecture on Pecha Kucha[5] in the company's headquarters, and one of the founders of Creatables in one of the Pecha Kucha sessions in Gothenburg. In his perception, the co-owner of Hans Andersson was a visionary leader; thus when the designers at Creatables communicated their interest in Hundred Offices, he thought it would be a good connection. Indeed, 'as soon as they met, they clicked' (Project Manager B, interview, 18 November 2011).

Hans Andersson AB is a family business involved in recycling. The company was founded in 1948 by the grandfather of the present owners, who went to Germany and started to collect and sell bottle caps. The concept of the business, which has grown to a organization with 500 employees and 20 recycling stations in Sweden and with headquarters in an industrial suburb of Gothenburg, remains the same: they collect recycling material and sell it to other companies. Their values are described on their website as 'business-like attitude', 'entrepreneurship' and 'focus on service'.

Creatables is a company founded in 2008 by three designers with small initial investments by family and friends. Two of them call themselves 'pop engineers', and devote their time primarily to designing new products; the third, the 'factory director', is in charge of public relations and develops business partnerships with factories which produce waste in their manufacturing processes and with their distributors. The goal of Creatables is to reduce waste; the company focuses on creating products from waste. They define their operations as 'reusing'; they examine manufacturing plants for produced waste, and try to find ways in which the wasted material can be used and transformed into functional products.

Even if the company's revenues have grown, it is still losing money, and the founders are not able to pay their own salaries. When I talked to them in the spring of 2011, they claimed that they were at the turning point, although they admitted that they had been saying this for a while.

Creatables' designers started their business in an apartment of one of the founders, where they were both designing and producing. When they were given notice in 2010, they found new space, but its availability was first postponed and finally cancelled. Thus, at the beginning of 2011, they had no place to work. They e-mailed the Hundred Offices project manager to ask him about the project, and he proposed a connection with Hans Andersson.

The factory director visited the company's offices for the first time in January 2011. Hans Andersson's headquarters is a building with two floors, with a spacious kitchen and common room on the ground floor, individual offices and a large conference room on the first floor, and a spacious and light corridor. The room that would be made available for Creatables was a smaller, rarely used conference room and a storage room on the first floor.

After his visit, the factory director was enthusiastic about the office space and the recycling station and about the owner he met. He convinced the other two designers to visit the facilities. After a short hesitation (the offices were some distance from the city centre, to be covered by bike every day), they took the chance. In describing the deal between Hans Andersson and Creatables, all the designers emphasized that the new office was free. It was thus their underflow of space and money that directed them to this connection.

The Hundred Offices project manager and a co-owner of Hans Andersson sat down with one of Creatables' designers to discuss a contract. The initial idea was that the creators should work 10 per cent of their time for Hans Andersson, but this condition made it more complicated to reach an agreement. A specific prescription, in which each other's obligations would be formally specified in terms of time, money and tasks, would run against the simplicity ideal of which the Hundred Offices boasted. Thus the parties skipped the 10 per cent work clause and wrote a simpler responsibility agreement, focusing on security issues that regulated the use of keys, Internet connections and computers.

In practice, however, the assumption of the natural interflowing of creativity and space turned out to be relatively fragile. Hundred Offices project management worked first on establishing the connection, and then on intervening in facilitation of the solution of practical problems.

To begin, the people at Creatables and Hans Andersson realized that the interflows of creativity and workspace were to take place in the midst of multiple cross-currents of other flows. There are a great many other flows within the materialities of everyday life – of things, people, money and publicity. No project can remain as simple as the Hundred Offices project managers wanted it to be.

Interflow of Things

The three designers, striving to revolutionize the world with their design products from waste, found themselves sitting in a small conference room at a bigger recycling management company in the suburbs of a Swedish city. They were expected to spill their excessive creativity over the walls of their room, as if it were an overflowing glass of water. But if they were to start creating, office furniture needed to flow in their conference room. Besides the conference table which was already there, Hans Andersson gave them another unused table and bought them a third table, so they could have three work stations in the room. Hans Andersson's office supplies and free breakfasts were also made available to Creatables.

Creatables have sometimes borrowed trucks for transporting material and products[6] and have even received waste material from Hans Andersson. They have also asked workers in the recycling station to put material that could be reused to one side so that it could be purchased from Hans Andersson.

Interflow of People

As the frames were opened, not only objects, but also people flowed through. The designers and company employees ate breakfast together every morning at 9:15 in the kitchen on the ground floor, and sometimes shared lunch breaks. As a result, as one of the designers told me, they had colleagues for the first time.

Besides this interflowing of colleagues, various daily work interactions occurred, involving the creators and Hans Andersson's employees. 'Creatables is good in refinements, whereas Hans Andersson helps them with structure and basic office bureaucracy', said one of the Hans Andersson owners. Creatables uses the recycling management company for support in bureaucratic tasks, consulting their administrative assistant for invoicing and accounting, and discussing business development issues with the owners. Hans Andersson has, in turn, consulted Creatables about designing new logos and brochures.

A number of new projects has also been developed in collaboration between Creatables and Hans Andersson. They are examining the possibility of cooperating in the redesign of the recycling stations, for instance, because they are rather ugly and, says Hans Andersson owner,

'This is not good. These, too, must be beautiful.' They are also planning to redesign recycling containers in order to adapt them to the products that need to be recycled. Furthermore, the administrative assistant is thinking of involving one of the designers in an internal education programme at Hans Andersson, called 'Learning Organization', in which key people in the organization attend a two-year programme about the organization and its operations. The creator could teach them about different materials and their recycling and reuse.

Interflows of Money

Not only things and people, but also money was flowing between Hans Andersson and Creatables' frames. The recycling management company bought a third desk, the Internet modem and a production machine for the creators: '5 or 10 000 SEK – not much money', said the administrative assistant. They have also pre-purchased large quantities of material on behalf of Creatables, in order to exploit economies of scale and obtain a lower price, selling it to them little by little as they had cash to pay. 'It is small money', says one of the owners, and 'we can help them by buying a little material in advance – 25 000 SEK, no big money' (Hans Andersson owner, interview, 20 January 2012).

Interflows of Publicity

Hans Andersson and Creatables have received mutual benefit in publicity from their connection, in the form of media attention. They were asked to present their case at a Pecha Kucha session in Gothenburg, and several local and specialized newspapers and online news publications have written about them. The Public Relations designer has been a guest on television morning news, and the Chamber of Commerce has published a report entitled 'Became roommate with a creator – get new energy' in its members' newsletter.

Apart from these common activities, on a number of occasions Creatables and Hans Andersson have benefited from the publicity of one other. Singapore School of Management included Creatables in a study visit to Gothenburg, together with Volvo, Lego and SKF. The visiting students were received in the large meeting room at Hans Andersson. As the factory director pointed out to me, they could never have held the meeting in such a room if they had not been hosted there. And at the same time, Hans Andersson received some attention. On another occasion one of Creatables' designers, who received the prize for Entrepreneur of the Year at the Swedish Recycling Award Gala, dedicated it to his mother and one of Hans Andersson's owners.

Hans Andersson's management seems to be aware of the inflow of publicity coming from Creatables and is planning to use it actively. As the administrative assistant said, 'There is a lot of talk about CSR (corporate social responsibility) nowadays. This is one way to do it. It will be written in next year's CSR report' (Hans Andersson administrative assistant, interview, 8 March 2012)

In turn, Creatables received attention through some initiatives organized by Hans Andersson. They have participated in fairs together. At the Beach Volleyball Fair in June 2011 in Gothenburg and at two real estate fairs in Gothenburg and Stockholm in September and November 2011, Hans Andersson hosted Creatables in its stand, and the designers used their production machine (which Hans Andersson had purchased for them) to make products from waste material. As a result, Hans Andersson's stand attracted a great deal of attention: 'People love it! They do re-use. We do re-cycling. It is not strange to have them in the stand', said a Hans Andersson owner (interview, 20 January 2012).

Another instance of interflows of publicity is a charity project for a school in India. In the spring of 2012, one of the designers and one of Hans Andersson's owners travelled together to visit the school that Hans Andersson had supported for many years. During their trip, they brought Creatables' production machine to show children how to use it and to test it with them. The children enjoyed playing with the machine and its products. Thus, Creatables will provide this school with several production machines, with the financial support of Hans Andersson's owner's Rotary Club.

In the midst of these multiple flows, the overflows of creativity and workspace were made into interflows, and the people engaged developed their own view of how it works. One of Hans Andersson's owners pointed out to me the visible differences in the way in which Creatables' and Hans Andersson's workspaces are organized: disorder and chaos on Creatables' side, order and tidiness on the other side. In the beginning, these differences caused some resistance among Hans Andersson's employees:

> At the beginning, they wondered why they should sit there, and it was tough [for Creatables]. Then, they changed their minds … Now they think it's great fun! (Hundred Offices Project Manager B, interview, 18 November 2011)

> When they moved in, people [at Hans Andersson] were grumbling because they were sceptical about them using their company's resources, especially Internet and the Network, and because it was a bit of extra work for people in

> the office. They weren't welcome at first. But now it's taken for granted that they can't move out. And they will do some projects with us. (Hans Andersson owner, interview, 20 January 2012)
>
> Not everybody was positive. In order to overcome this reluctance, it was important that everybody received information, both by e-mail and at breakfast. It was also important to underline that this was a temporary solution. Now they are work colleagues. (Hans Andersson administrative assistant, interview, 8 March 2012)

Even though Creatables keep their chaos within the physical boundary of their office, when Hans Andersson employees are passing by the untidy room they often stop and look in. Perhaps they may even get inspired just by walking by, suggested the owner. Just by creators being there, the 'visionarity' atmosphere spills over into the company, which within its bureaucratic frame had lost its visionary drive.

But it is not only differences that count. As the Hans Andersson owner said in the same interview:

> I like entrepreneurship. I like entrepreneurs. First and foremost, entrepreneurs who are not out for the money … Daniel Pink, I have read his book [*Drive: The Surprising Truth about What Motivates Us*, 2009] about entrepreneurs who are not primarily driven by money. It is not about money, but other things one wants to do. When [the Hundred Offices project manager] proposed the project to me, I said: 'Sure. See if you find somebody'. And he found Creatables, who do exactly what we do. They see to it that waste becomes a product. Thus, we can actually show a customer that we do see to it that material is re-used …
>
> [An employee] said that we should buy them in order to help them, but I am strongly against this idea, because it would not work. They have to decide themselves and manage their thing themselves. We can help them by buying a little material for them. (Hans Andersson owner, interview, 20 January 2012)

The success of the connection between Creatables and Hans Andersson seems to rely upon mutual identification and a common idealization of the heroic entrepreneur. Both Hans Andersson's co-owner and the factory director at Creatables define themselves as entrepreneurs. One is middle-aged and sits comfortably on the results of his successful entrepreneurship; the other is young and starving for success. The company owner sees in the young creator the epitomic entrepreneur, driven by a creative energy beyond the scarcity of economic resources, while the young creator sees the owner as the epitomic entrepreneur who has made it. They seem to display desires to have what the other has in excess, and what the other has lost through the years (creativity) or has yet to achieve (money).

All this sounds good, but one question remains. Lending the excess space to the designers, Hans Andersson ends up having less space. Is the effect symmetrical? Will Creatables become less creative, or perhaps 'just creative enough'?

DO FLOWS BECOME 'EVEN' AS A RESULT OF INTERFLOWING?

The Hundred Offices project brought together two organizations that differ in their ways of thinking and doing, with the purpose of managing overflows of workspace and creativity. Based on their own descriptions, I presented the hoped-for functioning of Hundred Offices as that of opening frames, as a result of which the unequally levelled fluids flow until they reach equal level in both vessels, as in communicating vessels. I have shown that this happens in the midst of other interflows, which may aid or hinder the hoped-for interflow.

Despite the simplicity of the concept and the apparently self-evident goodness of the idea, Hundred Offices has managed to create only three such connections in its first two years of existence. Differences in types of overflows and difficulties in opening frames may explain some of the complications in realizing the project. Reflecting on their experience, TILLT's CEO told me:

> It has been significantly more difficult than we thought. We thought it would be much easier. We go out and communicate artistic competences with the goal of developing creativity and ability to innovate at the workplace. It is difficult, but possible. This one [Hundred Offices project] we thought was easy, but it has not been realized. There are certainly a hundred reasons for that. (TILLT's CEO, interview, 10 September 2012)

As mentioned, one of the major difficulties in Hundred Offices project management is to engage companies. Trying to explain to me why that is so, TILLT's CEO reflected on the asymmetry between the two 'vessels' to be connected:

> The need is on the artists' side. They have already formulated the need. The companies have not done it yet. We have to formulate the need for them. We have to come up with the idea for it.
>
> If one has an empty surface in a company, one does not think … that there is an artist that can sit here, unless we come and propose it. It is there that our work efforts are mostly required, I think. (TILLT's CEO, interview, 10 September 2012)

Although the creators' underflow of workspace has been formulated as a concrete need, the companies' underflow of creativity and inspiration has not yet been formulated. Even if Hundred Offices project managers treat creativity as if it were a material thing which is possible to pass to new users when in excess, just like workspace, this way of thinking has not yet reached companies. It is worth noting here that the Hundred Offices project seems to conflate creators and creativity into one and the same thing. Creativity is materialized into the creators and cannot flow without them being physically present at the company's premises, whereas workspace is a property of the company and distinguished from its employees.

The asymmetry between creators and companies, as recognized by TILLT's CEO, may be due to the difference in the type of flow between workspace and creativity. The two flows are both treated and managed as if they were made of a similar material and considered as equal parts of a potential exchange. The physics of their interflowing may be quite different, however. While creativity may be considered unlimited and creative ideas shareable between two parties without limiting their use to either one of them, workspace may be used by either the company or the creator. The Hundred Offices project makes the previously excessive workspace inaccessible to its owner. For that reason, companies seem to be reluctant to relinquish control of and access to their own workspace. What if they suddenly need it again?

TILLT's CEO has identified another reason why the development of the Hundred Offices project has been a slow and difficult process – because the functioning of Hundred Offices depends on the type of creators they have solicited and the type of workspace they require:

> [I]t is easier to put architects, web developers and game developers into a company's office space than it is to place real artists. The artists, especially those born in the 1940s, want to have an atelier, big surfaces. What is often offered is a desk. (TILLT's CEO, interview, 10 September 2012)

So although creativity has a different kind of flow than workspace does that is not always readily understood. Furthermore, there are differences between types of workspace (atelier versus office space) and types of creativity: architects, web developers and game developers are easier to locate in the offices than 'real' artists are. Some creators are more compatible with business offices than others are.

Then, even when frames have been opened, as in the pilot project, there is one question left, even in the creators' mind: what is an 'even level' of creativity? One of the designers at Creatables expressed his concerns as follows:

> Having a free workspace is good for us. Then again, I don't know if this is the place where one is most creative. This conference room is so messy. One would need a wide clean desk. But then I don't know. There is no specific place where one is creative. (Designer at Creatables, interview, 23 May 2012)

It seems that he was worried that the overflow of a company's workspace in the creators' frame might have produced an underflow of creativity. Callon pointed out that 'objects and things, the theatre stage, its walls and sounds, all play a role in setting up' the frame and its interdependencies with the rest of the world, which, by providing cultural references for objects and situations inside the frame, is leveraged and mobilized for understanding the meaning of things inside (Callon, 1998a: 250). As another economic sociologist, Don Slater, formulated it:

> [F]raming 'extricates' agents and entities from the networks of interaction in which they have achieved some kind of social existence, in order to 'push' them onto a clearly demarcated 'stage'. However, like a prop or an actor placed on a theatrical stage, these entities retain their links with the outside world (as do all the actors, or audiences); indeed … it is hard to see how any entity could continue to be meaningful on stage or in the market without continuing to draw on its 'cultural' meanings. (Slater, 2002: 242)

Creatables makes sense of its activities in relation to the design field, including competing designers, engineering and design schools, and design competition. Hans Andersson makes sense of its activities in relation to its recycling field, including competing recycling companies, regulators and public administration. Each of these two organizational frames are able to produce overflows in its regular functioning. Forcing part of their overflows into a specific direction – companies' workspace into creators and creators' creativity into companies – may lead to an underflow of these 'fluids'. Opening the frame at one point – the point of encounter with Hans Andersson – may close or narrow other connections, such as the one between Creatables and the rest of the design world. That could prove crucial to fostering the production of excess creativity – creativity that may overflow into the company's frame.

NOTES

1. These terms are used by House of Win–Win to present its activities on its webpage (www.win-win.se). House of Win–Win is a privately owned creative office collective

in Gothenburg, gathering creative entrepreneurs and freelancers in an open office space, and offering consulting services to any and all companies for the development of their creativity.

2. These terms are used by TILLT on its website (www.tillt.se). TILLT is a consulting company using artistic competencies for producing organizational change and increasing innovation in organizations. It is an incorporated company, owned by the non-profit cultural association Skådebana, which reinvests any profits into TILLT operations.
3. These terms are used in SVID's 2011 activity report, published on its website (www.svid.se). SVID is a privately owned consulting organization, using design thinking to help companies in their change processes.
4. The Programme Leader of West Sweden Region Programme for Business Development of the Cultural Sector had a similar idea that he called Local Pool. He wanted to locate artists in unused spaces owned by real estate companies – garages or storage rooms on the ground floors of apartment buildings, for instance – and charge them cheap rent. At first, both ideas were included in the Region's Programme. The Programme Leader and his team quickly realized, however, that it was more difficult to establish Local Pool than it was to establish Hundred Offices, and they ended up focusing on Hundred Offices.
5. Pecha Kucha is a 'happening' format that has spread from Japan to other countries and is now performed in 550 cities around the world. Its motto is 20 × 20, and it is a popular public weekly gathering at which creative ideas, projects, businesses and initiatives can be presented in the format of 20 slides of 20 seconds each. Having experienced Pecha Kucha in Tokyo, the first project manager imported it to Gothenburg.
6. During my interview with one of the designers, he explained that there was no post office nearby. They needed to use a car or truck to mail or receive their packages.

10. Recycling food waste into biogas, or how management transforms overflows into flows

Hervé Corvellec

To throw away food is to invite virtually unanimous condemnation. Contemporary patterns of production and consumption, which allow tonnes of edible product to be discarded at every stage of production, distribution, consumption and post-consumption, has long been considered a sign of moral breakdown by members of the anti-hunger movement. Increasingly, these patterns are considered to be harbingers of ecological breakdown as well, for although discarded food never reaches the oesophagus, its production still requires the consumption of huge quantities of water, fertilizers, pesticides and energy.

Yet waste management companies claim that there is at least a partial solution to these moral and ecological breakdowns: the food that one cannot help but waste can be turned into a resource (Corvellec and Hultman, 2012) – the twenty-first-century equivalent of the late nineteenth-century oil rush: biogas! Uneaten food, waste management companies tell us, can become fuel for the buses and cars that take us to work. What is needed is an efficient system that separates food waste from other refuse and adequately processes waste.

Waste management authorities and waste management companies do not recommend that people oversupply themselves with food in order to support their local transportation company with a sufficient supply of biogas, of course, or that they throw food away rather than eating it, as a new type of diet. Rather they insist that food waste should be reduced at the source. The Swedish National Plan for Waste of the Swedish Environmental Protection Agency (Naturvårdverket, 2012), for example, considers the prevention of food waste to be a waste policy priority for the years to come.

At the same time, waste management companies and the Swedish Environmental Protection Agency underscore the fact that the recycling of food waste, regardless of its preventability, makes a significant contribution to sustainability and is, therefore, a responsible act. And when waste management companies and agencies convey this message, another, subliminal message emerges: an efficient recycling of food waste can preserve our mobile modes of living (Urry, 2007), even if fossil fuels become a rarity. Thus beyond all pious commitments to food waste prevention, the transformation of food waste into biogas binds two objects of gluttony – food and mobility – back to back. Food, which can be considered a proxy for life, feeds mobility, which one could call another proxy for life. As claimed by pre-Socratic Greek philosopher Anaxagoras of Clazomenae (c. 500–428 BC) and French chemist Antoine Lavoisier (1743–1794): nothing is ever lost, all is transformed. Let food that has become waste ensure sustainable mobility. Food waste is to evoke not only an image of hungry children and depleted soils; it is also to evoke, more ambiguously, environmentally friendly city buses. Paper bags for food recycling have become the heralds of transition to a sustainable mode of living.

French intellectual Georges Bataille's (1897–1962) theory of excess places the transformation of food waste into biogas in a critical light, however. For Bataille (1949/1988), the organization of destruction was a necessary accompaniment to the organization of production. He claimed that most societies produce in excess, and how a society handles this excess is essential to the way it conceives of itself and the way it functions as a society. So if one considers the transformation of food waste into biogas as a method of handling excess, it may provide a key to understanding how our society conceives of itself and its function.

It is a telling comment on our times that the transforming of wasted food into biogas is seen as an act of sustainable responsibility. As I claim in this chapter, this transformation project can be treated as an illustration of trust in the ability of the social practice of management to convert overflows into normal flows and, implicitly, to mitigate the social critique that excess may bring with it.

My claim is that management is a machine (Deleuze and Guattari, 1987) of control (Löfgren and Czarniawska, 2012), with a capacity to normalize overflows. Think of practices as diverse as the ostentatious funerals of nineteenth-century France, today's massive production of information or the abundant collection of domestic possessions in households of the First World (three examples detailed in Löfgren and Czarniawska, 2012). Think even of the construction of pyramids, the exaggerated clothing fashions of the eighteenth century or the massive deportation of slaves from Africa to the Americas. These historical examples demonstrate the practical rationality (Townley, 2008) underlying administrative practices with an established record of handling that which is 'too much' – in the non-exclusive sense of the extreme, the monstrous, the obscene or the absurd – and turning it into normality, often at a profit. Management is the name given to the contemporary state of this administrative rationality.

The framing of overflows as problems in need of a solution, and the claim that they can offer this solution, can be found in governance schemes; strategic plans; facilities development; project management procedures; education and training programmes; environmental monitoring systems; norms and certification frameworks; and, not least, a systematic work on language, classification and labels. Managerial technology offers the opportunity to remove the 'over' from overflows and transform them into mere flows. Management produces and establishes new frames of normality that accommodate what is out of frame and make it an integral part of what is current, actual and under control. If critics insist that the overflow persists, their voices are neutralized and silenced, by invoking the notions of duty or responsibility, for example. And when overflows are turned into flows, business can continue as usual. The transformation of food waste into biogas provides an example of the ability of waste management to transform the abnormal into something normal. The management machine turns excesses into something normal, and therefore something difficult to question.

The first section of this chapter describes the production of food waste and examines why it can be considered an overflow. The next section demonstrates how waste management companies frame the production of biogas as a solution to the issue of food waste. The third section presents George Bataille's economic theory of destruction and applies it to the transformation of food waste into biogas, in order to emphasize the classic industrial nature of this solution. And the fourth section explains why management can be seen as a normalizing machine. In conclusion, I ask the question: 'Is this normalization really a solution to the food waste issue?'

FOOD WASTE AS OVERFLOW

A report from the Swedish Institute for Food and Biotechnology (SIK) ordered by the Food and Agriculture Organization of the United Nations (FAO) presents an alarming description of the amount of food that is wasted worldwide:

> Roughly one-third of food produced for human consumption is lost or wasted globally, which amounts to about 1.3 billion tons per year … Food is lost or wasted throughout the supply chain, from initial agricultural production down to final household consumption. (Gustavsson et al., 2011: v)

To make things clearer, the report reuses the Parfitt et al. (2010) distinction between food losses and food waste:

> Food losses refer to the decrease in edible food mass throughout the part of the supply chain that specifically leads to edible food for human consumption. Food losses take place at production, postharvest and processing stages in the food supply chain (Parfitt et al., 2010). Food losses occurring at the end of the food chain (retail and final consumption) are rather called 'food waste', which relates to retailers' and consumers' behavior (Parfitt et al., 2010). (Gustavsson et al., 2011: 2)

This distinction enables the authors of the report to underscore key differences between richer and poorer parts of the world:

> In medium- and high-income countries food is to a great extent wasted, meaning that it is thrown away even if it is still suitable for human consumption. Significant food loss and waste do, however, also occur early in the food supply chain. In low-income countries food is mainly lost during the early and middle stages of the food supply chain; much less food is wasted at the consumer level. (Gustavsson et al., 2011: 4)

And, whereas the report does not touch on the moral dimension of food losses and waste, it does conclude that:

> [H]uge amounts of the resources used in food production are used in vain, and … the greenhouse gas emissions caused by production of food that gets lost or wasted are also emissions in vain. (Gustavsson et al., 2011: v)

All these claims are supported by quantified data, some of it evocative. Consumers in Europe and North America waste an estimated 95–115 kg of food per capita per year, whereas the comparable figure in sub-Saharan Africa and South/Southeast Asia is only 6–11 kg per capita per year (Gustavsson et al., 2011: 5). Furthermore, consumers in medium- and high-income countries discard between 15 and 30 per cent by mass of their fruit and vegetable purchases (Gustavsson et al., 2011: 7).

Food waste thus represents a typical instance of overflow, in the commonsense use of the term: a state of things to which one reacts with, 'It is simply too much!' (Löfgren and Czarniawska, 2012). Food waste stands for the irresponsible desire in contemporary Western societies for material abundance, regardless of the moral or environmental consequences.

This issue brings me to the second, more theoretical, sense of overflow: to Callon (1998a, 1998b), overflow refers to something that results from the action of framing, but does not stay within the frame designed to contain whatever this frame was designed to contain. Overflow refers to that which exists outside this frame – that which frames never succeed in enframing.

Food waste is food that does not serve its intended purpose, as it does not fulfil the human needs it is meant to fulfil. It is food that does not stay in the place it should stay; rather it leaves the frame of food and enters the frame of waste. Food waste is food that spills over the techno-bureaucratic frames that feature food as an essential commodity. It is food that has fallen from the grace of value into the generally despised wasteland of garbage.

But food waste does not need to remain valueless, specialists of waste management claim, because it can be transformed into biogas, which is economically and environmentally valuable. Food waste can even become an overflow in a third and positive sense of the term – in the form of wealth and abundance. Waste management companies describe this process and how this is likely to unfold.

THE BIOGAS RUSH

The European directive on the promotion of the use of biofuels for renewable sources sets mandatory national targets for the overall proportion of energy from renewable sources in the gross final consumption of energy in general and for the proportion of energy from renewable sources in transport in particular (European Union, 2009/28/EC, article 1). These mandatory national overall targets differ from country to country but are consistent with a target of at least 20 per cent of its energy from renewable sources in the Community's gross final consumption of energy in 2020. For Sweden, this target requires it to raise its proportion of energy from renewable sources in gross final consumption of energy from 40 per cent in 2005 to 49 per cent in 2020 (European Union, 2009/28/EC, Annex 1). This objective provides strong institutional support for the transformation of food waste into fuels.

Even if Sweden managed in 2010 to recycle as much as 20 per cent of its food waste (Avfall Sverige, 2011b), the country is still not reaching its national goal: at least 35 per cent of food waste from households, restaurants, institutional catering and shops to be recycled that year through biological treatment (Naturvårdverket, 2005). And in April 2012, the Swedish government set a new interim goal for food waste management: by 2018, food waste from households, institutional kitchens, shops and restaurants shall be separated and processed in such a way that at least 50 per cent of nutrients and 40 per cent of energy will be utilized (Regeringskansliet, 2012). The conversion of food waste into biogas is therefore a key element of Sweden's national waste strategy (Naturvårdverket, 2012).

Municipally owned solid waste management companies play a key role in this strategy, not least because municipalities have legal responsibility for the treatment of waste (SFS, 1998: 808). And these companies advertise intensively that food waste, if it cannot be avoided, can be turned into biogas. Southern and Western Swedish cities offer several examples. Sysav, in the city of Malmö, underscores the position that 'Food scraps and waste from cooking account for almost half the weight of an ordinary trash bag. Much of this waste can be sorted and utilized in new ways' (Sysav, n.d.). The company is currently developing a biogas plant and describes how biogas is to replace gasoline:

> Can replace gasoline
>
> Food waste which is not treated biologically is currently used as fuel in Sysav's incinerator, primarily to produce district heating. A biological treatment will instead utilize the energy content of food waste to produce biogas. This biogas can be upgraded to become vehicle fuel, which can be used as a substitute for gasoline and other fossil fuels. (Sysav, n.d.; translation is mine)

This quote illustrates how the company intends to reorient food waste away from the production of heat and electricity through incineration and towards the more valuable production of biogas for vehicles.

The NSR waste management company in Helsingborg has a long record of biofuel production and is a major producer of biogas. Its website states that '[b]iogas is a modern-day fuel that can generate significant environmental gains in the form of reduced carbon emissions', and that '[t]he demand for biogas as vehicle fuel is high in the Helsingborg region' (NSR, n.d.-b; translation is mine). A stick-figure pictogram reinforces their message (Figure 10.1).

People who throw their apple cores into a paper bag distributed by NSR for food waste can help get a bus moving in a way that respects flowers, and therefore benefits people. A banner affirms that 'it is easy to sort right'. And a link redirects visitors towards a description of how

Source: NSR, used with permission.

Figure 10.1 Food waste drives buses, NSR (www.nsr.se) (Sweden)

NSR produces biogas and upgrades it to vehicle fuel, richly illustrated with pictures and animated diagrams of the company's installations (NSR, n.d.-a). Consequently NSR insists on the importance of biogas production for a sustainable development of the region.

Renova (n.d.-a), a waste management company in Göteborg, states on its webpage that 'We have decided ourselves: Food waste will be biogas' and the company explains that it is developing a plant that will make it possible for people in the region to 'fill their tank with food' – literally (Renova, n.d.-b). This proclamation is supported by a two-minute-51-second film that follows what I assume to be a father, who is cooking and eating vegetable soup with his son, at home. The film begins with an off-voice stating that:

> In Sweden, we throw away an awful lot of food, nearly 100 kilos per person annually, that is 900 000 tons altogether. Much of it should not be thrown away. We are kind of afraid of sell-by dates. But if food does not smell strange, it is okay to eat it. (Renova, n.d.-b, transcription and translation are mine)

After this opening on the need to reduce food waste at source, the man in the film explains to the child how food waste is collected and processed to become biogas. Moving pictures of Renova's installations illustrate his explanations. At one point, the owner of a biogas-powered car declares, 'I can drive 250 kilometres on 60 household paper bags [of household food waste]'. And the film ends with the man joking with the child that it is not only cool, but indeed super-cool, that food waste can be used to bring cars and buses into motion.

The websites of most Swedish waste management companies portray the benefits of transforming food waste into biogas. The recurrent message is that this process can make a difference to our world. Biogas lessens the consumption of fossil fuels and our emissions of carbon dioxide; recycling food waste is amongst the most concrete things that inhabitants of the Western world can do to reduce their environmental footprint. Recycling food waste is a way for one's bad environmental conscience to glide, along with leftovers, into the paper bag for someone else to process. Sometimes reference is made to the waste hierarchy model (for example, Solna stad, 2010), which ranks landfill as the least-attractive waste management method; the best solutions, in increasing order, are deemed to be incineration with energy recovery, recycling, reuse and waste prevention (Hultman and Corvellec, 2012). But virtually no mention is made of the food versus fuel debate (for example, Aaron, 2010), which may be a legitimate oversight, as the transformation of food waste is not a focal point in this brand of criticism. More to the point, there is no questioning of the ability of biogas to become a major vehicle fuel (for example, Wetzstein and Wetzstein, 2011). The campaign for biogas leaves little room for critical voices. Rather, it conveys an orchestrated message: well-conceived and well-managed systems of biogas production will bring a responsible answer to the moral and environmental issues raised by food waste – and will make cars run.

COMMODIFYING EXCESS

Georges Bataille's theory of excess brings the transforming of food waste into biogas in a critical light. His provocative idea, as presented in *The Accursed Share* (1949/1988), is that economy is about expenditure and excess rather than production and scarcity. Perhaps Bataille took this idiosyncratic way of approaching economy because his inspiration came not from economists, but from an anthropologist such as Mauss (1902/2000) or a sociologist such as Weber (1904–1905/1958), although not from Veblen (1899/2001). Bataille aimed to define the rules of the 'general economy' of life, as distinct from the 'restricted economy' of monetary exchanges. With a distinct interest in the role of economy in social life rather than pure economic life, Bataille was a precursor of business in society as a field of study. Loosely inspired by Marx's theory that work produces more value than it consumes, Bataille suggested that a society should be characterized by the way it disposes of the surplus that it creates:

> On the whole a society always produces more than is necessary for its survival; it has a surplus at its disposal. It is precisely the use it makes of this surplus that determines it: The surplus is the cause of the agitation, of the structural changes and of the entire history of society. (Bataille, 1949/1988: 106)

Bataille's key claim is that the way members of a society waste things together keeps them together, and is integral to their cohesion and development. The Aztec society organized massive sacred sacrifices; Native American tribes on the Northwest coast organized lavish potlatch rituals; and Tibetan society maintained many unproductive monks. Furthermore, all societies resort to war as an ultimate means of disposing of their excesses. For Bataille, the function of sumptuous patterns of consumption was to manifest values and to connect wealth with the responsibility of manifesting those values. For him, the destruction of value did not indicate a breakdown or a failure, therefore, but an expression of the vitality of a society.

Bataille's reasoning invites questions, however. What does massive wasting of food say about contemporary Western societies? Does it contribute to social cohesion, and if yes, how? As a first answer, think of a restaurant's buffet: food from all over the world is on display in abundance, particularly rich in animal proteins, fat and sugar. A key principle of buffet maintenance is that the last guest should experience the buffet as richly supplied as the first guest found it. Because buffets are never to look empty, they are continuously refurbished, although much of the food must be thrown away uneaten. Because Swedish regulations require restaurants to dispose of all uneaten food that has been placed on display, at least one entire buffet must be discarded every day in a legally sanctioned sacrifice. In the name of which divinity is this sacrifice made? In the name of the freedom of choice, the pleasure of plenty and the spectacle of material abundance – all promises of the more-than-affluent societies.

The restaurant buffet represents concentrated consumption: 'Have more of everything' is the permissive narrative of overconsumption society – at least for those who are lucky enough to have the necessary purchasing power. But buffets also exemplify that the pleasure of consuming is conditioned by an intensive practice of wasting.

What about using food waste to produce biogas, then? Bataille's view on excess may provide an answer. Following Weber (1904–1905/1958) and Tawney (1926/1984), Bataille asserted that medieval economy differed from the capitalist economy in that the former was a static economy in which excess was consumed in a non-productive way, whereas the latter, under the influence of Calvinism, became a dynamic economy of accumulation oriented towards the growth of the production apparatus. The Reformation replaced the earlier ideal of idleness and luxury with an ideal of diligence and industry. To Bataille, industrial capitalism rests on a rationale that differs from the underlying principles of the economic systems that came before it: A rationale of a material accumulation in which things are always being turned into new things. The transformation of food waste into biogas is a classic case of this transformation. (See Figure 10.2 for a flow chart of NSR's biogas production plant.)

Food waste is collected from schools, restaurants and households and gathered in a reception tank (A in Figure 10.2). The bio-organic material is cleaned and separated from non-organic material such as packaging with the help of specially designed presses and filters, and processed into substrates that contain, among other things, the correct proportion of water (B). These substrates are then transported to biogas reactors, also called digesters or fermentation tanks, where they are kept under

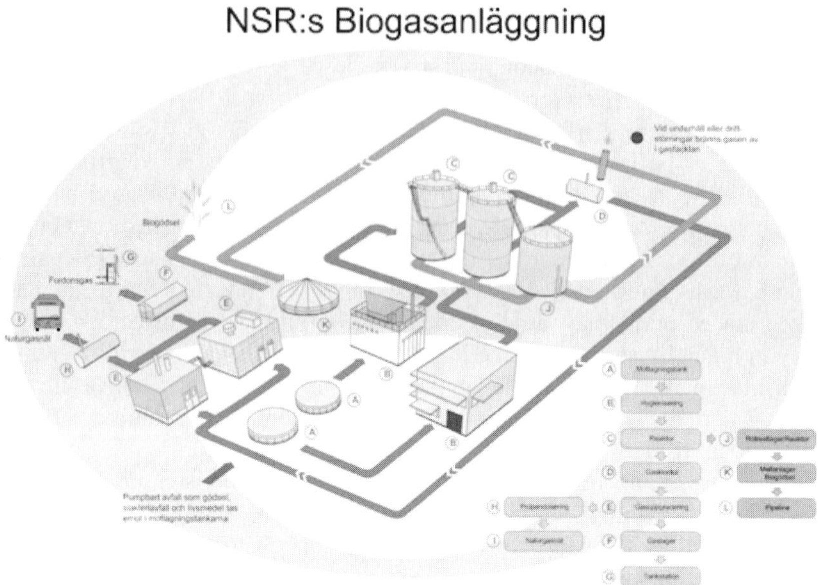

Source: NSR, used with permission.

Figure 10.2 NSR's biogas production plant, Helsingborg, Sweden

controlled conditions of anaerobe digestion (C; Figure 10.3). The substrates in the reactors are constantly heated and stirred in order to uphold their homogeneity and ensure the ideal conditions for the bacteria to work and, eventually, to allow a consistent production and discharge of biogas. The biogas is then led through pipes to a compressor (D) and transported to enrichment units (E) that raise the proportion of methane to the levels at which it can be used as biogas. In addition to the production of gas, a pipe guides the sludge into biofertilizer production units (J, K) and from there, through pipelines, to remote storage units (L). Finally, the enriched gas is sent to storage units (H, F), from which it can be distributed to the fossil gas distribution network (I) or to biogas pumps for cars and busses (G; Figure 10.4).

This transformation of food waste into biogas is a yet another example of the classic industrial capitalist rationale of endless transformation of things into new things. Waste is not to remain waste, and therefore food waste is not to remain wasted. It is to be transformed into something else – a fuel – that can be reinjected into the economy: an object of economic exchange.

Source: NSR, used with permission.

Figure 10.3 Three biogas reactors (on the left) and a compressor (on the right) at NSR's main installation site in Helsingborg, Sweden

Industrial installations such as biogas reactors (Figure 10.3) and biogas pumps (Figure 10.4) ensure that waste does not rest. Three key elements of the industrial process guarantee a consistent availability of gas at the pump: a careful monitoring of bacteria workings in the reactor, a provident planning of production and an efficient distribution system. The industriousness of waste managers ensures the systematic movement of waste and guarantees that it is put to work serving the public in another way. When waste management works fully, the transformation of waste into new stuff (Leonard, 2010) is total; waste is no longer waste. It has become biogas and biofertilizer, at the service of biomobility, bio-agriculture and sustainable capitalism.

As Rehn and Lindahl (2011) have suggested, Bataille could have claimed 'Waste, nothing but glorious waste!' But Avfall Sverige [Swedish Waste Management], which organizes the municipally owned waste management companies, claims that there shall be no such thing as waste (Avfall Sverige, 2011a). The avowed objective of the Swedish waste management industry is to see that the object of its management ceases to exist: that waste gives way to commodities that are fully able to participate in the movement of the economy.

Source: NSR, used with permission.

Figure 10.4 Biogas pump at NSR's main site in Helsingborg, Sweden

Sustainable capitalism is established not on wasting, but on reuse, recycling and transformation. The emerging promise of sustainability has no room for the spectacle of destruction: everything is to be reused, recycled or transformed. The chasing arrows of recycling symbols such as the German Der Grüne Punkt or the Universal Recycling Symbol are truly symbols of the ideal of a never-ending movement, of a constant circulation of materials. The circulation of commodities in which goods are exchanged for money is to be rendered as smooth as possible, so that it never pauses.

Management practice, and ultimately work, sees to it that the movement of goods and money runs as efficiently as possible. Management tools such as marketing plans and total quality management ensure that there is as little waste and spillage and as few leftovers as possible. And this movement will grow in pace and volume. (Mechanically, a movement that receives more impulses than resistance can only grow in pace or volume.) Whereas food waste is paradigmatic of the overproduction of everything that characterizes consumption-intensive societies, the transformation of food waste into biogas is typical of our current obsession with increasing mobilities (Urry, 2007). The new responsibility is to keep waste moving: the consumption show must go on and the recycling flow must increase. Sustainability brings with it moral and aesthetic imperatives of a submission to fluidity (Bauman, 2000). Variants of sustainable capitalism such as Natural Capitalism (Hawken et al., 1999) promise to handle the surplus of industrial capitalism; under sustainable capitalism, even waste shall fructify and produce value. The transience of waste (Thompson, 1979) should be overcome, so that it remains possible for buffets to stay open.

WASTE MANAGEMENT AS NORMALIZING MACHINE

The transformation of food waste into biogas represents an instance of overflow management. Huge quantities of food are wasted, but waste management companies claim to have found a sustainable solution to this havoc by recycling food waste into bio-energy. Through this transformation, they connect food waste to the three dimensions of sustainability: an economic dimension, in that they retrieve good economic value from food waste; an environmental dimension, in that they retrieve its energy and nutrient content; and a social dimension, in that they offer producers and consumers the possibility of quenching their eventual bad environmental conscience – concerning climate change, for instance.

The practice of waste management, starting with classifying and sorting (Bowker and Star, 2000), is a process of frame-building. The transformation of food waste into biogas inscribes waste in a series of such frames as sustainable growth, regional development plans, corporate strategies, investment budgets and quality insurance procedures. Food waste is no longer to remain as undifferentiated material. The care that waste management companies bring to food waste turns it into an object with specific qualities.

In a double movement of deterritorialization and reterritorialization (Deleuze and Guattari, 1987), waste management companies remove food waste from the vague territory of refuse and relocate it into the striated territory of economic, environmental and social responsibility. This double movement endows food waste with what Gregson (Gregson, 2009; Gregson et al., 2007; Gregson et al., 2010) calls a new socio-materiality – a new understanding (necessarily social) of the materiality of waste.

The transformation of waste into an energy resource begins with a repulsive substance of negative value (Hawkins and Muecke, 2003) and creates a desirable input for several techno-economic systems. Waste management companies inscribe food waste within a circular material economy (Hultman and Corvellec, 2012). By letting waste re-enter the economy (O'Brien, 1999), they embed it within a new regime of value (Appadurai, 1986), one that underscores the importance of not wasting and of reusing. Waste management companies give waste a new social life as a thing (Appadurai, 1986) – as fuel and as fertilizer – but also as a symbol and as hope.

The recycling of food waste into biogas rests on a successful redefinition, redesign and reorientation of waste from problem to resource (Corvellec and Hultman, 2012). A new frame (perhaps several frames) is created for food waste that brings energy and nutrients into evidence, the very energy and nutrients which, according to Bataille (1949/1988), are the sources of all surpluses. The potential of food waste to become energy and nutrients provides waste with finality and function. Once taken from the realm of waste, its energy and nutrient content become part of a new order of economic, environmental and even moral values. Food waste management creates a new ethic of food waste (Hawkins, 2006). Because it is possible, say the waste management companies, to recycle food waste, one has a duty and responsibility to do so. Recycling is a moral as much as a material economy.

The transformation of food waste into biogas is an example of the ability of the social practice of management to create and develop ad hoc frames that are able to accommodate excesses, surpluses and overspills. Overflow is not only to be controlled, but to be normalized, in the sense that its existence must enter the doxa of its time. The notion of doxa refers to the common opinion, common beliefs and accepted knowledge that circulate and impose themselves until they become indisputable (Barthes, 1975), until no one even thinks about questioning them (Bourdieu 1975/1984). In the case of food waste management, a new certitude is gaining ground: food waste is a problem, but the production of biogas is a decisive solution to this problem.

Management is akin to what Deleuze and Guattari (1987) call a machine: a purposeful assemblage of disparate elements that transform all types of inputs into all types of outputs in an unremitting flow of production. The management machine demonstrates a relentless potential to normalize overflows, the transformation of food waste into energy being only one example. Thanks to the technical efficiency of Sysav's pre-treatment installation, food producers in Malmö do not even need to open the containers of the food that they wish to throw away. A press at the biogas production plant separates the content from the container and a separation unit will orient the content towards the biogas reactor and the container towards the incinerator (Sysav, n.d. – 2009 or later). Thus the act of throwing away pallets of untouched food is no longer reprehensible, but has been turned into an act of sustainable resource management and energy production. The morals of consumption are redefined, excused or even encouraged, as customers need only to put the food they no longer want to eat in the brown paper bag at their arbitrary whim, at the purchase or the disposal point. Responsibility is redefined in terms of a correct sorting of waste. The brown paper bag is elevated to the status of a tool for the sustainable redemption of wasteful consumption. Recycling manages to unite spill and wealth, these diametrically opposed dimensions of overflows. The shame of wasting disappears behind the pride of recycling.

A PERSONAL REFLECTION: TO QUESTION OR NOT TO QUESTION?

As the reader has probably determined at this point, I find myself ambivalent about the transformation of food waste. It does bring an efficient, albeit partial, solution to the inextricably intertwined societal, moral and environmental issue of food waste; but this very efficiency deflects a more radical questioning of the interwoven social, moral and environmental logic of food waste production. Biogas production is an efficient solution to food waste; but its very efficiency contributes to the normalizing of a wasteful status quo and may alienate upstream efforts at preventing (in contrast to managing) the production of food waste. Yet there seems to be no critical voice about the transformation of food waste into biogas. It may be necessary to ask if the efficient systems of biogas production are not creating an infrastructural lock-in to a high volume of food waste production, just as the efficient waste incineration to fuel urban district systems has locked several Swedish municipalities into ever-increasing volumes of household waste (Corvellec et al., 2013).

Standing in front of the sink, I ask myself: 'Is the recycling of food waste into biogas really a solution to our intolerable food waste? Or is biogas production locking me into the ongoing massive production of food waste?' My answers depend on my stand on matters of political ecology.

Ecological modernization (Fisher and Freudenburg, 2001; Warner, 2010) orients me towards a positive view of food waste recycling, for energy is a superior order of justification (Boltanski and Thévenot, 1991) in consumption-intensive societies. It is difficult, therefore, to deny the relevance of producing more renewable fuels. The production of biogas from food waste appears to me to be a positive move that demonstrates the possibility of combining economic growth and sustainable development.

But radical ecology (Næss, 1989) orients me towards a more critical view. Can the recycling of food waste be an end-of-pipe measure which does not address the issue of aberrant food production methods – in terms of the accumulation of fertilizers and pesticides in soils and water? Could it be that the transformation of food waste into energy is nothing but a method, once again, of delaying a critical reassessment of our relationship to a consumption-intensive mode of living? I hesitate, as I scrape some more food waste from my plate.

There is a problem induced by the normalization of producing biogas from food waste: I may not even ask myself these questions. Of course, I am thinking of the repeated appeals made by public authorities and waste management companies to reduce food waste at the source. But immediately, right in front of me, an efficient management of overflow makes it difficult to question this particular overflow critically. As Barthes (1975) and Bourdieu (1975/1984) have noted, doxa brackets questionings and criticisms. It is not easy to question surpluses, excesses and, more generally, the exuberance of life so dear to Bataille (1949/1988), when these surpluses, excesses and exuberances have been turned into something predictable and controllable – into something normal. The successes of the practical rationality of management make it more difficult to adopt a critical stance towards the object being managed. The efficiency of management practices at transforming overflows into flows makes it difficult to ask such questions as, 'Is there an overflow here? What will I do with it?'

What is considered normal tends to be considered good and legitimate; and, inversely, what is good and legitimate tends to be considered normal (Boltanski and Thévenot, 2006). In practice, few people question such overflows as hypermobile styles of living, the oversupply of proteins or vitamins, the overabundance of clothes, oversized computer storage capacities or workaholic behaviour. Developing a social practice that questions flows which have become normalized is not an easy matter, even if, as the 'No Impact Man' (Beavan, 2009) project demonstrates,[1] it is possible. In practice, few people have the strength to question their intense consumption of energy or their use of drinking water to flush toilets.[2] The ability of management to turn overflows into normal flows makes it difficult to claim with credibility that something overflows. Critique – in the sense of a systematic examination of the implicit presuppositions, capacities and limits of one's ways of thinking (Butler, 2002; Foucault, 1990) – falls prey to the efficiency of management practice.

So, as I empty my plate into the food waste paper bag, perhaps the key question should not be 'Is the recycling of food waste into biogas really a solution to the issue of food waste?' It may not even be 'Why is so much food being wasted?' Perhaps the relevant questions are: 'How can I remind myself to ask, "Is this too much?"' and 'How can I resist the normalizing work of the overflow management machine?'

NOTES

1. As Colin Beavan describes the No Impact Man project: 'For one year, my wife, my 2-year-old daughter, my dog and I, while living in the middle of New York City, are attempting to live without making any net impact on the environment. In other words, no trash, no carbon emissions, no toxins in the water, no elevators, no subway, no products in packaging, no plastics, no air conditioning, no TV, no toilets' (http://noimpactman.typepad.com/blog/2007/02/the_no_impact_e.html). Although the No Impact Man project was not fully successful, given that the Beavan family were still using computers and other manufactured products from afar, it did demonstrate that, if one is really ready to change one's way of life, then it is possible to reduce a person's environmental impact considerably.
2. Maj-Britt Quitzau (2007) suggested that the systemic development of flushing toilets and the extent to which they have been imbedded into daily practice makes it difficult to create any other solutions.

FIELD MATERIAL

Avfall Sverige (Swedish Waste Management) (2011a), *Det finns inget avfall: En vision för Avfall Sverige* [*There is no Waste: A Vision for Swedish Waste Management*], Malmö, Sweden: Avfall Sverige.

Avfall Sverige (2011b), *Svensk avfallshantering 2011* [*Swedish Waste Management 2011*], Malmö, Sweden: Avfall Sverige.

Beavan, Colin (2009), *No Impact Man*, New York: Picador.

European Union (2009/28/EC), *Directive 2009/28/EC of the European Parliament and of the Council of 23 April 2009 on the promotion of the use of energy from renewable sources and amending and subsequently repealing Directives 2001/77/EC and 2003/30/EC*. Brussels: Official Journal of the European Union.

Naturvårdverket (Swedish Environmental Protection Agency) (2005), *A strategy for sustainable waste management: Sweden's waste plan*, Stockholm: Naturvårdsverket.

Naturvårdverket (Swedish Environmental Protection Agency) (2012) *Från avfallshantering till resurshushållning: Sveriges avfallsplan 2012–2017,* [*From waste management to resource management: Sweden's waste plan*] 2012–2017) Stockholm: Naturvårdsverket.

NSR (n.d.-a), 'NSR Biogas – Vi gör det lätt' ['NSR Biogas – We do it simple'], available at http://www.nsr.se/Default.aspx?ID=1645, accessed 3 February 2012.

NSR (n.d.-b), Startpage: NSR – Ett miljöföretag i världsklass [NSR – A world-class environmental company] available at http://www.nsr.se, accessed 3 February 2012.

Regeringskansliet (2012), 13 etappmål [13 intermediary targets], available at http://www.regeringen.se/sb/d/2055/a/191671, accessed 30 May 2012.

Renova (n.d.-a), 'Ett ledande miljöföretag inom avfall och återvinning' ['A leading environmental company within waste management and recycling, available at http://www.renova.se (startpage), accessed 3 February 2012.

Renova (n.d.-b), 'Matavfall blir biogas' ['Food waste becomes biogas'], available at http://www.renova.se/om-renova/matavfall-till-biogas/, accessed 3 February 2012.

SFS (Swedish Code of Statutes) (1998: 808), *Miljöbalk* [*Environmental Code*], Stockholm: Svensk författningsamling.

Solna stad (2010), 'Regelverk' ['Rules']. available at http://www.solna.se/sv/boende-miljo/avfall-atervinning/regelverk/, accessed 3 February 2012.

Sysav (n.d.), 'Matavfall och miljön' ['Food waste and the environment'], available at http://www.sysav.se/Templates/Page.aspx?id=4513, accessed 4 February 2012.

Sysav (n.d. – 2009 or later), *Från matavfall till nya resurser: Sysavs förbehandlinganläggning för matavfall* [From food waste to new resources: Sysav's pre-treatment installation for food waste], Malmö, Sweden: Sysav.

11. The discovery of relations to artefacts in the boundless process of moving

Karin M. Ekström

Since the 1950s, progression of the consumer culture (see, for example, Lury, 1996; Slater, 1997; Sassatelli, 2007) has paralleled the development of welfare in Sweden. The number of goods owned by consumers has increased rapidly, as manifested in larger but overflowing wardrobes, houses and garages, and ultimately causing waste problems. Apart from increased welfare, there are socio-cultural reasons for the abundance of goods, one being the fact that consumption during the last decades has become a stronger social marker. Zygmunt Bauman (1998) has argued that consumption has replaced work as a status indicator. The stronger emphasis on symbolic consumption is reflected in consumption for social comparison and for distinction (Bourdieu, 1984; Ekström and Hjort, 2009), although distinction is restricted by social norms, which limits one's ability to be unique (Ekström, 2007). Another factor influencing the accelerated pace of consumption is the reduced number of working hours and Sweden's regulated paid holiday (Eriksson, 1999), which has rendered shopping a leisure activity. Attitudes towards consumption and the borrowing of money has also changed over time. Whereas earlier generations saved money to buy things, greater opportunities for borrowing money have resulted in many people borrowing money for the attainment of consumer goods. All these factors have contributed to an abundance of things, particularly visible in Swedish middle-class homes. The overflow of things has also led to an increasing number of secondhand markets and private sales on the Internet (HUI Research, 2012).

Things are central to the understanding of consumer culture: 'To use the term "consumer culture" is to emphasize that the world of goods and their principles of structuration are central to the understanding of contemporary society' (Featherstone, 1991: 84). Although consumer culture is far from a recent phenomenon and is intimately tied to modern social thought (Slater, 1997), the increased abundance of 'stuff' (Miller, 2010) deserves greater attention by researchers trying to understand current consumption patterns. The abundance of goods becomes particularly apparent during such stages of transition as moving, divorce and death. Things or stuff, then, must be cared for, and many decisions must be made in the disposal of goods: giving them away, selling them, driving them to the recycling centre.

This chapter deals with the way middle-aged Swedes handle their excess of stuff when moving from a house into an apartment. Many of my informants represent the middle-class Swedish baby boom generation: they are relatively wealthy; they own a house or apartment, a car, a summerhouse or a boat – sometimes all of these. If they have debts, they are usually minuscule. They have acquired innumerable things during their lifetime, some of them have recently inherited more things from their parents, and an increasing amount of time is spent caring for all these things. At the same time, their children have left the nest, so their space feels empty. As members of the baby boom generation approach retirement, then, many of them decide to sell their home and move to a smaller place.

The purpose of this chapter is to describe how middle-aged Swedes in the process of moving deal with all the stuff they have acquired throughout life – stuff that must now be limited and disposed of in various ways. Relations with artefacts are of particular interest, because the move suddenly exposes ties, knots and tangles, and renders them visible in a new way. The move also necessitates a negotiation with existing relations and new relations to things.

Moving can reveal relations to things which have never been considered before. And deciding what to do with all the stuff acquired over the years is not always easy, as over time people appropriate things that they become closely attached to (Belk, 1988; Miller, 1997). Furthermore, moving decisions involve not only the individuals directly involved, but also negotiating with family members who develop strategies to cope with an abundance of goods.

This study is based on interviews and observations. In total, 12 families were interviewed, four of which are presented in this chapter. Interviewees were recruited through acquaintances who knew people who had moved. Two of the interviews took place at the families' homes and two at the university.[1]

FOUR FAMILIES – FOUR STORIES

Story One

Kerstin and Lennart are both retired and in their mid-60s. Because their two children have long left the nest, they decided about three years ago to move from a 176-square-metre country house plus basement to a 115-square-metre apartment in town. The move took them about a year, and was more intense towards the end. They were extremely tired after the move, to the point that they cancelled a planned trip. Lennart hurt his leg during the move and had to use crutches and attend physical therapy. He told me that the move was also difficult psychologically: 'You do not want to separate from some things'. They had accumulated a great deal of stuff over the years, something they fully realized during the process of moving: 90 flower pots under the kitchen sink and seven or eight axes for chopping wood, for example, requiring 11 totally filled trailers to be driven to the dump. Some things were given to their children, their son in particular, others to neighbours and to charity. Some things were sold. None of their children liked the coverlets that Kerstin's mother had crocheted, so they were given to Lennart's sister's son's girlfriend, who was a retro fan.

The move was not simple. Kerstin and Lennart were attached to the house which they had built and lived in for 30 years – crucial years of their lives when their children had been growing up and when memories were being formed. As Lennart put it: 'Both joy and sorrow have existed there.' As they were getting older, however, and the house would ultimately need repairs, it was time to move to a simpler form of living, particularly as they also have a camper that they use extensively. They were both aware of the difficulty in separating from the house, and as Lennart described, they were 'afraid of building their soul into the house, because then, you know, it will be difficult'. They looked for an apartment for some time; when they found the current one, it felt perfect, and they decided to sell the house.

The apartment is situated in an old house. They have renovated the bathroom and are in the process of renovating the kitchen. They kept some of their furniture and bought new furniture. They are planning to replace the old chairs around the dining room table that they brought from the house.

Kerstin emphasized that there was uncertainty associated with the move, because one never knows if one will feel at home – and then there is no returning. Their son was attached to the house and they offered to sell it to him, but he did not want to buy it. Before they moved, their son would walk around the new area to see how it felt. He now visits them more than he did when they lived in the house. Their daughter, who has a family, thought they should move. Now, the entire family enjoys the new home. Kerstin and Lennart mentioned that they brought some of their children's toys with them to the apartment so their grandchild can play with them when visiting.

In some ways, the move seems to resemble a cleaning, in that Kerstin and Lennart got rid of many things. Life is less filled with demands in their apartment. They are now retired and enjoy their new life, which gives them more time to meet with friends and go for walks, for instance. They have about one-third of the things they had before, have less to care for, and say that they do not miss anything.

They told me that they accomplished the sorting-out process in several steps. First they disposed of the things they felt sure about and put things they were uncertain about to the side. Then they took a new look at these uncertain things and sorted them again, putting aside those things they still viewed as uncertain. Their output progressed over time: 'The longer we kept going, the more we threw out', said Kerstin. Maybe it is easier to get rid of things when some things are already gone?

If they felt unsure about whether or not to keep something, they brought it with them to the apartment, placed it in the storage room in their apartment building, and decided later. The process of moving continues. They still plan to sort out the storage; they have four bicycles, for example, but need only two.

The couple shared the experiences involved with the move, by discussing what to keep and not to keep, for instance. Lennart found it more difficult to get rid of things than Kerstin did, but said that the move has made him reflect upon the meaning of material things. He concluded that material things mean little to him. Not that he finds them uninteresting – merely that he does not want to have too many things.

Kerstin and Lennart also told me that they are attached to the things they have kept, and they have carefully selected what to keep. Because they thought their children should know about the things they will eventually inherit, they decided to tell them the stories behind items that were moved to the apartment. Kerstin said that when her mother died, there was a beautiful dinner set to inherit, but that no one knew its origins.

Kerstin admitted that she occasionally missed some little thing in the kitchen and wondered, 'Maybe I should have saved it instead of the ten carafes.' She saved all the postcards she had received since she was 13 years old, but before the move she decided to burn all but a few. It wasn't fun, she said, but necessary because 'How much should you leave for the children? The postcards were of no interest to them.' The move and experiences of their parents' deaths made them realize that they did not want their children to have to deal with many things. Lennart has kept 130 telegrams that they do not want to discard. They are thinking of options. Maybe a museum would be interested?

The move has made them more cautious when seeing new things that interest them, and they are less likely to make purchases – something they could easily do when they had a large house. As Lennart said, 'We've been very close to buying, but we have said, "Should we have it? Why? Because we like it just now?"'

Lennart said that Kerstin 'is crazy about decorative pillows'. Kerstin told me that 'Lennart says, "No pillows now. We can't have more pillows. We can not have more pillows." And I think "But it's so nice. It's so nice. I can feel that I really want to have it." I have to discipline myself. "No, I can't have it. No! No!"'

Even though they do not miss the house, they said that they missed the garage, the tiled stove, the apple tree and the little green bush that Kerstin used to take branches from to decorate the house. They drive by their house to visit friends, but they do not want to go in, because they do not know how they would react. Lennart described his reaction when he found out that the new owners had changed things in the kitchen: 'Can they do that in my house? Oh, it's not my house! No!' The new owners have cut down the little green bush.

Lennart told me that he did not want to sell another house. No matter how careful and honest one is, it is possible that the inspection ordered by the buyers can find something wrong with a house. This involves worries for the seller – worries that something unexpected will be discovered. Even though it did not happen, it was a worry. Moving can involve an overflow of emotions in many ways.

Story Two

Björn is working part time and Anna is retired; they are both in their mid-60s. They met in their mid-50s and soon moved into a newly built 130-square-metre house. At that time, Björn brought with him many things from the 280-square-metre house that he had shared for a long time with his former wife, who had died. Anna, on the other hand, had moved many times before they met, and had often been faced with sorting and disposing of things. She brought very little to the newly built house, and stored some things at her son's house. For Björn, the move involved emotional decisions related to memories from earlier phases of his life.

After some years in the house, Anna decided that she did not feel happy in a suburb far from the city and initiated a new move. Björn resisted for some time, particularly because he appreciated the space for his motor vehicles. Eventually he agreed, however, and they moved into a 97-square-metre downtown apartment.

Moving involves leaving things behind, breaking up a former phase of life and entering into a new phase. Björn and Anna described this move as 'closing the books' in both a material and a psychological sense of the term. Another expression they used was that 'the move was a total drainage of history'. They got rid of all their old furniture and things from the past – particularly things that Björn had brought with him to the new house. The paintings that Björn had kept from his former wife were now given to a public institution.

To move into the apartment meant that they created a home together, mostly with things which they had decided upon and bought together. The apartment is located in a modern building with a great deal of light, many windows, an open design and only a few walls. They felt that their previous furniture from the 1970s did not fit the design of the new apartment, so they bought modern furniture. They brought only a few things from the old house – a digital piano, a paraffin lamp and a dinner set – personal things, two of which Anna had inherited from relatives. Everything else was given to their children or charity, sold or thrown away. The only thing that Anna regrets getting rid of is an old chest of drawers from her grandmother. Björn did not think it would fit in with the new things they bought, and it was therefore sold on the Internet.

In general, however, the decisions to get rid of things seem to have been more difficult for Björn than for Anna, perhaps because Björn had so many more things – things related to memories from the past. Or perhaps Anna had moved so many times and had sorted and disposed of things so often that she had less emotional attachment to possessions. She said that things that have emotional meaning for her are related to her grandmother and her parents, and that she sorted things herself because she did not want anyone else to have to do it after her death.

It seems as if the last move has affected the way Björn thinks about the meaning of material things; he says that they matter very little to him now. Yet he and Anna have put a great deal of effort into finding new furniture for their apartment. They also talked about the chest of drawers that Anna misses and the vehicles that mean a lot to Björn. Anna suggested that Björn was more interested in status than she was.

The modern layout of the new apartment has little storage space, and they have bought two extra wardrobes to accommodate that situation. They have 9 square metres in the basement which is filled to the brim, but well organized by Anna. They are planning to get rid of more things from the storage room – things that they are not using: 'Many things just sit there, just as they did in the house.' They rent extra storage for Björn's motor vehicles.

Neither Björn nor Anna regret the move. Anna visited the house once after the move, and she said that she did not find it difficult to do.

Story Three

Birgitta, who is in her early 70s, is retired and has two children who left the nest long ago. Until 1999, Birgitta had lived for 30 years in a 120-square-metre house. By then she had been divorced for some time and decided to move into a 94-square-metre apartment, after noticing an ad in the paper that someone wanted to exchange an apartment for a house. There was a great deal of rubbish: wood from carpentry and other garbage accumulated in the storage space. Some of these things were given to her children who had started university, and to charity. She gave clothes to a secondhand charity, adding that she never throws clothes away if they can be used. She took most of the furniture, apart from a bed and desk, to the apartment.

Birgitta said that she could not afford to buy new furniture, but she remembered buying a stereo, a bicycle and a coat. When I asked her if there was anything she regretted getting rid of during that move, she said that she never grieves things from the past. She did miss the ability to hang washed clothes outside to dry, however, and to be able to sit and read the paper in the garden. Even though the apartment had a balcony, it did not have the same feeling to her as a garden did.

The children did not have any opinions about the move, apart from the son mentioning now and then that 'he did not have a home any longer'. In Birgitta's opinion, however, he was over 20, and the house was just an ordinary house, although the children had stored things from their childhood there. But Birgitta has kept a bag of soft cuddly toys that she will give them sooner or later.

Birgitta really enjoyed the move to the apartment, not least because of its central location. As she admitted, 'The first two weeks I was standing at the windows looking out almost before I unpacked because I could see far, far away over town – all the way to the Angered Bridge,[2] I think, in good weather.'

Birgitta's second move occurred about six years ago from that 94-square-metre apartment to a 64-square-metre apartment in the same area. The reason for the move was economic: the first apartment was too expensive when she retired, and it was a good selling market then. This time around, she did not get rid of many things, apart from a bed and some shelves. She bought a dishwasher, a new bed, a dining room table, a side table, new carpets and a small kitchen cabinet. She also bought a used table and bookshelves from her former husband. The move between apartments involved more changes of furniture than did the move between the house and the apartment, but the second move went quickly. She still had to sort things after the move, however, which made it possible to see how her possessions looked in a new environment: 'Then you see what fits and what you don't need at all and what you need to complement.' The apartment was built in the 1940s, and its design is highly functional. There are a great many cupboards, wardrobes and storage spaces, both in the attic and the basement.

Birgitta spoke warmly about her five Lundqvist bookshelves.[3] She has many books, but she got rid of pocket books and debate pamphlets when moving. Now she reads e-books and likes them, exactly because they do not require a bookshelf. She decided to keep the books from her working life because the thought of getting rid of them was too disturbing: 'When I stopped working, oh, God, I thought for a while to get rid of most of my sociology books, but then I thought, "I will lose my identity totally." So I still have them, but I don't open them.' Her books are closely connected to her identity. As she put it: 'You have some books that you don't return to, but you still don't want to get rid of them. They mean something.'

Birgitta told me that she was attached to some of her things, but not to material goods in general. She mentioned the bookshelves and some chairs that she finds both attractive and functional – that combination seems to be crucial. Some of her furniture is of good quality and has lasted for many years. She did not consider it necessary to exchange things that actually work: 'I have decided to keep the furniture that I think is worthwhile', she said. My impression was that material things were not irrelevant to Birgitta, but that in comparison to her former husband and his family of origin – people who have many things – they did not matter much. Her ex-husband and his family 'are so involved with the material things that it could drive one mad, but at the same time, it can be nice sometimes'.

Birgitta enjoys reading books, going to the cinema and painting. Even though she thinks moving gets tougher the older one gets, she would still like to find an apartment with an extra room – for painting – if she could afford it.

Story Four

Monica and Göran are in their early 60s, and had never considered moving from the house that they had lived in for 31 years. They had paid off their loans and they liked the neighbourhood. But after seeing an apartment with an outstanding view which an acquaintance was going to sell, they decided to move. Although they liked the apartment, it was not an easy decision to move from a place where they had had their family and where they lived for many years. But their youngest child had moved away from home, 'the house felt strange' without children, and they did own a summer house. They realized that they were getting older and would have trouble in the future maintaining both a house and summer house. So they went to look at the apartment and the surroundings one more time to see if they still had the same positive feeling. As Monica told me, 'I said, let's do it. We'll never get this chance again. We'll never find this location.' Still, it was a big decision, as moving often is.

The legal possibility for the buyer of the house to reconsider the purchase within a certain period was difficult, as the selling was not yet final. Furthermore, their children had spent all their childhood in the house and considered it home. Their youngest child, who had moved out of the house some time before they sold it, walked around saying goodbye to the house. Still, they do not regret selling. The house looks completely different today than it did when they lived there.

It is four years since they moved, and they still remember the move as being extremely difficult. It felt as if the process was never going to be finished. They had acquired many things over the years and filled all the spaces. In Monica's opinion, the most difficult thing about the move was the fact that they never got around to sorting things, and finally had to throw things away. As Göran remembered it:

> After the major vanload of things had been moved, we said that we should go back and finish it. And I think we did this seven times. Now we are ready! Then we looked in that storage room, and there were a lot of things left, which we took. Then we went up [to the house] another time and opened a wardrobe. It wasn't empty. Then we looked into the attic, but there were still things left.

They organized the move, sorting things into categories: things to keep, to sell, to give away or to throw out. Some things, like the garden furniture, were taken to the summer house. Their children had little interest in acquiring their things, but Monica and Göran saved some things they thought their children would appreciate later in life: clothes that their future grandchildren could wear, for example, and children's books.

There were many possessions that they found difficult to separate from. Monica, in particular, had a hard time getting rid of things. She found memories and affectionate value important; Göran believes that he is more rational than she is. One solution to the problem of having to separate from things was Göran's storage at work, where he could put 23 boxes and some clothes. The boxes are all catalogued, so they will know where to find things they need.

The couple decided to bring some furniture to the new apartment to see how it looked, and then, after some time, possibly to replace it with new furniture – which they have done. At the time of the interview, they were trying to sell a chair on the Internet. They told me that it would have felt strange to move into a new home with only new things.

The apartment is relatively new, with an architectural style that permits few walls and few wardrobes. They had to add a few extra wardrobes. Overall, they found it difficult to locate places to store things; they had to store the vacuum cleaner in a built-in closet full of clothes, for instance. The same applied to recycling material, which was much easier to store in the house. There is no room in the apartment to store empty packages and bottles, which means that they have to visit the recycling station more often. As a result, they recycle fewer things now than they did previously: empty milk packages are no longer recycled, for example.

They have a small storage space in the basement filled with boxes and clothes. Göran said that he had a difficult time finding things after the move. He missed the garage and places in the house where he had been able to keep more things; he even finds it difficult to vacuum the apartment, as there is so little room to move around. Living in a smaller place requires better organization.

The move has changed the couple's consumption patterns. When they lived in the house, they would buy things in larger quantities and store them, but there is not enough space to store things in the apartment. They belong to a generation that has been able to buy things throughout their lives, and they inherited things from their parents. They admitted to having three generations' worth of Christmas decorations. The move made them realize just how many things they owned. The fact that Monica's mother died some time after the move has also affected their relations to things. Monica does not want to keep many possessions for her children to deal with when she dies.

At the time of the interview, the move was not finalized, and they were still sorting things. Monica emphasized that she felt relieved about getting rid of things. In the coming years, before Göran retires, they will need to sort the 23 boxes at his workplace. He claimed that he was not tempted to buy anything today. It seems as if the move and the smaller storage space have made him reconsider his purchases.

They, particularly Göran, disposed of many books when they moved. They had bookshelves in their study and the attic in the house. But because of a shortage of storage space in the apartment, Göran decided that from now on, if he buys a book, he will keep it for six months to a year, and then probably get rid of it.

Monica keeps several boxes of books at Göran's workplace. The new apartment building has a little library shelf in the basement where the tenants can dispose of books they no longer want, and one tenant ensures that the library is tidy.

MULTIPLE OVERFLOWS RELATED TO MOVING

These stories show how four families in their 60s or early 70s experience a move to apartments that are much smaller than their former homes. Overflow of stuff, a result of consumerism – the desiring, purchasing, owning, using, maintaining and repairing of goods over a number of years – is suddenly exposed. But there is also an overflow of decisions that must be made regarding what to do with all the stuff acquired over time. What should be kept and what can be discarded? Moving is one of the biggest decisions in life and produces an overflow of emotions. It is impossible for people to know if they will feel at home in their new home, and this problem can involve an overflow of worries about making the right decision. There is no guarantee that the move will be successful.

These four stories show that the feelings associated with seeing the new apartment for the first time was a key factor in the decision to move. Two couples also expressed worries related to the selling of their houses, relating to uncertainties before the final sale. The move also involves the overflow of physical tiredness or even pain. Lennart and Kerstin, for example, described how tired they were after the move and that it resulted in their having to cancel a planned trip. Lennart also hurt his leg and had to attend physical therapy.

Life Situation

These stories revealed that the experiences of moving differed, depending on life situations. People who move on their own, as Birgitta did, make their own decisions. But people who move with their partner must negotiate and make joint decisions about what to keep or not to keep. This process may be easier for couples like Kerstin and Lennart or Monica and Göran, who have spent most of their lives together, learned each other's preferences over the years, and learned how to navigate through the decision-making process – easier than for couples like Anna and Björn, who met later in life.

Apart from the persons who are moving, there are other family members who may influence the move, directly or indirectly. Göran and Monica said that 'the house felt strange' without children, which affected their decision to move. Various family members have different reactions to the move. As the stories demonstrated, if the children had grown up in the house, the departure from the house seemed to be more difficult. Birgitta, Kerstin and Lennart, and Monica and Göran all said that their children found the move difficult at the beginning.

Baudrillard (1998) suggested that everything possessed is relativized in relation to others. Interactions among family members are often related to artefacts and become more apparent during a move. These stories revealed that decisions had to be made about such things as children's toys, which had been stored at a home that the children had left long ago. Birgitta, Kerstin and Lennart, and Göran and Monica all brought their children's toys along with them during the move.

Moving from one home to another in a transitory stage of life such as retirement entails a break from a former phase in life to a new phase, which in turn involves lifestyle changes. Kerstin and Lennart have more time to meet with friends since they retired. Their move to an apartment also means that life has become less demanding for them. For Björn and Anna, both moves symbolized a new start in life together. The second move was unusual, in that it involved leaving things from the past behind and buying new things together to create a new home together.

Attachment to Things

The overflow of emotions related to the move seems to be related to the overflow of attachments involved. As things accumulate throughout life, people are likely to establish relations with their things, a dependency that can be difficult to break. Over time people make a home with their stuff, a gradual transformation process that Miller (1997) called 'to appropriate'. To break up a home can be difficult, as possessions become part of one's identity over the years. Lennart said that he and his wife were 'afraid of building their soul into the house'. Things related to special experiences can be particularly difficult to relinquish. Birgitta talked about her working life and the books that had become part of her identity. Things related to people we hold dear can also be difficult to part with. Anna spoke of the paraffin lamp and the chest of drawers that she inherited, and both Anna and Kerstin mentioned dinner sets from their parents in that context.

Russell W. Belk (1988) has argued that an object could become part of the self. Possessions that have become part of one's extended self are not merely part of the self, but can also be seen as instrumental for development of the self. Psychological theories of self-concept (for example, Sirgy, 1982) posit that people's self-concepts are based on how they perceive themselves (actual self) and how they want to be seen (ideal self). Psychologists Mihaly Csikszentmihalyi and Eugene Rochberg-Halton (1981) interviewed 80 families in Chicago about their feelings towards common household objects and concluded that things shape identities in contemporary societies.

Objects influence people – and not only in the construction of their self-identity. Using certain objects and not others also exerts an influence on the outside world, the societal context. Elliott (1997) has suggested that the symbolic meaning of products can operate inward and outward. By inward, he meant construction of our self-identity or self-symbolism; by outward, the construction of the social world, or social symbolism. Anna said that Björn was more interested in status than she was. Such matters are difficult to study, however, as people may be unaware of them or unwilling to admit to them. Both Kerstin and Monica showed interest in home decoration, but as this is a declaration made in an interview, it is difficult to say if it is an expression of self-identity or social symbolism – or perhaps both?

Strong attachments to things make it more difficult to separate from them. Kerstin burned most of her collection of postcards before moving. They were personal, and she did not want her children having to deal with them later. Lennart had a collection of telegrams that he considered giving to a museum. Collections tend to be more difficult to dispose of, for many reasons. First, there is a strong connection between the individual and the objects collected. As Corrigan (1997: 48) wrote: 'It becomes hard to know whether you are collecting French clocks, or they are collecting you – there is a tight connection between the individual subject and the object.' Second, collectors are concerned with what will happen to their collections. As Belk et al. (1991) have suggested, collectors express a desire for immortality through their collections. Third, it is not a given that family, friends and museums can or will take care of a collection. To inherit a collection usually requires both space and responsibility.

The consequences of disposing of products by giving them away, selling them or throwing them in the garbage cannot always be foreseen, but are usually realized afterwards. Anna, for example, regretted having sold her grandmother's old chest of drawers when moving to the apartment. Because people's identity is formed in relation to things, relinquished possessions can be missed and create a loss of self. As Goffman (1961) claimed in a similar context, some institutions deprive people of their possessions, thereby causing a loss of self.

The consequences of keeping and bringing things to a new home are not always foreseen at the time of the move, either. Björn kept many of his former wife's paintings when he and Anna moved into their first home together, but decided to part with them during their second move – to an apartment.

The overflow of strong attachments is also visible in a concern about what will happen to things that are given away. Kerstin, for example, gave the coverlets that her mother had crocheted to someone who appreciates them and likes retro style. There is also responsibility involved for the person who receives a gift from someone who has formed strong attachments to that gift.

The stories also indicated attachments to houses. Some people wanted to visit their old home after the move; others did not. Anna visited the house she had moved from, but neither Kerstin nor Lennart would consider doing that. Lennart mentioned that their former house was changed; his reaction when he heard that the new owners had changed the kitchen was 'Can they do that in my house? Oh, it's not my house! No!' The little green bush that Lennart and Kerstin liked has been cut down by the new owners. Göran and Monica mentioned that their house looks different today than it did when they lived there. Maybe the appropriation process gets stronger the longer something is kept – a house lived in for a long time, for example – and it makes disposal more difficult the longer things are kept? Or do some people find it easier to relinquish stuff they have had for a long time than others do?

Perhaps a difficult process of separation during a move can make people less likely to become attached to things again. Björn, Lennart and Göran all mentioned that their moves have made them think about the meaning of material things, and have concluded that these things actually mean very little in life. They seem to be more careful about such attachments after their moves; they think twice before buying, and consider more carefully the necessity of their purchases. Before their moves, both Björn and Lennart had stronger ties to things, it seems, than their wives did, which may have created a stronger impact from the move.

Materialism as a way of seeking happiness through consumption has attracted researchers' attention over the years. Belk (2001) explicitly stated that materialism can bring unhappiness, and posited that consumption can become an obsession, leading to unbearable debt, low self-esteem and environmental damage. Although negative attitudes to materialism exist, however, people may still have the desire to consume (Ger and Belk, 1999). Both Anna and Björn seemed to think that material things did not matter, yet they put a great deal of effort into finding new furniture for their apartment. Miller (2010) presented a view opposite to that of Ger and Belk, by arguing that things could be looked upon as having a capacity for enhancing humanity. In another work, Miller (1998) suggested that the importance of things for social interaction must not be overlooked, as a lonely person without things may indicate a lack of capacity to create relationships.

Storage

An overflow of stuff is suddenly noticeable during a transitional phase in life, such as moving. Kerstin and Lennart, for example, talked about 90 flower pots under the kitchen sink. Relations to artefacts can be exposed – relations that the persons moving were unaware of or did not have to consider because of the spacious homes they previously enjoyed. Monica and Göran said that their house had a great deal of storage space, and that there was always room somewhere for things in their old house. It was easy, therefore, to keep track of where things were. In a smaller place, it seems that one must be better organized. Löfgren (2012) suggested that one way to battle domestic overflow is to create storage space, which determines how much can be brought from the former place of living to the new one. Storage makes a move easier, as a separation can be postponed, or the necessity to separate may never arise. The older apartment buildings that Birgitta and Kerstin and Lennart moved to had a great deal of storage. Göran and Monica, and Björn and Anna, on the other hand, moved to apartments with modern architecture, many windows, few walls and limited storage space. Apartments built during the last few decades, with a focus on minimalistic interior design, suffer from a shortage of storage space. Architects' opinions on the role of storage varies over time, as reflected in different architectural styles at different historical periods. Birgitta's apartment was built in 1945 in a functionalist style, when storage was considered a key ingredient.

When there is little storage space, the solution is either to dispose of things or to find storage elsewhere. Göran and Monica had the opportunity to store things at Göran's workplace, but also found that lack of storage space affected their recycling behaviour.

The Boundless Process of Moving

The time to move also affects how stuff is handled. If there is a long time between the decision to move and the actual move, as was the case for Kerstin and Lennart, there is more time to sort things before the move and less risk of impulsive decisions to discard things that may be regretted later. Birgitta explained that the last move did go relatively quickly, so rather than making hasty decisions, things were brought to the new place to be sorted there.

The process of moving starts from the date one decides to move, but continues after the move has been completed. All the interviewees talked about their continuing to sort things long after the move had occurred. The opportunity to store things will prolong this process even longer – maybe forever, or at least until the next move – thereby revealing the boundless character of the moving process. And different people probably have different skills for discarding, rearranging, layering, sorting and circulating stuff. These skills may also develop over time.

The stories also indicate that the process of eliminating things seems to intensify over time. As mentioned previously, having once thrown things away, it may be easier to dispose of things in the future. As Kerstin put it, 'the longer we kept going, the more we threw out'. Maybe it is easier to throw things away when some are already gone? For Kerstin and Lennart, the move was not a simple one, as they had many memories associated with the house. Maybe an overflow of memories makes it more difficult to move? They now feel relieved not to have so many things to take care of.

Monica mentioned that she felt relieved when getting rid of things. An overflow of stuff can be oppressive. The stories show that things require both physical and emotional place. The fewer things one has, the less one has to care for – physically as well as emotionally. In some ways, moving does resemble cleaning, involving many strategies for the way things are divested: by driving to the recycling centre, for instance, or giving things away.

Creating a New Home

Moving involves not only leaving behind, but bringing old things to a new context and thus creating new meaning in a new home. Artefacts affect each other and are affected by their surroundings – the design of the apartment or house, for instance. As Boyd and Levy (1963: 130) noted, '[t]he use behaviour for a particular product is bound to be affected not only by … the task to be performed with the use of that product, but also by the related products and their use behaviours that make up the total consumption system'. Products in a consumer's habitat can influence the perception of a specific product; an old toaster may look different in a high-tech kitchen than in an old kitchen (Ekström and Karlsson, 1998). Anna and Björn thought that their 1970s furniture would look odd in their modern apartment, so they bought new furniture.

All the interviewees had bought some new furniture in constructing their new home. Scholars with a material-culture perspective emphasize that by consuming objects, people also construct themselves (Miller, 1998). By surrounding oneself with new possessions, a new self may develop. Several of the interviewees claimed, in fact, that a move can feel like a new start in life.

Societal Values

Societal values are expressed in design (Forty, 1992; Woodham, 1997). At certain times in history, for example, wear and tear may represent damage and diminished value; whereas at other times it is considered beautiful patina. The fact that the importance of consumption as a social marker has increased over the past few decades may have contributed to making home interiors more socially uniform. The focus on minimalism is noticeable in interior decoration magazines, in advertisements for apartments and houses for sale, and in many Swedish homes.

One example of minimalism is the lack of books in many Swedish homes – in sharp contrast to a few years ago. Göran got rid of his books when he and Monica moved, because the apartment did not have enough space for them. Still, the decision to perceive an artefact as superfluous, unneeded, uninteresting and therefore discardable, is highly individual. Birgitta talked about her books and bookshelves, and it was clear that her books are a critical part of her identity.

CONCLUSIONS: CONSUMPTION AND OVERFLOW

Overflow as a result of consumption is noticeable during transitional phases in life, such as moving. People moving from a house to an apartment particularly need to think about what to do with all the stuff they have acquired over the years. Their relations to artefacts are now suddenly exposed – to family members and other people, but also to themselves. There is suddenly an overflow of stuff, an overflow of decisions to be made and an overflow of emotions, on top of the overflow of worries involved in selling the former home and concern if the new home will be as good or better than the former home.

The interviews indicated that relations to artefacts were discovered during the moving process. The move made it necessary to deal with all the stuff acquired over the years and to consider what was important to keep. As things accumulate throughout life, it is likely that people establish relations to things, a dependency that can be difficult to break. It can also lower the probability that the person will become attached to things again.

The interviews also showed that the experiences of moving were varied, depending on the life situation: moving on one's own differs from moving with a partner. Family members also influenced the move. For several of the interviewees, the move meant a new start in life. Moving is not merely a moment in time; the process begins on the day one decides to move and continues after the move – a boundless process. In general, the length of time between the decision to move and the actual move seems to determine whether things are sorted before the move or kept and sorted at the new residence. Storage space will also affect the experience of moving. If it is too small, the solution is either to get rid of things or to find storage elsewhere.

Even though decisions regarding interior design are affected by societal values, they are also affected by individual preferences. Moving involves not only leaving behind, but also creating new meaning and maybe even a new self in a new home.

NOTES

1. Although the interviews consisted of informal discussions, an interview guide was used as a point of departure. Each interview was tape recorded and later transcribed by the interviewer. Each interview took approximately 1–2 hours.
2. Angered Bridge is a 930-metre-long bridge that joins downtown Gothenburg with the Island of Hisingen, one of the city districts.

3. The Swedish company Lundqvist Woodworking was started in 1939 by the innovative carpenter Harald Lundqvist. In the 1940s, the company designed a bookshelf series called Klassika – the first mass-produced bookshelf for both private home and office use.

FIELD MATERIAL

Eriksson, Thomas (1999), *Älskade pryl! Reklam- och prylhistoria för rekordårens barn*, Stockholm: Bokförlaget Prisma.

HUI Research (2012), *Begagnatbarometern*, available at http://www.hui.se/nyheter/begagnatbarometern, accessed 9 November 2012.

12. Managing inflows, throughflows and outflows: mothers navigating the baby stuff scape

Helene Brembeck

> The first thing I did [when I found out that I was pregnant] was to book a date with a friend who has children. Together we wrote a list of what was necessary to acquire on two A4 pages. Then it remained just to start checking off the list. (Kajsa)

Today, the market for things for the baby – clothes, toys, blankets, watchers, gyms, nappies, baby bottles, strollers – is expanding. This chapter demonstrates that parents, and particularly mothers, are engaged in continuous and time-consuming work to manage the inflows, throughflows and outflows of baby stuff, and that this work is necessary in order to maintain control and prevent overflow in the home. The chapter also highlights the new digital market of buying, selling and barter sites on the Internet, a market which can be perceived as a response to and a necessity for the management of these flows that are increasing in size and rapidity.

Judging from the introductory quote and similar statements from women in this study, they appeared to be well-informed and rational consumers, demonstrating no sign of the impulsiveness that is often ascribed to female consumers. There are, however, other more intriguing ways of conceptualizing their utterances. When applying an overflow perspective, the managing of the acquisition process emerges as part of the regulation of inflow of baby things in the home. It also becomes apparent that this process is not simply about managing stuff, but also about managing motherhood and childhood – ways of being and acting as mother and child. Thus the managing process is occurring in what has been termed commercial culture (Jackson et al., 2001) – the intermingling of markets and everyday life – and it is only from this perspective that the course of events can be understood.

MATERIALS AND METHODS

This chapter builds primarily upon stories from 14 women collected during the first year of their babies' lives. I met the women at an open preschool,[1] where they visited the 0–6-month-old babies' group once a week during their parental leave. Thanks to the generosity of the staff, I was given the opportunity to visit the centre several times in January 2011, to meet with the women, to present my project and to recruit 'coresearchers'. The story-writing method was not obvious from the start. Rather my idea was to meet with the women at the preschool or in their homes. But after discussing this option with the women, I soon discovered that writing and e-mailing stories to me was a better approach. The babies, all of whom were born in the autumn of 2010, were 3–4 months old. The mothers were constantly required to attend to their needs at the preschool, and because at-home routines for sleeping and eating had not yet been set, it was difficult to book times for peaceful interviews at the preschool or at home. Writing stories was easier. The women regularly used their computers to keep in touch with friends while their children slept, and it was simple for them to answer my questions at the same time. That is how I came up with the idea of writing assignments: short stories on themes like 'planning for the baby', 'the first Christmas', 'the Christening/name-giving', 'spring wardrobe', 'the first birthday', 'the first year – concluding comments'. I also asked the women to send me photographs of gifts that the baby received during the first year.

Of the 14 women who accepted the invitation, nine wrote stories that were relatively short and concise, and I had little contact with them between assignments. But the others – Kajsa, Anna, Linda, Malin, Sara and Rebecca[2] – whose words will appear in this chapter, wrote extensive stories, sometimes several pages long. I also kept in touch with them between assignments, asking them follow-up questions or just chatting. I asked if I could visit them in their homes and discuss the baby's first year rather than have them complete the final writing assignment; except for Sara, who was moving to another city, they all agreed. I usually visited them in the evening when their children were sleeping.

Guided by the frequent mention of magazines, Internet sites and shops in the women's stories, I decided to include them in the material I used. I followed in their footsteps and surfed the Internet, browsed through magazines and visited physical and online shops. I was particularly interested in one of these sites: Loppi.se. I registered as a member, followed its activities and received newsletters for most of the fieldwork year. And because my granddaughter was only slightly older than the children of my informants, discussions with my daughter and her female friends gave me valuable personal insight into the baby stuff scape. This method required to me to pick bits and pieces from the baby stuff scape, guided by the women and my own increasing acquaintance with this field – a kind of 'triangulation' or 'multi-local fieldwork'. As with any qualitative study, the story that unfolds in this chapter does not provide representativeness and generalization. Rather, my goal was to present a grounded story about living and handling life as a young mother in the midst of constant inflows and outflows of things for the baby.[3]

IN, THROUGH AND OUT

Departing from our previous work on overflow management (Czarniawska and Löfgren, 2012), my goal in this chapter is to use and expand upon the concepts discussed there. For this purpose, I focus on the three phases of the management process that are clearly visible in the women's stories: the inflow, the throughflow and the outflow. To some extent, this resembles another type of inflow and outflow that has been previously studied in the programme: the input and output of information at news agencies (Czarniawska, 2011, 2012). From Czarniawska I borrow the ideas of cybernization and filtration to conceptualize the inflow. To describe the throughflow, I borrow from Orvar Löfgren's studies of everyday coping techniques (2012; and Chapter 14 in this volume), in addition to those techniques I found in my research material. My analysis of outflow builds upon studies of waste and waste management (Åkesson, 2012; Corvellec, Chapter 10 in this volume; Ekström, Chapter 11 in this volume), but also adds new dimensions by focusing not on the discarded, torn and tattered, but on the nearly new that is sent back into circulation, largely through the Internet. This story also pinpoints the 'essence' of the management of baby stuff as I have come to know it: it is not a straightforward and linear process of inflows and outflows; rather it is about circulation or 'interflows: flows and overflows in different directions, creating new patterns, new realities along the route of the flows and swirls, whirlpools, cross-currents, undercurrents, and breaking waves' (Kunda, 2012: 99).

REGULATING INFLOW

Just like the dispatchers at news agencies in Czarniawska's study, the women and their partners used techniques and devices to regulate the inflow. But unlike the devices at the news agencies, although many of them were digital, not all were. Most obvious was the shopping list which was e-mailed among friends and which could be in the form of an Excel document. This made the process 'cybernized', with the Internet and software serving as extensions of the human body. This cybernized process of managing began long before the Excel lists were made, during the search for items to be acquired on the Internet – an activity which started several months before the baby was due. I was not able to follow this process from the beginning, but from the stories I heard it was obvious that it required distinctive skills and familiarity with digital technology, which these young adults had acquired. They were already attuned to cybernized practices. And, as Robert Willim noted, the software menuing also has its own framing power, and computer programs create their own routines, storage and retrieval habits (Willim, 2006; Löfgren, 2012).

Filtering Devices: The List

For the purpose of this chapter, I depart from the list. As Czarniawska showed in regard to news agency staff, cyborgs primarily manage overflow through categories. The lists can be regarded as one of the devices used in the filtering of information, and two other related processes – accreditation and verification – are visible in the creation of these lists. Accreditation concerns the credibility of the sources; it is obvious, for example, that these women turn to *Råd & Rön*, a commercially independent magazine that offers product testing, or to the National Society for Road Safety Promotion (NTF) as trustworthy sources of information about safety issues and safe products. Verification refers to the items that actually get on the list and the items that can wait or be omitted, that I interpret as part of another type of filtering: peer filtering, which serves a critical function in the lives of these women. This peer filtering – or my perceived peer filtering – comes close to the 'gut feelings' or intuition that Czarniawska's news agency respondents described as essential to the managing process.

Linda's list, which follows, distinguishes among items borrowed, purchased secondhand, purchased new and received as gifts and bought new. It also includes prices and, in the case of secondhand items, both the price actually paid and the selling price in store. She told me the story behind the list:

> It emanates from an Excel list I received from a friend and then adjusted. Here you can see that we made a column for what we needed to buy, what we

> bought secondhand, what we borrowed and so on. We thought we would monitor how much we saved [buying secondhand] sometime, but we haven't done that yet. I'm a control freak, so I thought it was nice to have it [the list].

From Linda's list (Figure 12.1) one can see that she and her husband hired a baby sitter and bought a baby gym and a carrier of the Swedish quality brand, Baby Björn, from the sell-and-buy site, Blocket.[4] They borrowed a bathtub and a car seat from Linda's sister, Åsa, and her parents gave them a crib. They also bought several items from baby stores.

Linda's list is similar to those of the other women. Preparing for the baby is not only about buying new stuff. Rather, the baby's room is filled with a mixture of something bought new or received from relatives; something secondhand given by or borrowed from family and friends or bought at Internet sites, like Blocket or Tradera;[5] and even something hired (such as a car seat from NTF).

One can also see that the total of the items amounts to approximately 20 000 SEK (€2000). The other women spoke of similar sums. The sum of the items on Anna's extensive three-page list was almost €3500, but it included a complete wardrobe for her baby's first months and costs for courses in prophylaxis and pregnancy yoga. These lists included everything from inexpensive items such as nappies and baby oils to expensive ones, the most expensive being the pram.

The technique of making lists was used throughout the babies' first year to manage the inflow of stuff, whether supplied by the parents or by others. All the women made lists of things they wanted for the baby for Christmas, baptisms and birthdays, and gave the lists to friends and relatives – especially to grandparents. Among relatives and friends with children of the same age, there was often an agreement about price and number of presents for the little newcomers: 'From Grandma and Grandpa, we wanted a car seat for the first birthday, and from my grandparents rainwear and boots from Polarn & Pyret. Sturdy and good things – quite expensive – that we really needed' (Malin).

Sometimes the requests were extremely explicit: 'The Stokke chair from grandmother and grandfather was well planned; we had been on the Net and checked the possible colours; and the chair was ordered in good time, so that it would arrive for Christmas' (Rebecca).

Parents, siblings and other relatives often asked what presents the mothers wanted for the baby. Linda had a constant list which she produced for those occasions. It included such items as 'money at Amanda's account, pants … right now there is a Sacco sack on the list, it works really well'.

Inhandla	Prio	OK	Purchase	Borrow/Bought In st	Price New	Prel. Prices(20 00
Baby Björn Babysitter 1-2-3	Prio	OK	300	Blocket	1295	1295
Baby Björn Sling Active backplate	Prio	OK	350	Blocket	1195	1195
Baby gym	Prio	OK	300	Blocket	660	660
Bath tub	Prio	OK	0	Lena	0	0
Car seat	Prio	OK	0	Lena	0	0
Stroller seat unit and carrycot (UJ)	Prio	OK	8598	Babyproffsen Gbg	8598	8598
Sheep skin grey (Tranås	Prio	OK	1500	Mellangården Öland	1795	1795
Pillow crib	Prio	OK	119	Babyproffsen Gbg	119	119
Pillow stroller	Prio	OK	109	Babyproffsen Gbg	109	109
mattress	Prio	OK	599	Babyproffsen Gbg	599	599
Raincover carrycot included	Prio	OK	0	Babyproffsen Gbg	0	0
Diaper Bag	Prio	OK	528	Polarn och Pyret	695	695
Crib	Prio	OK	0	Linda's Parents	0	0
Crib Swing for legs	Prio	OK	299	Babyproffsen Gbg	299	299
Quilt	Prio	OK	239	Babyproffsen Gbg	239	239
Changing table	Prio	OK	1295	Baby&Björn Mölndal	1300	1300
Waste bin nappies etc.	Prio	OK	0			
bumpers crib	Prio	OK	379	Babyproffsen Gbg	379	379
Pillowcases stroller	Prio	OK	89	Baby&Björn Mölndal	89	89
Blanket PoP	Prio	OK				
Wheel Cover (Teutonia)	Prio	OK			120	120
Pee protection cot-plastic toweling	Prio	OK				
Puke protection IKEA	Prio	OK				
Paper napkins	Prio	OK				
Changing table mattress	Prio	OK				
Baby wipes	Prio	OK				
Footmuff	Prio	OK			1000	1000
Quilt cover cot	Prio	OK				
Rain cover seat unit		OK	449	Babyproffsen Gbg	449	449
Music box cot		OK	149	Babyproffsen Gbg	149	149
Blanket fleece		OK	299	Baby&Björn Mölndal	299	299
Bags for the trash bin (3 ex)		OK	249	Babyproffsen Gbg	299	299
Diapers (Libero newborn 2-4kg)		OK				
Drop-down blackout						
Baby watch		OK				
Bath towel						
Baby oil (Ica Maxi mfl.)		OK				
Baby oinment f ex.. Inotyol (pharmacist)		OK				
High chair						
Car seat older children						
Boxes toys Brio						
Thermometer (pharmacist)						
Stuffed animals						
Bip						
Learning-go-cart Brio						
Mosquito Protection						
Pacifiers (Latex)						
Feeding bottles						
Travel cot						
Side sunscreen car						
Seat Protection stroller					ca 350	
Sun screen						
Plate/cutlery						
SUM			15850			19677

Notes: The second page shows baby clothes and the third page highlights things to bring to the delivery ward. Prices are in Swedish krona (SEK; December 2012 exchange rate: 100 SEK = approximately €10).

Figure 12.1 The first page of Linda's list: baby things

Cultural Filtering: Becoming a Mother

Another type of filtering is cultural and deals with discourses and traditions related to stuff, babies and parenthood that are generally considered self-evident. Ethnologists and anthropologists, who have pointed to the communicative, symbolic function of the objects involved, have frequently noted that the markings of life, from baptisms to funerals, have become major consumer events. These objects become extensions of parents' and/or society's aspirations, desires and feelings. The process Daniel Miller called 'objectification' consists of objects externalizing – giving form to – emotions embedded in social processes; by making them visible, they are made available for negotiation (Miller, 1987). This process gives strollers, pacifiers and baby clothes the role not only as mediators of childhood – social and personal feelings and ideas about how the child should be and behave – but also as the designer of the elusive transformation into parenthood.

Today, mothering and consumption have become mutually constitutive phenomena (Taylor et al., 2004), as witnessed in the story of the pram. The pram was generally bought new, and the price for a new pram could easily amount to €1000. The cost of Linda's Urban Jungle carrier was €850, and Anna and Kajsa spent almost €1100 on their I-Candy prams. The pram was also the item that the women spent the most time and effort selecting. Here is an excerpt from Rebecca's written story:

> The thing that we've spent the most money on is definitely the buggy. A lot of thought went into it, and I started asking around among friends for tips and advice early in my pregnancy. We realized quite early what we wanted (thanks to tips, I should add …): a carrier with four wheels, with the top two hinged, and with soft fabric, so that we could carry it up to our flat on the third floor. (There is no lift.) There weren't many models to choose from, and we actually chose the first carrier that a friend recommended: Teutonia Fun. We'd already started watching for prams five months before Hedda was born, if I remember correctly. After the first visit to a pram store (it felt almost a little sacred to step in there, as a prospective first-time parent), we realized how much money we would have to spend on the carrier. We checked a little on Blocket after the model we wanted, and my partner also surfed around German and US stroller sites to see if it would be cheaper to order from abroad. But eventually we realized that the price would be the same if we ordered it from a shop in Gothenburg, because we had some discount vouchers. We soon decided to buy a new carrier rather than a used one – mainly because we wanted to, but we justified the cost by thinking that hopefully we'll have another child in the future and number two will inherit the stroller. Now, it only remained to decide on the colour. I wanted one with colours or patterns; my partner wanted a classic carrier (i.e., black … a recurring theme whenever we make choices …). Because we didn't know the gender of the child, we didn't want to have either a red or blue stroller. Therefore we agreed on a brown one, with patterns in white and brownish-gray, and we were both really happy with it when it arrived. We ordered it ten weeks before delivery and received it a month before Hedda was born. My

> partner's parents said they could keep it in their garage, but we wanted to look at it every day (at least I did …), so we had it on display in the living room waiting for the new family member.

Rebecca's story is definitely about money, functionality, brand, colours and asking around and surfing the Internet in the process of making the right choice. She is the epitome of a rational consumer. But her story is equally about emotional investments and about becoming a mother with the help of this object. It is also about becoming a father, as witnessed in Rebecca's partner wanting a 'classic', black and presumably 'manly' stroller, and his surfing of international stroller sites.

There are other examples of male partners actively involved in the planning process. Malin's partner bought a bag on eBay to bring to the delivery ward several months before their son was born, for example, and he was the one who planned what to pack. But this chapter focuses women, who, according to these stories, were by far the most committed to the acquisition of baby stuff.

All the hours devoted to the search for and decision about the right pram certainly revolved around becoming a mother. And Rebecca's desire to display the pram in the living room for a month before the baby was due – her daily watching ritual – can be interpreted as a way of working her way to motherhood and gradually coming to know herself as a mother. Linda Layne has described how women who lost their babies could, by buying baby things, construct the child as a real baby and themselves as real mothers (Layne, 2000). For Rebecca, the baby became real, and she enacted the role of a mother by watching the pram. And this was not happening in a 'pure' cultural sphere of sentiments and traditions, but in the midst of the market, in a highly commercial scape.

Peer Filtering: Making Sameness

It has been argued that social research has largely ignored, or at best underestimated, the significance of women's social contacts as mothers (Bell and Ribbens, 1994). Becoming a mother is as much a cultural as a biological process (Layne, 2000), whereby the commercial culture (in the form of gift objects: clothing, services, foods) is paramount in transforming domesticity into specific types of meanings and solidarity within mothering. It is during the early infancy of their children that mothers are most likely to seek solidarity with other women. For Alison Clarke, the interaction between mothers is about 'making sameness': the generation of sociality whereby mothers, through the appropriation of the market, find their own ways of being mothers (Clarke, 2007). This phenomenon can be clearly witnessed in a quote from Rebecca:

> During the first year I met with my parents' group[6] often – several times a week – and we gave each other tips and advice on flashy toys. It often ended with the children having exactly the same toys. In addition, we often took buggy walks around town and used the opportunity to peek into the shops and buy something small (= cheap). Had I not had the parents' group, I might have used the Internet more, but now we were eight who associated closely (and three other friends who had a baby almost in the same month), so I thought I got so much out of it.

Linda recounted a similar experience about the purchase of Sophie the Giraffe:

> When I was in Stockholm, I bought Sophie the Giraffe. She's very popular. It was a truly fashionable toy in Stockholm, and one that all the mothers wanted to have. It's a giraffe that beeps, and the children can suck and chew on it. And it's supposed to taste a little of vanilla, which is supposed to be organically grown or something … I think it cost 25 EUR – for that little thing! But I wanted it because it was so trendy. So that was a thing I really swallowed. As it was written about on blogs and everything [giggles]'.

On the webpage of Lollopard, a company specializing in ecologic designer toys where Linda guided me, Sophie the Giraffe is marketed as a 100 per cent natural bite toy for the child:

> Sophie is handmade from natural rubber. She is hand painted with food-based paint. She does not contain phthalates or other chemicals. Sophie is the right size and easy to handle. Sophie's legs, neck, the ears and the horns are easy to grip. The natural rubber is comfortable and soft in the child's hand. It is perfect even when your child gets teeth, and soothes the child's irritated gums when teeth begin to grow out. (www.lollopard.se)

A look into Sophie's history reveals that Sophie the Giraffe, or Sophie La Girafe in French, has been a favourite teething toy in France for more than 40 years. Since her creation in 1961, more than 40 million copies have been sold, and nine out of ten newborn babies in France are currently receiving their own Sophie La Girafe (http://en.wikipedia.org/wiki/Sophie_the_Giraffe). She has also conquered the British, US and Australian baby toy markets.

Now this precious toy has obviously reached Sweden. Sophie the Giraffe seems perfect for creating motherhood and sameness. It has all the required qualities: it is popular among mothers, trendy, ecologically sound, a designer toy, from Paris, soft, easy for the child to handle, and even soothing at teething time.

Setting Levels of 'Enough'

In terms of overflow, it is obvious from the stories that women friends discuss, test, contest and regulate the content and size of the inflow from early pregnancy onward. And it was within this context that the levels of what was considered 'enough' was set – that the shopping lists could be regarded as a list of the content and size of the normal inflow of things needed for the transformation to motherhood in one's social environment. Thus to become a mother is not merely to perform a predetermined script or to assemble it from bits and pieces. Within a circle of friends, adaptations are made, transformations occur and levels of 'enough' are set. A key aspect is that levels of enough alleviate the pressure of a potlatch culture and oppressive forms of competitive motherhood; it is an equalizing device in the management process.

Floodgates Opening: When Managing Fails

However much the women tried to regulate the inflow of stuff, their restrictions were not enough to keep it at the low, sensible and manageable level they had initially intended – probably because this process was not merely about rationality, techniques and devices, but was happening in the midst of social and cultural currents and swirls of desire, of commercial culture. The inflow en masse started as soon as the baby was born. By the time the baby was a few months old, the women had acquired numerous things.

'I got a lot from friends and family', said Linda, 'a bunch of pacifiers ("binkies") and loads of clothes. I almost panicked.' She also had three bags of used baby clothes from her sister. In addition to gifts for Christening, Christmas and the first birthday, both grandmothers and even Linda bought 'month-birthday gifts' throughout the first year. There was a constant flow of baby stuff into the house, she wrote.

Although her daughter was only three months old at her first Christmas, she received more gifts than anyone else in the family, Anna told me: 'We could hardly get into the car, we had so much stuff with us on our way back home.' And on her first birthday the baby received 'a xylophone, a gray jacket and skirt, an Astrid Lindgren CD, puzzles, textile blocks, a basket of plastic fruit, a Hello Kitty backpack, a Pippi Longstocking doll and flag, four pairs of pajamas, soft cupcakes, Hello Kitty leggings and a Barbapapa walking bike'.

Potlatch and the Power of Cuteness

The myriad clothes and playthings that the babies received during their first year from parents, relatives (mainly grandmothers and aunts) and the mother's best friends can be understood in many ways. They can be conceived of as an almost constant potlatch, at which parents, grandparents and other relatives and friends 'burn' their excess money by buying gifts for the child, notably as a sign of affection and relationship-building; or, referring to Bataille (1949/1988), wasting excess energy, which is an inevitable part of any economy, on sumptuous consumption for the innocent child. Corvellec, in Chapter 10 in this volume, agrees with Bataille: destruction of excess is a necessary consequence of production. Buying for the child is fun, and a legitimate way to eliminate some of the steam built up by our desire to acquire, which is usually restrained in Sweden's Lutheran morality of moderation.

It is also obvious that clothes and toys provide an attraction. They are cute, small and soft, in lovely colours; and, resembling babies as they do, they are almost irresistible. The women had a difficult time tearing themselves away from storefronts with gorgeous little things, as sweet as candy – and as cheap as candy, too. As Rebecca said, 'I think little dresses are so cute, I just can't help myself, even though it is not the most practical item of clothing a child could use.' Their women friends fall for the cuteness of baby clothes as well. To quote Sara: 'When my friends buy clothes for her, I often hear "I bought this 'cause it was so CUTE".'

As becomes obvious from many of these quotes, cheap prices were definitely not an irrelevant factor in the purchasing of baby stuff. Michele Lee has argued that the market for garments is swamped with cheap clothes, which she refers to as 'McFashion'. These women would probably not agree with Lee's judgement that these clothes are 'unsatisfying, commonplace, and utterly forgettable' – the baby clothing equivalent of fast food (Lee, 2003). For them baby clothes represented value for money; their price and easy accessibility was definitely part of their attraction. Yet the metaphor is one of the candy store with a large variety of colourful, tasty and tempting items, rather than the standardized and easily consumed assortment of the fast-food restaurant. 'You really feel the urge. So, I close my eyes when I pass some of this stuff, because they are so cute; and they only cost 50, 70 SEK [€5, €7]. It's really cheap', Linda said.

Something similar can also happen regarding toys, although seldom as often or as intensely. Linda confided, for example, that the last time she went to Ullared (a huge shopping mall 100 kilometres from Gothenburg) she bought too many small plastic toys, attracted by the price, although she realized that her daughter would have fun with them for only 'five minutes'.

The women also bought more baby clothes and toys than necessary to satisfy their feelings of responsibility for the well-being of their children; some of them were uncertain about how to keep their babies warm in the winter and protect them from the sun in the summer. As Linda said about shopping for her daughter's first summer outfits: 'I bought a bunch of summer clothes, because they are so cute, and then I got the idea that she would probably have to have three shirts and three short sleeve bodysuits and many dresses'. Linda had imagined that her daughter would be sitting quietly, playing under a parasol wearing cute short-sleeved dresses. But that did not happen, of course. As soon as her daughter learned to crawl, she did not want to sit under a parasol at all, so she needed clothes that enabled her to move around, clothes that covered her body to protect her from the sun.

One way the women found to make the flow of things manageable while restraining their desire to shop (besides walking quickly past shop windows or not going downtown at all) was to distribute the gifts across the year – as in the month-birthday gifts from parents and grandparents. Anna told of another type of distribution: her best friend, who is also is the godmother of her daughter Olivia, and who desperately longed for a child herself, gave her a new collection of clothes for every size the baby grew out of the first year (besides presents for Christening, birthday and Christmas). To give the babies in-between presents on their name day – usually two or three – was another strategy to distribute desire and the flow of gifts.

MANAGING THE IN-BETWEEN: STORING, DISTRIBUTING AND CIRCULATING

The Skills

One of the lessons learned from the previous volume dedicated to managing overflow (Czarniawska and Löfgren, 2012) is that people do manage. Through routinization, they integrate and absorb new tasks, new skills, objects and ideas into their everyday lives (Löfgren, 2012; McCloskey, 2012). This was also true for the women in this study. They used various techniques to manage baby stuff in their homes, and said that they seldom felt overloaded. Anna, for example, told me that she never felt overloaded by children's stuff at home: 'Because I sort and divide the toys in boxes in different rooms, I don't experience this at all'. Anna's method can be regarded as physical categorization, as compared to the digital categorizations of the Excel list.

This compartmentalization is something Anna had in common with the rest of the women: they all stored baby stuff in boxes and distributed them all over the house – especially toy boxes. If the children of most people 100 years ago could be happy with a corner or a small box of their own, 50 years ago a room shared with their siblings, and the last 30 years or so their own room to keep their things, today there are boxes with playthings and children's play corners in every room of the house, even for babies. As Anna told me:

> Olivia plays mostly in her room in the morning. She has a small kitchenette in the room that she likes. There she also has a box of toys and a shelf for toys. Then I have a large box of toys in the living room and a doll and doll carriage. I have a toy box in the TV room, too. I vary the contents of the boxes from time to time, so Olivia won't be playing with the same toys all the time.

Kajsa told of a similar situation:

> We have some toys in a basket here [the kitchen]. And we have a basket in the living room, and a play blanket. And then in his room there are small barrels with toys. So at any time we can produce something new, and it works for a while. And this weekend, we will prepare his room, buying a shelf at IKEA. And then we'll set up some toys there so he can go there spontaneously and play with them. He prefers to be where we are.

Anthropologists have frequently noted the importance of keeping the baby stuff in the right place to prevent feelings of overload and chaos. As Lynn Åkesson (2012: 146) has remarked: 'Just what is the right place is a result of cultural conditioning and varies with time, space, and social affiliations. But, generally speaking, there is an overhanging threat of chaos when things become homeless or end up in the wrong place.' In her study of the handling of waste, Åkesson demonstrated that new orders are established in order to manage the large amounts of trash that threatens to overflow. The same goes for toys in these women's stories. New orders were established whereby children's toys were neatly placed in boxes and corners in every room of the apartment; at least they look neat and tidy in Figures 12.2 and 12.3, before the children started playing with them or when they were tidied up in the evening after the children had gone to sleep.

Figure 12.2 In the corner of Kajsa's living room; her son Otto was then eight months old

As can be witnessed in the quotes from these women, they prevented the overflow of baby stuff by keeping it in constant circulation – the opposite of framing, a managing technique discussed in Czarniawska and Löfgren's (2012) first book on the management of overflow. The main point was that the stuff must be used. Overflow, according to these women, happened when there were heaps of clothes that the baby had never worn or mountains of toys that the baby had never played with. The trick was to keep these items in constant circulation so everything had the opportunity to be used at least once.

The women agreed that it was stressful if there was not enough time to use all the baby's clothes before the baby outgrew them or they were out of season. To prevent this from happening, they kept changing the baby's clothes – not merely when they were dirty. Every day the baby appeared in new outfits. As Linda told me: 'Mum said that "You've got different constellations on her every day". But I said she had to use the clothes.'

Regarding toys, the trick was to spread them in boxes in every room of the apartment, and to change the contents of the boxes so that it was enough for the child to handle – that there were always new things to attract the child and that every toy was played with, at least for a while.

Figure 12.3 *Left: Assembly of toys for Olivia, 11 months, in the TV room; right: Olivia's room with stove and cupboard*

Cultural Ideals and Learning the Skills to Handle Overflow

Underlying the mothers' practices are ideas of children, toys, clothes and motherhood. Clothes should be soft and functional and should keep the child comfortable (not too warm, not too cold); but they should also be desirable for the mother: cute, trendy and fashionable. And children should be amused. Toys are needed to amuse the child, but also to foster the child's development, and they are also vessels of nostalgia for the parents. Nostalgia is certainly one of the reasons for the heroic status of Sophie la Girafe in France. So whether or not the parents had Sophies as children, Sophie la Girafe has an aura of nostalgia connected to her.

During their babies' infancy, mothers can dress them in any clothes they want to, without the child protesting. Before long this cooperativeness will give away to the increasing agency of the child, who demands clothes of special colours and styles. Toys are a bit trickier from the beginning, because playing requires agency even for these young children. The child must like the toys and be interested in playing with them or they will be ignored. Consequently, these mothers were eager to learn about the toys that are likely to be enjoyed by children of a certain age, and they often ended up with the same toys as the children of their friends had. Each mother also watched intensively to learn what her baby liked to play with when visiting friends or at the open preschool. As Anna said, 'What is Olivia playing with at the open preschool or with friends? What does she think is fun? That's mostly what guides me.'

From these practices, children learn specific competencies: how to handle the constant tide of things flowing through their lives, how to use toys and clothes for only a brief period and then move to new ones. When I met with some of these mothers after the fieldwork, when their children were approximately 18 months old, they told me that one of their children's favourite activities was changing clothes. That children of that age like to try their motor skills by putting on trousers and jumpers on their own is nothing new. But that clean clothes should be changed for new ones directly from the wardrobe is clearly not an innate characteristic. As Orvar Löfgren writes in this volume, these skills are basically about forgetting, letting go and not committing oneself too much. This is also something I noticed in a study of children's birthday parties at McDonald's (Brembeck, 2007). After the party, there were many half-eaten burgers and boxes of fries on the tables and heaps of trash on the floor, with little evidence that the children cared about the mess that was being left behind. This attitude of negligence could be interpreted as the behaviour of spoilt children, and compliant staff and parents. From the perspective of overflow management, however, it emerges as a pivotal technique for handling everyday life in a society overflowing with objects. As we can see from this study, this competence is learned at a very young age.

But just as the children at McDonald's could easily switch to dedicating themselves to things of importance to them, so did these babies (and their mothers). The babies had tattered favourite stuffed toys or blankets that followed them around wherever they went. The women also found this behaviour to be natural, and encouraged their babies to connect to certain stuff. The competence of getting emotionally involved in and clinging to certain stuff was important to the mothers, and they also had favourite toys or children's garments that they wanted to keep.

Managing Outflows

When they felt that there was really too much stuff around, the first thing the women did was to pack things into bags or boxes and store them in attics and basements. To begin with, it was mostly clothes the babies had outgrown, but also the first baby toys such as comforters and rattles. As Rebecca said:

> Every time Hedda grew out of a clothing size, I usually washed all the clothes of that size and put them in one or more bags that I marked with the size and then put in a removal box that is in the attic. I am already on the second removal box, so she has obviously used a lot of clothes since she was born… I have no thought of selling them yet, because we are planning for a sibling to Hedda. I am happy to lend them to friends from time to time, however, should they need them. After a potential sibling, I can well imagine selling most of the clothes at, for example, Blocket or Tradera and save only a few favourite pieces, or perhaps, more likely, give them to friends or to my sister.

'That's a tricky question', said Malin, in response to my question about what happens when they find out that there are too many toys around: 'From time to time, not too often, we clean up Otto's toys, throw away whatever is half broken, pack away what he has been playing with for a long time and store them in a box in the attic. Now we have a small warehouse in the attic.' So things were saved for the next child. Another preferred route was saving stuff for friends and relatives, especially sisters. Yet another common way to do away with stuff was to sell them at Blocket or Tradera. To return to the metaphor of filtering, there was a great deal of peer and cultural filtering going on before passing certain items on to Blocket or Tradera.

At a first glance, these practices seem almost identical to what has been described before. English geographer Nicky Gregson showed how family members inherit some stuff, other things are thrown away and yet others end up at charity organizations (Gregson, 2011; Åkesson, 2012). She also demonstrated that there are special routes or channels for clothes. They often go by the relatives channel. Only if they have no receiver among relatives, are they given to secondhand sales or charitable organizations. Worn or tattered clothes are thrown in the trash (Gregson, 2011). To some extent, the women in this study adhere to this system. Linda did not feel right selling clothes at Blocket, although she planned to dispose of other baby equipment that way: 'I have a little nostalgia with clothes,' she told me. 'I feel I'd rather give them to friends.' And Anna admitted that she would never buy clothes that had been worn by someone she did not know. Clothes were personal. Sara's reason for not selling clothes at Blocket was more prosaic: 'You don't get much money for clothes at Blocket, and it's too much trouble going to the post office etc.' So she saved a pile and gave it away to a women's home close to where she lived. Rebecca, Kajsa and Malin, on the other hand, and in fact most of the 14 women in this study, readily bought and sold children's clothes at Blocket and similar sites – not just overalls and boots, but more intimate clothes such as onesies, pants and jumpers. As Malin said, 'We bought cheap pants and shirts on Tradera from brands like MiniRodini, Polarn o Pyret, Småfolk and Katvig. When I was shopping in a store, it was in Åhléns, Lindex, KappAhl. Then it's mostly small purchases such as socks.'

All the brands Malin mentioned are for fashionable children's clothes. Katvig, for example, is a Danish company manufacturing children's organic fashion clothing. To some extent, two approaches to secondhand goods appeared: an older approach, by which secondhand clothes were considered tainted by their former user and difficult to relate to; and a newer approach by which sites like Blocket were viewed in the same way as any shop with easy access to a never-ending assortment of branded quality clothes at a good price.

Making Money on the Net

This exposé of inflows, throughflows and outflows of stuff during the baby's first year begins and ends at the Internet. The digital market for baby stuff and sites such as Tradera, Blocket and Loppi.se (a site recommended by the women), has specific importance as the enabling 'device', 'machine' or 'place' that maintains the circulation of stuff. The market for secondhand goods is often considered the end station for objects in the chain from acquisition to use and divestment. Listening to the women in this project and reading their stories, it became obvious that Internet sites were largely where it all happened, it was 'the' market for baby stuff. The women were equally likely to buy and to sell stuff on the Internet. In the final section of this chapter, two aspects of the digital market are briefly touched upon: the quality of the stuff, and a seemingly new and more commercial mentality among young parents with regard to becoming a trader and earning money on the Internet.

From a perspective suggested by Michel Callon (1998b) and elaborated upon in this volume in Chapters by 5 and 6 by Norén and Tarim, the buy-and-sell sites can be considered the result of an overflowing market of baby stuff. It is because there are so many nearly new items available that this market can flourish. It is notable that the things bought and sold on the Internet are nearly new and in extremely good condition, as a look at Loppi.se. makes obvious. Things for sale are also often branded: 'If you are looking for a diaper bag from Skip Hop, an ergonomic baby carrier from ERGObaby, a baby sitter from Baby Bjorn or other practical item for your child, then you have come to the right place!'[7] There is an upsurge of nearly new items sold for a reasonable price on the site (see Figures 12.4 and 12.5 for examples). Many of them have never been used:

- Brand new and not previously packed up feeding chair from Baby Bjorn (€160).
- Baby nest washed once – otherwise like new (€30).
- Completely unused breastfeeding pillow (could not breastfeed) for twins (€55).
- Go-to-toilet seat with bar code left and used only a few times (€5).
- Completely unused Nike trainers, size 20 (€5).[8]

Figure 12.4 Blue baby cardigan size 74 (275 SEK; €2.75); completely unused, the price tag still attached (price in store: 700 SEK; €7)

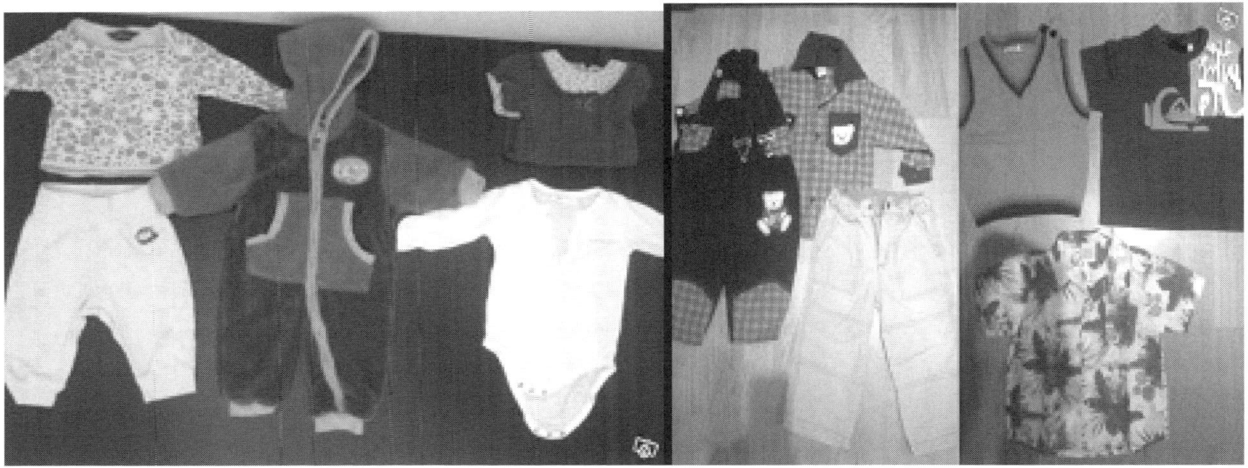

Figure 12.5 *Left: Clothes package designer clothes, girl size 62/68: set with pink shirt (Oilily) and matching pink shorts (Alfie Atkins), outerwear, fleece-lined suit (Me Too), two bodysuits with long sleeves, white and brown/pink (200 SEK; €2). Right: Coat package set, bib and matching shirt, size 80 (Linus & Lotta), pants, khaki (POP), size 80 pullover, pink (Name It). Size 80 T-shirt, gray (Quicksilver), size 1 year; Hawaiian shirt, size 1 year (120 SEK; €1.2)*

It is also because of the overflowing market of baby stuff that women are inspired to start their own blogs or buy-and-sell sites. New Internet sites for buying, selling, bartering, lending and swapping are sometimes regarded as expressions of an alternative economic system, and part of what has been named 'collaborative consumption'. Activists and spokespersons Botsman and Rogers (2010) describe how collaborative consumption is about creating value from shared and open resources through such methods as swap trading, time banks, local exchange trading systems (LETS), bartering, social lending, clothing swaps and toy sharing. It is difficult, however, to see the Internet trading that the women are involved in and sites such as Blocket, Tradera or Loppi as part of this movement; basically these mothers are interested in making and saving money. As Kajsa said, 'We saw it as an investment to buy a good pram. We figured if we buy a good, new pram we can use it for the next child. And because the resale value of prams is high, we thought we could always sell it if we don't want it any more.'

The two young mothers who created Loppi.se obviously regarded their site as a way of making money for themselves and others. In a newspaper interview, one of them stated that she and her business partner wanted to run a profitable business, even if they were not quite there yet. They started Loppi because they themselves could not find 'a niche site where families can do good business with a clear conscience' (*Göteborgs-Posten*, 31 October 2010).

Marketing Stuff Online

The young women in my study are not merely consumers (buyers and users) of things for the baby; they are also marketers and retailers. It obviously requires training to learn these skills, and Loppi.se is there to give a helping hand. The site provides a crash course on online marketing and ways of producing an attractive and saleable ad. The user is reminded that every word in the ad is searchable; therefore, it is valuable to have an informative header that allows the buyer to find the item. Trademarks are key: 'A trademark can be attractive – sometimes a Baby Bear harness sell better than "just" a baby carrier'. Loppi.se also advises the user to keep the ad text short:

> Be relatively brief: describe clearly what it is you are selling, but no essay writing. It is not the most important thing in the world, for example, to find out why you are selling. 'Now, my youngest daughter has outgrown her first skates that she got for Christmas from her grandmother two years ago.' Hello? Is the ad reader still there?[9]

Moreover there are pricing tips and photo tips. A photo of items to sell can be the difference between getting them sold or having them remain in storage; many buyers sift out ads without photos, Loppi.se warns. Photos should be sharp, with visible details and a clean background. Gadgets should be photographed individually. But if the prospective seller has many small clothes to sell, the advice is to photograph a composite package of the clothes, nicely displayed. It obviously requires the learning of skills and techniques to become a versatile user of the digital baby stuff market.

As I see it, the quality of the stuff and the money-making aspect are key reasons for the central position of the Internet and sites such as Tradera, Blocket and Loppi in the circulation of baby stuff. For some people, the monetary aspect may be more important than other factors, and for some the critical issue is getting rid of stuff. But all in all this combination of abundance, the joy of cute stuff, digital technology and commerce, is what makes the baby stuff world go round, the stuff never piling up and parents not being overwhelmed. On the other hand, if these mothers did not involve themselves in this constant managing of stuff they would soon be overloaded and lose control. It is not merely an offer or a fun game; it is a necessity for handling everyday life, motherhood and babyhood in the commercial culture.

CONCLUSION

I have demonstrated in this chapter how young mothers are engaged in continuous and time-consuming work to manage inflows and outflows of baby stuff, and have shown that this work is necessary in order to maintain control and prevent overflow in the home. But this process is also highly social and cultural, happening as it does in the midst of commercial culture. I have also demonstrated the importance of the digital market of buy, barter and sell sites on the Internet. Preventing overflow is basically about maintaining the circulation of things, never allowing stuff to pile up in unused heaps, and preserving the baby's interest in a never-ending supply of new things – which turns out to be an essential prerequisite to handling life in affluent societies. In order to accomplish this task, the parents must acquire all the skills mentioned by Löfgren in Chapter 14 in this volume: skimming and skipping, developing scan paths, and more. New forms of economic activity on the Internet are a prerequisite – forms generated by the overflowing market. Some events in the lives of these young mothers clearly belonged to the moral economy (Jackson et al., 2001): investing emotionally only in specific, selected items, such as the pram, and allowing others to flow through their lives with little investment; or enjoying something, like cute little baby clothes, for a short while, then letting go – competencies learned from a young age. These skills and technologies form assemblages through which new identities for stuff and new ways of being a consumer can be performed. My basic argument is that these handling techniques and the expansion of the new, largely consumer-driven market require an understanding of production and consumption as inseparable. Consumers produce, producers consume, consumers become retailers, marketers and producers produce for themselves (Löfgren and Czarniawska, 2012).

NOTES

1. Open preschool organizes free, open activities for children 0–5 years old who are not attending kindergarten. The staff organizes activities, but parents are responsible for their children. Children are not enrolled; rather the parents choose when and how often they want to participate. Open preschools are popular, and serve as regular meeting places for parents and their babies during parental leave, which lasts for 18 months in Sweden.
2. The women represented 'inner-city mums', but were socio-economically diverse. They represented a wide variety of professions: child minder, administrator, teacher and designer with an academic degree.
3. I recognize that many fathers play a large role in their babies' lives, including the purchasing of stuff, and if it appears in this chapter that mothers are these babies' only parents, it is because it was mothers I worked with in this study.
4. Blocket started in 1996 as a regional digital market for gadgets for Scania. As of 2012, the Norwegian media group Schibsted owns Blocket; it is the largest buy-and-sell site in Sweden and the third-largest media site in all categories. Blocket reaches about 4 million unique visitors a week; 95 per cent of Sweden's population know of Blocket and nearly seven out of ten Swedes have bought or sold something on Blocket (http://www.blocket.se/omblocket.htm).
5. Tradera is one of Sweden's leading buy-and-sell sites, with over 2.5 million members in 2011. Tradera was founded in 1999 by Kaplan's Auctions, but was purchased by the international e-commerce group, eBay, in 2006. Tradera was initially an auction site, but is now an e-commerce site for both private and commercial operators, where they can buy both new and secondhand items via auction or fixed price (http://sv.wikipedia.org/wiki/Tradera).
6. All first-time parents in Sweden are invited to attend parents' group meetings at maternity care centres during their pregnancy and the first months after the delivery. It is usually the mothers who meet, especially during the first months after delivery, when it is the mother who most often stays at home. But groups of fathers sometimes continue to meet during the last part of the parental leave, when they are often the ones in charge of their babies.

7.–9. Loppi.se, accessed 27 August 2012.

FIELD MATERIAL

Göteborgs-Posten (2010), 'Guide till begagnat på nätet', 31 October.
http://en.wikipedia.org/wiki/Sophie_the_Giraffe, accessed 27 October 2012.
http://www.lollopard.se/Shop/ProductList.aspx?ProductID=8d825563-d9c8-469b-ae67-a435c92d965c, accessed 29 October 2012.

13. Lost in the archive: the business historian in distress

Susanna Fellman and Andrew Popp

Perhaps the most commented upon example of overflow in contemporary society is in relation to information. Informational overload is often associated with our own digital era but the proliferation of information as a key marker of modernity was presaged in and led by the industrial revolutions of the nineteenth century and the giant corporations to which those revolutions gave birth. In *Control through Communication: The Rise of System in American Management* (1989), JoAnne Yates traced how firms in key industries, such as services, transport, utilities and manufacturing, were enabled in their growth by new densities, volumes, genres and technologies of information (and its communication) that knitted together and coordinated organizations of unparalleled scale, scope, complexity and ambition. Information, produced and made increasingly storable and retrievable by a dizzying onrush of technological change and development, itself became a key technology. Corporations were to an extent defined and made (or broken) by their control (or lack of it) over information. But this proliferation of information has a dark side. As a manager once reported to one of the current authors, 'I am swamped in information but starved of data.' Mixing metaphors of both surfeit and dearth, this is a powerful image of a peculiarly modern condition; the possibility of knowing too much. Is this a condition that might afflict the historian – especially the historians of those very corporations?

In historical research, scarcity of empirical sources and archival material is the most common problem. This is particularly the case the further we go back in history. It is no surprise that it has been primarily historians of the medieval and the early modern period who have been interested in the question of sources, source criticism and how to combine fragments of sources of very different kinds into a compelling and convincing narrative. Historians of more recent periods of time occasionally run across the problem that there is ample archival material, but not the material that enables them to answer the research question at hand.

In business history, which is also usually focused on more contemporary periods of time, the problem might be of another type, however. Given the developments in information technologies and the growth of corporations as large-scale, enduring and highly bureaucratized organizations, business archives, especially private archives of big firms which have existed over a long period of time, are often extensive. As a result there might be an abundance of material and the business historian is overwhelmed by sources, swamped with information. We are not the first to identify this phenomenon. Kobrak and Schneider describe a 'paradoxical dilemma of having too many and too few sources' (2011: 411). However, we want to go further in exploring both what this dilemma means and how it is met. It is a dilemma, we would suggest, that might be experienced as a distressing phenomenon, in which control slips away – historians have spoken to us of their emotions on confronting large archives, emotions that can include panic even – just as the modern citizen sometimes feels control slipping away amidst a plethora of consumer goods or social network interactions. At the same time, time schedules in the archive are often limited, especially in the case of commissioned histories but also increasingly so in scholarly research. Thus, the business historian has to deal with questions such as: how might we handle this amount of material, without losing the focus? How can we go about selecting material in a systematic fashion? How are we to select the (most) relevant material, or even to know what is (most) relevant?

In this chapter we are concerned, first, with the archival practices of business historians. To an extent these practices are merely pragmatic – in the sense that they are a way of coping – but, more fundamentally, we contend that they also reflect a series of underlying biases or normative positions within the discipline. Thus, these practices are not just a question of 'tactics' or even of 'strategy' but, more fundamentally, of forms of knowledge. Historians are used to working inductively from sources and within realist or naturalistic paradigms. They begin with the rooted, the local and the specific and look out only tentatively towards larger patterns; they are cautious about generalization, modelling and theory and are as apt to emphasize contingency, specificity and change as they are continuity and the universally applicable. It is commonly thought that historians begin with the sources and not the question. However, today many historians are also driven by research questions, but especially within business history, due to its closeness to neighbouring social sciences and particularly business and organizational studies, it is more common to start from scientifically motivated research questions and then proceed to search for suitable archival and other empirical material that can help answer the questions at hand. Thus, as against some historians in other subdisciplines, the stance might be reversed; we might begin with the question and then go in search of the data. Nevertheless, the availability of sources and the empirical evidence is always guiding the work and the research process of the historian.

In this chapter we will deal with the question of how business historians go about their work in this situation of 'swamping'. We will also confront the issue of how they understand the work they do. So, for example, do they still adhere to a notion of the 'historian's craft', in line with work of Marc Bloch (1954) and others? We adopt two tactics. First, we study a sample of business history publications in order to analyse how the authors have dealt with this issue in practice, studying their use of sources and their reflections, if any, on sources and methods. Second, we interview a small sample of business historians with experience of archival work, about their own work practices. These interviews focus on both pragmatic and strategic questions of doing large scale archive work as well as on more fundamental epistemological questions. Indeed, one important question might be the extent to which business history confronts these issues at all, either explicitly or implicitly through its practices. Thus our research focuses on the question of how historians researching in large corporate archives work to produce historical knowledge in a context of overflow. We take this to be, in some ways, quite a practical question – a matter of practices – but believe those practices reflect underlying epistemological positions. A second set of questions begins to open up those positions. This work is important because, we contend, the discipline of business history has been reluctant to reflect on its sources, methods and epistemology. Without this work the claims we make for the knowledge we produce may remain unclear, particularly to others.

SOURCES AND METHODS

We are both established business historians. We thus draw on our existing knowledge of the business history literature in formulating the arguments presented here. Moreover, between us we have held a range of editorial and institutional positions allowing an overview of recent developments across the field. One may think of this as equivalent to the deep contextualizing knowledge that the historian 'naturally' develops in relation to their area of specialism. We also draw on fresh empirical work, which we briefly describe here. This empirical research, designed to be neither exhaustive nor conclusive but instead exploratory and indicative, has two dimensions. First, we have undertaken a bibliometric survey of four of the leading English language journals in the field of business history: *Business History* (BH), *Business History Review* (BHR), *Enterprise and Society* (E&S) and *Management and Organizational History*. Taking the last five complete volumes (for example, 2007–2011) we surveyed published research articles, searching for explicit discussion of sources used and research methodology. Our judgement as to whether an article did or did not include discussion of these issues was kept informal and subjective. The bar was not set high. Articles did not need dedicated, headed sources or methods sections in order to qualify. Dissertation summaries, review articles and articles based on specific symposiums were excluded, but articles from special issues were included. The period covered is perhaps too short to show any meaningful trends over time but does cover years during which the discipline's institutional shift towards schools of business and management intensified. Moreover, three of the four journals (BH, BHR and E&S) experienced changes of editorial leadership in this period and published statements that set out both editorial positions and overviews of the current state of the art and likely future directions.

Second, we have conducted interviews with five active business historians. These took the form of semi-structured face-to-face interviews. All interviews were taped and subsequently transcribed. These interviews aimed to develop an understanding of the particular historian's practical approaches to archival work. Third, the interviews moved on to a consideration of underlying epistemological principles, and in particular the relationship between the archive and the research question or topic. Here we begin to approach to the core of the practice of historical research as a discipline. Are we driven in the first instance by the archive or by a question or theoretical position? From this point the interviews moved on to consider, third, the subjects' understandings of what it is to be a (business) historian, how they came to that understanding in their own careers, and what (if any) sort of training they received both as a historian and specifically in how to work in an archive. In this last area we aimed to get at whether business historians share either a tacit sense of the so-called historical method or any sort of professional identity.

The selection of candidates for interview relied on the authors' personal contacts and thus was not by any means random. Nonetheless, our sampling aimed to identify a group varied in age, length of career and seniority, gender, nationality and research interest. We have anonymized our interviewees in line with social science practice. Once transcribed, the interviews have been treated much as we would approach other source documents and have not been subject to formal methods of content or discourse analysis. Our sources and methods could thus be summarized as qualitative, triangulated and interpretive – appropriate for an exploratory piece of research aimed at a first mapping of an underdeveloped research domain, namely the working practices of professional business historians.

PROBLEMATIZING THE ARCHIVE(S)

For the historian, the archive is the key place in their search for sources – even a place of dreams where they can discover records and voices that have been hidden or lost (Giles, 1996; Steedman, 1998, 2011). Part of the thrill of the historian is to make these long-lost voices speak. While non-historians perhaps consider the archives as unexciting and dusty places, and the slow work with the documents tedious, the archive is for many historians a place where they feel at home or feel a sense of belonging (Steedman, 1998; Bradley, 1999). The historian can also suffer from an 'archival fever', in the words of Jacques Derrida (1995: 6). Although Derrida's notion relates to the broader phenomenon of the memories and experiences of human nature, especially in relation to the psychoanalytic process, the historian often find a similar fundamental need – or obsession – to reach back to the origin, where everything started, before the archive; to 'the absolute commencement' where it all began (Derrida, 1995: 91; for interpretation see Steedman, 2001: 4–6). However, an irreducible historical past is as inaccessible as the human mind 'before the archive' (memories, feelings, experiences). Moreover, it is inaccessible not only because only traces remain in the archive, but also because the process of accessing it is not available to us. Whether the historian considers the archive a necessity, or a place of dreams, the archive becomes over the years a familiar place, and when the historian goes to the archive they often sense, beside familiarity or happiness, also that 'soon there will be some work done'.

Archives are important places also for business historians, but business historians are seldom 'archive fetishists'. Archival material is rarely considered superior to other types of material and many business historians work with, for example, statistics, newspapers, diaries and memoirs, pictures and audiovisual material, interviews and so on, making the archive only one type of material. Nonetheless, the business archive is important for most business historians.

But what is an archive and what role does it play in the creation of historical knowledge and narratives? The archive is commonly understood as a place for storage of documents, but also as the actual collection of documents within. Thus, it is both an institution and the content of this institution. An archive, however, is not only an accumulation of papers, but a result of active creation or collection, even if the documents in the archive have not been created for the purpose of being archived. Thus, not all collections of documents or other records of human activity constitute an archive. On the other hand, in order to be 'an archive', the place does not have to be well organized, with professional archivists employed. Archives can be both messy and unorganized. Moreover, some archives, especially private business archives, are not neat collections, systematically deposited into one particular place of storage – a feature familiar to many business historians and especially those who write about small companies. The various documents the scholar has to hunt for in the company managers' offices or in corridors and basements can certainly be considered as constituting the company's archive. Finally, the digitalization of archives and documents challenges the whole idea of what an archive is, and especially the archive of a physical place with documents stored in one place (cf. Burton, 2005: 2).

This obviously raises the question of what conditions need to be met in order for something to be considered an archive and not a mixed heap of documents. A related question is the source of the authority given to 'official' archives in comparison to documents kept outside such sanctioned archives (Blair and Milligan, 2007).

Thus, when talking about archives, one often thinks of the site of official government records (Blair and Milligan, 2007; Featherstone, 2006). The history of the archive is also to a great extent the history of public records. Throughout history, however, private individuals and organizations have also established places for the storage of documents created by their activities. So archives are important sites for creating both national and corporate memory (Steedman, 1998; Bradley, 1999; Deserno, 2009). At the same time, the archive cannot be studied without raising the question of power over history and over memory. Or vice versa; as Jacques Derrida noted, 'there is no political power without control of the archive, if not of memory' (Derrida, 1995: 4, footnote 1).

However, the archive also has important symbolic or metaphoric meanings to historians. It is not simply a place or thing in which or through which work can be done. Some scholars distinguish between 'the archive' in the singular and 'the archives' in the plural. The archive is used as a metaphor, symbolizing human knowledge, memory, identity and so on. The archives are the actual organizations containing documents and records. This distinction is especially made by those that want to problematize the archives, and they argue that archives are not passive storehouses of documents, but are sites of power and agency, where the content has been interfered with, both by its creators and by the – allegedly neutral – archivists. Similarly, business historian Stephanie Decker, working within a post-colonial framing, pointed to differentiation between pragmatic and Foucauldian definitions of archives, namely between masses of 'materials specifically collected for the purpose of preserving a history and housed in a distinct location' as against a 'poststructuralist definition of an *archive* as a complex system of embedded rules that determines the production of knowledge'. Knowledge, in other words, is not neutral. Within postcolonial history and subaltern studies that production of knowledge would often be held to involve the 'othering' or silencing of particular voices marginalized within or completely excluded from the archive. Thus, however cumbersome the 'archive/*archive*' distinction, as acknowledged by Decker, it does at least alert us to how power is inscribed in the archive. As Decker observes, 'the sensemaking and storying of the historians begins in the archive, not in the construction of the narrative on the page' (Decker, 2012: 6).

Thus, though the scholar often looks at their engagement with the archive from a relatively technical point of view: trying to cope with the lack of some documents or information – or with a massive amount of relevant material – it is essential to recognize that the archives are constructed by someone and that the preservation of archival material is not accidental. There was for long among archivists a positivist view of the archive. That is, the documents have come about as a result of 'natural' processes and activities, not from the perspective of some outside reader; and, moreover, that they reflect these activities accurately and in a neutral way (Trace, 2002). However, this is not correct. As Carolyn Steedman noted, the archive can be both 'a consciously chosen documentation of the past' and a 'mad fragmentation that no one intended to preserve' (Steedman, 2001: 66). Although it is the historian who selects what becomes important for their narrative, the selection and organization of the archive and the record is not irrelevant. The archive itself, its content, its construction and the (re)arranging of its material, influences the work of the historian and their questions and interpretations. They are not neutral arenas, consisting of objective 'historical facts' which existed prior to interpretation, or unproblematic storehouses of records awaiting the historians, but are sites of agency and power reflecting the needs and desires of their creators (Trouillot, 1997; Bradley, 1999; Trace, 2002; Cook, 2009).

Moreover, the archives are important for both creating remembrance and forgetting. It is not the case that all the material which is in the archive will ever be read: 'The act of rendering memorable does not mean that at any stage it will be remembered' (Bowker, 2006: 12). At the same time, as Derrida noted, the process of archivization 'produces as much as it records the event' (Derrida, 1995: 17). Thus, the ordering and classification actually also classifies the remembering (Bowker, 2006: 13).

It is also interesting to dwell for a moment on the nature of the archive in relation to the metaphors and insights framing the much wider project of which this chapter is just one small part. As Löfgren and Czarniawska (2012) point out, the term 'overflow' necessarily invokes metaphors and images of flow, fluidity, change, flood and flux. In contrast the archive seems to have a stilling effect – often literally, archives being notably still and silent places. The flow of historical time is stilled and stopped, pools form, sediment sinks and accumulates. It is no surprise that Steedman (2001) entitled her meditation on the archive *Dust* – they are places where layers build up, again both literally and metaphorically. This is important because in imposing boundary conditions (like the dams that enclose a mill pond so that this pooling and settling can take place and power be stored and harnessed) the archive becomes a framing device, an everyday practice of routinization and coping. In becoming a place 'out of time', the things stored are stored because their time has elapsed and been completed; the archive can become part of what Löfgren and Czarniawska called the cultural dynamics of the overflow dramatization. The archive helps us to hold back the threat of the flood.

These questions are particularly important for scholars meeting the 'overflowing' archives from which, out of necessity, a considerable share of the material will most likely already have been cleared out and the rest has been organized and classified according to categorizations not chosen by the historian and potentially now opaque or lost. Records in archives of big organizations – like corporate archives – have, as a rule, been consciously collected (or not collected) for various reasons. These archives are often considered as reflecting the hierarchical structures of the organization, and so the bureaucratic and the hierarchical order are preserved in the archival structure. The archivist and the archival system often created orders and hierarchies out of apparent chaos and the ad hoc. Moreover, material from activities which were considered most significant is more likely to be preserved, while material from activities seen as marginal or peripheral may be and often is simply destroyed. Going further, deliberate silences may be created where activities, behaviours, discussions or decisions might be considered sensitive, perhaps unethical, or even shameful. Only what has been stored can be located, and thus the voices which are allowed to speak to the historian are often already selected (Bradley, 1999) – they are typically those that in life were also the most privileged, as much within corporations as within colonial societies. However, the degree of significance was of course always from somebody's perspective. In the business archives, for example, managerial records from the head office are seen as of more importance than materials produced in more remote departments. Thus, it also important to consider when visiting abundant archives what is not to be found. Even in the corporate archives in Western capitalism voices have been silenced, but those silences might be particularly difficult to observe, due to the seemingly 'completeness' of the archive. Do business historians recognize these issues, and if so, how do they confront them?

OUT OF THE ARCHIVE AND BACK IN AGAIN: AN 'ARCHIVAL TURN' IN BUSINESS HISTORY?

Within history there has been what could be considered a revival of evidence proper and source criticism (for a review, see Rahikainen and Fellman, 2012b). Carolyn Steedman has talked about an 'archival turn' within the field (2011).[1] One reason for this 'turn' is obviously a counter reaction to other 'turns', not least the linguistic turn. However, several important events during recent decades have also restored the archive to its central place within the history field. Antoinette Burton (2005) gives as an example some notable cases of plagiarism in the US, which have made documentation of sources and proper referencing a key virtue. More importantly, however, as Wolfgang Ernst (2008) argues, significant political transformations during the last decades have stimulated a debate about the politics of the archive. In Europe this was most notable in the case of the STASI archives after the fall of the iron curtain, but similar cases of political changes and the opening up of new archives have enabled or demanded reinterpretations of other national histories. Obviously, these occurrences have also concretely led to access to new sources for historians with less spectacular tasks. Nevertheless, it can even be claimed that archival research is a little fashionable.

Although most historians would claim they were never out of the archive, the archive as the empirical foundation of research and the 'historian's basic craft' are again a focus of discussion. As part of this revival it is argued that the historian should not conceal the rules of the games followed, but instead openly declare the process by means of which history is constructed, 'by showing both the fruitful paths and the dead-ends, the manner in which questions were formulated and answers sought' (Levi, 2012: 124–5).

In business history there is currently something of a 'historical turn' (Jones and Khanna, 2006; Popp, 2009; Decker, 2012). But, contrary to other historians, business historians are seldom very explicit about their sources or how they have selected and processed their empirical material – they have been largely absent from the debate on the 'archival turn'. One reason is perhaps that the empirical foundation for business history – the business archive itself – is taken as self-evident. The abundance of material also makes the single piece of evidence less valuable than in cases where archive material is very scanty. The support for conclusions is, from the scholar's point of view, overwhelming. As a result, the need for explicitly explaining how material has been gathered, systematized, processed and analysed is not considered important or necessary.

Another reason for this neglect may lie in the business history community itself. Discussion within the field has long focused on the need for theoretical rigour and an urge to move beyond the isolated narrative case study; in the process the question of methods has been sidelined in favour of a preoccupation with 'theory'. There has also been a growing tension around the direction in which business history should go: should it be a subfield to economic history (applying economic theory), or should it shift towards management and organization studies, borrowing concepts, theories and methods from this field (Forum, 2009)? In either case, there has been little imperative to question the positivist epistemology that is held to by many business historians. Finally, a third reason might be a very practical one, namely the increasing tendency within the field to write articles, which does not allow for lengthy discussions of sources and methods.

We want to stress that we do not doubt the empirical rigour of the vast majority of business history writing. But we do argue that business history has a strong tendency to naturalize the archive – or the empirical sources more broadly – and, in turn, the relationship between the archive and the historical narratives created from it. Is this refusal to problematize the archive actually problematic? If business historians are doing careful, painstaking archival work, then is that not enough? Perhaps not always. Unquestioning attitudes to notions of objective truth might see business history confined to acting as a supplier of useful applied cases illustrative of theory developed elsewhere in the academy. We have also already seen that the archive is a socially constructed artefact containing biases, gaps and silences. Thus the archive needs to be problematized through recognition of it as a place through which power is embedded and transmitted (Trouillot, 1997). To naturalize the archive and its contents as a neutral repository of documents directly representative of an/the objective truth is to fail to engage with many possible questions, as convincingly demonstrated by Hansen (2012). Only on rare occasions, such as in the case of corporations accused of complicity with the Nazi regime, have business historians been forced into a consideration of these issues – and at the same time into a renewed and refreshed relationship with the archive. Similarly those business historians working with foci once seen as relatively marginal to the field (such as gender, race or post-colonialism) are often also those who point us to the need for a less easy or unquestioning relationship with the archive and its contents.

SO, WHAT HAVE THE BUSINESS HISTORIANS BEEN UP TO?

As Kobrak and Schneider would have it, 'One of the primary tasks of an historian is to be aware and explain to his reader how he came to believe what he thinks he knows' (2011: 410). Do business historians fulfil this task and responsibility, and if so, how do they do it? It soon becomes apparent there is little consensus. Per Hansen (2012) was clear that 'Historians use all sorts of empirical evidence, and the determinant for what kind of evidence we use and how we use it is our research question', while Decker was equally clear that history 'as a discipline has a methodology of reconstruction from archival material'. Hansen and Decker are both experienced and thoughtful researchers who have reflected on the nature of business history's relationship to sources and archives and yet they disagree on this fundamental point. In another answer, Franco Amatori (who was frank enough to 'admit that I am not one of those people who becomes ecstatic when the word "archives" is pronounced… I do not like archives and would much prefer to sit in my library and read books'; Amatori, 2009: 8) provided one immediate answer, and a recognition of the problem of overflow with which we are concerned here, stating that:

> As business historians, we usually have access to an infinite variety of sources … An historian cannot be afraid to wade through all these sources, even though he or she must always follow a precise focus, a focus on the

> other end that becomes sharper and sharper in the confrontation with sources in a continuous coming and going between sources and problems. (Amatori, 2009: 9)

Attempting to look at what business historians actually do in the archive, we soon discovered that whatever business historians are doing in (and out of) the archive, they seem reluctant to tell anybody about it. In the period 2007–2011 in *Business History*, which might be considered one of the two leading journals in the field, nearly 60 per cent (57 per cent) of 207 research articles contained no meaningful discussion of either sources or methods. A mere 20 per cent carried extensive discussion of either sources and/or methods – and not all of those contained a dedicated, subheaded section on sources and methods. In the same period, just under half (47.3 per cent) of research articles in the typically more reflexively oriented *Management and Organizational History* (M&OH) carried substantive discussion or sources and/or methods. (And, it should be noted, that when these issues were discussed they tended to receive much more extensive coverage, often within a dedicated, subheaded section of the text, than in the other journals. Furthermore, *M&OH* also tends to carry a larger proportion of conceptual papers in which discussion of sources and methods can obviously play no meaningful part.) In the areas of management sciences and organization studies, to which *Business History* in particular aspires to make a contribution, it is probably impossible to publish in a leading journal without an explicit discussion of sources and methods. In *Enterprise and Society* and *Business History Review*, about one-third of the articles (34 per cent and 31.8 per cent, respectively) included some discussions of the sources and methods applied, but only a small share of the articles went into a lengthy discussion or problematized the material. In this analysis review articles and some specific types of articles in which such discussions could not be expected to be found (for example the articles in the special issue paying tribute to Alfred D. Chandler Jr in 2008), were excluded. Though quite a number of articles in *BHR* addressed conceptual and theoretical arguments among empirical research articles it was nonetheless still extremely rare to find more than a short mention of what type of material had been used, not to mention a whole subsection on 'data and method'. Symptomatically, the *Oxford Handbook of Business History* (Jones and Zeitlin, 2008) does not contain chapters on either sources or methods. Clearly there is a reluctance to make explicit research strategies, to ground findings in an explicit explanation of how sources support claims, or to openly confront possible biases, weaknesses and ambiguities in evidence.

This does not mean that the scholars did not use archival and/or other forms of empirical material as a basis for their argumentation, or that their work has to be considered inadequate historical research. On the contrary, in many cases the work was excellent; it merely did not present or comment on the selection of the empirical material, its strengths or weaknesses, or its relevance for or relationship to their research question. Are there any explanations for this reluctance? One problem with journal articles is obviously the limited space for dealing with various problems and questions relating to archival work and the choice of empirical sources. Traditionally, historians publish books as it is difficult to fit the historical narrative into a short article. Publishing in scholarly journals has, however, become a priority in universities all over the world. The need to compete in the scientific world has become a guiding rule, whether it suits the history field or not. The growing demand to publish articles has also narrowed research questions – and thus also the necessary archival effort. Moreover, journal articles are typically becoming shorter, so why use the few words to discuss issues which many historians consider rather self-evident? In any case where the problematization of the sources could be considered a key issue, it can be assumed that it would receive at least a short note. At the same time, management scholars do manage to find space for their own methodological discussions.

These silences might also reflect the fact that archival work is today a luxury. Large-scale projects are replaced by smaller and more focused 'stand-alone' studies leading to one or two publications. Thus, researchers are rarely – often to their own dissatisfaction – 'swamped' by the archive. Short-term project funding and heavy administrative work-loads have also led to less time for in-depth archival research (for a discussion and comments by historians on this, see Rahikainen and Fellman, 2012a: 2). The business historians have perhaps taken a new approach to the work: rapidly in and out of the archive. The pattern also shows, however, some limited variation between the journals. The traditions and foci differ between individual journals. But still, the silence about sources and methods is a shared characteristic reflecting a view that the 'historian's craft' is taken as self-evident. If 'flirting' with the management and social sciences has made business historians 'uneasy' about the purpose and nature of their field, as claimed by Decker (2012: 2), then it has not gone so far as to make them more explicit or assertive about their methods and sources.

We have also looked more closely at some of the articles in which the author(s) explicitly deliberated on the empirical material. Although they often dealt with the sources and research material relatively scantily, some interesting notions and reflections concerning the source material are found. The most common notions about the empirical material concerned its relevance for the research question, often combined with a comment that the material had been underutilized, or that this was new material never accessed before. The material thus opened up new possibilities and provided new perspectives (for example, Godley, 2006; Abdelrehim et al., 2011). When a more lengthy discussion was found it was often when, for instance, a new extensive data set (de Jong et al., 2011) had been collected; but also in cases where a more elaborate method was adopted, the material was often discussed at greater length (see for example, Stanziani, 2010). Obviously, in this case the main focus was on the limitation or the suitability of the material in relation to the method. But at the same time some general reflections on the material was usually provided. In cases where a multitude of diverse types of sources were used, where sources were atypical for business history (for example, Popp and French, 2010; Ivory and Genus, 2010) or where a topic might be seen as relatively marginal to the 'core' of the discipline (Sanderson et al., 2010), the comments were in general more abundant. This was also the case where sources were rather fragmented and had to be reassembled (Trompette, 2011).

However, most tellingly for our purposes, articles very rarely, if ever, touched upon the question of the immensity of the material, or upon difficulty in selecting what to utilize. Moreover, no one discussed the origins of the archive either, or how it had been kept, administered or organized. It is also interesting to note that critical comments about the empirical material were scarce. Actually, the comments on the material were usually presented in a very positive tone. Obviously, in the limited space of an article it is probably considered unnecessary to deal with all dead-ends the scholar had experienced, and all the material which had been discarded as not useful. But it appears that it is considered important to advertise the usefulness of the material; and thus, indirectly, also advertise the significance of the results. Source criticism does not seem to be the strongest virtues among business historians. It is true however that more extensive discussions about both sources and methods are to be found in monographs, and especially in those based on Doctoral dissertations. The dissertations are still some kind of journeyman's test, in which the Doctoral candidate has to show how they have proceeded and in which way they have developed the arguments.

MAPPING THE CONTEXT AND THE GEOGRAPHY OF THE ARCHIVE

If business historians will not tell us about their research strategies and methods, where else can we turn in order to try and understand what they get up to in (and out of) the archive? One group of people who have investigated this issue is the archivists themselves. In order to improve their services, their finding tools and their classification systems, archivists and information scientists have been interested in how scholars go about their work in the archive, how they use catalogues and search tools, how they find and use their materials. These investigations have led to a number of publications, often based on interviews with active historians (though not, so far as we are aware, business historians), from which we can draw a number of preliminary conclusions that help us situate what we learnt from our own interviews with business historians. We may think of these as themed around: orientation and mapping, building context, unfolding phases, dealing with concerns, emerging syntheses, and the purpose or nature of the research. Even experienced historians report mixed feelings when they entered a new archive for the first time; both a feeling of having been there before and a feeling of being lost – of visiting a foreign country, to extend the old metaphor. The 'archive' as an ideal-typical space is a familiar and even loved place but its reality can overpower the scholar. Interviewees reported, for instance to Duff and Johnson (2002), that a new archive can simply be overwhelming. There are ways of beginning to come to terms with this sense of being lost. That archival classification systems have common features (business archives and public office records often follow a certain hierarchy), combined with the professionalism of archivists themselves, provides a sense of familiarity that can allow the historian to more quickly settle down to work. Scholars' initial strategies are often directed at building a picture of the totality or – in the words of one interviewee – the 'geography' of the archive.

This mapping not only gives a sense of the outline of the archive but also starts the process of building context. All the studies on the working methods of historians stress the building of contextual knowledge as one of the key issues in their research and information-seeking processes. Context is important not only for understanding and interpreting the phenomena, but also for the search for material of relevance (Cole, 2000). The building of the context seems to have been a common strategy among our interviewees as well. Of course there are individual or idiosyncratic behaviours but research often starts out with a vague feeling of what is needed, and later becomes more and more certain about information needs as contextual knowledge increases over time and searches become more efficient (Cole, 2000). Thus archival work often unfolds over four phases: the first is one of orientation; the second, a familiarization with known materials or collections; the third, building contextual knowledge; and the fourth, identification of relevant materials. These phases do not necessarily follow any given order, but depend on a multitude of issues (topic, previous knowledge of the topic, availability of sources and so on) and can be iterative or cyclical.

Still, despite these practices, historians almost always fear overlooking important sources, a serious flaw that might brand them as unprofessional or poor researchers. There also still exists in the field of history an idea that you should 'see it all'. Returning to the archive, however, is not always easy or practical; sometimes it is simply not possible. There is always a balance to be struck between depth and efficiency. These fears notwithstanding, many historians interviewed in studies by archivists remained broadly confident in their ability to identify and locate all necessary, relevant materials. Later synthesis was viewed as much more difficult (Case, 1991).

Unsurprisingly the archivists also found that historians did not enter the archive completely unprepared. Most of the interviewees emphasized that a good research question is critical. Typically historians start searching for material around the actual topic. If historians just look for specific documents directly related to a very narrow research question, it might limit their gaze – and discoveries. Moreover, archives can be like jigsaws: a single document may make little sense without those that surround it (Trace, 2002). As Featherstone noted, innovative scholars such as Michel Foucault went into the French national libraries reading partly haphazardly – what Foucault himself called 'on the diagonal' – across the collections over a wide range of material, creating new connections. Thus, it might be still be crucial to get acquainted with the totality of a particular collection in order to create a convincing interpretation; in doing so most historians rely on past experience and information gleaned informally from colleagues and archivists.

The usefulness of a good relationship with the archivist was pointed out by many of the interviewees (Duff and Johnson, 2002). Archivists can point out relevant material that one would not find in any ordinary ways. This was also stressed by all our interviewees.

Many of Duff and Johnson's interviewees had made use of finding aids and they appear to have found less serendipity in the search process and more deliberate action in the information-seeking behaviour. The informality in the information-seeking process does not mean that it is ad hoc, but rather that it follows unique paths and is difficult to verbalize. Interviewees reported building a 'picture' in their memory in which to store data from the reading they did, but also as a way to train the eye to search for new and relevant data in the following texts. But Cole's study showed that some also considered the process of searching for relevant material as more like a jigsaw puzzle, a process of filling in missing pieces, but a puzzle that never becomes complete. There were always new links and new ideas to follow up (Cole, 1998). To what extent are the findings of archivists replicated in our own interviews with practising business historians?

ENCOUNTERING THE ARCHIVE

Naturally, archivists were most focused on what happens inside the archive rather than what happens outside, both prior and after. Our interviewees focused on the inside–outside split more equally. Yet they did replicate or echo many of the findings of the archivists. Very evident in terms of concrete working practice was the centrality of orientation, mapping and context-building. All our respondents reported this as vital, perhaps unavoidable. All also noted its processual, iterative and cyclical character. Processes of learning, even for very experienced historians, remain vital each and every time a new archive is encountered. In part this is a pragmatic response but in part it is also a coping mechanism; one triggered explicitly by the overflow experienced in corporate archives. William is a senior member of the business history community in Britain. He described how and why, early on in his research career, his working methods had to change:

> It was just the sheer impossibility of working with [with the archive] because you may look at Board Minutes, which is a fairly obvious starting point to look at, also the Annual Reports and so on, and very quickly you get into trouble because literally you are in a room, or a series of rooms, and you are walking about and you can see you are not going to manage this task … I was just completely overwhelmed by that.

Similarly Claire, who at the time of our interview was working as a research assistant on a major UK corporate history, initially 'started out naively thinking that I could go through it all, read every minute and somehow trudge all the way through it and not be buried in detail'. A change was required, one that Claire described as occurring through 'trial and error'. A sense of the outer margins of the archive, however vague and sketchy, was needed. In particular, the team she worked as part of began a pragmatic process of sampling combined with a reformulated and refined division of labour: 'Well one of the first things that we did was to do a divide and conquer effort in which each of us took, roughly a 50-year period.' Through these changes of working practice a sense of calm and order was gradually restored to the project and Claire began to feel more comfortable and in control, able 'to stop and say, "ok what are the key issues"... because by then we had gone through enough of the stuff to say, "we are starting to see these themes across this broad area of time"'. Those processes of orientation, contextualization and mapping described in the research undertaken by archivists were taking place and imposing a shape on the project and, in a sense, the archive. Maria is a young but established Nordic scholar, who wrote a PhD thesis on consumption in the nobility based on an extensive eighteenth-century family archive consisting of both private and business material. Her experience was not dissimilar to Claire's. Maria is a historian trained in a humanities faculty and, perhaps due to her scholarly background, she has received a more profound education in the traditional skills of a historian – that is, archives, source criticism, old handwritings and so on – than the other interviewees. Moreover, her Master's thesis had involved extensive archival work. But she had not received any systematic teaching or any hands-on instruction in how to go about being in an archive.

Her first encounter with the archive was not very systematic, although she knew what she was interested in and had some training on which to rely. But still at first she felt unsure about where to start, so she went to the archive and asked the archivist: 'What shall I do? How shall I do it?' And so she got the archive lists to start with. However, previous scholarly work and senior scholars were also of use. She had been guided to this archive by a professor: 'I think it was Professor NN who told me "start with this, it is an interesting family and start with the probate records, which all students of consumption do"'. She also used previous research as a guide and looked at what type of material previous scholars had used to study the nobility's consumption patterns during the eighteenth century. This also helped her to decide what material could be relevant to look at.

One of our interviewees, Henrik, who is a senior scholar within business history with a high reputation in the field, had actually been close to dropping a topic due to the overwhelming feeling on first seeing the archive:

> I was about to write about X and the archival list was not detailed enough so I was granted access from the public records office in XX to go to their storehouse and take a look for myself and I think there was about three-four-five hundred meters and I just went out again and thought, 'I cannot do this',

> because they were somehow all relevant, I would have taken a look at it all, and I don't know how many documents there are in three-four-five hundred meters, but that's more than a million, I mean, there was no way I could do that for writing an article. But other times, it is simply, you know, you have all these boxes, and you know just as well as I do that you start at page one and then you start turning them.

However, in the end he wrote an article on the topic, but with another angle, and thus did not have to enter that archive again. Moreover, overflow does not only stress the historian in the archive, but also the abundance of research going on overflows the scholars:

> my interest right now is in [X] and, I think never ever in history have so many working papers and so many articles and books and stuff been published on that topic. There is no way I can read everything. So the way I deal with that is that most often I print everything that I, you know, am aware of, and then it sorts of piles high on my table and at some point in time I say, 'ok, this is not going to work', and then I throw it all out, and then I hope that some bright person … will be able to write a little review or something like that in two years' time or so.

Given the mapping metaphor, it is worth noting at this point that all our interviewees possessed a sharp sense of the archive as a very real, physical place, a place moreover populated by people and with histories of their own. This knowledge was generally acquired during the research process and added important depth and appreciation to the more surface but immediately pressing issues of gaining familiarity with, for example, a new catalogue or classification system. But in fact two of our interviewees also had some formal qualifications as archivists. Claire undertook a certificate in Archives Management as part of her Masters-level studies, which means she brings with her some understanding of how archives are organized and 'what the priorities [are] from the archivists perspective and I think it certainly helps me in dealing with archives and archivists and knowing where to look and how to look through catalogue archives'. Indeed, as the archive she works in continues to make new acquisitions Claire is able to help in the cataloguing process. Thor – a young Scandinavian post-Doctoral researcher, who wrote a dissertation based on an extensive amount material from several big archives – had received training as an archivist and also worked as an archivist for some years before starting his PhD, which made him feel very secure about going about into the archives he later needed. For him, archival work was a very essential part of the research, and he was perhaps more archive- and source-driven in his research than some of our other interviewees. But he had also had his ordeals when he first started out as young Master's student:

> When I first went to the archive, as a fresh student, I was completely green and I had to find my way around things … I tried to look for what is significant, 'can I use this in any way at all?' So I spent quite a lot of time developing those skills by learning by doing, actually. So I hadn't been taught about it, but you were thrown out in the big sea, and you learn to sink or swim, I guess.

Henrik emphasized one important notion, which we also address earlier in the section 'Problematizing the archive': namely that sources are actually something the historians create and construct. The material stored in an archive, or other material used by the historians, becomes sources only through the questions they ask and by utilizing this material for answering these questions. Otherwise it is only a heap of papers (or pictures or artefacts). However, as he concluded, the most important thing is not the sources as such, but how we can contextualize that information and create a narrative out of it.

WORKING WITH THE MATERIAL

As the archivists emphasized, mapping, orientation and context-building allow new phases of work to begin and unfold. William, for example, painted a vivid portrait of himself and his team settling into a pattern of near ruthless efficiency in this description of a recent working trip to an archive in the US:

> For reasons of efficiency we have had had two month long trips to X, three of us and we have two scanners permanently based there and so we get the scanners out and we do an awful lot of scanning. What we are doing there is to follow the search strategy that I set and so it is a bit like a slave ship and I am trying to beat out work and the other two are working with a scanner each to the tune of [my rhythm], we are doing this series, that series we are working on this issue, we are working on this, now we are doing the letters, now we are doing diaries, now we are doing Opening Events for X or whatever and that is how we do it.

Despite this advanced use of modern copying technologies, extensive on-site reading of documents is not precluded: 'you are reading enough of the material – I am scanning ahead and doing all the check lists and the ticking and then the farming out – that is the way it works'. Moreover, because this work was undertaken away from home, evenings in the hotel were spent reading through recently scanned material and preparing for the following day's search and copying strategy. And, of course, 'you make choices constantly'. Naturally, all of the interviewees had difficulty in explaining how those choices were made. Indeed, it was common to our interviewees that they had difficulty in verbalizing how they 'know' what to look at.

These pragmatic strategies, perhaps best thought of as 'tactics', do not smooth out all the bumps in the road, as Claire attested: 'I usually have a pretty good idea of "can I get through two years today" … I think I have gotten used to the panic or comfortable with the level of panic [but] yes, I still feel swamped.' Doing archive work brings with it concerns and anxieties. Claire admitted to powerful emotions:

> Panic – how can I manage to write something about this if I cannot … get through all this stuff and there is always the fear of what you are going to miss, isn't there! But there is that fear no matter what – if you are feeling tired in the archive, whatever the size of the archive, and your eye skips over what could be the statement that blows open the whole subject.

As this quotation suggests, the archives also have a physicality to them that cannot be separated from the emotional experience – the work undertaken there is variously back-breaking, boring, worrisome, but also stimulating and inspiring, even exhilarating. Claire's tactic is one of 'rigid time discipline'. Unburdened by administrative or teaching duties she is able to approach time in the archive as a job, putting in regular working hours most days. Even so, Claire admitted that the archive work is a 'moving target', one that will never be complete. Perhaps this acknowledgement is another tactic. Other researchers are enabled to cope differently. Maria stressed the luxury of not having to be in a hurry when she did the archival studies for her PhD. During several years she worked only part-time with her PhD as she was full-time employed in another job, but what she then did was to immerse herself in the archival material. This is not a luxury that many later on in their career can indulge in. We have already seen William admit to a sense of being 'overwhelmed'. His reaction, at least at first, was the simple admission that the work 'was way beyond me'. The dam or dyke of the archive promises only temporary protection from the flood – in fact threatens to make the flood worse when it finally breaks. On the other hand, being a professional historian probably contains – or at least the interviewees seem to feel so themselves – the ability to avoid the flood, to cope. For instance, Maria told us that after she got acquainted with the family archive in detail, and especially with the records on the family's various income, consumption and expenditure groups, she decided to use benchmark years. She understood that she did not need to read or see everything. But again, after a while, she realized that she also occasionally had to divert from this principle as she would have missed out some very important incidences heavily affecting the family's consumption expenditures over several years. As a result she looked at such incidences separately. In general, she was able to narrow down the material quite extensively. When asked about when she obtained these insights, she said she had difficulty in putting it into words, but that it sprang from knowledge about and sensitivity to the material, which was constituted of 'several components': knowledge about the context, about the research field, about the archive and about previous research. Finally, she concluded – with a laugh – 'when one knows, one is a scholar'. However, other historians might sneer at such research strategies. For example, Stephanie Decker was on one occasion accused of doing 'small n-studies' (2012: 18), when narrowing down the material by using samples.

Thor had a slightly different strategy than the other interviewees. He seems to have enjoyed, even indulged, in gathering as much material as possible, without getting a sense of panic or about having 'too much'. When he came to an archive, he also worked very fast and aimed to collect as much as possible, without thinking very much. This strategy was possible because he:

> was lucky enough to have quite a lot of time in all of the main corporate archives. So I had the luxury of being able to look at basically everything that I thought would be interesting. So that meant that I didn't really have to make too hard choices when in the archives … I took a lot of pictures, but by the end of my stays I felt pretty confident that I had seen everything that related to what I was interested in, and that's all.

In one of the foreign archives he visited, he took pictures of everything which he considered relevant, without thinking whether he would need it later or not: in all over 1000 pictures. And that was just the first archive.

With the new technology, particularly scanning and digital photography, now allowed by many archives, enabling historians to work fast, the overflow is not felt so strongly in the archive because one can go through the folders and quickly take pictures, but the feeling comes later. The sense of being overwhelmed is displaced or delayed, but not avoided. In fact feeling overwhelmed may be exacerbated as one no longer feels the need to exercise choice or discernment while in the archive itself. It is for this reason that some more senior historians still rely on in-situ reading and transcription, and eschew or minimize the use of technology. Thor continued:

> Then you start to read … I usually read it on the screen, and I will take notes in a Word document on the side, writing down every letter or minutes of the board … what was important in each one of them … I would have a document that would tell me what are the important things in here, whom is writing to whom and what is this about, what are they discussing? And then I would … take all these documents and try to create the time-lines, the chronology, the sequences, to get a feel for what is happening. And while you are reading through all the documents that you photographed, you really lose all the sight, completely … Because it's very time-consuming and you can't really remember what you have read after a couple of days. So when you have done that, and then you go back to your notes, then you really see what you have been reading and you get a much clearer picture of what is going on here.

Asked if he considered that the many diverse archives he worked with was a stressful factor, Thor answered 'no', and claimed that he considered it an advantage to have access to 'different archives, with different pieces of information, which made it easier to compose a bigger story … I didn't have to rely on only one archive. I would not have been comfortably with that.' When asked how he set out to combine the abundant material from many different archives in order to construct the story, he explained:

> I set up time-lines, plotted in the different events and linked them to archival material, combining different archives, so, when I was for instance writing about [X], I would combine four or five different archives and put them in the time-line, to get a feel for what is happening when, what is the sequence of the events, so that was my working method, I would say.

THE ARCHIVE AS A PLACE FOR EMOTIONS

We have already seen that working in the archive can be an emotional experience and we have tended to stress some negative emotions, such as panic and stress. Still it is worth noting that the emotional experiences encountered in the archive can also be very positive. Claire talked about being 'lucky' and 'fortunate' to be able to devote so much time to archival work, concluding with a hint of self-effacement, 'Well, I suppose that says a lot about my breed.' William too reported near euphoric states in which he found total absorption. In the end, Claire acknowledged, 'I am a very happy person doing the research.'

Thus there is considerable correspondence between our respondents and those interviewed by the archivists; in particular all stressed the importance of orientation, mapping and contextualization, leading to phases of work that do not banish but help to soothe anxieties and concerns and lead to a preparation of the ground for syntheses that hope to answer to the original purposes and design of the project. William for example talked extensively about the coding of data that, for him, if the work is to remain history, must always take place after rather than prior to the archive work. Overarching all of this is a sense of process and learning that takes place day to day at, in Claire's words, 'the coal face'; that is, at work with documents in the archive. However, our respondents also dwelt in depth on much more long-run learning processes spanning the breadth, and more, of a total research career.

For instance Maria's story resembles an 'exploration' – to use the old metaphor once more – both in the way she became a scholar, and in the way she went about in her research. She felt that when she began her dissertation project, she had started out on a trip that took her to unknown places, unknown material and unknown phenomena. And an unknown life. She had never had big plans of becoming a scholar, but these visits to the archive, where she experienced feelings like: 'wow, this is interesting' and 'this must be important', drove her forward and towards becoming a professional historian.

For William the process of learning had deep roots in childhood influences in the home, at school, in the local environment and in initial forays in to the world of work. These influences have worked to create a very powerful dispositional attitude towards not simply archive work but also to the wider epistemological framework within which archive work is carried out. In turn that framework structures the relationship between evidence and argumentation, the framing and structure of a specific project, and the selection of methodology. Central here is William's unabashed self-identification as an 'empiricist':

> I have never changed course in my career at all, [in] my interest … [as] an empiricist in what goes on in the world and why the world is configured as it is and my search, which is unending, and can never end, is to better understand the world and why it has evolved in a particular way.

Indeed, he later stated that in his opinion an 'historian is an empiricist' and asserted that reliance on large volumes of evidence is a 'peculiarity of method within the discipline'. Critically, as a way of relating to the world, his empiricism forms the very ground from which his research can begin. Research, he suggests, begins then not from a specific research question but something rather broader that 'doesn't have to constitute, at that stage, a theory … [rather] it has to constitute something in the empirical world that is worth explaining, is worth understanding and … tackling'. We might call his stance here the empirical imperative. It goes to the very heart of, and might provide one answer to, our question about the relationship between the evidence contained in the archive and the research question or problem. For William the empirical world, as represented in the archive, is prior (though still not to be mistaken for an objective truth). For William, translating this empirical epistemology into practice produces: 'what I believe in is the inducto-deductive cycle and I believe in a process of refinement – refinement and understanding'. This takes us back, ultimately, into the cyclical, iterative and phased work actually in the archive that we have already seen all our respondents discuss.

As well as defining himself as an 'empiricist', William also claimed to be a 'structured thinker' who enjoys aspects of research such as design and coding and who is quantitatively skilled, even though most of his work is broadly qualitative. Henrik, on the other hand, was more sceptical about our ability to reach an accurate knowledge of the past or, provided we have enough historians and enough work is done, that the gaps in our knowledge would eventually be filled, and we would 'know everything'. This stance comes, Henrik claimed, from a mistaken idea that history is an accumulative science. For him it is not, but instead historians construct and reconstruct history all the time. Moreover, he emphasized that the material in the archive itself is a construction. Thus, the traces of the past are not direct windows to the past, but a construction of the construction.

For William the most powerful formative influences were probably located, as we have indicated, in his childhood spent in an industrial region of the UK in the 1950s, a world:

> of which I was part and so I was enthralled by that and by the sense of history, the sense of place, the sense of being in the world … So that was my starting point, which was I enjoyed looking at the world – observing the world and thinking about the world.

Our respondents recognized their own place in a more immediate chain of transmission involving other scholars. Claire noted how her Doctoral studies included no formal methods training, concluding that 'was probably expected to have occurred by now'. William, with many successful Doctoral supervisions to his name, claimed to take a highly structured approach to the induction of new scholars to the field, but much of what he has to say on the subject often remains – perhaps deliberately – vague. At the same time William also spoke of how 'I feel incredibly comfortable with fellow historians because we are on the same wavelength dispositionally… because we have the same set of practices and we have the same values and so there is a historical method.' This emphasis on the dispositional as a structuring element in the conduct of scholarship – that is, on pre-existing, almost inherent or inborn attitudes towards the world and how it is observed, experienced, studied and understood – seems to us a somewhat unexpected but important finding.

In the final analysis, all of this effort, learning and emotion is directed towards one aim. As William noted, 'it is very sensemaking, isn't it, and if you are talking about overflow and weight of information – what you are actually doing is condensing: that is what you are doing, you are "condensing" so as to make sense'. Here we come to the very nub of the issue we are most interested in: overflow can only be coped with through a process of condensing, and perhaps stylization and simplification as well. But overflow is also in a way considered essential for historical research, as the overwhelming material gives us the strong base to stand on in our argumentation.

CONCLUSIONS

This chapter has dealt with how the business historians approach, prepare for and go about work in the archive, especially in the case of an abundance of material. However, it has also discussed the historians' emotions towards the archive, as the archive tends to become for many historians a very special – occasionally even mythical – place. We learned from the discussions that most of them thought very seriously about their work and the archive and the sources, although they might seldom have expressed it explicitly in their published work. Also people from outside the field often visualize a historian as a person sitting in an archive with heaps of material, who is meticulous about the reliability and relevance of the material. Why are historians writing so little about this process, although it is so vital for our work?

We could observe that one reason for the silence of the business historians about their work in the archive was a feeling that what they are doing there is somehow a self-evident issue; self-evident to themselves, to other historians and to people outside the field. However, it was also common to all the interviewees that their silence on these issues also originates in a difficulty in putting their practices into words. The interviewees also stressed that they had learned the practices by doing them. However, this does not make the lack of reflexivity about the material and its limits, or about the working methods or choice of material in case of abundance, less problematic. Nonetheless, not all the silence we found in the articles we surveyed should be interpreted as neglect of these questions. It would be interesting, if a wider study of business historians were possible, to discover whether this perhaps previously unobserved reflexivity is widespread or even common in the community.[2]

We also learned many other things when carrying out the interviews. Most of our interviewees claim that they had definitely started out with a research question. This is an interesting and somewhat different idea about what historians do than is the usual notion. Importantly, our interviews confirmed the archivists' emphasis on learning and phases, but extended it in several ways. First, the dimensions of learning are multiple; at the micro level in the specific archive; at the meso level from one project to another; and at the macro level across the scholarly life. Moreover these learning cycles and processes are not only strategic, tactical or wisdom-based but are also complex emotional processes, rooted in basic dispositional attitudes and formative influences filtered through subsequent experiences.

The stress on a basic disposition towards doing this work – and being able to do this work, to cope with it – seems an important finding to us. It relates to several issues. First, it helps make sense of the relatively tacit and informal ways that the majority of historians are still introduced to and inducted into being a professional historian. It also helps us make sense of the fact that all of interviewees share a strong enjoyment of doing archive work as a vital, indispensable part of their practice and their professional identities as business historians. In this respect it is also notable that all of our respondents welcomed and enjoyed a perhaps rare opportunity to talk about and reflect on what they do; though, of course, this may merely reflect a bias in our far from random sampling procedure. Still, for all involved, interviewers and interviewees, this research was experienced as a worthwhile and positive process – just as being in the archive generally is. So there are important rewards that should not be forgotten; some are tangible, such as publications and career, but others, perhaps just as important, are psychic, an inherent satisfaction.

We believe our contribution opens up to discussion several under-researched topics. Overflow is seen to be a fact of life for the practising business historian but one for which no carefully delineated strategy is available. For the most part our interviewees could be said to work with the grain of the archive, to ride the flood. It is the only tactic available.

The literature on the working practices of business historians is particularly sparse and we make a contribution in showing how they go about doing that work and how they come to know how to do it. A further contribution lies in beginning to raise the question of the relationship between those practices and both underlying epistemologies and then the knowledge produced. Again, as with the tactics for coping with overflow, these do not seem to be relationships that are closely or tightly delineated; instead they emerge as relatively ad hoc. This second set of questions provides a rich avenue of potential future research; perhaps one that business historians will not be able to ignore as they continue to engage more deeply with other disciplines in history and the social sciences, in both of which greater reflexivity is becoming more prominent.

Finally, running silently through all we have said, is that in the final analysis we do find a way, however imperfect, to cope, as we all must, with the overflow. And this is true for the business historian, not least because the challenge cannot be avoided. If we wish to be business historians then we must go to the overflowing archive.

NOTES

1. With this 'turn' scholars do not necessarily mean a turn back to traditional archival research, but rather an emphasis on the basic idea that historical scholarly research requires archives (Götselius, 2008: 10).
2. According to Stephanie Decker (2012: 17), strong resistance against having to explicate practice was expressed at a panel discussion at the Business History Conference in 2011.

14. Selective knowledge: learning to forget and ignore

Orvar Löfgren

ACADEMIC SKILLS OF OVERFLOW MANAGEMENT

> There was a young faculty member in our sociology department who was called to sit on all kinds of committees, because he read – thoroughly – all the material sent out, unlike his older colleagues, who just skimmed the stuff distributed, from memos to research applications. I told him: 'You'll never survive if you don't develop the skills they have; all this work will kill you!'

My chapter explores this world of crucial but elusive academic skills used for surviving various types of overflows, as described in the interview quoted here.[1] Scholars create overflow in many ways: downloading files, photocopying papers, buying books that may never be read but 'may come in handy'. Office desks and filing cabinets are bursting with material; hard disks are overloaded and demanding more memory. In examining the ways in which these types of overflow are handled, my main interest lies in the social and cultural organization of selective knowledge in academia. Thesauruses equate 'select' with synonyms such as: choose, single out, distinguish, limit, favour. We are reminded that it is a concept loaded with cultural norms. What is important, unimportant, irrelevant or noteworthy in a given setting?

The focus of this chapter is on the way routines and skills are produced and maintained as academics learn to ignore, forget, overlook and neglect. I explore the concept of selective knowledge from various angles: the constant selection and deselection of available knowledge and the ways in which we practise selective sensitivities – the selective attention of hearing, sight and memory. Ignoring, overlooking or forgetting are often seen in negative terms, but in the form of creative oblivion, organized forgetting and strategic ignorance, they are crucial resources in the production and management of knowledge.

I am interested in the everyday practices of academic work, the ways in which people gradually develop routines for handling information, collecting materials and producing texts. The skill perspective is key, because it focuses on constant training, the acquisition of new competencies and increased skills. How do you acquire the motoric dexterity of rifling through a filing cabinet, skimming Google pages, deleting e-mails, judging a book by holding in it your hands, learning to grasp the gist of the matter?

Selective knowledge is not an easy topic to explore, for at least two reasons. First of all, many of these skills are embedded in everyday routines which have been naturalized into invisibility. They rest more in the body than in the mind, and even if you can bring them into consciousness, they are difficult practices to verbalize. Second, although academia is a work setting with strong emphasis on teaching and instruction, skills of selective knowledge are rarely found in textbooks or manuals. They represent a self-taught understanding acquired through situated learning and often formed as tacit or at least implicit knowledge (Collins, 2010). But although scholars often develop what they see as individual strategies of selective knowledge, it is an intensely cultural field, shaped by local and current norms about the relevant, the important or the necessary. This cultural dimension also brings the dimensions of power into the field. Who is setting the rules and routines for what can be ignored or deleted?

To gain perspectives on informal and non-verbal learning processes, one must turn mainly to a research literature focusing on artisan skills, gleaning the empirical material primarily from trade settings. Here we find stuff on carpenters and car mechanics rather than on sociologists or philosophers. The focus is on the acquisition and communication of 'silent knowledge'; it is a world of nimble fingers, coordinated body movements and interaction with all types of tools (see for example, Sennett, 2008; Ehn, 2011; Marchand, 2010).

It is not surprising that the research on more elusive academic skills has, above all, focused on laboratory experiences. How does one acquire what is sometimes called 'lab fingers': learning to work efficiently, quickly, but also innovatively, in a laboratory setting? There is a vast ethnographic literature here, from the classic works of Bruno Latour and Steve Woolgar (1987) and Karin Knorr-Cetina (1981), on to more recent studies (see the overview in Nicolini, 2009; Viteritti, 2012).

My focus, however, is on the academic sector of the cultural and social sciences – a world without white coats, test tubes, machines or lab diaries. On the surface, the everyday life of a cultural analyst or a sociologist may seem less material, but the materialities of the social and cultural sciences are, of course, as critical as those of any other settings, although they may be present in forms less obvious than the lab.

To access these elusive materialities and sensibilities, I have used tools from research traditions based upon prediscursive or non-discursive aspects of everyday life, from post-phenomenological interest in mundane activities (Verbeek, 2005) and actor-network theory (Latour, 2005) to practise theory (Shove et al., 2012) and non-representational theory (Anderson and Harrison, 2010).

I have been looking for situations in which mundane practices are brought to the surface and become visible and problematized (Ehn and Löfgren, 2010: 79ff.) That is why it seems fruitful to focus on academic situations in which new technologies are introduced and old ones abandoned. Once skills and competencies are mastered, they often cease to be seen as skills or knowledge, turning instead into 'epistemic wallpaper' as Nigel Thrift (2004) has called it. This situation makes it helpful to compare different generational experiences (Eyerman and Turner, 1998) of handling overflow in the social and cultural sciences. Every academic generation – whether in the 1630s or the 2010s – has a tendency to see its own life history as revolutionary, because it has encompassed so many dramatic changes.

My main focus will be on scholars who have lived with both analogue and digital technologies. The generations born in the 1940s and 1950s faced several specific challenges. They began their careers in a world of analogue tools and techniques, hammering on typewriters, cutting and pasting manuscripts, producing stencils, writing letters, handling rolls of film and tape. Later they became 'digital immigrants', exposed to a wide range of new ways of handling knowledge. The term 'immigrants' may represent a tendency to overdramatize this changeover in knowledge production, a watershed idea of a drastically different 'before' and 'after'. Because there have always been new media calling for striking adjustments, one should be wary of talking about a digital revolution, but I use the concepts of analogue and digital in this chapter as they serve as a broad metaphor for generational experiences in handling overflows of academic knowledge. Is it possible to talk not only about analogue and digital skills for storing and retrieving knowledge, but also, in a more playful manner, about analogue search routines or digital forgetting?

To access these generational differences, I started by interviewing scholars who entered academia at various stages of the analogue–digital transformation. I have also used material from an earlier ethnography of everyday life in academia (Ehn and Löfgren, 2004, 2007) as well as autobiographical accounts. To provide further contrast, I have moved back to the literature on earlier historical periods, when similar complaints about 'information overload' were being aired and new strategies of selective knowledge had to be developed.

In what follows, I map out a research territory that still is relatively underdeveloped, by exploring a number of themes and providing the reader with more questions than answers. I start with a classic analogue medium – the printed text – examining the ways in which various strategies for handling that medium evolved and remain valuable today. I then move to processes of selecting, highlighting and excerpting material in a flow of possibilities and looking at various forms of search engines, both analogue and digital. The next theme concerns the ordering, storing and retrieving of research material, and from there I turn to questions of remembering and forgetting, deleting and ridding. The last theme is about strategies of ignoring and overlooking, and in the conclusion I suggest ways in which this field of everyday practices in selective knowledge can be further developed.

SKIMMING AND SCANNING – SELECTIVE READING

'In our time the multitude of books becomes an immensity', a scholar complained, in speculating about ways to navigate through a new and threatening overflow of knowledge. A colleague urgently called for new routines of selection and deselection: 'What books must we throw away or "leave in oblivion", and how can we know what is useful or not among those that we decide to read?'

The quotes in the previous paragraph come not from twenty-first-century academics, but from seventeenth-century debates, at a time when 'the print revolution' had created an unprecedented expansion in knowledge production and circulation, or as one 1630 scholar noted, what earlier took ten people a whole year to write by quill, was now printed by four men in a day (Blair, 2010: 47, 57). These utterances came from scholars who saw opportunities in this situation of stressful overflow and who were engaged in such new forms of information management as the rapidly growing genre of compilations, reference books and guides to selecting books.

As a new medium, the printed texts of books and pamphlets colonized the scholarly world of the sixteenth and seventeenth centuries, and a whole infrastructure of tools and routines developed around the consumption of book knowledge. But as Blair (2010: 11) reminded readers, this revolution was not the simple result of technological change. There were parallel processes at work: the discovery of new worlds, the recovery of ancient texts and the quest for more and more information – what Blair has called 'infolust' – but also a more critical and reflexive stance towards knowledge. The new and lucrative trade in books produced a great deal of shoddy work, plagiarism and badly edited texts, which increased the need for a critical eye.

New genres and technologies of information management were developed or medieval ones made more sophisticated. I am talking about storage technologies such as the bookcase and the library; search methods such as pagination and indexing, genres of encyclopaedias, book abstracts and reading guides; the hiring of research and library assistants; and new forms of information circulation, such as group note-taking, learned journals and book reviews.

As early as the sixteenth century, scholars were investing in new equipment to improve reading and information management. One such item was the book wheel, which was placed on a table, allowing the reader to turn quickly from book to book; another was the swivel chair, which made it possible to combine several desk spaces. These investments served two functions: they produced research advantages to the scholar, but they also imparted a feeling of superiority over less high-tech colleagues (Grafton, 1999: 210).

But what about the skills? Forms of reading began to change: silent reading replacing reading aloud, slow reading becoming faster, during what sometimes was called the 'Reading Revolution' of the eighteenth century (Cavallo and Chartier, 1999). Scholars learned to skim and browse texts, leafing through the pages, developing different levels of attention in their reading. The eighteenth-century scholar Samuel Johnson identified four types of reading styles: 'hard study' for learned books read with pen in hand, 'perusal' for searching information, 'curious reading' for novels, and 'mere reading' for browsing and scanning 'without the fatigue of close attention' (DeMaria, 1997: 1–15). By then there was an ongoing debate over the merits and dangers of fast and selective reading, a debate that is still with us (Currell, 2007; Jackson, 2008: 153ff.).

By fast reading, I mean techniques of skimming texts (looking for specific stuff and skipping over what is deemed irrelevant). Research on eye movements has shown how individuals develop 'scan paths' when leafing through a text or clicking on the Internet (Holmqvist and Nyström, 2011: 253ff). Skimming and scanning were the survival techniques used by veteran faculty members in the sociology department mentioned in the introduction. Interviewees often stressed their use of these techniques, almost in a bragging manner. How long does it take to evaluate a thesis or a research application? 'I have learned to do it in x minutes or y nanoseconds!' said one academic. The skimming of books could result in such micro-choreographies as starting from the back, checking the blurbs, running through the references, glancing at the contents list and the rifling through the pages to get 'a feel of the book'. One of my colleagues described his skimming technique:

> I have a look at the cover, check the publisher … is it a well-established one? Next I go to the introduction, read the first lines and then scan through the rest, always skipping quotes. If the intro is long-winded, I get impatient; it's a bad sign. Then I move to check the table of contents. Are there some attractive headings? I start leafing through the chapters to see if there's something that catches my eye. It can be a sentence that makes me start thinking – good sign! After getting the smell of a couple of chapters, I decide: Is this a book for me to read or should it just go back into the shelf?

Another scholar used a similar olfactory metaphor for skimming: 'sniffing a book or an article to see if it is worth consuming' A third said that he sometimes read books by 'osmosis'. Just by having them in a pile on his desk and shuffling them about, he could eventually convince himself that he had actually read them.

It is sometimes argued that reading skills are about constant acceleration, both in history and in personal careers, but academic literacy is striking in that it consists of a number of intensive and extensive modes of reading which are mixed and combined.

SELECTING, MARKING AND EXCERPTING

As the number of available texts grew rapidly, skills of highlighting, summarizing and excerpting had to be cultivated. Over the centuries, scholars developed their own routines to mark useful knowledge, from torn-out or dog-eared pages, through underlining passages or writing comments in the margins, to the development of various note-taking systems. During the print revolution, the new availability of paper became key, but above all, note-taking called for the development of storage systems, from notebooks and bundles of loose papers held together by ribbons, to the first attempts, in the seventeenth century, at developing filing cabinets. As early as the sixteenth century, the notebook had become a key tool for collecting quotes, comments and ideas. The bound book or the bundle of commentaries had its limitations, however, and techniques of cutting and pasting were developed for the orderly rearranging of notes. One radical breakthrough was the systematic use of the paper slip, which made it possible to rearrange knowledge in various ways. Note collections turned into a new resource, sometimes jealously guarded, sometimes transformed into a market commodity.

Later generations of scholars developed their own, often personalized systems for organizing knowledge, ideas and excerpts, but there is also a striking continuity. The notebook has survived into the digital age. New tools for underlining emerged, from the revolutionary innovation of the pencil in the late eighteenth century to the coloured felt pen and the electronic marker of the late twentieth century. Similarly the seventeenth- and eighteenth-century experiments with filing cabinets resulted in the birth of the box for index cards. The seemingly simple idea of paper slips – either as torn pieces of paper or bundles of sheets – and, later, cards opened a new world of research possibilities, in which materials were combined in novel ways, as the cards could be sorted and selected differently. More sophisticated mixing and indexing came with systems like the late nineteenth-century filing cabinet, the carbon copy, the twentieth-century punch card and other forerunners of computerized data handling (Burke, 2012), but the simple card box remained a powerful research tool for centuries, right up to present times (although now also transformed into new digital forms). Claude Levi-Strauss was a scholar who could not work without a card box:

> I get by when I work by accumulating notes – a bit about everything, ideas captured on the fly, summaries of what I have read, references, quotations … And when I want to start a project, I pull a packet of notes out of their pigeonhole and deal them like a deck of cards. This kind of operation, where chance plays a role, helps me revive my failing memory. (after Krapp, 2006: 361)

Roland Barthes was another researcher for whom the mixing and dealing of index cards was a key research technology. During his career, he collected more than 12 000 cards, which were constantly reorganized. To 'shuffle and deal' became a significant activity for finding new ideas and combining findings – so much so that Barthes argued that his index card collection should appear as a co-author in his texts (Krapp, 2006: 363).

COLLECTING AND STORING

The history of selective reading and excerpting and tools such as the card box or the filing cabinet bring us into the domain of memory and storing practices. Ways of remembering are, of course, a major form of selective organization of knowledge, and there is a rich interdisciplinary literature on both the history and the social and technological contexts of memory practices (Bowker, 2006; Connerton, 2009). Concepts such as 'memory regimes' and 'epochs' are used to understand how people organize collective and individual memory in different settings.

One major theme here is the history of archives. As Geoffrey Bowker (2006: 26ff.) has noted, the start of every new archive or archival principle is an inaugural act of forgetting and remembering that wipes out certain aspects and materials of the past. It represents organized oblivion.

But archives exist in many forms, from central institutions to the ways in which individual scholars turn their offices into mini-archives, trying to maintain order, not only in their filing cabinets and on hard disks, but also on the desk or in the bookcase.

Archives are based upon systems of storage and classification. There is an abundant literature on archives as an institution, but here I am interested primarily in the informal ways in which individual scholars tend to be their own archivists. Research stuff is often organized and stored in idiosyncratic ways. There are many examples of people starting ambitious organizing and ordering projects, only to have them slowly peter out. The seventeenth-century philosopher Leibniz was one such person: 'After having done something, I forget it almost entirely within a few months, and rather than searching for it amid a chaos of jottings that I do not have the leisure to arrange and mark with headings I am obliged to do the work all over again' (after Blair, 2010: 88).

These half-hearted or unfinished ordering projects, which interest me greatly, surfaced more than once in the interviews. Another theme that some scholars stressed was the importance of early training. Reflecting on her own skills and priorities, a media researcher in her 40s remembers the archival training of her teenage years:

> My parents were office workers, and I loved to hang around their workplaces, getting familiar with office routines and new technologies. During my early teens, I created my own personal archives. I had ring binders on the shelves in my room for every hobby: horses, flowers. I loved creating this kind of order and became a very well organized person. I guess those skills have been important in my later academic career … I was like a sponge, sucking up all kinds of information, collecting everything, reading everything. And I guess I am still sponge-like, having my tentacles sticking out in all directions. Always looking for new stuff.

Later she became less obsessed with organizing her personal research materials, relying more and more on access to the Internet, but also finding short cuts to archiving. Obtaining a new computer meant a time-consuming procedure of discovering which files from the old computer should be transferred to the new: 'I stopped doing that. Now I never delete anything – just use my old computers as archives, where I can search for old stuff.'

SEARCH ENGINES

As knowledge is outsourced to archives, to libraries and later to databases, selective knowledge depends heavily on routines of searching for and retrieving information. The digital age created a whole array of tools in the form of search engines, but similar techniques existed, of course, in different forms in analogue times.

Some of the academics I interviewed tended to stress the move from analogue to digital search techniques as one of the most radical changes they had undertaken. In an analogue world, many search techniques were combined: browsing in libraries and bookshops, asking colleagues, skimming indexes, reviews and abstracts, locating journals. All kinds of stuff had to be excerpted or photocopied.

Looking back on his research career in neuroscience, one professor remembers the cumbersome work of searching for relevant literature during his PhD work:

> There was this sea of journal articles we had to search. Our department subscribed to a weekly newsletter, *Current Contents*, where medical journals were abstracted. It was a thin little booklet that we all queued up to read. We scrutinized it for interesting stuff and copied the authors' addresses, which were also provided. From the department, we got preprinted postcards asking for offprints, with a flap with a return address that the receiver could tear off. Over the period of a week, we could send out 5 to 15 such cards; and if we were lucky, we got offprints from half of our requests. Slowly we built up our own research library.
>
> There was also the possibility of going to the university library and paying for a literature search. But it was expensive, and I spent quite a bit of time thinking about how to go about it. It felt rather solemn to walk up to the librarian to place my search profile, returning home with a bunch of abstracts printed out.
>
> Today, it's all done on the Net. I have long since stopped printing out texts; I do all my searching and copying on the screen. I still receive printed journals, but I just throw them away. No room for them and never time to read them. I have almost stopped reading articles in full. It's abstracts that I read.

For a long time, the academic circulation of offprints was a specific kind of gift economy, a trading of information, a chance to expand one's own selective information base and academic network. But this type of search had strong time and cost constraints.

Although many of the analogue search techniques have survived, they now live in the shadow of surfing the Internet for information. Many digital immigrants have described the exhilarating, liberating feeling of entering cyberspace, with a new world of knowledge and possibilities presenting themselves. But as Wanda Orlikowski (2012) has suggested, Google searches tend to overemphasize the freedom of the user. Behind the screen is a world of software programming that selects information and organizes knowledge production in subtle and often opaque ways. Google searches have their own unique framing, shaped in a constant interaction among databases, indexes, search algorithms and the constant input of millions of other searches. Thus the selection process is constantly changing, for both the display of web pages and the order in which they are ranked. 'The information obtained with a Google search done today will shape research practices differently than had the Google search been done next week or last month' (Orlikowski, 2012: 1440; see also Puschmann, forthcoming) As ethnologist Robert Willim (2010: 35) has written: 'Together with the technology, we are joined in a kind of cognitive and epistemological feedback-loop, which influences our creativity'. He argued that there is far too little reflection on the subtle consequences for our daily research practices. Willim has also discussed the framing power of software 'menuing', and the ways in which computer programmes create their own routines, storage and retrieval habits, 'providing both a relief from frequent choice situations, and a major constraint on freedom' (Willim, 2006: 129).

All search methods – from walking along library shelves to navigating the Internet, are of course preprogrammed, but in very different ways. Lev Manovich has identified another kind of structural difference:

> As a cultural form, database represents the world as a list of items and it refuses to order this list. In contrast a narrative creates a cause-and-effect trajectory of seemingly unordered items (events). Therefore, database and narrative are natural enemies. Competing for the same territory of human culture, each claims an exclusive right to make meaning out of the world. (Manovich, 2001: 225)

But this battle among various forms of organizing and retrieving knowledge has a longer history. When documents were bound or written in volumes in chronological order – outgoing and incoming correspondence, for example – the temporal structure became specific. Innovations such as the paper slip and card box, the folder and the filing cabinet, made it possible to rearrange materials in new combinations. This technique was furthered by the production of several handwritten copies, and later, by carbon copies followed by photocopying. Old archival narratives gave way to new ones, as materials could be arranged in several ways.

It is striking that digital information management also produced new metaphors for searching. 'Navigation' was the term given to searches along set pathways in early databases – databases with elements of a narrative structure. Later, new metaphors emerged: 'data mining', and 'trawling for information' (Bowker, 2006: 29; Jackson, 2008: 164). Such metaphors have framing powers in the quest to conceptualize the cyberworld of information.

With the domesticating of new digital technologies came radically new habits for storage and retrieval. Retrieval was made easy through new kinds of software, but it is noteworthy that many of the digital innovations rested firmly on old analogue and well-established ways of organizing knowledge. 'Googling', for example, is based upon the singular way of organizing knowledge represented by list-making (Belknap, 2004).

Trawling for information on the Internet is also a striking example of a gradually acquired skill which is difficult to verbalize. Clicking one's way from link to link calls for swift decisions about what is or is not of interest, and this part of the research process is seldom documented or reflected upon. Ethnologist Hanna Jansson (2010) has attempted to reconstruct her own learning process, when surfing the Internet for research material on hobby crafts. She reflected upon the ways in which she developed a selective clicking, navigating through blogs and home pages, ignoring some links, following others. She felt the need to create her own analogue database by cutting and pasting on the screen and ending up with stacks of printouts in order to shuffle texts, mark, underline and circle them on paper. This transformation from digital to analogue form transforms the material, freezes the blog flow. It becomes a pale and one-dimensional reflection of the lively and colourful screen activities. Jansson was struggling to capture the dynamics of blog exchanges by creating a type of field diary. She noted that 'nethnography' calls for a sharp awareness of the constant need to select and ignore in order not to be swamped by all the material 'out there'.

Scholars develop their own strategies and tactics for selective surfing. Search routines may often seem unorganized. Lorie Roth collected printouts from student searches in library trash cans: 'I finally arrived at the conclusion, in fact, that there was no process; that there was no logical, clear systematic inquiry' (after Jackson, 2008: 164). But on another level, the traces of such searches may tell one a great deal about culturally acquired conventions and routines, about where to look and when to give up.

It can be difficult for people to verbalize the development of their search profiles. One sociologist put it this way:

> I wanted to hire a research assistant to go through newspaper and other media material for a specific project. He asked me: So, what should I be looking for? I answered: 'Look for interesting stuff.' Then I realized I couldn't tell him more. Now that I've worked with the material myself for some time, I could go back and be more specific. But then I was relying more on a gut feeling that couldn't really be converted into clear instructions.

Search routines – whether analogue or digital – emerge as a strong example of skills that are difficult to verbalize. Body and mind work together, and it is not only the eyes that are set to work. Fingers flip quickly through print paper, scroll and click for screen material, run along the spines of books in the library, making split-second decisions of stopping or moving on.

SELECTIVE MEMORY

In his discussion of memory practices in various scientific settings, Geoffrey C. Bowker noted that one must not focus too much on memory institutions like archives, but see remembering as a many-stranded activity: 'it is a way of framing the present; a mode of acting. We exude, sketch, form, design memory traces of all kinds; these work together in complex ecologies' (Bowker, 2006: 25). Rather than tracking the site of memory, like the archive, the researcher should focus on the ways in which memories in research settings are circulated and processed through a number of media. Bowker studied the technological, social and cultural organization of remembering in academia by looking at different memory regimes in history. The ways in which remembering and forgetting are valued in different academic settings and epochs is a challenging topic, which can draw on more general discussions of memory politics, such as 'collective amnesia', 'structural forgetting', 'frames of remembering' (for a discussion of this vast field see for example, Misztal, 2003; Connerton, 2009).

In earlier times, the art of remembering produced academic experts who were often consulted. As a student, I remember how I was directed to this or that authority, often to scholars who were not necessarily prolific producers, but who had a reputation for immense personal knowledge or fantastic collections of excerpts – walking encyclopaedias.

A good personal memory was an important research asset throughout the history of scholarly activity, but its value decreased with new technologies for outsourcing memory. To burden oneself trying to remember references, scholars and research arguments was no longer as important as it had once been. Scholars could travel lighter by forgetting stuff they knew they could retrieve from many types of storage facilities – from a stack of notes on a desk to analogue archives and digital databases.

Forgetting can be defined simply as just 'not remembering', as Bowker and Star (2000: 256ff.) noted in their discussions of selective forgetfulness and organizational forgetting. The verb 'forgetting' tends to have a negative spin, linked to neglect, repression or disinterest. But Bowker and Star have focused on the necessities of proactive modes of forgetting in academia. Total recall is neither desirable nor possible, they reminded us, and moved on to discuss how forgetting is organized in different milieux, through processes such as 'clearance' (the ways in which barriers are erected to prevent information or knowledge from leaking out into the present) or 'erasure' (the ongoing destruction of selective traces in the present). Their analysis of shifting academic settings often takes as a starting point the production of classification systems, to show how knowledge is filtered, rearranged or deleted. They also observed that rediscovery is sometimes an easier strategy than remembering in many organizational contexts, thereby rendering systematic forgetfulness a creative tool (Bowker and Star, 2000: 257).

Bowker and Star's focus, however, was mainly on the memory practices of institutions, with little attention paid to the materialities and sensibilities of remembering and forgetting in everyday work life. In an ethnographic study of a university office, Yli-Kauhaluoma and Pantzar (2012) analysed such informal routines and personal skills of remembering and forgetting, storing and retrieving knowledge. Their focus was on the mundane material of paper, which turned out to have a crucial and often creative role in organizing memory in this heavily digitalized workplace. In this hectic work setting, where the staff often felt an overflow of incoming tasks and documents, the researchers found three dominant remembering practices based upon paper: reminding, verifying and back-up practices. There were such short-term memory devices as Post-it notes, printouts and paper piles with special mnemonic qualities. People kept making printouts of e-mails and e-documents: 'It is much better to have it on paper, because it stays here', one of them argued. It was soon drowned in the e-mailbox among all the other incoming mails, and lost, 'slowly sinking down to the bottom'.

There was a skilful use of positioning Post-it notes, printouts and stacks in ways that made matters visible. Long-term memory techniques were also based on printouts of electronic documents, often in order to remember that the work had been done. In the same way, various strategies of piling stuff on desks and shelves often turned out to be more effective than the use of binders or filing cabinets. To begin with, more systematic archiving was sometimes believed to be too time-consuming.

Similar practices are discussed in Sellen and Harper's (2002) classic study, described in *The Myth of the Paperless Office*. The authors' motto is: 'Do you want to know if an organization works well? Check the wastepaper baskets – they should be full.' They visited a computer research lab, where the researchers were ordered to hide all the piles of paper and printouts when visitors arrived. Theirs was meant to be a workplace of the future; paper was obsolete. Before visitors arrived, there was a frantic hiding of paper stacks in boxes and closets until, with a sigh of relief, the masses of papers could be returned to the desks again, and effective research could continue.

In both these studies, it is critical to note the haptic dimension: remembering by holding a document in your hand or scribbling a note is a way of using one's fingers, not merely one's eyes, to remember. Sorting through a pile can be quicker than scrolling a library on the screen.

Forgetting is not merely a general option. The interlocutors in this study mentioned many informal strategies for remembering at work, often creating personal memory crutches and routines which ranged from Post-it notes on the computer screen to stacks of books placed the night before on the staircase to be taken to work the next morning. Or, as one scholar reflected, 'I remember books by their colours' – thus echoing the medieval technique of colouring letters or parts of the manuscripts to help the memory.

Tactics such as these can also be explored by examining the memory techniques used in specific offices or work desk spaces: stacks of loose paper arranged in various ways, plastic folders in different colours, books arranged in certain ways. It all constitutes a landscape that is constantly choreographed and rearranged to attract attention and create hierarchies of importance or unimportance, urgency or lack of urgency. Different strategies and aesthetics organize this work, from ideas of 'the creative mess' (Abrahamson and Freedman, 2007) to neatness and order.

DELETING AND RIDDING

> Imagine yourself streaming through time shedding gloves, umbrellas, wrenches, books, friends, homes, names. This is what the view looks like if you take a rear-facing seat on the train. Looking forward you constantly

> acquire moments of arrival, moments of realization, moments of discovery. The wind blows your hair back and you are greeted by what you have never seen before. The material falls away in onrushing experience. It peels off like skin from a molting snake. (Solnit, 2005: 23)

In Rebecca Solnit's *A Field Guide to Getting Lost*, she observed that social sciences had placed greater emphasis on all the new that is constantly in the making, than on all that must disappear in order to make room for the new. In my interviews, scholars often found it difficult to capture the ways in which old knowledge was continuously cleared away to make room for the new.

Some of the academics I interviewed talked about the promise of the digital revolution to solve the problems of storage and archiving: merely by obtaining access to endlessly expanding storage space through the utilization of more powerful hard disks or online servers, the problem of ridding could be ignored or at least postponed. Take, for example, the classic case of computer researcher and innovator Gordon Bell. For many years, he had been engaged in a process for remembering all the bits and pieces of his life for a Microsoft project called MyLifeBits. He scanned most of his paper notes and health records, kept copies of all of his 120 000 incoming e-mails and an image of every webpage he visited. He recorded many of the conversations he had with others and wore a small digital camera around his neck to take a photograph every 30 seconds, or whenever someone approached him. By 2007 he had acquired more than 100 000 of these snapshots. All this was to demonstrate that modern digital storing can allow us to collect a great deal of stuff. What it fails to tell us, however, is what to do with this flood of knowledge, texts and images.

The example of Bell is taken from Viktor Mayer-Schönberger's (2009: 50) book *Delete: The Virtue of Forgetting in the Digital Age*. It describes the hoarding of digital information on personal hard disks and on the servers of universities, governments and corporations. Mayer-Schönberger discussed the potentials and problems of this hoarding: it is easier in this new world to store information than to delete it. A click downloads every photograph from a camera, eliminating the cumbersome job of deciding which ones to keep. 'Forgetting – the three seconds it takes to choose – has become too expensive', he argued (2009: 68). As the computer asks sternly: 'Do you really want to delete this?'

Although Mayer-Schönberger also told the history of storing, organizing and retrieving information, he did not explore all the facets of the verb 'delete'. The *Oxford Dictionary* defines it as 'destroy, annihilate, do away with, cross out, cancel, remove, erase'. What kinds of deleting processes are open to scholars in a given social and historical context, and how is body and mind set in action to dispose of different kinds of knowledge, a memory, a text or an idea?

I was reminded by the differences between analogue and digital ridding when I encountered the task of moving office, which meant that I had to sift through years of accumulated research stuff, trying to decide what to keep and what to eliminate. Much of it I had stored and forgotten, many things had become invisible, even though (or because) they had been staring directly at me for years. In a sense, the cleaning-out process made me aware of my own history of storage and ridding. I constantly found myself sitting with a stack of papers or a book in my hand, trying to decide what to do with it. Get rid of it or save it? But where and how and why? Some stuff is harder to relinquish than other stuff. Books of course. There are stacks that the library won't accept, I won't keep and nobody else wants, but it is still difficult to throw books into the recycling container.

I felt like an archaeologist excavating the ruins from my old analogue days: carbon copies of letters (a great innovation at the time), old stencils and photocopies, video cassettes, taped interviews, typewritten manuscripts covered with cutting and pasting to save retyping, handwritten notes, a box of punch cards, boxes of slides and floppy disks, piles of overhead acetates, and of course loads of computer printouts and stacks of offprints. All this stuff represents technologies calling for different storage techniques. The bookshelves and the filing cabinets carry traces of my earlier and often half-hearted attempts at organizing and classifying. Other scholars I interviewed often mentioned the situation of moving office as a crucial moment of ridding and keeping. An anthropologist in her 30s thus reflected on her strategies of deleting:

> When I changed office, I started to throw things away – all my lecture notes from my student days, for example – but I found it hard to get rid of books and papers. Earlier I was very good at organizing everything in binders and folders, but now my hard disk stuff is much more neatly organized than my desk. I find it hard to delete stuff from the computer, apart from some e-mails. I keep my texts in myriad versions, can't throw them away, even though I know I'll never read them. But then I have all the memory space I want.
>
> I'm good at keeping computer files under control. When I'm too tired to do other work, I often sit down and organize materials on the hard disk.

Another colleague complained that after moving office and organizing her stuff in perfect order, rows of binders in the bookcase and a clean desk, she found that her research creativity had disappeared with the old disorder. 'I just couldn't work in this new, well organized setting.'

Others use the strategy of having double work places and therefore double archives: 'Important stuff and books I keep in my study at home – that's where I really work. In the office are just books, journals and papers that I never use, but find it hard to throw away.' Similar to this strategy, is the idea of double burials introduced by Kevin Hetherington (2004) in his discussion of ridding. There are, he argues, the 'first burial places' of a discarded object – the basement or the digital 'wastepaper basket' of the computer – stations that give people a chance to adapt to the transformation or loss. An unread memo must rest in the filing cabinet for a suitable period before it can be run through the shredder.

When I interviewed managers in a city administration on the topic of overload, they kept coming back to the stress they were experiencing from all the materials that came pouring in and landing on their desks and in their computers: suggestions, plans, surveys, memos. Like Rebecca Solnit, they rarely glanced backwards to see what was disappearing from their office at the same time. A new memo could not be thrown directly into the wastepaper basket, but by placing it in the stack on the far corner of the desk, its journey to oblivion had begun. Slowly the printouts started gathering dust and slid towards oblivion as well. After travelling to the bottom of the stack or being temporary filed away, they were getting ready for the wastepaper basket. This slow journey was hardly ever noticed.

How do we actually lose stuff, and why is that we mislay certain books, forget certain colleagues' names or cannot remember certain ideas? Utz Jeggle (1969) asked himself this question in a paper on the unconscious in research. He claimed that losing or misplacing stuff is often a much more active process than people acknowledge. By framing disappearances in terms of unintentional loss, people do not have to assume responsibility: 'I have no idea how that disappeared.' The passive disappearance is often described as a slow process. Objects slip away, relations become weaker, memories pale. All of a sudden they are gone, but how did that happen?

Again, remembering and forgetting are influenced by the ways in which human senses handle materialities. Pounding the keyboard, underlining a text, touching the screen, all represent different kinds of memory work. In a similar manner, analogue ridding means hard body work, handling stuff, leafing through contents, sorting through stacks, carrying material to the new office, organizing new filing systems or making the journey to the dust bin or the recycling station. Digital ridding, like reorganizing the hard disk, calls for other sensory inputs.

Cleaning up and reshuffling research stuff is also about producing new knowledge by finding surprising combinations. The old book one has forgotten, the lost file, the hidden offprint – all of a sudden something happens. The reshuffling of research materials is another way of reshuffling ideas. In a sense, it can be the remaking of both past and present.

STRATEGIES OF IGNORING

Discussions about ridding plunge us into the territory of organized ignorance. The recently coined term 'agnotology' focuses on the ways in which activities such as ignoring, overlooking and forgetting knowledge are culturally organized in different settings and periods (Proctor and Schiebinger, 2008; see also the discussion in Burke, 2012). Activities like these are, of course, necessary survival techniques both at home and in academia.

Writing about the history of attention, Jonathan Crary (1999) has pointed to the parallel history of inattention. It is striking that much of the early theorizing about learning to ignore centres around the modern urban experience. Scholars such as Simmel, Wirth, Goffman and Milgram all tackled the survival strategies of selective ignorance in their discussions of the way new generations of city dwellers learned to handle the sensory overload of impressions, information and people that flooded them in public life (see the discussion in Nippert-Eng, 2010: 203ff.).

In his parody of the über-academic society, Jonathan Swift describes the kingdom of Laputa, one of the stations in the travels of Gulliver. Here the absent-minded scholars live so intensively in their own thoughts that they need a servant, carrying a bladder with dried peas on a stick, called a *climenole*. By discreetly rattling this stick, the servant reminds the scholar when it is time to talk or listen to a colleague, but also to prevent the learned man from bumping into a lamppost or another person.

We need to take a closer look at how patterns of inattention, disinterest and distraction are part of selective knowledge. How do people learn not only to overlook or overhear, but also to desensitize themselves in other ways? Any form of focusing or attention is also a way of not registering or ignoring. Or, as has been said: 'A way of seeing is also a way of not seeing.' Some things manage to slip by unnoticed or be effectively camouflaged (Proctor and Schiebinger, 2008: 7). Generations create different kinds of *climenole* techniques and tools, in order to organize their attention or inattention.

Ignorance can be organized on different levels of consciousness: knowing that we do not know as opposed to not knowing we don't know.

Ignorance has the same tension between active and passive as in the discussion of deleting. In academia, we can map various ecologies of ignorance: ignorance as a resource, an empty space or a vacuum that it is attracting research attention; ignorance as inattention or disinterest, resistance or repression. This approach also calls for a closer look at the micro-processes of specific orientations and disorientations, as Sarah Ahmed (2006) has noted in her discussion of the philosopher and his writing table. All these small movements of the body, the eyes or the mind may open or block the view.

In everyday academic life, ignorance is not only what we do not (yet) know; it includes knowledge lost, abandoned or redefined as irrelevant or unimportant – and this process can be both active and passive, ranging from conscious engineering to accidental omission. Any scholar is constantly rearranging an ecology of knowing, clicking past some links, avoiding some arguments, deciding not to include certain texts or viewpoints. Here we may observe the constant (and changing) definitions of what is irrelevant, unimportant or uninteresting. In a given academic situation, what types of ignorance are encouraged or discouraged? One major way of organizing ignorance is to fence in a given research topic or arena, creating barriers to other research traditions or disciplines that need not be considered. Perhaps the case of disciplinary boundaries is the most forceful example of this active strategy. ('No need to worry about what the scholars on the other side of the fence have to say about this'). Local or national academic traditions can also create boundaries between the relevant and the irrelevant.

A cultural geographer who started his training in Germany but finished his PhD in France was struck by the different demands in the two countries. His German colleagues often got bogged down in the need to cover everything about their topic, searching and reading widely, anxious not to overlook anything. Demonstrating their extensive knowledge of the field was important but extremely time-consuming and resulted in long introductory chapters. In France he was confronted with a more bohemian attitude, told to focus on his own ideas and not to bother too much about what others had written before him. (A comparison of the length of the bibliographies in German and French dissertations demonstrates these different attitudes.) 'I was moving between two very different academic traditions. And both seemed a bit extreme', he said.

The selective mechanisms behind words such as 'uninteresting' or 'irrelevant' stuff can be observed through the ways in which scholars rapidly work their way through a bibliography, for example. One colleague demonstrated his technique. It took him an average of 30 seconds to get through a page of references with pen in hand. 'Lots of unknown authors here', he said:

> I'm looking for interesting or mystifying titles. Look at this one; it sounds intriguing. Might check it out. This one also sounds interesting, but is too old – from 1974. I'm looking for new or recent stuff. I'm looking for material on contemporary everyday culture, if there's 'media' in the title, I skip it. Same with books that smell of cultural history or seem to come from the wrong kinds of disciplines.

In the end, he had marked three out of 200 titles, which he would examine more closely later.

Another field concerns the conscious use of filters to stem information overflow. In *Islands of Privacy*, Christena Nippert-Eng (2010) discusses the extremely complex systems some Americans, and especially professionals and academics, have developed to block, filter or select incoming information or contacts, in everything from e-mails and leaflets to phone calls. People learn to delete e-mails without even looking at them, or throw unopened letters in the waste paper basket with a glance. Some establish several phone lines and e-mail accounts to eliminate spam and contacts they do not want. As Nippert-Eng shows, this filtering and blocking can sometimes become rather troublesome or time-consuming, and require the installation of filtering software or the purchase of new gadgets.

COPING WITH OVERFLOWS AND THE POWER OF ROUTINES

> Files pile up on desks, accumulate in offices and fill attics and basements. Though registered, their order collapses time and again; though collected, quashed, dispatched, sold, shredded, or destroyed in some other way, they keep mushrooming. Their incessant proliferation seems a natural phenomenon. Masses of paper rise and merge into mountains that join together to form entire mountain ranges. Floods of paper empty into oceans. (Vismann, 2008: 1)

In the introduction to her book on the workings of filing systems, Cornelia Vismann (2008: 1) points to the ways in which files take on a life of their own. In this chapter, I have called for closer attention to the materialities of selective knowledge and the ways in which a given academic setting handles, selects, stores or ignores research materials. In a Latourian sense, elements of the material infrastructure become significant co-actors (or actants): the philosopher viewing the world from a desk (Ahmed, 2006); the index card box that is not only a storage tool but also a 'creativity machine' (Wilken, 2010); the Google list that subtly ranks knowledge.

The often-elusive everyday organization of selective knowledge is a research territory still awaiting development. I have pointed to the importance of a skill perspective in order to avoid technological determinism. Why? Because skills are created at the intersection of technologies, personal habits and specific socio-cultural contexts. People create their own strategies for coping with overflow, thereby acquiring new skills – skills such as navigating through potential material and making nanosecond-long decisions about what seems worth noticing. A slowly accumulated competence of cutting corners, skimming and skipping; knowing what e-mails to answer, what memos to read; judging a book by holding it in one's hand. Many of the skills I have discussed may not even be recognized as skills by the actors themselves, but rather some of their survival techniques in situations of overload, of information and tasks.

How are such competencies acquired? The skill perspective requires a focus on processes of learning and unlearning, which brings cultural and social dimensions into practices that may at first seem individual, but are actually based upon local academic norms, conventions and understandings. This cultural dimension also surfaces in situations in which certain skills are made visible or challenged.

The skill perspective also emphasizes the fact that we are talking about practices at which people constantly improve their performance, increase their skill level. But how? Much of the research debate on skills focuses on well-organized processes of learning – as in the classic Dreyfusian five-stage model of skill acquisition, for example, moving from novice, advanced beginner, competent user, then proficient user and on to expert status (see the discussion in Collins, 2010: 101ff.). The kinds of academic skills I have discussed do not follow such a neat model. The learning process is much messier and, above all, difficult to pinpoint. Many of the skills I have discussed hover between the conscious and the unconscious. In his discussion of tacit knowledge, Collins (2010: 103) uses the classic example of people mastering touch typing – typing without looking at the keyboard. When asked to write down the order of letters on the keyboard without looking, most touch typists will fail. This knowledge now rests in the fingers, not in the mind. In his critique of the Dreyfusian model, Collins reminds us that what may look like the same skill to the outsider may be accomplished through very different and individual learning processes of a knowledge which is often difficult to verbalize.

In searching for the material and sensory dimensions, I have found a historical perspective to be helpful in two ways. First, the generational outlook underlines the importance of the way new skills are learned and old ones are abandoned or adapted. Second, historical contrasts are helpful in making patterns emerge – similarities and striking differences. To avoid getting trapped in a watershed model of before and after, as in debates about 'the digital divide', such comparisons need to be put into perspective by looking at similar, earlier discussions of radical adjustment – among the first generations after the print revolution, for example. In any such historical comparison, one must avoid seeing developments through the lenses of nostalgia (such as the loss of sensuality or authenticity). Members of every generation will tend to experience their own life as one of dramatic changes in the ways of handling knowledge and being confronted by new technologies. In this process, new sensibilities are developed.

The generational perspective also introduces questions of power. Who in academia is allowed to cut corners; to merely skim texts; to neglect, ignore and overlook certain stuff or certain aspects? Not only are many skills gradually mastered, but the ways they can be put to use also depend on one's academic position. How much selecting of knowledge can a graduate student get away with compared to an old professor? As Nancy Tuana suggests (2008: 109), this is a question linked to issues of cognitive authority, doubt, trust, silencing and uncertainty (see also Diley, 2010).

Power dimensions are also found in the ways in which research routines are permeated by changing aesthetic values: a nice print-out, a cogent argument, a good-looking diagram, a well-balanced text, a scholarly approach, a pleasing order or creative disorder in the office. As Michael Herzfeld (2007) has noted, this aesthetic dimension is often tied to ideas of academic work as a craft and thus to questions of position, skills and authority. How do we know when enough is enough materials, references and argumentation? The politics of aesthetics also appears in the ways that organizing and selecting research material create polarities of neatness and importance, as opposed to the trash, mess or residue that represents unappetizing and unimportant stuff.

Questions of selective knowledge are also embedded in the ways in which academic competencies are evaluated, words such as 'scholar', and adjectives such as 'learned' or 'erudite' have changing cultural content. Warnings about speed reading producing shallow knowledge were common in the nineteenth century, whereas skimming texts or the Internet began to be perceived as a more positive skill during the next century (Currell, 2007). There is an fascinating shift from being knowledgeable to becoming knowledge-able in attitudes towards selective knowledge: the shift from analogue to digital modes of handling materials, but, more importantly, shifts in evaluating various types of academic knowledge.

A major lesson to be learned from the study of undercurrents in everyday academic routines is that power positions and normative charges are often safely hidden in seemingly insignificant habits. Here hierarchies of, for example, gender, class and age or other positions of authority may go unchallenged.

The ways in which texts are read and materials handled, selected or deselected are also dependent upon changing scientific paradigms, but are also related to tools of information management. The card index is, in a sense, 'a quintessential structuralist tool, in that it simultaneously combines the paradigmatic (selection) with the syntagmatic (combination) in one mechanism', as Wilken (2010: 12) has argued. Similarly, one may discuss the ways in which digitalization influenced post-structuralist academic writing and the world of hypertexts.

Finally, my explorations stress the importance of looking at the microphysics of selective knowledge. Of special interest here are the trajectories of transformation and selection, as research materials and ideas move through the academic terrain and are contained in different material forms, as in Latour's (1999b) classic study, *Sampling the Soil in the Amazon Forest*. His study of an analogue trajectory can be compared to the digital world of transformations that Hanna Jansson (2010) touched in her auto-ethnography of using cyberstuff and seeing digital material on the screen transformed into analogue stacks of printouts on her desk.

Returning to the dictionary, there are several things to note. Many of the verbs depicting processes of selection are active – people doing something – but, as we have seen, selective knowledge exists in a strong tension between the active and the passive, the conscious and unconscious. Sometimes the unconscious helps us by blurring the boundary between losing and leaving behind, ignoring and missing – turning the active into passive. It is striking how many of these verbs focus on small moves, on a choreography of neglect: over-look, dis-regard, pass over, leave out, slip up on, for-get, e-rase, ob-scure. Often the senses and the body are used to describe such processes: turning a blind eye or a deaf ear to, taking a half-hearted interest in, brushing off, being unaware of or insensitive to. Or as Thomas Pynchon has put it: 'Ignorance is not just a blank space on a person's mental map. It has contours and coherence, and for all I know rules of operation as well' (after Proctor, 2008: 1).

NOTE

1. My discussion is part of an ongoing project on everyday academic skills. I am grateful for the constructive comments of Gösta Arvastson, Peter Burke, Billy Ehn, Ron Eyerman and Jonas Frykman.

15. Afterword: overflows as boundary events between organizations and markets

Franck Cochoy

Considered as a dynamic and abstract variant of Star and Griesemer's (1989) famous notion of 'boundary objects', any overflow could be called a 'boundary event'. Whatever its form and content, the occurrence of an overflow connects, but also challenges, the external market-like flows and the internal organizational frames: It leads the flows to excess and chaos and urges the frames to bring it back to control and stability.

As this book demonstrates, the overflows which actors must manage are incredibly pervasive and varied. They range from financial surplus (Czarniawska, Donatella and Solli) and stock trading moves (Tarim) to such everyday objects as baby 'stuff' (Brembeck) and adult 'stuff' (Czubaj; Ekström); from essentially material entities like biogas (Corvellec), office space (Raviola), music (Wenzer) and white noise (Willim) through such anthropological entities as human utopia (Pantzar), academic knowledge (Löfgren) and business archives (Fellman and Popp) to human beings in the form of patients (Norén) – and, of course, human feelings, moral concerns and emotions, which most of these authors have addressed in their own ways. This volume also presents an impressive array of techniques and strategies aimed at managing such overflows. These techniques range from managerial tools (Czarniawska, Donatella and Solli; Tarim), filtering and sorting methods (Löfgren; Ekström; Brembeck; Wenzer) and the 'freezing' of past flows as a way of stabilizing them (Fellman and Popp); converting procedures, which succeed in shifting useless, wasteful or negative overflows into valuable new entities (Corvellec; Willim; Raviola); and even paradoxical magic-like tricks – when generating overflows appears to be the way to control them (Norén), when rarefying goods raises curiosity about them (Wenzer) or when spending money is presented as a way of saving it (Czubaj).

In order to control this overflowing diversity of overflows and related techniques, I propose in this Afterword to rely on my own filtering devices, by highlighting a selection of five independent but related insights to be found in this collection of chapters. The first of them unveils the subjective dimension of overflow management; the second reflects on the type of this involved agency; the third stresses the role of time in such operations; the fourth explores the way overflow management makes sense of traces; and the fifth addresses the importance of combining calculating and narrative approaches.

FROM COLLECTIVE ORGANIZATION TO SUBJECTIVE ORGANIZING

Whereas economics still believe that the world is controlled by organizational or market tools and models, social scientists and organization theorists suggest that the management of overflows loosens the power of organizations and reintroduces, at least momentarily, the subjective point of view and efforts of individuals who have to reorganize their network and reinvent organizing procedures to cope with these overflows which disrupt the structures they relied on previously.

Of course, several contributions to this book present classic organizational ways of handling overflows: health management (Norén), financial services (Czarniawska, Donatella and Solli; Tarim), recycling companies (Corvellec) and non-profit organizations (Raviola) are collective bodies dealing with overflows of patients, money, waste and space, respectively. But even in these cases, we discover that the disruptions introduced by overflows present a challenge to organizational routines, and thus favour within them the emergence of individualized creative solutions. This is particularly true in the case of financial services, in which accountants and traders take the lead in inventing appropriate argumentations; or, in the case of the Hundred Offices initiative, in which the exchange between space and creation works only through strong individual involvement. In fact, in most cases, be it organizational or otherwise, overflow management is handled, first and foremost, at the personal level: parents cope with the invading amount of baby stuff (Brembeck); couples deal with the profusion of things they must discard when moving to smaller houses (Ekström); consumers face the flow of goods and services (Czubaj; Wenzer; Willim); business historians and other scholars struggle with the abundance of archives, materials and sources (Fellman and Popp; Löfgren).

It is noteworthy that, in most cases, an overflow presents itself as an unexpected fact, event or shock. Ekström's example of families moving and downsizing makes it particularly clear: because people continue to see themselves as embedded in social, cultural and institutional matters, they pay less attention to the flow of the innumerable things which can proliferate, despite but also thanks to them. But later in life, these people come to realize how things have invaded their lives, to the point where they find it difficult and even painful to get rid of them. Because overflows present themselves as an unthought or unexpected matter of fact, they are first received by people without any mediation and thus lived as a subjective encounter – as something several persons first experience alone, usually before they can share it and deal with it collectively.

In this respect, the case of historians and scientists is particularly illuminating. There is a strong discrepancy, a tension, if not a contradiction, between scientific norms, in the Mertonian sense, which impose a general and systematic treatment of an exhaustive set of data, and scientific practice, in the Latourian sense, which immerses each scientist in the middle of an overwhelming flow of facts and questions. This situation echoes Herbert Simon's classic opposition between synoptic and bounded rationality: science as an institution prescribes the adoption of a synoptic view, but science as a practice requires the bounded approach to be followed. Fellman and Popp's and Löfgren's contributions show that researchers have to behave in a schizophrenic way: they have no choice but to acknowledge their professional commitment to systematic knowledge publicly, while privately behaving in the only manageable way – which is of course by obeying the pragmatic rule to select, sort, discard and forget any excess data, more or less arbitrarily. It is only through anonymous interviews that people confess that individualized overflow experiences pave the way towards scientific knowledge ('There is no way I can read everything': Fellman and Popp). In transgressing this taboo, this volume has a most welcome emancipatory character: it helps us to realize that denying or fighting overflow is not the proper strategy. Rather than cheating or lying in staging an encyclopaedic knowledge no one can have, instead of exhausting oneself swimming against the stream, we should better accept that scientific conduct, and more generally any professional behaviour, particularly in the economic sector, requires acceptance of being carried by the flow and swimming into it properly. One of the most illuminating lessons of this book, albeit implicit, is that workable overflow management is less about resisting the flow, containing it, framing it, stopping it behind dams and dikes, than it is about accepting the evidence and force of the flood, abandoning oneself to it, but then trying to avoid drowning in the stream – rather staying on the surface, keeping clear of obstacles, favouring serendipity and peripheral vision in order to choose the appropriate bifurcations, and eventually reach calmer waters and reflect upon the travel accomplished after reaching more promising banks.

But how does one swim through an overflowing stream? Several highly original solutions emerge from this book. One goes beyond individual versus organizational solutions in redefining the subject; the second enriches the previous framework of the management of externalities by giving it a temporal dimension; the last one stresses the importance of meaning and narratives as a way of making sense of the apparent quantitative problem raised by overflows.

BEYOND INDIVIDUAL AND ORGANIZATIONAL ACTION: 'CYBORGIZED' OVERFLOW MANAGERS

At least since Rousseau, we have known that organizational arrangements emerge when individuals, eager to accomplish a task they cannot fulfil on their own, have no solution other than signing a 'social contract' with partners who are willing to join their efforts. But the dispossession of some of their freedom and their correlative submission to the agreed-upon rule is the price they must pay to benefit from collective action as a means of acting more efficiently and attaining larger objectives. Yet, does not the move back to personalized overflow management that I have just noted contradict the Rousseauist solution? Is it possible to manage overflow alone? In fact, the contradiction fades away when we discover, through the contemporary situations addressed in this collection, the existence of an alternative to both individual and organizational action. In several cases, the individuals who are lost in front of the various types of overflows with which they must deal, rest not only on their individual skills or on organizational frames, but also on various external entities such as stories (Tarim), accounting devices (Czarniawska, Donatella and Solli), shopping lists (Brembeck), indexes (Fellman and Popp; Löfgren) and web browsers (Wenzer). To a certain extent, such an observation is trivial and well-known: the power of technique is as old as human history. In order to do more and perform better, individual tools have always been if not an alternative, at least a powerful complement to collective endeavours.

The situations examined in this book subtly displace and redefine this classic result, however. First, some of the overflows at stake help tracing the displacement I refer to. Brembeck's study on baby stuff management, for instance, shows that even someone as simple and clearly delimited as a baby enters society not merely as a little individual, but rather as an amazing bundle comprising various entities. Indeed, the naked singularity of a new-born baby lasts only for the first few seconds of life and is almost immediately redefined as the nexus of an incredible web comprising lovely body parts and human expressions, of course, but also varied clothes, nappies, toys, prams, strollers, and other material goods. Parents believe at first that they are waiting merely for a beloved person to arrive, but they quickly discover, usually even before the birth, that they must also welcome all the stuff that accompanies the baby. Second, what is true for some of the managed overflows (such as baby stuff) is also true for some overflow managers, such as researchers and their data. Here comes the displacement I want to highlight. The very process of overflow management reshapes the involved entities. The individuals facing today's overflows are not merely equipped with the external tools available to manage the task; rather, overflow management rests on the hybridization of people and their tools. The examples of sound production (Willim) and music consumption (Wenzer) demonstrate it well: sound producers and music amateurs believe that they create their own sound or express their inner tastes, but in fact, the contemporary listening entity is neither individual artists nor listeners and their music devices. More and more it is a 'cyborg' agency – a combination of the two. Indeed, modern subjects combine their internal/human brain and external/artificial cognitive prostheses in the forms of samplers, filters, algorithms, computers, web browsers and automatic indexes. The iTunes Genius device and Amazon's suggestions build and express networks of preferences; contemporary 'quantified selves' spread their lives between their individual experiences and their electronic cognitive equipment (Licoppe, 2013). The opposite philosophies of Google versus Duck Duck Go algorithms decide beyond us how to sort our data. (Whereas Google bases its suggestions on our past requests, its recent challenger, Duck Duck Go, bets on anonymous amnesic exploration.) These devices, once external, have become part of us. Notice how our smartphones have become an indispensable secondary brain, helping us to solve our overflow management problems. More importantly, such tools manage to dilute the 'quantified self' (Licoppe, 2013) into an overflow of larger cognitive networks (Serres, 2012). All in all, contemporary issues about the protection of 'privacy' within the Internet economy (Kessous, 2012) are raised and denied simultaneously. The endangered private isolated actors no longer exist, but have already melted into an overflow of monads – public webs of private traces … or private knots of public links (Latour et al., 2012).

SPACE AND TIME: FROM EXTERNALITIES TO TEMPORALITIES MANAGEMENT

The rise of these hybrid entities challenges the classic opposition among internal actors, whether individuals or organizations, and external 'invading' events – the overflow that actors have to manage. In several situations, of course, the game between organizational frames and external flows still prevails and is worthy of study. Norén makes a strong contribution, for instance, in showing that overflows, far from being mere emergent events, can be provoked and used as a way to manage organization 'by outside overflows'. The managers of health services, he demonstrates, deliberately transform the overflow of patients from an undesired event into a voluntary construction, which is supposed to press organizational structures to adapt and improve themselves accordingly. The more patients exist as a real stream (and the same is true for all market 'crowds' of customers), the more they can be used as a rhetorical device, as a way to have people do what classic administrative authority no longer obtains by itself (Cochoy, 2005). But yet, the general tendency is rather that of the dissolution of the dialectic of frames and flows (Callon, 1998b) into more, larger and flexible actor-networks, or action nets (Czarniawska, 1997). Ironically, the management of overflows often leads to fluxing organizations.

In this respect, the processes that really matter may well be less spatial than temporal, as Czarniawska, Donatella and Solli suggest: several overflow problems now rest less on mobilizing organizational resources to cope with market or public events than they do on playing temporal tricks to balance overflows. See how the financial specialists of the municipality of Northtown managed to turn 'too much money' into 'too little money'. They did so by cleverly combining provisions, tariff reserves, present taxes and future projects. In other words, the 'inside–outside' dichotomy is replaced by a 'before–after' dichotomy; the internalization of externalities is supplemented by a management of temporalities. In this game, a key feature is that of buffering – creating an atemporal zone where things may be extracted from the flow of time, apart from the past, the present and the future, so that the decision of their conservation or discarding may be postponed. This transitory buffering process plays a prominent role in private life, when families move to smaller homes and are forced to deal with the overflow of things and with the emotions attached to them (Ekström) – but also in more professional contexts, as when a researcher places an 'unread memo …

in the filing cabinet for a suitable period before it can be run through the shredder' (Löfgren).

MAKING SENSE OF OVERFLOWS: FROM TRACEABILITY TO 'MAPPABILITY'

Overflow buffering reveals the reflexive power of overflows. Surprise, embarrassment or puzzlement are the first feelings experienced when facing an overflow. But soon such troubles lead the overflowed actor to think and make sense of what he or she faces. Behind this cognitive pattern lies a major evolution that contemporary organizations and markets are currently experiencing: I once proposed calling this evolution the shift from 'traceability' to 'mappability' (Cochoy and Terssac, 2000).

The meaning and potential of these two notions is best captured in referring to a literary metaphor. In his novel *City of Glass*, part of the *New York Trilogy*, US writer Paul Auster (1989) featured a private eye, Quinn, who is paid to follow the comings and goings of a fellow named Stillman. Professionally, Quinn's behaviour is perfect. He follows Stillman daily, without ever being noticed, without ever losing his trace, while methodically documenting all Stillman's actions in a small notebook: where he goes, what he collects, and so on. Quinn works as a perfect traceability manager. And yet, this perfect traceability – a discrete, continuous and exhaustive recording – leads to nothing; the private eye may well follow his target like his shadow, but the retrospective review of the collected evidence proves completely meaningless. Annoyed after days and days of this sterile manhunt, the detective is about to give up when he suddenly gets the idea to write on a map of New York the names of the streets and avenues travelled by Stillman and methodically recorded in Quinn's notebook. By retracing Stillman's footsteps, Quinn realizes that each daily course drew a letter of the alphabet. The chronological sequence of these letters ultimately discloses the purpose which animated the apparent meaningless of Stillman's ramblings, which spell the words 'TOWER OF BABEL'. The lesson is clear: traces make sense only when reported on a map. To overcome the overflow of traces, then, one must move from traceability to mappability, a move that requires a 90-degree rotation. The idea is not only to save the links among various entities, but to gain height and build a comprehensive larger picture from the collected traces.

Performing a successful mappability operation – making sense of archivists' traceability efforts – is, of course, the traditional challenge which any historian tries to meet. As Fellman and Popp have so nicely put it, historical work is precisely about '[m]apping the context and the geography of the archive'. But the historian's effort aimed at mapping the overflows of traces is now shared in the form of a more general movement of 'data mining', which, far from being restricted to historical or academic pursuits (Löfgren), has become a pervasive activity in innumerable organizations. This movement relies on the convergence of a long-lasting evolution and the appearance of new ad hoc technologies. As far as the evolution is concerned, the twentieth-century economy has been marked by the production and management of traces, from the invention of product labelling and brand names, which helped to connect producers and consumers (Strasser, 1989), to modern traceability systems, aimed at guaranteeing and improving quality (Cochoy, 2005). But for a long time, traces were kept 'just in case', as a blind safety corpus that was neglected in ordinary situations but that one would consult if, under extraordinary circumstances, a problem occurred or someone were interested in re-examining the past. Consequently, a collection of traces ended up as overflows of forgotten data that only police officers, historians or lawyers would explore from time to time according to their respective objectives. Today, the novelty is the emergence of what could be called 'mappability technologies', such as automatic indexes, statistical software or network analysis algorithms, which help to make sense of the previously unmanageable overflow of traces now converted in valuable maps and new economic resources. Note the recent development of the 'big data' industry and market, based on systematic mapping of the gigantic overflow of traces collected from our smartphones and cloud computing activities. For long time, overflow was a matter of too many (things), and not enough (meaning). The dream of big data management is to reduce the two: with big data, every piece of information is supposed to be controllable yet meaningful.

QUALCULATING OVERFLOWS

However big they may be, data never fully cover the world they refer to. Reality will always overflow (or escape) the web of references that are supposed to account for it (Latour, 1999a). Here, we reach a second taboo of scientific overflow management. As we already saw with Fellman and Popp, the first taboo is the impossibility of embracing everything. The second taboo is the symmetric counterpart of the first: if analysts are unable to welcome all data and are yet obliged to pretend that they do (first taboo), the data they have are often not enough to support the results fully, yet they must present them as such. Historians cannot but present their work in the terms of official science, as a body of knowledge stemming from rigorous methods and objective data, for instance. Yet they know perfectly well that it is possible to reach that objective only by implementing an amazing practice of literary creation. Historians' accounts largely consist of filling the overflowing gaps of missing data with words, linking the available facts with appropriate guesses, writing a coherent and continuous story from erratic and discrete traces, discovering the flow of past events through narrative and creative inventions (second taboo). In other words and as far as overflow management is concerned, the scientific and the literary, the real and the imaginary, the calculative and the qualitative go hand in hand. One cannot account for the flood of things without appropriate 'qualculation' procedures: procedures which combine numbers and words, or replace statistical figures with rhetorical ones when the former are missing (Cochoy, 2008). Several contributions to this book brilliantly illustrate the pervasiveness of this scheme: the talent of smart accountants is not limited to computing skills, but extends to and rests upon a virtuous ability to embed numbers with proper notions and stories of mergers, tariff reserves and budget expenditures (Czarniawska, Donatella and Solli); even the traders of financial markets that everyone acknowledges as the wizards of pure economic calculation are also frenetic storytellers. As Tarim demonstrates, markets professionals do not calculate; they 'formulate' the economy. Formulation is really the right word (Callon, 2013); it brings together the formulas (the famous Black and Scholes equation performed on derivative markets; MacKenzie and Millo, 2003), the forms (in which numbers are recorded) and the narrative 'formulations', without which the formulas could have no performative effects. Last but not least, the urban planners of Tapiola frame and reinvent city overflows at the same time, showing us how the cold analytics of modern technocracy can be combined with the poetic dreams of pure utopia (Pantzar).

CONCLUSION: THE AMBIVALENT POLITICS OF OVERFLOWS

The key question is, of course, 'Where do such combinations lead?' As I have already noted, if overflows are first considered a problem, they eventually appear as an extraordinary resource for reflexivity, awareness and invention. Management often suspends thinking because of its primary reliance on given procedures and routines (Cyert and March,

1963); the emergence of overflows stops automatic answers and opens the way for criticism, reassessment and innovation.

The lessons learned are ambivalent. On the one hand, the collection of chapters stresses the surprising creativity attached to overflow management. Overflows are largely unexpected events. Largely, but not completely. See what happens in consumer markets: the unexpected flow of goods experienced on the demand side (Brembeck; Ekström; Czubaj) is fully controlled on the organizational side. Management is about producing, and products and services are produced to overflow markets. In the marketing economy, overflows are neither side effects nor the unwitting results of excessive framing; they are voluntary productions. For a long time, historians of consumption have shown the extent to which the production of marketing overflows paralleled the industrial revolution (McKendrick et al., 1982). Significantly, the Protestants, who as we all know were ascetically saving at work, were also frenetically consuming at home, at least by proxy (Mukerji, 1983; Campbell, 1987). To a certain extent, this volume celebrates creativity, in describing overflow producers as contemporary versions of Michel Serres' (1982) parasite. In several situations, managing overflows is a parasitic activity, in Serres' positive sense of the term: an activity aimed at giving value to that which others discard.

To use another metaphor, overflow managers can thus be presented as modern alchemists who succeed if not in turning lead into gold, at least in turning noise into positive sound (Willim), waste into biogas (Corvellec), and space emptiness into full human exchange (Raviola). Management is often acknowledged as a matter of framing, channelling, organizing a given entity. Here, we discover that management is also a matter of invention or transmutation. At least when facing overflows, management hybridizes with engineering, and powerfully contributes to human creativity.

But, on the other hand, the production of overflows goes with an overflow of new problems and questions. For Czubaj, who meets Naomi Klein's (2000) former conclusions, the consumerist overflow of goods is produced as a pure sham. We think that we face infinite choices, but each item is merely an illusory variation of a same product. If Czubaj is correct, one could say that the Western capitalist economy ironically reinvents the old Soviet supply of unique generic products in a more perverse way, as the uniqueness of each good is now hidden behind the overflowing shams of diversity. If not illusory, creative overflows are at least ambiguous, upstream as well as downstream. Waste can well be converted into biogas, for instance, but this apparently positive production cannot exist without more questionable overflows of waste upstream

(Corvellec) and green gas emission downstream. Even when neither illusory nor ambiguous, overflows run badly. In Raviola's Hundred Offices case, however astute may be the decision to pair artists with empty business space, this creative scheme proves difficult to implement, even in the most favourable cases, because of the difficulty of playing the 'connecting vessels' game with 'non-homogeneous' liquids. And even when implemented, overflow management is often bypassed by the emergence of new types of overflows: The 'overplanning' of Tapiola's garden city is submersed by the prosaic forces of noise disturbances and car traffic flood (Pantzar). Last but not least, several overflow management schemes must face more discrete 'leaks' – problems or promises – when music escapes the dikes of property management systems, for instance (Wenzer). This issue introduces a fascinating distinction between two notions that are often confused. An overflow goes above a dike; a leak goes beneath or through it. An overflow often comes from the outside; leaks come from the inside. If less spectacular, are not leaks more frequent than and as transformative as overflows? In this respect, it would probably be worthwhile to avoid any leak from this project, to stick with the flow of research it opened, and to complement the study of overflow with the study of leak management.

References

Aario, Leo (1986) The original garden cities in Britain and the garden city ideal in Finland. *Fennia*, 164(2): 157–209.

Aaron, Leopold (2010) The changing constellation of power and resistance in the global debate over agrofuels. *Innovation: The European Journal of Social Science Research*, 23(4): 389–408.

Abdelrehim, Neveen, Maltby, Josephine and Toms, Stephen (2011) Corporate Social Responsibility and corporate control: The Anglo-Iranian Oil Company, 1933–1951. *Enterprise & Society*, 12(4): 824–862.

Abolafia, Mitchel Y. (1996) *Making markets. Opportunism and restraint on Wall Street*. Cambridge, MA: Harvard University Press.

Abolafia, Mitchel Y. (1998) Markets as cultures: An ethnographic approach. In Callon, Michael (ed.) *The laws of the markets*. Oxford: Blackwell, 69–85.

Abolafia, Mitchel Y. (2010) Narrative construction as sensemaking: How a central bank thinks. *Organization Studies*, 31(3): 349–367.

Abrahamson, Eric and Freedman, David H. (2006) *A perfect mess: The hidden benefits of disorder*. New York: Little, Brown & Company.

Ahmed, Sarah (2006) Orientations: Toward a queer phenomenology. *GLG: A Journal of Lesbian and Gay Studies*, 12(4): 543–574.

Åkesson, Lynn (2012) Waste in overflow. In: Czarniawska, Barbara and Löfgren, Orvar (eds) *The management of overflow in affluent societies*. New York: Routledge, 141–154.

Amatori, Franco (2009) Business history as history. *Business History*, 51(2): 142–156.

Anderson, Ben and Harrison, Paul (2010) *Taking place. Non-representational theories*. Burlington, VT: Ashgate.

Anell, Anders (2005) *Primärvård i förändring*. Lund: Studentlitteratur.

Anell, Anders (2011) Choice and privatization in Swedish primary care. *Health Economics, Policy and Law*, 6: 549–569.

Anthony, Robert N. (1985) Games government accountants play. *Harvard Business Review*, 63(5): 161–170.

Anton, Thomas J. (1967) Roles and symbols in state expenditures. *Midwest Journal of Political Science*, 11(Feb): 27–43.

Appadurai, Arjun (1986) Commodities and the politics of value. In Appadurai, Arjun (ed.), *The social life of things. Commodities in cultural perspective*. Cambridge: Cambridge University Press, 34–43.
Auster, Paul (1989) *The New York trilogy*. London: Faber and Faber.
Ballantine, Joan; Forker, John and Greenwood, Margaret (2007) Earnings management in English NHS hospital trusts. *Financial Accountability and Management*, 23(4): 421–440.
Barthes, Roland (1975) *Roland Barthes par Roland Barthes*. Paris: Éditions du Seuil.
Bataille, Georges (1949/1988) *The accursed share: An essay on general economy (Volume 1: Consumption)*. New York: Zone Books.
Baudrillard, Jean (1998) *The consumer society. Myths and structure*. London: Sage.
Bauman, Zygmunt (1998) *Work, consumerism and the new poor*. Buckingham: Open University Press.
Bauman, Zygmunt (2000) *Liquid modernity*. Cambridge: Polity.
Bauman, Zygmunt (2003) *Razem osobno*. Kraków: Wydawnictwo Literackie.
Baym, Nancy K. (2011) The Swedish Model: Balancing markets and gifts in the music industry. *Popular Communication: The International Journal of Media and Culture*, 9(1): 22–38.
Belk, Russell W. (1988) Possessions and the extended self. *Journal of Consumer Research*, 15(2): 168.
Belk, Russell W. (2001) Materialism and you. *Journal of Research for Consumers*, 1: 1–7.
Belk, Russell W.; Wallendorf, Melanie and Sherry, John Jr. (1991) The sacred and the profane in consumer behavior: Theodicy on the Odyssey. In: Belk, Russell W. (ed.) *Highways and buyways: Naturalistic research from the consumer behavior Odyssey*. Provo, UT: Association for Consumer Research, 59–101.
Belk, Russell W.; Wallendorf, Melanie; Sherry, John Jr. and Holbrook, Morris (1988) Collectors and collecting. In: Houston, Michael J. (ed.) *Advances in consumer research*. Provo, UT: Associations for Consumer Research, 548–553.
Belknap, Robert E. (2004) *The list. The uses and pleasures of cataloguing*. New Haven, CT: Yale University Press.
Bell, Linda and Ribbens, Jane (1994) Isolated housewives and complex maternal worlds. *Sociological Review*, 42(2): 227–262.
Benedict, Ruth (1934/2006) *Patterns of culture*. Boston, MA: Mariner Books.
Benkler, Yochai (2006) *The wealth of networks: How social production transforms markets and freedom*. New Haven, CT: Yale University Press.

Bergmark, Åke (2008) Market reforms in Swedish health care: Normative reorientation and welfare state sustainability. *Journal of Medicine and Philosophy*, 33(3): 241–261.

Beunza, Daniel, and Stark, David (2005) How to recognize opportunities: Hierarchical search in a trading room. In: Knorr Cetina, Karin and Preda, Alex (eds) *The sociology of financial markets*. Oxford: Oxford University Press, 84–101.

Blair, Ann M. (2010) *Too much to know. Managing scholarly information before the modern age*. New Haven, CT: Yale University Press.

Blair, Ann and Milligan, Jennifer (2007) Introduction. *Archival Science*, 7(4): 289–296.

Bloch, Marc (1954) *The historian's craft*. Manchester: Manchester University Press.

Boje, David M. (1991) Organizations as storytelling networks: A study of story performance in an office-supply firm. *Administrative Science Quarterly*, 36(1): 106–126.

Boje, David M. (2001) *Narrative methods for organizational and communication research*. London: Sage.

Boltanski, Luc and Thévenot, Laurent (2006) *On justification: Economies of worth*. Princeton, NJ: Princeton University Press.

Botsman, Rachel and Rogers, Roo (2010) *What's mine is yours. How collaborative consumption is changing the way we live*. London: HarperCollins.

Bourdieu, Pierre (1975/1984) Pour une sociologie des sociologues. In: Bourdieu, Pierre (ed.) *Questions de sociologie*. Paris: Minuit, 79–85.

Bourdieu, Pierre (1984) *Distinction. A social critique of the judgement of taste*. Harvard, MA: Harvard University Press.

Bowker, Geoffrey C. (2006) *Memory practices in the sciences*. Cambridge, MA: MIT Press.

Bowker, Geoffrey C. and Star, Susan Leigh (1999) *Sorting things out. Classification and its consequences*. Cambridge, MA: MIT Press, paperback 2000.

Boyd, Harper W., Jr and Levy, Sidney (1963) New dimensions in consumer analysis. *Harvard Business Review*, 41(November–December): 129–140.

Bradley, Harriet (1999) The seduction of the archive: Voices lost and found. *History of the Human Sciences*, 12(2): 107–122.

Brembeck, Helene (2007) To consume and be consumed. In: Brembeck, Helene; Ekström, Karin M. and Mörck, Magnus (eds) *Little monsters. (De)coupling assemblages of consumption*. Berlin: LIT Verlag, 183–205.

Brembeck, Helene (2012) Cozy Friday: An analysis of family togetherness and ritual overconsumption. In: Czarniawska, Barbara and

Löfgren, Orvar (eds) *Managing overflow in affluent societies*. New York: Routledge, 125–140.

Brorström, Björn (1997) *För den goda redovisningsseden*. Lund: Studentlitteratur.

Brorström, Björn (2007) Den finansiella redovisningens utveckling och kvalitet. In: Siverbo, Sven; Andersson-Felé, Lena; Karlsson, David and Nilsson, Viveka (eds) *Demokratisk och effektiv styrning: En antologi om forskning i offentlig förvaltning*. Lund: Studentlitteratur, 143–158.

Brorström, Björn; Eriksson, Ola and Haglund, Anders (2008) *Kommunal redovisningslag: Beskrivning och tolkning*. Lund: Studentlitteratur.

Brown, Richard Harvey (1978) Bureaucracy as praxis: Toward of political phenomenology of formal organizations. *Administrative Science Quarterly*, 23(3): 365–382.

Bruner, Jerome (1986) *Actual minds, possible worlds*. Cambridge, MA: Harvard University Press.

Brunsson, Nils (1989) *The organization of hypocrisy: Talk, action and decision in organizations*. London: Wiley.

Brunsson, Nils (1991) Politisering och företagisering – om institutionell förankring och förvirring i organisationernas värld. In: Arvidsson, Göran and Lind, Rolf (eds) *Ledning av företag och förvaltningar*. Stockholm: SNS, 20–41.

Burke, Peter (2012) *From the Encyclopédie to Wikipedia: A social history of knowledge*. Oxford: Polity Press.

Burridge, Kenelm (1960/1995) *Mambu. A Melanesian millennium*. Princeton, NJ: Princeton University Press.

Burton, Antoinette (2005) Introduction. Archive fever, archive stories. In: Burton Antoinette (ed.) *Archive stories. Facts, fictions, and the writing of history*. Durham, NC: Duke University Press, 1–24.

Butler, Judith (2002) What is critique? An essay on Foucault's virtue. In: Ingram, David (ed.) *The political: Readings in continental philosophy*. London: Basil Blackwell, 212–229.

Caldwell, Nigel; Walker, Helen; Harland, Christine; Knight, Louise; Zheng, Jurong and Wakeley, Tom (2005) Promoting competitive markets: The role of public procurement. *Journal of Purchasing and Supply Management*, 11(5–6): 242–251.

Callon, Michel (1986) Some elements of a sociology of translation: domestication of the scallops and the fishermen of St Brieuc Bay. In: Law, John (ed.) *Power, action and belief*. London: Routledge & Kegan Paul, 196–223.

Callon, Michel (1998a) An essay on framing and overflowing: Economic externalities revisited by sociology. *Sociological Review Monograph*, 46, 244–269.

Callon, Michel (1998b). Introduction: The embeddness of economic markets in economics. In: Callon, Michel (ed.) *The laws of the markets*. Oxford: Blackwell, 1–57.

Callon, Michel (1999) Actor Network Theory – the market test. In: Law, John and Hassard, John (eds). *Actor Network Theory and after*. Oxford: Blackwell, 181–195.

Callon, Michel (2013) Sociologie des agencements marchands. Paris: Presses des Mines.

Campbell, Colin (1987) *The romantic ethic and the spirit of modern consumerism*. New York: Basic Blackwell.

Campbell, Colin (2003) I shop therefore I know that I am. In: Ekström, Karin and Brembeck, Helen (eds) *Elusive consumption: Tracking new research perspectives*. Oxford: Berg, 27–44.

Carlin, Tyrone M. (2005) Debating the impact of accrual accounting and reporting in the public sector. *Financial Accountability and Management*, 21(3): 309–336.

Cascone, Kim (2000) The aesthetics of failure: 'Post-digital' tendencies. *Computer Music Journal*, 24(4): 12–18.

Case, Donald Owen (1991) The collection and use of information by some American historians: A study of motives and methods. *Library Quarterly*, 61(1): 66–82.

Cavallo, Guglielmo and Chartier, Roger (eds) *A history of reading in the west*. Amherst, MA: University of Massachusetts Press.

Cetina, Karin K. and Preda, Alex (2007) The temporalisation of financial markets: From network to flow. *Theory, Culture, and Society*, 24(7–8): 116–138.

Clarke, Alison, J. (2007) Making sameness: Mothering, commerce and the culture of children's birthday parties. In: Casey, Emma and Martens, Lydia (eds) *Gender and consumption. Domestic cultures and the commercialisation of everyday life*. Aldershot: Ashgate, 79–95.

Cochoy, Franck (2005) A short history of 'customers', or the gradual standardization of markets and organizations. *Sociologie du travail*, 47(1): 36–56.

Cochoy, Franck (2008) Calculation, qualculation, calqulation: Shopping cart's arithmetic, equipped cognition and the collective consumer. *Marketing Theory*, 8: 15–44.

Cochoy, Franck (2009) Driving a shopping cart from STS to business, and the other way round: On the introduction of shopping cards in American grocery stores (1936–1959). *Organization*, 16(1): 31–55.

Cochoy, Franck (2012) '*In datamatrix veritas?*' Managing wine flow and information overflow with a two-dimensional barcode. In: Czarniawska, Barbara and Löfgren, Orvar (eds) *Managing overflow in affluent societies*. New York: Routledge, 52–67.

Cochoy, Franck and Terssac, Gilbert de (2000) Au-delà de la traçabilité: la mappabilité. Deux notions connexes mais distinctes pour penser les normes de management. In: Serverin, Évelyne and Berthoud, Arnaud (eds) *La production des normes entre État et société civile*. Paris: L'Harmattan, 239–249.
Cole, Charles (1998) Information acquisition in history PhD students: Inferencing and the formation of knowledge structures. *Library Quarterly*, 68(1): 33–54.
Cole, Charles (2000) Inducing expertise in history doctoral students via information retrieval design. *Library Quarterly*, 70(1): 86–109.
Collins, Harry (2010) *Tacit and explicit knowledge*. Chicago, IL: University of Chicago Press.
Connerton, Paul (2009) *How modernity forgets*. Cambridge: Cambridge University Press.
Cook, Terry (2009) The archive(s) is a foreign country. Historians, archivists, and the changing archival landscape. *Canadian Historical Review*, 90(3): 497–534.
Corrigan, Peter (1997) *The sociology of consumption. An introduction*. London: Sage.
Corvellec, Hervé and Johan Hultman (2012) From 'less landfilling' to 'wasting less' – Societal narratives, socio-materiality and organizations. *Journal of Organizational Change Management*, 25(2), 297–314.
Corvellec, Hervé; Zapata Campos, María José and Zapata, Patrik (2013) Infrastructures, lock-in, and sustainable urban development: The case of waste incineration in a Swedish metropolitan area. *Journal of Cleaner Production*, 50(1): 32f C.
Cova, Bernard; Kozinets, Robert and Shankar, Avi (2007) *Consumer tribes*. Amsterdam: Elsevier.
Cox, Christoph and Warner, Daniel (2004) *Audio culture: Readings in modern music*. New York: Bloomsbury.
Crary, Jonathan (1999) *Suspensions of perception. Attention, spectacle, and modern culture*. Cambridge, MA: MIT Press.
Csikszentmihalyi, Mihaly and Rochberg-Halton, Eugene (1981) *The meaning of thing. Domestic symbols and the self*. Cambridge: Cambridge University Press.
Currell, Sue (2007) Streamlining the eye: Reading and the revolution of words, 1870–1940. In: Acland, Charles R. (ed.) *Residual media*. Minneapolis, MN: University of Minnesota Press, 344–360.
Cyert, Richard M. and March, James G. (1963) *A behavioural theory of the firm*. Englewood Cliffs, NJ: Prentice Hall.
Czarniawska, Barbara (1989) *Economic decline and organizational control*. New York: Praeger.

Czarniawska, Barbara (1996) Changing times and accounts: Tales from an organization field. In: Munro, Roland and Mouritsen, Jan (eds) *Accountability: Power, ethos and the techniques of managing*. London: Thomson International Business Press, 307–328.
Czarniawska, Barbara (1997) *Narrating the organization. Dramas of institutional identity*. Chicago, IL: University of Chicago Press.
Czarniawska, Barbara (2002) *A tale of three cities*. Oxford: Oxford University Press.
Czarniawska, Barbara (2004) *Narrative in social science research*. London: Sage.
Czarniawska, Barbara (2007) *Shadowing and other techniques for doing fieldwork in modern societies*. Malmö: Liber.
Czarniawska, Barbara (2008) *A theory of organizing*. Cheltenham: Edward Elgar.
Czarniawska, Barbara (2009) Distant readings: anthropology of organizations through novels. *Journal of Organizational Change Management*, 22(4): 357–372.
Czarniawska, Barbara (2011) *Cyberfactories: How news agencies produce news*. Cheltenham, UK and Northampton, MA, USA: Edward Elgar.
Czarniawska, Barbara (2012) News agencies: The place where information permanently overflows. In: Czarniawska, Barbara and Löfgren, Orvar (eds) *Managing overflow in affluent societies*. New York: Routledge, 31–51.
Czarniawska, Barbara and Löfgren, Orvar (eds) (2012) *Managing overflow in affluent societies*. New York: Routledge.
Czarniawska, Barbara and Sevón, Guje (eds) (2005) *Global ideas: How ideas, objects and practices travel in the global economy*. Malmö/Copenhagen: Liber/CBS Press.
Czubaj, Mariusz (2007) *Biodra Elvisa Presleya. Od paleoherosów do neofanów*. Warszawa: Wydawnictwa Akademickie i Profesjonalne.
Czubaj, Mariusz; Drozda, Jacek and Myszkorowski, Jakub (2012) *Postfutbol: antropologia piłki nożnej*. Gdańsk: Wydawnictwo Naukowe Katedra
Daunton, Martin (2007) *Wealth and welfare: An economic and social history of Britain 1851–1951*. Oxford: Oxford University Press.
de Certeau, Michel (1988) *The practice of everyday life*. Berkeley, CA: University of California Press.
De Graff, John; Wann, David and Naylor, Thomas (2001) *Affluenza. The all-consuming epidemic*. San Francisco, CA: Berret-Koehler Publishers.

Dechow, Patricia; Ge, Weili and Schrand, Catherine (2010) Understanding earnings quality: A review of the proxies, their determinants and their consequences. *Journal of Accounting and Economics*, 50(2–3): 344–401.
Decker, Stephanie (2012) The silence of the archive: post-colonialism and the practice of historical reconstruction from archival evidence. NPRA paper No 37280, http//mpra.ub.uni-muenchen.de/37280/, accessed 2012-02-19.
Deland, Mats (2001) *The social city. Stockholm 1900–1945*. Stockholm: Studier i stads-kommunhistoria 23, Stads-och kommunhistoriska institutet.
Deleuze, Gilles and Guattari, Felix (1987) *A thousand plateaus: Capitalism and schizophrenia*. Minneapolis, MN: University of Minnesota Press.
DeMaria, Robert Jr. (1997) *Samuel Johnson and the life of reading*. Baltimore, MD: Johns Hopkins University Press.
Derrida, Jacques (1995) *Archival fever. A Freudian impression*. Chicago, IL: University of Chicago Press.
Deserno, Ineke (2009) The value of international business archives: the importance of the archives of multinational companies in shaping cultural identity. *Archival Science*, 9(3–4): 215–225.
Deuze, Mark (2006) Participation, remediation, bricolage: Considering principal components of a digital culture. *Information Society*, 22(2): 63–75.
Diderichsen, Finn (1995) Market reforms in health care and sustainability of the welfare state: lessons from Sweden. *Health Policy*, 32: 141–143.
Diley, Roy (2010) Reflections on knowledge practices and the problem of ignorance. In: Marchand, Trevor H.J. (ed.) *Making knowledge. Explorations of the indissoluble relation between mind, body and environment*. London: Wiley-Blackwell, 167–182.
Donabedian Avedis (1966) Evaluating the quality of medical care. *Milbank Memorial Fund Quarterly*, 44: 166–206.
Donabedian, Avedis (2003) *An introduction to quality assurance in health care*. New York: Oxford University Press.
Du Gay, Paul and Salaman, Graeme (1992) The (cult)ure of the customer. *Journal of Management Studies*, 29(5): 561–691.
Duff, Wendy M., and Johnson, Catherine A. (2002) Accidentally found on purpose: Information-seeking behaviour of historians. *Library Quarterly*, 72(4): 472–496.
Eco, Umberto (1985) The modern concept of symbols. *Social Research*, 52(2): 383–402.
Ehn, Billy (2011) Do-It-Yourself ethnography. *Ethnologia Europaea*, 41(1): 53–64.

Ehn, Billy and Lafgren, Orvar (2004) *Hur blir man klok Do-It-Yourself et* Lund: Studentlitteratur.

Ehn, Billy and Löfgren, Orvar (2007) Emotions in academia. In: Wulff, Helena (ed.) *Emotions: A cultural reader.* Oxford: Berg, 101–118.

Ehn, Billy and Löfgren, Orvar (2007) *The secret world of doing nothing.* Berkeley, CA: California University Press.

Ekström, Karin M. (2007) Participating in the catwalk of consumption. In: Ekström, Karin M. and Tufte, Birgitte (eds) *Children, media and consumption. On the front edge*. Gothenburg: Nordicom.

Ekström, Karin M. and Hjort, Torbjörn (2009) Hidden consumers in marketing – the neglect of consumers with scarce resource in affluent societites. *Journal of Marketing Management*, 25(7–8): 697–712.

Ekström, Karin M. and Karlsson, MariAnne (1998) *Fitting the pieces of the jig-saw puzzle. The art of understanding the customer in product development*. Workshop, Customer Research Academy, Manchester School of Management, Manchester, UK.

Elliott, Richard (1997) Existential consumption and irrational desire. *European Journal of Marketing*, 34(4): 285–296.

Encyclopaedia Britannica Online Academic Edition (n.d.) Noise.

Ernst, Wolfgang (2008) *Sorlet från arkivet. Ordning ur oordning*. Munkedal: Glänta Produktion.

Eyerman, Ron and Turner, Brian (1998) An outline of a theory of generations. *European Journal of Social Theory*, 1(1): 91–106.

Featherstone, Mike (1991) *Consumer culture and postmodernism.* London: Sage.

Featherstone, Mike (2006) Archive. *Theory, Culture and Society*, 23(2–3): 591–596.

Fehérváry, Krisztina (2009) Goods and states. The political logic of state-socialist material culture. *Comparative Studies in Society and History*, 51. 2426–2459.

Fisher, Dana R. and Freudenburg, William R. (2001) Ecological modernization and its critics: Assessing the past and looking toward the future. *Society and Natural Resources*, 14(8), 701–709.

Forssell, Anders and Jansson, David (2000) *Idéer som fängslar: Recept för en offentlig reformation*. Malmö: Liber.

Forty, Adrian (1992) *Objects of desire. Design and society since 1750.* New York: Thames & Hudson.

Forum (2009) Forum: History, a useful science for management? From polemics to controversies. *Enterprise and Society*, 10(4), 831–836.

Foucault, Michel (1990) Qu'est-ce que la critique. *Bulletin de la société française de la philosophie*, 84(2): 35–63.

Frykman, Jonas and Löfgren, Orvar (eds) (1985) Modärna tider. Malmö: Liber.

Gabriel, Yiannis (2000) *Storytelling in organisations*. Oxford: Oxford University Press.

Gabriel, Yiannis (2008) *Organising words*. Oxford: Oxford University Press.

Ger, Güliz and Belk, Russell W. (1999) Accounting for materialism in four cultures. *Journal of Material Culture*, 4: 183–204.

Giles, Geoffrey J. (ed.) (1996) *Archivists and historians: The crucial partnership*. Washington, DC: German Historical Institute Occasional Paper No. 17.

Godley, Andrew (2006) Selling the sewing machine around the World: Singer's international marketing strategies, 1850–1920. *Enterprise and Society*, 7(2): 266–314.

Goffman, Erving (1961) *Asylums. Essays on the social situation of mental patients and other inmates*. New York: Anchor Books.

Goffman, Erving (1974) *Frame analysis: An essay on the organization of experience*. London: Harper & Row.

Götselius, Thomas (2008) Förord. In: Ernst, Wolfgang (ed.), *Sorlet från arkivet. Ordning ur oordning*. Munkedal: Glänta Produktion, 7–15.

Grafton, Anthony (1999) The humanist as reader. In: Cavallo, Guglielmo and Chartier, Roger (eds) *A history of reading in the West*. Amherst, MA: University of Massachusetts Press, 179–212.

Gregson, Nicky (2009) Recycling as policy and assemblage. *Geography*, 94(1): 61–65.

Gregson, Nicky (2011) *Living with things. Ridding, accommodating, dwelling*. Canon Pyon, UK: Sean Kingston Publishing.

Gregson, Nicky; Metcalfe, Alan and Crewe, Louise (2007) Moving things along: The conduits and practices of divestment in consumption. *Transactions of the Institute of British Geographers*, 32(2): 187–200.

Gregson, Nicky; Watkins, Helen and Calestani, Melania (2010) Inextinguishable fibres: Demolition and the vital materialisms of asbestos. *Environment and Planning A*, 42(5): 1065–1083.

Gustavsson, Jenny; Cederberg, Christel; Sonesson, Ulf; van Otterdijk, Robert and Meybeck, Alexandre (2011) *Global food losses and food waste: Extent, causes and prevention*. Rome: Food and Agriculture Organization of the United Nations.

Hall, Edward T. (1976) *Beyond culture*.New York: Anchor Books.

Hannerz, Ulf (1996) *Transnational connections*. London: Routledge.

Hanning, Marianne (2005) *Maximum waiting-time guarantee – a remedy to long waiting lists. Assessment of the Swedish waiting-time guarantee policy*. Uppsala: Uppsala University.

Hansen, Per (2012) Business history: A cultural and narrative approach. *Business History Review*, 86(Winter): 693–717.

Hawken, Paul; Lovins, Amory B. and Lovins, L. Hunter (1999) *Natural capitalism: The next industrial revolution*. London: Earthscan.

Hawkins, Gay (2006) *The ethics of waste: How we relate to rubbish*. Lanham, MD: Rowman & Littlefield.

Hawkins, Gay and Muecke, Stephen (2003) *Culture and waste: The creation and destruction of value*. Lanham, MD: Rowman & Littlefield.

Healy, Paul M. and Wahlen, James Michael (1999) A review of the earnings management literature and its implications for standard setting. *Accounting Horizons*, 13(4): 365–383.

Heinonen, V. and Pantzar, Mika (2002) Little America: Modernizing Finnish consumer society in the 1950s and 1960s – some paradoxical findings. In: Kipping, Matthias and Tiratsoo, Nick (eds) *Americanisation in 20th century Europe: business, culture, politics*. Lille: Centre d'Histoire de l'Europe du Nord-Ouest.

Herman, David (2003) *Narrative theory and the cognitive sciences*. Stanford, CA: Stanford University, CSLI Publications.

Hernandez, Maria Padrón (2012) *Beans and roses. Everyday economies and morality in contemporary Havana, Cuba*. Gothenburg: University of Gothenburg, School of Global Studies.

Herzfeld, Michael (2007) Deskilling, 'dumbing down' and the auditing of knowledge in the practical mastery of artisans and academics: An ethnographer's response to a global problem. In: Harris, Mark (ed.) *Ways of knowing: New approaches in the anthropology of experience and learning*. Oxford: Berghahn Books, 91–112.

Hetherington, Kevin (2004) Secondhandedness: Consumption, disposal, and absent presence. *Environment and Planning D: Society and Space*, 22: 157–173.

Hines, Ruth D. (1988) Financial accounting: In communicating reality, we construct reality. *Accounting, Organizations and Society*, 13(3): 251–261.

Hirschman, Albert O. (1970) *Exit, voice or loyalty: Responses to decline in firms, organizations, and states*. Cambridge, MA: Harvard University Press.

Hjortsberg, Catharina and Ghatnekar, Ola (2001) *Health care systems in transition: Sweden*. Brussels: European Observatory on Health Care Systems.

Holmqvist, Kenneth and Nyström, Marcus (eds) (2011) *Eye tracking: A comprehensive guide to methods and measures*. Oxford: Oxford University Press.

Hopwood, Anthony and Miller, Peter B. (eds) (1994) *Accounting as social and institutional practice*. Cambridge: Cambridge University Press.

Horney, Karen (1937) *The neurotic personality of our times*. New York: W.W. Norton.

Howard, Ebenezer (1898/1965) *Garden cities of to-morrow*. Cambridge, MA: MIT Press.

Hultman, Johan and Corvellec, Hervé (2012) The waste hierarchy model: From the socio-materiality of waste to a politics of consumption. *Environment and Planning A*, 44(10), 2413–2427.

Ivory, Chris and Genus, Audley (2010) Symbolic consumption, signification and the 'lockout' of electric cars, 1885–1914. *Business History*, 52(7): 1107–1122.

Jackson, Maggie (2008) *Distracted. The erosion of attention and the coming Dark Age*. New York: Prometheus Books.

Jackson, Peter A.; Lowe, Michelle; Miller, Daniel and Mort, Frank (eds) (2001) *Commercial cultures. Economies, practices, spaces*. Oxford: Berg.

Jacobs, Jane (1961/1993) *The death and life of great American cities*. New York: Modern Library.

Jansson, Hanna (2010) Digitala texter och analoga fältarbetare – Internetetnografins metodologiska dilemma. *#Nätverket*, 2010:17-29-53. (http://natverket.etnologi.uu.se, accessed 2012-11-30).

Jeggle, Utz (1969) The lost track. On the unconscious in folklore. *Journal of Folklore Research*, 40(1): 73–94.

Jerram, Leif (2011) *Streetlife. The untold history of Europe's twentieth century*. Oxford: Oxford University Press.

Jones, Geoffrey, and Khanna, Tharun (2006) Bringing history (back) into international business. *Journal of International Business Studies*, 37(2): 453–468.

Jones, Geoffrey and Zeitlin, Jonathan (2008) *The Oxford handbook of business history*. New York: Oxford University Press.

de Jong, Abe; Sluyterman, Keetie and Westerhuis, Gerarda (2011) Strategic and structural responses to international dynamics in the open Dutch economy, 1963–2003. *Business History*, 53(1): 63–84.

Jönsson, Bengt; Arvidsson, Göran; Levin, Lars-Åke and Rhenberg, Clas (2004) *Hälsa, vård och tillväxt*. Stockholm: SNS.

Jönsson, Sten (1996) *Accounting for improvement*. Oxford: Pergamon.

Jönsson, Sten; Nilsson, Lennart; Rubenowitz Sigvard and Westerståhl, Jörgen (1999) *The decentralized city – democracy, efficiency, service*. Gothenburg: Bokförlaget BAS.

Kahn, Douglas (2001) *Noise, water, meat: A history of sound in the arts*. Cambridge, MA: MIT Press.

Kelly, Caleb (2009) *Cracked media: The sound of malfunction*. Cambridge, MA: MIT Press.

Kelman, Ari V. (2010) Rethinking the soundscape: A critical genealogy of a key term in sound studies. *Senses and Society*, 5(2): 212–234.

Kessous, Emmanuel (2012) *L'attention au monde. Sociologie des données personnelles à l'ère numérique*. Paris: Armand Colin.

Klein, Naomi (2000) *No logo: Taking aim at the brand bullies.* New York: Picador.

Knorr Cetina, Karin (1981) *The manufacture of knowledge. An essay in the constructivist and contextual nature of science.* New York: Pergamon Press.

Kobrak, Chris and Schneider, Andrea (2011) Varieties of business history: Subject and methods for the twenty-first century. *Business History*, 53(3): 401–424.

Krapp, Peter (2006) Hypertext *avant la lettre.* In: Chun, Wendy Hiui Kyong; Chun, Thomas Chun and Keenan,Thomas W. (eds) *New media old media.* New York: Routledge, 359–374.

Krapp, Peter (2011) *Noise channels: Glitch and error in digital culture.* Minneapolis, MN: University of Minnesota Press.

Kristeva, Julia (1980) *Desire in language: A semiotic approach to literature and art.* New York: Columbia University Press.

Kroen, Sheryl (2006) Negotiations with the American way: The consumer and the social contract in post-war Europe. In: Brewer, John and Trentman, Frank (eds) *Consuming cultures, global perspectives.* Oxford: Berg, 251–278.

Kunda, Gideon (2012) Scenes from a marriage: Regulating flows between work and home. In: Czarniawska, Barbara and Löfgren, Orvar (eds) *Managing overflow in affluent societies.* New York: Routledge, 88–100.

Kusek, David and Leonhard, Gerd (2005) *The future of music: Manifesto for the digital music revolution.* Boston, MA: Berklee Press.

Lapsley, Irvine; Mussari, Riccardo and Paulsson, Gert (2009) On the adoption of accrual accounting in the public sector: A self-evident and problematic reform. *European Accounting Review*, 18(4): 719–723.

Latour, Bruno (1993) *We have never been modern.* Cambridge, MA: Harvard University Press.

Latour, Bruno (1999) *Pandora's hope. Essays on the reality of science studies.* Cambridge, MA: Harvard University Press.

Latour, Bruno (2005) *Reassembling the social – an introduction to actor-network-theory.* Oxford: Oxford University Press.

Latour, Bruno; Jensen, Pablo; Venturini, Tommaso; Grauwin, Sébastian and Boullier, Dominique (2012) 'The whole is always smaller than its parts' – a digital test of Gabriel Tardes' monads. *British Journal of Sociology*, 63(4): 590–615.

Latour, Bruno and Woolgar, Steve (1987) *Laboratory life: The social construction of scientific facts.* Princeton, NJ: Princeton University Press.

Layne, Linda L. (2000) He was a baby with real things. A material culture analysis of personhood, parenthood and pregnancy loss. *Journal of Material Culture*, 5(3): 321–345.

Lee, Michele (2003) *Fashion victim: Our love–hate relationship with dressing, shopping, and the cost of style.* New York: Broadway Books.

Lefebvre, Henri (1991) *Critique of everyday life*, Vol. 1, London: Verso.

Le Feuvre, Lisa (ed.) (2010) *Failure*. Cambridge, MA: MIT Press.

Lehtonen, Turo-Kimmo and Pantzar, Mika (2002) The ethos of thrift – The legitimisation of bank saving in Finland during the 1950s. *Journal of Material Culture*, 7(2): 211–232.

Leonard, Annie (2010) *The story of stuff: How our problem with overconsumption is trashing the planet, our communities and our health – and what to do about it.* London: Constable.

Levi, Giovanni (2012) Microhistory and the recovery of complexity. In: Fellman, Susanna and Rahikainen, Marjatta (eds) *Historical knowledge. In quest of theory, method and evidence*. Newcastle upon Tyne: Cambridge Scholars Publishing, 121–132.

Levin, Peter A. (2005) Information, prices, and sensemaking in financial futures trading. In: Elbasch, Kimberly D. (ed.) *Qualitative organizational research*. Charlotte, NC: Information Age Publishing, 205–225.

Lévi-Strauss, Claude (1977) The effectiveness of symbols. In: *Structural Anthropology*, Harmondsworth: Penguin, 186–205.

Libby, Robert, and Seybert, Nicholas (2009) Behavioural studies of the effects of regulation on earnings management and accounting choice. In: Chapman, Christopher S.; Cooper, David J. and Miller, Peter B. (eds) *Accounting, organizations, and institutions: Essays in honour of Anthony Hopwood*. Oxford: Oxford University Press, 290–314.

Licoppe, Christian (2013) *Formes de la présence et circulations de l'expérience. De Jean-Jacques Rousseau au quantified self.* Telecom ParisTech, working paper.

Lipovetsky, Gilles (2006) *Le bonheur paradoxal. Essai sur la soci société d'hyperconsommation*. Paris: Gallimard.

Löfgren, Orvar (2012) It's simply too much! Coping with domestic overflow. In: Czarniawska, Barbara and Löfgren, Orvar (eds) *Managing overflow in affluent societies*. New York: Routledge, 101–124.

Löfgren, Orvar and Czarniawska, Barbara (2012a) The inherited theories of overflow and their challenges. In: Löfgren, Orvar and Czarniawska, Barbara (eds) *Managing overflow in affluent societies*. New York: Routledge, 1–12.

Löfgren, Orvar and Willim, Robert (eds) (2006) *Magic, culture and the new economy*. Oxford: Berg.
Löwy, Ilona (1992) The strength of weak concepts – boundary concepts, federative experimental strategies and disciplinary growth: the case of immunology. *History of Science*, 30: 371–395.
Lury, Celia (1996) *Consumer culture*. Oxford: Polity Press.
Lynd, Robert S. and Lynd, Helen M. (1929) *Middletown: A study in contemporary American culture*. New York: Harcourt, Brace, & Company.
Lynd, Robert S. and Lynd, Helen M. (1937) *Middletown in transition: A study in cultural conflicts*. New York: Harcourt, Brace, & Company.
MacKenzie, Donald (2009) *Material markets: How economic agents are constructed*. Oxford: Oxford University Press.
MacKenzie, Donald and Millo, Yuval (2003) Constructing a market, performing theory: The historical sociology of a financial derivatives exchange. *American Journal of Sociology*, 109(1): 107–145.
Mann, Peter (1954) The concept of neighborliness. *American Journal of Sociology*, 60(2): 163–168.
Manovich, Lev (2001) *The language of new media*. Cambridge, MA: MIT Press.
Marchand, Trevor H.J. (ed.) (2010) *Making knowledge. Explorations of the indissoluble relation between mind, body and environment*. London: Wiley-Blackwell.
Mauss, Marcel (1902/2000) *The gift: The form and reason for exchange in archaic societies*. New York: W.W. Norton.
Mayer-Schönberger, Viktor (2009) *Delete: The virtue of forgetting in the digital age*. Princeton, NJ: Princeton University Press.
McCann Eugene (2003) Framing space and time in city: Urban policy and the politics of spatial and temporal scale. *Journal of Urban Affairs*, 25(2): 159–178.
McCloskey, Deirdre N. (2012) Afterword: Keep calm and carry on? The economic history of overflow. In: Czarniawska, Barbara and Löfgren, Orvar (eds) *Managing overflow in affluent societies*. New York: Routledge, 155–164.
McKendrick, Neil; Brewer, John and Plumb, John Harold (1982) *The birth of a consumer society. The commercialization of eighteenth-century England*. Bloomington, IN: Indiana University Press.
Menkman, Rosa (2011) *The glitch moment(um)*. Amsterdam: Institute of Network Cultures.
Miller, Daniel (1987) *Material culture and mass consumption*. Oxford: Berg.
Miller, Daniel (1997) Consumption and its consequences. In: Mackay, Hugh (ed.) *Consumption and everyday life*. London: Sage, 1–50.

Miller, Daniel (1998) *A theory of shopping*. Cambridge: Polity Press.
Miller, Daniel (2010) *Stuff*. Cambridge: Polity Press.
Misztal, Barbara A. (2003) *Theories of social remembering*. Maidenhead, UK: Open University Press.
Mol, Annemarie (2008) *The logic of care. Health and the problem of patient choice*. London: Routledge.
Mukerji, Chandra (1983) *From graven images: Patterns of modern materialism*. New York: Columbia University Press.
Næss, Arne (1989) *Ecology, community and lifestyle: Outline of an ecosophy*. Cambridge: Cambridge University Press.
Nicolini, Davide (2009) Zooming in and out: Studying practices by switching theoretical lenses and trailing connections. *Organization Studies*, 30(12): 1391–1418.
Nikula, Riitta (ed.) (1994) *Sankaruus ja arki. Suomen 1950-luvun miljöö* (Heroism in Finnish architecture of the 1950s). Helsinki: Suomen rakennustaiteen museo.
Nippert-Eng, Christena (2010) *Islands of privacy*. Chicago, IL: Chicago University Press.
Norén, Lars (2010) The private interest of consumers in the health care market. *International Journal of Public Sector Management*, 23(4): 364–371.
O'Brien, Martin (1999) Rubbish values: Reflections on the political economy of waste. *Science as Culture*, 8(3): 269–297.
O'Dell, Tom, and Willim, Robert (eds) (2011) *Irregular ethnographies* (Special issue of *Ethnologia Europaea*, 41:1). Copenhagen: Museum Tusculanum Press.
Olson, Olov and Sahlin-Andersson, Kerstin (1998) Accounting transformation in an advanced welfare state: The case of Sweden. In: Olson, Olov; Guthrie, James and Humphrey, Christopher (eds) *Global warning! Debating international developments in new public financial management*. Oslo: Cappelen, 241–275.
Orlikowski, Wanda J. (2012) Sociomaterial practices: Exploring technology at work. *Organization Studies*, 28(09): 1435–1448.
Orr, Julian E. (1995) *Talking about machines. Ethnography of a modern job*. Ithaca, NY: ILR Press.
Osborne, David and Gaebler, Ted (1993) *Reinventing government. How the entrepreneurial spirit is transforming the public sector*. New York: Penguin Books.
Ossowska, Maria (1956/1986), *Bourgeois morality*. London: Routledge & Kegan Paul.
Pantzar, Mika (2003) Tools or toys. Inventing the need for domestic appliances in post-war and postmodern Finland. *Journal of Advertising*, 32(1): 81–91.

Pantzar, Mika (2010) Tapiola as a breeding ground for modern consumption and consumers. In: Aav, Marianne and Savolainen, Jukka (eds) *Modernism*. Helsinki: Helsinki Design Museum, 104–124.

Parfitt, Julian; Barthel Mark and Macnaughton, Sarah (2010) Food waste within food supply chains: Quantification and potential for change to 2050. *Philosophical Transactions – Royal Society. Biological Sciences*, 365(1554): 3065–3081.

Péteri, György (2006) Introduction. In: Péteri, György (ed.) *Nylon Curtain. Transnational and transsystemic tendencies in the cultural life of state-socialist Russia and East-Central Europe*. Trondheim: Trondheim Studies on East European Cultures and Societies, no. 18: 1–13.

Peters, Thomas and Waterman, Robert (1982) *In search of excellence: Lessons from America's best run companies*. New York: Harper & Row.

Pilcher, Robyn A. and Van Der Zhan, Mitchell (2010) Local governments, unexpected depreciation and financial performance adjustment. *Financial Accountability and Management*, 26(3): 299–324.

Pinch, Trevor (2012), Book reviewing for Amazon.com: How socio-technical systems struggle to make less from more. In: Czarniawska, Barbara and Löfgren, Orvar (eds) *Managing overflow in affluent societies*. New York: Routledge, 68–87.

Pink, Daniel H. (2009) *Drive: The surprising truth about what motivates us*. New York: Penguin.

Piore, Michael and Sabel, Charles (1984) *The second industrial divide*. New York: Basic Books.

Polkinghorne, Donald E. (1988) *Narrative knowing and the human sciences*. Albany, NY: State University of New York Press.

Popp, Andrew (2009) History, a useful 'science' for management? A response. *Enterprise and Society*, 10(4): 831–836.

Popp, Andrew and French, Michael (2010) Practically the uniform of the tribe: Dress codes among commercial travelers. *Enterprise and Society*, 11(3): 437–467.

Power, Michael (1994) From science of accounts to financial accountability of science. In: Power, Michael (ed.) *Accounting and science. Natural inquiry and commercial reason*. Cambridge: Cambridge University Press, 1–33.

Power, Michael (1997) *The audit society. Rituals of verification*. Oxford: Oxford University Press.

Preda, Alex (2009) *Framing finance: The boundaries of markets and modern capitalism*. Chicago, IL: University of Chicago Press.

Proctor, Robert (2008) Agnotology: A missing term to describe the cultural production of ignorance. In: Proctor, Robert and Schiebinger,

Londa (eds) *Agnotology. The making and unmaking of ignorance.* Stanford, CA: Stanford University Press, 1–35.

Proctor, Robert and Schiebinger, Londa (eds) (2008) *Agnotology. The making and unmaking of ignorance.* Stanford, CA: Stanford University Press.

Puschmann, Cornelius (forthcoming) Beyond the filter bubble: From consumers to curators. *Global Perspectives on Digital History.*

Quitzau, Maj-Britt (2007) Water-flushing toilets: Systemic development and path-dependent characteristics and their bearing on technological alternatives. *Technology in Society*, 29(3): 351–360.

Rahikainen, Marjatta and Fellman, Susanna (2012a) Introduction. In: Fellman, Susanna and Rahikainen, Marjatta (eds) *Historical knowledge. In quest of theory, method and evidence.* Newcastle upon Tyne: Cambridge Scholars Publishing, 1–4.

Rahikainen, Marjatta and Fellman, Susanna (2012b). On historical writing and evidence In: Fellman, Susanna and Rahikainen, Marjatta (eds) *Historical knowledge. In quest of theory, method and evidence.* Newcastle upon Tyne: Cambridge Scholars Publishing, 5–44.

Ranerup, Agneta (2008) In what ways does web technology support the individual in choice reforms in healthcare? A comparison among Norway, Denmark, and Sweden. *International Journal of Healthcare Information Systems and Informatics*, 3(2): 48–68.

Rehn, Alf and Lindahl, Marcus (2011) Georges Bataille: On his shoulders (and other parts of the body of knowledge). In: Jensen, Tommy and Wilson, Timothy L. (eds) *On the shoulders of giants.* Lund: Studentlitteratur, 25–38.

Riesman, David (1951) The nylon war. *Common Cause*, 4(February): 279.

Ritzer, George (1993/2008) *The McDonaldization of society.* Los Angeles, CA: Pine Forge Press.

Ritzer, George (1996) *The McDonaldization of society.* Thousand Oaks, CA: Pine Forge Press.

Rose, Nicholas (1993) Government, authority and expertise in advanced liberalism. *Economy and Society*, 22(3): 283–300.

Rose, Nicholas (1999) *Powers of freedom. Reframing political thought.* Cambridge: Cambridge University Press.

Saarinen, Eliel (1943/1958) *The city.* New York: Reinhold Publishing Corporation.

Sahlin-Andersson, Kerstin (1996) Imitating by editing success: The construction of organizational fields and identities. In Czarniawska, Barbara and Sevón, Guje (eds) *Translating organizational change.* Berlin: de Gruyter, 69–92.

Saltman, Richard (2006) Drawing the strands together: Primary care in perspective. In: Saltman, Richard; Rico, Ana and Boerma, Wienke (eds) *Primary care in the driver's seat? Organizational reform in European Primary Care*. Buckingham: Open University Press, 268–282.

Saltman, Richard and von Otter, Casten (1992) *Planned markets and public competition. Strategic reform in Northern European health systems*. Buckingham: Open University Press.

Sanderson, Kathy; Boone Parsons, Donna; Helms Mills, Jean and Mills, Albert J. (2010) Riding the second wave: Organizing feminism and organizational discourse – stewardesses for women's rights. *Management and Organizational History*, 5(3–4): 360–377.

Sassatelli, Roberta (2007) *Consumer culture. History, theory and politics*. London: Sage.

Sassen, Saskia (2005) The embeddedness of electronic markets: The case of global capital markets. In: Cetina, Karin K. and Preda, Alex (eds) *The sociology of financial markets*. Oxford: Oxford University Press, 17–37.

Schafer, R. Murray (1994) *The soundscape: Our sonic environment and the tuning of the world*. Rochester: Destiny Books.

Schafer, R. Murray (2004) The music of the environment. In: Cox, Christoph and Warner, Daniel (eds) *Audio culture: Readings in modern music*. New York: Bloomsbury, 29–39.

Schwarz, Hillel (2011) *Making noise. From Babel to the big bang and beyond*. New York: Zone Books.

Schön, Donald A. (1984) *The reflective practitioner. How professionals think in action*. New York: Basic Books.

Sellen, Abigail J. and Harper, Richard H.R. (2002) *The myth of the paperless office*. London: MIT Press.

Sennett, Richard (2008) *The craftsman*. London: Penguin.

Serres, Michel (1982) *The parasite*. Baltimore, MD: Johns Hopkins University Press.

Serres, Michel (2012) *Petite poucette*. Paris: Le Pommier.

Shove, Elisabeth; Pantzar, Mika and Watson, Matthew (2012) *The dynamics of social practice*. London: Sage.

Sirgy, M. Joseph (1982) A self-concept in consumer behavior: A critical review. *Journal of Consumer Research*, 9(3): 287-300.

Slater, Daniel (1997) *Consumer culture and modernity*. Cambridge: Polity Press.

Slater, Don (2002) From calculation to alienation: disentangling economic abstractions. *Economy and Society*, 31(2): 234–249.

Smith, Charles W. (1998) *Success and survival on Wall Street: Understanding the mind of the markets*. Oxford: Rowman & Littlefield.

Solnit, Rebecca (2005) *A field guide to getting lost*. New York: Viking.
Stalebrink, Odd J. (2007) An investigation of discretionary accruals and surplus-deficit management: evidence from Swedish municipalities. *Financial Accountability and Management*, 23(4): 441–457.
Stanziani, Alessandro (2010) Economic information on international markets: French strategies in the Italian mirror (Nineteenth–early twentieth centuries). *Enterprise and Society*, 11(1): 26–64.
Star, Susan Leigh and Griesemer, James (1989) Institutional ecology, 'translations' and boundary objects: Amateurs and professionals in Berkeley's museum of Vertebrate Zoology. *Social Studies in Science*, 19: 387–420.
Steedman, Carolyn (1998) The space of memory: In an archive. *History of the Human Science*, 11(4): 65–83.
Steedman, Carolyn (2001) *Dust*. Manchester: Manchester University Press
Steedman, Carolyn (2011) After the archive. *Comparative Critical Studies*, 8(2): 321–340.
Strasser, Susan (1989) *Satisfaction guaranteed. The making of the American mass market*. New York: Pantheon Books.
Sulima, Roch (2000) *Antropologia codzienności*. Kraków: Wydawnictwo Uniwersytetu Jagiellońskiego.
Szlendak, Tomasz (2004) *Supermarketyzacja. Religia i obyczaje seksualne młodzieży w kulturze konsumpcyjnej*. Wrocław: Wydawnictwa Uniwersytetu Wrocławskiego.
Szlendak, Tomasz and Piotrowicz, Krzysztof (eds) (2004) *Na pokaz: o konsumeryzmie w kapitalizmie bez kapitału*. Toruń: Wydawnictwo Uniwersytetu Mikołaja Kopernika.
Szpakowska, Małgorzata (2004) *Chcieć i mieć. Samowiedza obyczajowa w Polsce czasu przemian*. Warszawa: W.A.B.
Tarim, Emre (2010) Two waves of globalisation in the Istanbul Stock Exchange since 1985 and the evolution of the domestic retail investor. *Competition and Change*, 14(3–4): 343–362.
Tawney, Richard Henry (1926/1984) *Religion and the rise of capitalism: A historical study*. Harmondsworth: Penguin.
Taylor, Frank (1966) Tapiola amerikkalaisin silmin (Tapiola as seen from the American point of view). *Valitut Palat* (*Reader's Digest* in Finnish), 2: 9–15.
Taylor, Janelle S.; Layne, Linda and Wozniak, Danielle F. (2004) *Consuming motherhood*. New Brunswick, NJ: Rutgers University Press.
Thompson, Michael (1979) *Rubbish theory: The creation and destruction of value*. Oxford: Oxford University Press.

Thrift, Nigel (2004) Movement-space: the changing domain of thinking resulting from the development of new kinds of spatial awareness. *Economy and Society*, 33(4): 582–604.

Tilly, Charles (1999) Trouble with stories. In: Aminzade, Ronald and Pescosolido, Bernice (eds) *The social worlds of higher education: Handbook for teaching in a new century*. Thousand Oaks, CA: Pine Forge Press, 256–270.

Toffler, Alvin (1980) *The third wave*. London: Collins.

Toop, David (2004) *Haunted weather. Music, silence and memory*. London: Serpent's Tail.

Vanhanen, Janne (2003) Virtual sound: Examining glitch and production. *Contemporary Music Review*, 22(4): 45–52.

Townley, Barbara (2008) *Reason's neglect: Rationality and organizing*. Oxford: Oxford University Press.

Trace, Ciaran (2002) What is recorded is never simply 'what happened': Record keeping in modern organizational culture. *Archival Science*, 2(3): 137–159.

Trentman, Frank (2009) Crossing divides. Consumption and globalization in history. *Journal of Consumer Culture*, 9(2): 187–220.

Trompette, Pascale (2011) Political exchanges in the French funeral market. *Management and Organizational History*, 6(1): 3–35.

Trompette, Pascale (2012) Pompes funèbres and the overflowing of ostentatious funerals. In: Czarniawska, Barbara, and Löfgren, Orvar (eds) *Managing overflow in affluent societies*. New York: Routledge, 13–30.

Trouillot, Michel-Rolph (1997) *Silencing the past: Power and the production of history*. Boston, MA: Beacon Press.

Tschmuck, Peter (2006) *Creativity and innovation in the music industry*. Dordrecht: Springer.

Tschmuck, Peter (2009) Copyrights, contracts and music production. *Information, Communication and Society*, 12(2): 251–226.

Tuana, Nancy (2008) Coming to understand. Orgasm and the epistemology of ignorance. In: Proctor, Robert and Schiebinger, Londa (eds) *Agnotology. The making and unmaking of ignorance*. Stanford, CA: Stanford University Press, 108–145.

Urry, John (2007) *Mobilities*. Cambridge: Polity Press.

Veblen, Thorstein (1899/1994) *The Theory of the Leisure Class*. Mineola, FL: Dover.

Verbeek, Peter Paul (2005) *What things do: Philosophical reflections on technology, agency and design*. University Park, PN: Pennsylvania State University Press.

Vismann, Cornelia (2008) *Files: Law and media technologies*. Stanford, CA: Stanford University Press.

Vitale, Patrick (2009) Learning to be suburban: the production of community in Westwood Hills, Pennsylvania, 1952–1958. *Journal of Historical Geography*, 35: 743–768.

Viteritti, Assunta (2012) Sociomaterial assemblages in learning scientific paradigm: Margherita's first PCR. *TECNOSCIENZA: Italian Journal of Science and Technology Studies*, 3(1): 29–48.

Von Eckardt, Wolf (1967) *A place to live. The crisis of the cities*. New York: Delacourte Press.

Walsh, Keiron (1995) *Public services and market mechanisms. Competition, contracting and the New Public Management*. London: Macmillan.

Ward, Stephen (ed.) (1992) *The Garden City: Past, present and future*. Oxon: Taylor & Francis.

Warner, Rosalind (2010) Ecological modernisation theory: Towards a critical ecopolitics of change? *Environmental Politics*, 19(4): 538–556.

Weber, Max (1904–1905/1958) *The protestant ethic and the spirit of capitalism*, New York: Scribner's Sons.

Weick, Karl E. (1979) *The social psychology of organizing*. Reading, MA: Addison-Wesley.

Weick, Karl E. (1995) *Sensemaking in organizations*. London: Sage.

Wetzstein, Michael E. and Wetzstein, Hazel Y. (2011) Four myths surrounding US biofuels. *Energy Policy*, 39(7): 4308–4312.

White, Hayden (1973) *Metahistory: The historical imagination in nineteenth century Europe*. Baltimore, MD: Johns Hopkins University Press.

Wikström, Patrik (2009) *The music industry: Music in the cloud*. Cambridge: Polity Press.

Wilk, Richard (2004) The binge in the food economy of nineteenth-century Belize. In: Lysaght, Patricia (ed.) *Changing tastes: Food culture and the processes of industrialization*. Basel: Verlag der Schweizerischen Gesellschaft für Volkskunde, 110–120.

Wilken, Rowan (2010) The card index as creativity machine. *Culture Machine*, 11: 7–30.

Willim, Robert (2006) Menuing. In: Löfgren Orvar and Wilk, Richard (eds) *Off the edge: Experiments in cultural analysis*. Copenhagen: Museum Tusculanum Press, 39–46.

Willim, Robert (2010) Nillim, Robert (2010) Culatmiska och irreguljära metoder. *#nätverk*,17: 34–38.

Willim, Robert (2013). Out of hand. Reflections on elsewhereness. In: Schneider, Arnd and Wright, Christopher (eds) *Anthropology and art practice*. Oxford: Berg.

Womack, James and Jones, Daniel (1996) *Lean thinking. Banish waste and create wealth in your corporation*. New York: Simon & Schuster.

Woodham, Jonathan M. (1997) *Twentieth-century design*. Oxford: Oxford University Press.

Yates, JoAnne (1989) *Control through communication: The rise of system in American management*. Baltimore, MD: Johns Hopkins University Press

Yli-Kauhaluoma, Sari and Pantzar, Mika (2012) *Remembering as a sociomaterial practice in back-office work*. Paper presented at the 7th Organization Studies Summer Workshop, Rhodos, Greece, May 24–26.

Zaloom, Caitlin (2003) Ambiguous numbers: Trading technologies and interpretation in financial markets. *American Ethnologist*, 30(2): 258–272.

Index